Diplomatic Asylum

Laura Hughes-Gerber

Diplomatic Asylum

Exploring a Legal Basis for the Practice Under General International Law

Springer

Laura Hughes-Gerber
Law School
Lancaster University
Lancaster, UK

ISBN 978-3-030-73045-1 ISBN 978-3-030-73046-8 (eBook)
https://doi.org/10.1007/978-3-030-73046-8

This Springer imprint is published by the registered company Springer Nature Switzerland AG.
The registered company address is: Gewerbestrasse 11, 6330 Cham, Switzerland

For my grandfather,
Martin Malachy Hughes

Acknowledgements

First and foremost, I would like to thank my doctoral supervisor, Prof. Dr. Dr. h.c. Stephan Hobe for all of his help, support and encouragement, as well as for all of the opportunities he has provided me with. In this regard, thanks also go to Prof. Dr. Bernhard Kempen for acting as my second marker.

Moreover, I would like to gratefully thank the *Kölner Gymnasial- und Stiftungsfonds* for financially supporting this research.

Thanks also go to all of my friends and former colleagues at the Institute of Air Law, Space Law and Cyber Law/Chair for Public International Law, European Union Law, European and International Economic Law of the University of Cologne for all of their help, support and encouragement over the years. Special thanks go to Anja Nakarada Pecujlic and Dr. Benjamyn Scott for their very helpful advice and to Matina Jozi for the fruitful discussions. In this regard, thanks must also go to Arne Gerber for his invaluable advice.

I would also like to wholeheartedly thank David Crow and Frances Russell for sacrificing their time to assist in the proofreading of this document.

Additionally, I wish to thank my colleagues at Lancaster University Law School for their encouragement and support. Particular thanks in this regard go to Prof. Sigrun Skogly, Prof. Steven Wheatley, Dr. James Summers and Dr. Noel McGuirk.

I would also like to gratefully thank the Springer Nature team, in particular Anke Seyfried, Julia Bieler and Abdus Salam Mazumder.

Last but certainly not least, I wish to thank my parents, my family and my husband for their unfailing support, without which this endeavour would never have been possible.

Contents

Abbreviations

ACHPR	African (Banjul) Charter of Human and Peoples' Rights
AdV	*Archiv des Völkerrechts* (Archive of Public International Law)
AFDI	*Annuaire français de droit international* (French Yearbook of International Law)
AJIA	Australian Journal of International Affairs
AJIL	American Journal of International Law
ALR	Adelaide Law Review
Am Univ Int Law Rev	American University International Law Review
AP	Associated Press
Apr(.)	April
APSR	American Political Science Review
Art.	Article(s)
ASIL	American Society of International Law
ASILI	American Society of International Law Insights
ASLJ	Arizona State Law Journal
AUG	August
BBC	British Broadcasting Corporation
BCICLR	Boston College International and Comparative Law Review
BDGIR	*Berichte der Deutschen Gesellschaft für Internationales Recht* (Reports of the German Society for International Law)
BDGVR	*Berichte der Deutschen Gesellschaft für Völkerrecht* (Reports of the German Society for Public International Law)
BIICL	British Institute of International and Comparative Law
BGBl.	*Bundesgesetzblatt* (German Federal Law Gazette)

BJIL	Brooklyn Journal of International Law
B.V.	*Besloten Vennootschap met beperkte aansprakelijkheid* (Dutch private company with limited liability)
BVerfGE	*Entscheidungen des Bundesverfassungsgerichts* (decisions of the German Federal Constitutional Court)
BVR	*Verfahren über Verfassungsbeschwerden* (proceedings regarding constitutional complaints)
BYIL	British Yearbook of International Law
C./Chap.	Chapter
Ca.	Circa
CBC	Canada Broadcasting Corporation
CDILR	Cumulative Digest of International Law and Relations
Cf.	*Confer* (compare)
CIA	Central Intelligence Agency (United States of America)
CILJ	Cornell International Law Journal
CJGG	The Chinese Journal of Global Governance
CJICL	Cambridge Journal of International and Comparative Law
CJIL	Chinese Journal of International Law
CLJ	Coventry Law Journal
CNN	Cable News Network
Co.	Company
COPEI	*Comité de Organización Política Electoral Independiente* (Venezuela)
COPIPSL	Cologne Occasional Papers on International Peace and Security Law
CWILJ	California Western International Law Journal
CWRJIL	Case Western Reserve Journal of International Law
D.C.	District of Colombia
Dec	December
dec.	Decision on Admissibility (ECHR)
Diss.	Dissertation
DJCIL	Duke Journal of Comparative and International Law
Doc.	Document
Docs	Documents
Dr(.)	Doctor
ECHR	European Convention on Human Rights (Convention for the Protection of Human Rights and Fundamental Freedoms)
ECtHR	European Court of Human Rights
Ed.	Editor
Edn	Edition
Eds	Editors
e.g.	*exempli gratia* (for example)

EJIL	European Journal of International Law
et al	*et alii* (and other people)
etc.	*et cetera* (and so on)
EU	European Union
EWCA	England and Wales Court of Appeal
EWHC	High Court of England and Wales
f.	And the following pages
FAZ	*Frankfurter Allgemeine Zeitung*
FBI	Federal Bureau of Investigation (United States of America)
Fn.	Footnote
FRG	Federal Republic of Germany
GA	General Assembly
GDR	German Democratic Republic
George Wash. Int Law Rev	The George Washington International Law Review
GJICL	Georgia Journal of International and Comparative Law
HHJ	His/Her Honour Judge (UK)
HICLR	Hastings International and Comparative Law Review
HILJO	Harvard International Law Journal Online
HLR	Harvard Law Review
HMS	Her Majesty's Ship (United Kingdom of Great Britain and Northern Ireland)
HRQ	Human Rights Quarterly
IACtHR	Inter-American Court of Human Rights
IALR	University of Miami Inter-American Law Review
IBP	International Business Publications (United States of America)
ICCPR	International Covenant on Civil and Political Rights
ICJ	International Court of Justice
ICLQ	The International and Comparative Law Quarterly
ICSID	International Centre for Settlement of Investment Disputes
i.e.	*id est* (that is)
IJIL	Indonesian Journal of International Law
IJLLJS	International Journal of Law and Legal Jurisprudence Studies
IJRL	International Journal of Refugee Law
ILA	International Law Association
ILC	International Law Commission
ILM	International Legal Materials
ILS	International Legal Studies
Inc.	Incorporated
J Third World Stud	Journal of Third World Studies
JIA	Journal of International Affairs
JIDS	Journal of International Dispute Settlement
JLAS	Journal of Latin American Studies

Jr.	Junior
JuS Schriftenreihe	*Schriftenreihe der Juristischen Schulung* (Publication Series of Legal Training)
KJIS	The Korean Journal of International Studies
KLRI	Korea Legislation Research Institute
LA	Los Angeles
lit.	*littera*
LJIL	Leiden Journal of International Law
LNTS	League of Nations Treaty Series
LQR	The Law Quarterly Review
Lt.	Lieutenant
m	Million
MA	Massachusetts
Mar(.)	March
MJIL	Michigan Journal of International Law
MLR	Michigan Law Review
MPEPIL	Max Planck Encyclopedia of Public International Law
MPICPLIL	Max Planck Institute for Comparative Public Law and International Law
MQR	Methodist Quarterly Review
Mr	Mister
N.	North
NCJIL	North Carolina Journal of International Law
NCJILCR	North Carolina Journal of International Law and Commercial Regulation
NJIHL	Northwestern Journal of International Human Rights
NJIL	Nordic Journal of International Law
NLI	National Library of Ireland
No. (s)	Number(s)
NUS	National University of Singapore
N.V.	*Naamloze vennootschap* (Dutch public company)
NYUJILP	New York University Journal of International Law and Politics
OAS	Organisation of American States
Oct	October
OEA	*Organização dos Estados Americanos* (Organisation of American States)
Oxon	Oxford(shire)
p.	Page
para. (s)	Paragraph(s)
PC	Police constable
PCIJ	Permanent Court of International Justice
PKK	*Partiya Karkerên Kurdistanê* (Kurdistan Workers' Party)
PLCJR	Plymouth Law and Criminal Justice Review

PLJ	Philippine Law Journal
pp(.)	Pages
Proc ASCE	Proceedings of the Association for the Study of the Cuban Economy
PSQ	Political Science Quarterly
R.	Regina (The Crown)
Ref.	Reference
RSQ	Refugee Survey Quarterly
RTL	Radio Television Luxembourg
S.	South
SAJHR	South African Journal on Human Rights
SBS	Special Broadcasting (News) Service (Australia)
Sect(s).	Section(s)
Sept	September
Ser.	Series
Sic	*sic erat scriptum* (thus it is written)
SLR	Stanford Law Review
S.p.A.	*Società per azioni* (Italian company with shares)
Sr.	Senior
St.	Saint
TAPSR	The American Political Science Review
TICLJ	Temple International and Comparative Law Journal
Trans. Grotius Soc.	Grotius Society Transactions
UBC	University of British Colombia
UDHR	Universal Declaration of Human Rights
UFRGS	*Universidade Federal do Rio Grande do Sul* (Federal University of Rio Grande do Sul)
UK	United Kingdom of Great Britain and Northern Ireland
UKSC	Supreme Court of the United Kingdom
UMLR	University of Miami Law Review
UMNSACLR	University of Miami National Security and Armed Conflict Law Review
UN	United Nations
UNALIL	United Nations Audiovisual Library of International Law
UNCLOS	United Nations Convention on the Law of the Sea
UNHCR	United Nations High Commissioner for Refugees
UNTS	United Nations Treaty Series
UPI	United Press International
UPJIL	University of Pennsylvania Journal of International Law
U. S.	United States Supreme Court
U.S./US	United States (of America)
USA	United States of America

UWALR	University of Western Australia Law Review
v	Versus
VCCR	Vienna Convention on Consular Relations
VCDR	Vienna Convention on Diplomatic Relations
VCLT	Vienna Convention on the Law of Treaties
VJTL	Vanderbilt Journal of Transnational Law
VLR	Virginia Law Review
Vol. (s)	Volume(s)
VS	*Verlag für Sozialwissenschaften* (Publishing House for Social Sciences)
WBHR	West Bohemian Historical Review
World Aff	World Affairs
YJIL	Yale Journal of International Law
ZaöRV	*Zeitschrift für ausländisches öffentliches Recht und Völkerrecht* (Heidelberg Journal of International Law)
ZfP	*Zeitschrift für Politik* (Journal of Politics)
ZJS	*Zeitschrift für das juristische Studium* (Journal of Legal Studies)

Chapter 1
Introduction

The question of whether a right to diplomatic asylum exists under public international law is one which has confounded international law for centuries. It is equally one which has not diminished in either salience or prevalence in recent times, not least considering the controversy surrounding the legality of Julian Assange's recent claim to asylum based upon his near seven year residence in the Ecuadorian embassy in London.[1] The international reception this case, and others like it, has garnered has in turn led to an increase in discussion of the topic. This is an area of law which has long sought both clarification and codification in the light of the case law of the ICJ and the unsuccessful codification attempts of the ILC.[2]

In determining the existence of such a right, which is to be ascertained taking into consideration a wealth of historical practice, one must necessarily weigh the interests of the so-called sending state, that is the foreign state setting up its diplomatic premises on the territory of another, against those of the host or receiving state, i.e. the state upon whose territory the diplomatic premises reside.

On the one hand, one has the interest of the host state in upholding its jurisdictional sovereignty, as enshrined for example in Art. 2 (1) UN Charter,[3] and territorial integrity, anchored in Art. 2 (4) UN Charter: an important part of which includes the enforceability of its domestic criminal and civil jurisdiction over those persons in its territory. On the other hand, one must consider the interests of the sending state in

[1] Assange entered Ecuador's London embassy on 19th June 2012. He was arrested by the British police after they were invited into the embassy by the Ecuadorian mission on 11th April 2019. Cf. Chap. 7: Annex, Table 7.1, Case No. 188. For further information on the Assange case, see Chap. 1: Sect. 1.1.

[2] Cf. Kitschenberg (1965), Einleitung describing diplomatic asylum as one of the most controversial areas of public international law.

[3] Charter of the United Nations 1945, Adopted in San Francisco on 26 June 1945, Entered into Force on 24 October 1945.

L. Hughes-Gerber, *Diplomatic Asylum*,
https://doi.org/10.1007/978-3-030-73046-8_1

upholding and preserving its sovereignty over its diplomatic premises.[4] This is most notably protected by the concept of the inviolability of the diplomatic premises in Art. 22 (1) Vienna Convention on Diplomatic Relations[5]—the cornerstone of diplomatic law.[6]

In essence, in order to determine whether or not such a right exists, one must not only analyse the sources of international law, codified in Art. 38 (1) ICJ Statute,[7] in particular international treaty law (a)[8] and custom (b),[9] but also determine the level of international legal protection afforded to both the interests and the sovereign rights of the host state and, on the other hand, the interests and sovereign rights of the sending state.

1.1 Relevance of the Topic

Any regulation of the practice of diplomatic asylum is notably absent from the Vienna Convention on Diplomatic Relations and although it was discussed in the context of the draft articles to this convention, ultimately it was decided that the concept of asylum should not be included in Art. 22 VCDR concerning the inviolability of the mission premises.[10] Denza attributes this absence to the inability of states to agree on specific rules with regard to diplomatic asylum.[11] Furthermore, codification attempts by and before the International Law Commission have so far been fruitless.[12]

Nevertheless, the practice has not been absent from international jurisprudence. In the following three contentious cases, the International Court of Justice has been confronted with the practice:

---

[4]Defined by Art. 1 (i) VCDR as: "the buildings or parts of buildings and the land ancillary thereto, irrespective of ownership, used for the purposes of the mission including the residence of the head of the mission."

[5]Vienna Convention on Diplomatic Relations 1961, Adopted in Vienna on 18 April 1961, Entered into Force on 24 April 1964, UNTS Vol. No. 500, p. 95.

[6]This concept has been described by the ICJ as a "fundamental prerequisite": Case Concerning United States Diplomatic and Consular Staff in Tehran (United States of America v Iran), Request for the Indication of Provisional Measures, Order of 15 December 1979, No. 64, p. 19, para. 38.

[7]Statute of the International Court of Justice 1945, Adopted in San Francisco on 24 October 1945.

[8]Cf. Chap. 4.

[9]Cf. Chap. 5.

[10]Yearbook of the International Law Commission, 1957, 394th Meeting, 3 May 1957, p. 55, para. 54 and 411th Meeting, 5 June 1957, p. 144, para. 61.

[11]Denza (2016), p. 3.

[12]See Chap. 3: Sect. 3.5.

- in the Columbian-Peruvian Asylum case of 1950[13]
- its request for interpretation of the same year[14]
- in the Haya de la Torre case of 1951.[15]

Though an application regarding a dispute arising from the practice was also filed more recently, by Honduras on 28 October 2009,[16] the application was discontinued and the case was then removed from the list.[17] These judgments, in addition to the lack of explicit treaty regulation of the practice on a universal level, have failed to bring about the clarity sought—indeed the request for interpretation of the first judgment came about because the parties had failed to understand said judgment and its implications.[18]

In recent years the topic has been increasingly prominent in the international arena due to the abundance of notable cases. First and foremost, the case of Julian Assange,[19] which came to an abrupt end with his arrest on 11th April 2019,[20] continues to attract intense media attention and warrant an in-depth academic discussion of the topic, particularly as it concerned two states (Ecuador and the United Kingdom) with opposing views on the practice of diplomatic asylum. Ecuador, on the one hand, is a long-time supporter of the practice even going as

[13]Colombian-Peruvian Asylum Case (Colombia v Peru), Judgment of 20 November 1950, ICJ Reports 1950, No. 7, p. 266 f. In its judgment, the Court acknowledged that there had been "so much fluctuation and discrepancy in the exercise of diplomatic asylum and in the official views expressed on various occasions:" Colombian-Peruvian Asylum Case (Colombia v Peru), Judgment of 20 November 1950, ICJ Reports 1950, No. 7, p. 277.

[14]Request for Interpretation of the Judgment of November 20th 1950 in the Asylum Case (Colombia v Peru), Judgment of 27 November 1950, ICJ Reports 1950, No. 13, p. 395 f.

[15]Haya de la Torre Case (Colombia v Peru), Judgment of 13 June 1951, ICJ Reports 1951, No. 14, p. 71 f.

[16]See Certain Questions concerning Diplomatic Relations (Honduras v Brazil) Application Instituting Proceedings by the Republic of Honduras against the Federative Republic of Brazil, 28 October 2009.

[17]Certain Questions concerning Diplomatic Relations (Honduras v Brazil), Order of 12 May 2010, No. 147, ICJ Reports 2010, pp. 303–305. Also see Chap. 3: Sect. 3.7.3 for the background to the case, which gave rise to the dispute.

[18]Request for Interpretation of the Judgment of November 20th 1950 in the Asylum Case (Colombia v Peru), Institution of Proceedings by the Republic of Colombia, 20 November 1950, p. 466.

[19]See Chap. 7: Annex, Table 7.1, Case No. 188. It is interesting to note that the case of Assange is not always classified as a case of diplomatic asylum due to the questionability of Assange's fundamental human rights being at risk, which some hold to be a prerequisite for diplomatic asylum. Whilst the risk of U.S. extradition would fulfil this condition, the Swedish arrest warrant would not: cf. Kau (2019), pp. 198–199, para. 75a. On the definition of diplomatic asylum, see Chap. 2, Sects. 2.1, 2.1.3.

[20]See The Guardian (11 April 2019), Julian Assange arrested at Ecuadorian embassy in London.

far as to make provision for the right to asylum in its constitution,[21] whilst the United Kingdom remains traditionally sceptical and dismissive thereof—going so far as to reject it altogether in recent times and certainly with regard to Assange.[22]

Furthermore, the case concerned Assange, an Australian[23] national whose exploits as founder of the website Wikileaks, renowned for whistleblowing and the release of confidential and sensitive national information, dominated the headlines for a number of years before he sought refuge in the premises of Ecuador's diplomatic mission in London in June 2012.[24] Assange, for whom a European arrest warrant was issued due to (now partially time-barred) sexual assault charges in Sweden[25] which have since been dropped,[26] feared that upon exercise of this warrant by the United Kingdom, he would not be extradited to Sweden to face such

---

[21]Art. 41 Ecuadorian Constitution, Republic of Ecuador, Constitution of 2008, Last Updated 31 January 2011, Published in the Official Register, 20 October 2008, Political Database of the Americas; Statement of the Government of the Republic of Ecuador on the asylum request of Julian Assange, News Release, No. 1. https://web.archive.org/web/20130615201655/http://www.mmrree.gob.ec/eng/2012/com042.asp. Last Accessed 13 Dec 2020. Ecuador's position was shown a degree of support by the OAS in: OAS, Resolution of the 27th Meeting of Consultation of Ministers of Foreign Affairs, 24 August 2012, Reference E- 67. Also see IACtHR, Advisory Opinion OC-25/18 of 30 May 2018 Requested by the Republic of Ecuador, The Institution of Asylum and its Recognition as a Human Right in the Inter-American System of Protection (Interpretation and Scope of Articles 5, 22.7 and 22.8 in Relation to Article 1(1) of the American Convention on Human Rights), p. 3 f.

[22]UN General Assembly, Question of Diplomatic Asylum, Report of the Secretary-General, 2 September 1975, A/10139 (Part I), paras 155, 191, 228; William Hague, U.K. Foreign Secretary, Statement on Ecuadorian Government's Decision to Offer Political Asylum to Julian Assange (16th August 2012). Available at: https://www.gov.uk/government/news/foreign-secretary-statement-on-ecuadorian-government-s-decision-to-offer-political-asylum-to-julian-assange. Last accessed 13 Dec 2020: "The UK does not accept the principle of diplomatic asylum." Also see McNair (1956), p. 76.

[23]Regarding Australian practice and its stance on diplomatic asylum, see Chap. 5: Sects. 5.3.6; 5.4.1.3 and 5.4.2.6.

[24]Cf. The New Yorker (31 May 2010), No Secrets: Julian Assange's mission for total transparency, The Guardian (14 July 2010), Julian Assange: the whistleblower; Forbes (29 November 2010), An interview with Wikileaks' Julian Assange; FAZ (13 December 2010), Wikileaks: Nichts verschweigen; Vanity Fair (6 January 2011), The man who spilled the secrets; The Guardian (28 January 2011), Wikileaks: The Guardian's role in the biggest leak in the history of the world; The Guardian (30 January 2011), Julian Assange: the teen hacker who became insurgent in information war; Die Zeit (3 February 2011), Wikileaks: Übernächtigt und unrasiert; Die Zeit (29 September 2011) Julian Assange: Er rechnet mit Vernichtung.

[25]On the appeal before British courts against his extradition due to these sexual assault charges, see Julian Assange v Swedish Prosecution Authority (2011) EWHC 2849 (Admin) and Assange v Swedish Prosecution Authority (2012) UKSC 22.

[26]Swedish Prosecution Authority, Press Release, The investigation against Julian Assange is discontinued, 19 November 2019. https://www.aklagare.se/en/news-and-press/press-releases/2019/november/the-investigation-against-julian-assange-is-discontinued/. Last Accessed 13 Dec 2020. Also see The Guardian (19 November 2019), Sweden drops Julian Assange rape investigation.

charges,[27] but instead to the U.S., where he argued he could face torture and/or inhuman treatment because of the publications of Wikileaks.

These publications, many of which relate to the U.S. and its governmental machinery, have been highly controversial, in particular those leaked by former U.S. army intelligence analyst Chelsea Manning.[28] Manning was sentenced to 35 years imprisonment for espionage charges, later commuted to 7 years total confinement—rendering Manning eligible for release due to time served—by President Obama.[29] Assange alleges that he, as the founder of Wikileaks, would face a much worse fate were he ever to be surrendered to the American authorities.[30] Before Assange's arrest, the U.S. had not publicly commented on the possibility of Assange being brought to trial there and what charges he could face.[31]

Assange's detention itself has also dominated the headlines—initially due to the high cost borne by the UK for policing the embassy 24/7 in order to promptly arrest Assange were he ever to leave,[32] then due to the continuous length of his detention and the findings of the UN Working Group on Arbitrary Detention, which in 2015

---

[27]The UK Supreme Court upheld the validity of this extradition request by Sweden in 2012: Assange v The Swedish Prosecution Authority (2012) UKSC 22, On appeal from: (2011) EWHC Admin 2849, para. 80. Also see Cullen and Burgess (2015), p. 214 f.

[28]Cf. CBC News, (16 May 2017), Chelsea Manning's controversial journey to freedom; The Washington Post (16 September 2017), The uncompromising debate at the heart of the Harvard-Chelsea Manning controversy.

[29]Manning was, however, jailed again in March 2019 for her refusal to testify before a grand jury in regard to Wikileaks: The Guardian (8 March 2019), Chelsea Manning jailed after refusing to testify to grand jury in Wikileaks case. She was then released in May 2019: The Guardian (10 May 2019), Chelsea Manning released after 62-day confinement in jail. Just over a week later, Manning was jailed again for refusing to testify in the Wikileaks enquiry: The New York Times (19 May 2019), Chelsea Manning Ordered Back to Jail for Refusal to Testify in Wikileaks Enquiry. She was eventually released in March 2020: cf. United States District Court for the Eastern District of Virginia, Alexandria Division, United States of America v John Doe 2010R03793, Grand Jury 19-3, Case No. 1:19-dm-12-AJT-, Order of March 12, 2020; also see The Washington Post (13 March 2020), Chelsea Manning is released from jail.

[30]See for example BBC News (17 December 2010), Wikileaks' Julian Assange 'fears extradition to US' from before Assange entered the embassy.

[31]See for example: U.S. Department of State, Special Briefing, Steve Goldstein and Brian Hook, Press Briefing Room, 11 January 2018: "And we don't discuss whether we are considering bringing Julian Assange to the United States for trial." See also The Guardian (16 November 2018), Julian Assange charged in secret, mistake on US court filing suggests; The Guardian (23 January 2019), Julian Assange launches legal challenge against Trump administration; The Independent (3 March 2019), Chelsea Manning ordered to testify before grand jury in Julian Assange investigation; Lacey (2011), pp. 202–226; Thebes (2012), pp. 889–915 (though it must be noted that this article was written before Assange entered the embassy).

[32]Estimated to total £16m: cf. R v Julian Assange (Bail Act offence), Sentencing Remarks of HHJ Deborah Taylor, Southwark Crown Court, 1 May 2019, p. 2. The round the clock policing of the embassy eventually ceased due to concerns as to its proportionality, nevertheless the UK would still have sought to arrest Assange if he had left the embassy of his own accord: The Guardian (12 October 2015), Julian Assange: Police Removed from outside Ecuadorian Embassy.

held that Assange was being arbitrarily detained by virtue of his continued residence in the embassy.[33]

Moreover, Assange continued to reside in the embassy despite the relevant statutory time limitations having lapsed with regard to the alleged sexual assault charges in Sweden, though an outstanding arrest warrant still remained for his failure to surrender to the court. This was despite Assange being granted Ecuadorian citizenship in January 2018, a futile attempt by Ecuador to facilitate Assange's exit from the embassy,[34] though Ecuador's request for Assange to be granted diplomatic status was duly rejected by the UK.[35]

Assange's residence in the embassy came to an abrupt end when, on the morning of 11th April 2019, he was arrested by the British Metropolitan police, who had been invited into the embassy by the Ecuadorian ambassador.[36] Assange was subsequently transported to a police station, where he was further arrested on behalf of the U.S., with the Metropolitan police confirming what had long been suspected—that Assange is subject to a U.S. extradition warrant.[37] A previously sealed U.S. indictment against Assange for charges of cyber hacking was also published.[38] Assange's arrest has been met with widespread criticism.[39] The prospect of Assange

[33]Human Rights Council, Working Group on Arbitrary Detention, Opinions adopted by the Working Group on Arbitrary Detention at its seventy-fourth session, 30 November–4 December 2015, Opinion No. 54/2015 concerning Julian Assange (Sweden and the United Kingdom of Great Britain and Northern Ireland), p. 17, para. 99. On this opinion, see Happold (2016) and Lazarus (2016).

[34]This citizenship was revoked before Ecuador invited British police into the embassy in order to arrest Assange: Yahoo News (11 April 2019), Quito withdraws Assange's Ecuador citizenship.

[35]The Guardian (10 January 2018), Julian Assange's bid for diplomatic status rejected by Britain.

[36]See Metropolitan Police, Arrest update—SW1 (11 April 2019).— at the time of writing in April 2021, this statement was no longer available online; The Guardian (11 April 2019), Julian Assange arrested at Ecuadorian embassy in London. On the lead-up to Assange's arrest, see: Die Zeit (5 April 2019), Assange könnte Botschaftsasyl verlieren; The Independent (5 April 2019), Julian Assange: WikiLeaks says founder to be expelled from Ecuador embassy within 'hours to days.'

[37]See Metropolitan Police, UPDATE: Arrest of Julian Assange (11 April 2019).—at the time of writing in April 2021, this statement was no longer available online.

[38]See The United States District Court for the Eastern District of Virginia, Alexandria Division, United States of America v Julian Paul Assange, 6 March 2018.

[39]UN News (11 April 2019), UN experts warn Assange arrest exposes him to risk of serious human rights violations. Available at: https://news.un.org/en/story/2019/04/1036491. Last Accessed 13 Dec 2020. Former Ecuadorian President Rafael Correa, who originally granted Assange asylum, described the decision of sitting President Moreno to permit the arrest of Assange as "a crime that humanity will never forget": cf. Reuters (11 April 2019), Factbox: Reaction to arrest of Julian Assange in London. Assange's subsequent detention has also dominated the headlines: cf. Spiegel Online (12 May 2019), Pamela Anderson über Julian Assange, "er sagte zu mir: Rette mein Leben!"; BBC News (13 September 2019), Julian Assange to stay in prison over absconding fears; The Guardian (14 September 2019), Julian Assange to remain in jail pending extradition to US; The Independent (28 September 2019), Julian Assange 'subjected to every kind of torment' in Belmarsh prison as he awaits extradition; France24 (1 November 2019), Prison conditions for Julian Assange are putting his life 'at risk': UN expert; Reuters (18 November 2019), WikiLeaks founder Assange has unsuitable computer in jail, court told; The Guardian (25 November 2019), Julian Assange's health is so bad 'he could die in prison', say 60 doctors.

being handed over to the U.S. authorities remains a distinct possibility, despite a Magistrate's Court's recent denial of the United States' extradition request due to grave concerns as to Assange's mental health.[40]

The length of Assange's residence in the small flat in the building Ecuador shares with Colombia for the purpose of providing diplomatic premises, which Ecuador at one point declared to be untenable,[41] has continually given rise to discussion as to the legitimacy of the practice of diplomatic asylum. Arguably, it depicts a use of the diplomatic premises inconsistent with those provided for in Art. 3 (1) Vienna Convention on Diplomatic Relations.[42] These functions include:

> (a) Representing the sending State in the receiving State;
> (b) Protecting in the receiving State the interests of the sending State and of its nationals, within the limits permitted by international law;
> (c) Negotiating with the Government of the receiving State;
> (d) Ascertaining by all lawful means conditions and developments in the receiving State, and reporting thereon to the Government of the sending State;
> (e) Promoting friendly relations between the sending State and the receiving State, and developing their economic, cultural and scientific relations.

Any use of the premises of the diplomatic mission inconsistent with the functions provided for in Art. 3 (1) VCDR, other rules of general international law or any special agreements in force between the sending state and the receiving state would necessarily constitute a breach of Art. 41 (3) VCDR, which provides:

> 3. The premises of the mission must not be used in any manner incompatible with the functions of the mission as laid down in the present Convention or by other rules of general international law or by any special agreements in force between the sending and the receiving State.

---

[40] See District Judge (Magistrates' Court) Vanessa Baraitser, Westminster Magistrates' Court, The Government of the United States of America v Julian Paul Assange, 4 January 2021. Specifically, it was held that Section 91 of the 2003 Extradition Act was constituted (on this point cf. para. 278 f). At the time of writing in April 2021, a decision as to the permissibility of the U.S. appeal before the High Court was still pending.

[41] The Guardian (9 January 2018), Julian Assange's stay in London embassy untenable, says Ecuador. It is also of note that Ecuador temporarily cut off Assange's internet connection in March 2018 due to his alleged interference in other states' affairs: The Guardian (28 March 2018), Ecuador cuts off Julian Assange's internet access at London embassy. For further information on the friction between the state of Ecuador and Assange, particularly in the last year of his residence in the embassy, see for example: The Guardian (15 May 2018), How Julian Assange became an unwelcome guest in Ecuador's embassy; The Guardian (16 October 2018), Ecuador tells Assange to avoid political activity online—and feed the cat; The Guardian (19 October 2018), Julian Assange launches legal action against Ecuador; The Guardian (24 October 2018), Ecuador says Assange must sort out own issues with Britain; The Guardian, (29 October 2018), Assange must follow new Ecuador embassy rules, says judge; The Telegraph (6 December 2018), Julian Assange rejects UK-Ecuador deal for him to leave the embassy; The Guardian (11 April 2019), The seven-year itch: Assange's awkward stay in the embassy.

[42] Cf. Chap. 4: Sect. 4.1.4.

Any such use of the diplomatic premises would constitute an abuse thereof, this being inconsistent with the purposes of the diplomatic mission.[43]

The case of Chen Guangcheng,[44] although less prominent in the media, has also brought the practice to the forefront of the international legal arena in recent years.[45] Guangcheng, a Chinese political activist, fled alleged persecution by the Chinese authorities to the U.S. embassy in Beijing in May 2012. This is despite the U.S., the *de facto* granting state, generally not recognising the practice of diplomatic asylum,[46] though it has been known to grant individuals such a right in exceptional cases.[47]

Guangcheng was afforded diplomatic protection by the U.S., though he left the embassy after a short time to travel to the U.S. to study. Interestingly, Guangcheng was not granted political asylum but was permitted to travel to the U.S. on the basis of a study visa[48]—he is thought to remain resident there to the present day (April 2021).

This case, which took place around the same time as Assange's, is evidentiary of the use of the practice as an interim solution for a political offender. Such an offender may be seeking diplomatic asylum until political asylum can be realised—i.e. until the asylee can reach the territory of the granting state. The Guangcheng case tested relations between the U.S. and China but is important in demonstrating that even states sceptical of the practice afford those persecuted for political offences diplomatic protection, in some cases as a prelude to political asylum.

Furthermore, the cases of Assange and Guangcheng by no means stand alone. In the annexed table, Table 7.1,[49] twentieth/twenty-first Century diplomatic asylum cases have been listed in order to illustrate both how widespread the practice is in terms of geography[50] and also in terms of the number of cases.[51] Notably, most of

---

[43]These purposes are reflected in the Preamble to the VCDR.

[44]See Chap. 7: Annex, Table 7.1, Case No. 186.

[45]Cf. Chisholm (2014), pp. 528–555.

[46]E.g. "The United States is not a party to the 1954 OAS Convention on Diplomatic Asylum [of Caracas] and does not recognise the concept of diplomatic asylum as a matter of international law," U.S. State Department Statement regarding Julian Assange's residence in the Ecuadorian embassy in London. The original statement is no longer available via the website of the U.S. state department but excerpts can be found in various media reports, for example: Foreign Policy (17 August 2012), State Department: The U.S. does not recognize the concept of 'diplomatic asylum.'

[47]See Chap. 7: Annex, Table 7.1. One notable example is the case of eminent Chinese scientist Fang Lizhi, his wife Lu Shuxian and son Fang Ke, who sought asylum in the U.S. asylum in Beijing in early June 1989, where they remained until 25 June 1990 (see Case No. 112 of Table 7.1 of Chap. 7: Annex for more details). For further information on this case see: Rubin (1990), pp. 84–89.

[48]The New York Times (9 May 2012), Behind Twists of Diplomacy in the Case of a Chinese Dissident. Also see Bhargava Ray (2013), pp. 1217–1218.

[49]See Chap. 7: Annex, Table 7.1.

[50]Encompassing states from all six major continents granting such a right.

[51]This stands at 209. See Chap. 7: Annex, Table 7.1.

these cases did not use the term diplomatic asylum, instead more regularly favouring the terms "shelter", "refuge" or "diplomatic protection".

Table 7.1[52] illustrates the granting of a *de facto* right to diplomatic asylum by states in all six of the world's major continents within the last century,[53] though the prevalence of both European and Latin American states in this regard cannot fail to go unnoticed. This gives rise to the question as to whether the widespread geography, in addition to the longstanding nature, of the practice suffices to constitute the state practice element of customary international law—which may in turn provide the practice with a legal basis.

Moreover, the historical and political significance of many of the cases is also immediately apparent e.g. the cases of Ferenc B. Farkas and Judith Maléter,[54] Imre Nagy[55] and József Mindszenty[56] against the backdrop of the Hungarian revolution, the case of Erich Honecker[57] following German reunification or the more recent cases of the Venezuelan judges,[58] Freddy Guevara,[59] twenty-five Guaido supporters,[60] Leopoldo López and his family,[61] eighteen national guardsmen,[62] Américo de Grazia, Mariela Magallanes and five others[63] and Franco Manuel Casella[64] due to continuously heightened political tension in Venezuela. In Hungary and in the context of the holocaust, many European legations are also reported to have used diplomatic asylum as a mechanism to save lives.[65] Such cases depict the use of the practice at times of political instability—a theme common to the practice since its inception.[66]

[52]See Chap. 7: Annex.

[53]For the convenience of the reader, cases have been organised according to the continent (though the continent of South America has been replaced by the wider region of Latin America and the continent of North America has been replaced accordingly by Northern America) of the granting state.

[54]See Chap. 7: Annex, Table 7.1. Case No. 52.

[55]See Chap. 7: Annex, Table 7.1, Case No. 53.

[56]See Chap. 7: Annex, Table 7.1, Case No. 54.

[57]See Chap. 7: Annex, Table 7.1, Case No. 137.

[58]See Chap. 7: Annex, Table 7.1, Case Nos 199 and 200.

[59]See Chap. 7: Annex, Table 7.1, Case No. 201.

[60]See Chap. 7: Annex, Table 7.1, Case No. 204.

[61]See Chap. 7: Annex, Table 7.1, Case Nos 205–206.

[62]See Chap. 7: Annex, Table 7.1, Case No. 207.

[63]See Chap. 7: Annex, Table 7.1, Case No. 208.

[64]See Chap. 7: Annex, Table 7.1, Case No. 209.

[65]Kovács and Ádány (2017), pp. 187–189.

[66]Dupuy (1976), p. 744. See also: Executive Order No. 5956, Unsanctioned Asylum, Herbert Hoover, White House, 1 December 1932, CDILR 2:104.

Many of these cases also depict diplomatic asylum being used as an (at times merely intended) interim solution until territorial political asylum can be realised by the asylum seeker in the granting state e.g. *inter alia* in the cases of Leonardo Argüello Barreto,[67] Jacobo Árbenz and family,[68] Reino Häyhänen,[69] Humberto Delgado,[70] Chen Guangcheng[71] or Julian Assange.[72]

Furthermore, Table 7.1 also demonstrates the extent to which the practice occurs in the modern day. It provides for at least two hundred and nine such cases having occurred in the twentieth and twenty-first Centuries and naturally does not provide for undocumented cases, the existence of which is strongly assumed.

An analysis of the duration of each case is also interesting: indeed, this differs from a matter of hours such as in the cases of Wang Lijun[73] or the Burundian students[74] to nearly fifteen years in the well-documented case of József Mindszenty.[75] It is clear that cases only short in duration cannot command the same media attention as enduring cases such as that of Mindszenty or Assange. However, their relevance cannot be overlooked. Such cases, despite their interim nature, are equally indicative of states granting (at least *de facto*) asylum to individuals in the context of their diplomatic premises[76] and thus constitute important examples of state practice in relation to diplomatic asylum.

1.2 Legal Context

Most authors addressing the issue of diplomatic asylum are critical of both state practice in relation to the claiming of such a right,[77] as well as the lack of clarity brought by the jurisprudence of the ICJ.[78] It is imperative to clarify the issue not only

[67] Cf. Chap. 7: Annex, Table 7.1, Case No. 46.

[68] Cf. Chap. 7: Annex, Table 7.1, Case No. 50.

[69] Cf. Chap. 7: Annex, Table 7.1, Case No. 55.

[70] Cf. Chap. 7: Annex, Table 7.1, Case No. 58.

[71] Cf. Chap. 7: Annex, Table 7.1, Case No. 186.

[72] Cf. Chap. 7: Annex, Table 7.1, Case No. 188.

[73] See Chap. 7: Annex, Table 7.1, Case No. 184.

[74] See Chap. 7: Annex, Table 7.1, Case No. 194.

[75] See Chap. 7: Annex, Table 7.1, Case No. 54.

[76] Cf. Accioly (1961), p. 292 holding that even states which do not recognise the concept of diplomatic asylum have endorsed it.

[77] E.g. Duxbury (2012), p. 1; Hobe (2020), p. 308; Schack (2014), p. 386; Stein et al. (2017), pp. 221, 277; Värk (2012), pp. 256–257; von Arnauld (2019), p. 258, para. 586. Cf. Colombian-Peruvian Asylum Case (Colombia v Peru), Counter-Memorial Submitted by the Government of the Republic of Peru, 21 March 1950, p. 121.

[78] E.g. Evans (1951), pp. 755, 761; García-Mora (1951), pp. 927, 930; Värk (2012), pp. 245–246.

to contribute to the sparse scholarly debate[79] surrounding the issue in general but more importantly to avoid further international disputes in the future. Such disputes include that which surrounded Assange, where one state purports to claim such a right upon the territory of a state which does not recognise its universal existence. The latter thus perceives the granting of asylum as an unlawful interference in its domestic affairs and a frustration of the course of its domestic legal system.[80]

The stalemate created by the recent Assange case is indicative of the legal conundrum posed by the issue of diplomatic asylum in general, the absolute sanctity of the diplomatic premises[81] facilitating the practice even without a formal legal basis recognised by the sending state.[82] This legal loophole is highly undesirable as it enables sending states to circumvent the local jurisdiction of the receiving state by sheltering an individual/a group of individuals from being subjected to the local justice system. This not only constitutes an intervention into the domestic affairs of the receiving state,[83] but also directly conflicts with the purpose of the Vienna Convention on Diplomatic Relations, which is not to benefit individuals but rather to facilitate the efficient functioning of the mission.[84]

The issue of diplomatic asylum could equally be indicative of a shift in international law in the twenty-first Century, denoted by achieving a new balance between the traditional principles of international law such as state sovereignty and non-interference on the one hand and newer human rights obligations on the other. In the light of the ever-increasing importance of human rights and the bolstered status of the individual in international law, the Assange and the Guangcheng cases may prove to be indicative of a growing trend.

[79]Extensive works are no longer current: see Carrie (1994); Kitschenberg (1965); Puthikampol (1990); Ronning (1965); Sinha (1971); Urrutia-Aparicio (1960) and, to a lesser extent, even Klepper (2009). More recent literature strongly places the focus on recent high profile cases particularly that of Julian Assange: see Ambos (2012); Chisholm (2014); Den Heijer (2013), pp. 399–425; Duxbury (2012); FAZ (22 August 2012), Mit Unlauteren Mitteln; Frank (2014); Happold (2012); Kristiyati (2013), pp. 217–230; Lavender (2014), pp. 443–486; Marauhn and Simon (2012), pp. 593–601; Nur Kayacan (2016); Schiffbauer (2013); Tawiah (2013), pp. 125–130; Tye (2016), pp. 218–238; Värk (2012), pp. 240–259. Also see Evans (1965), p. 674 where it is noted that the bulk of literature on the subject is from Latin America.

[80]Colombian-Peruvian Asylum Case (Colombia v Peru), Judgment of 20 November 1950, ICJ Reports 1950, No. 7, p. 284. Cf. Dahm et al. (1989), p. 291; Kitschenberg (1965), p. 2; von Arnauld (2019), p. 258, para. 586; Foreign Ministry Spokesperson Liu Weimin's Remarks on Chen Guangcheng's Entering the US Embassy in China, 2nd May 2012.

[81]Cf. Art. 22 (1) VCDR. McClanahan goes as far as to say that inviolability is set forth in such a way that it leaves open the possibility for asylum: McClanahan (1989), p. 54. Cf. Accioly (1961), p. 291.

[82]Cf. Kimminich (1961), p. 236 holding that diplomatic asylum is without legal foundation in general international law.

[83]Cf. Art. 41 (1) VCDR and Art. 2 (1) UN Charter.

[84]Cf. Preamble to the VCDR.

1.3 Outline

In order to explore whether a right to diplomatic asylum exists in general international law,[85] it is necessary to establish both the historical and the present context of the term "diplomatic asylum" in the international legal system. In this regard, Chap. 2 will establish a definition for the term "diplomatic asylum", drawing herewith on the term's component parts.

Chapter 3 will then detail the history of the practice in the context of diplomatic law from its inceptions in the fifteenth Century to the present day, placing a particular emphasis on recent practice from Latin America in order to ascertain the central features of the practice in this context.

Chapter 4 will examine international treaty law as a primary source of international law[86] in order to determine the extent to which a right to grant diplomatic exists hereunder. In this regard, relevant universal and regional treaty law will be evaluated, with the VCDR being of central importance with respect to the former and the regional Latin American treaty law framework on diplomatic asylum being constitutive of the latter. Latin America remains the only world region in which such a treaty framework exists.

Chapter 5 will evaluate whether a legal basis for the right to diplomatic asylum can be identified in customary international law. In this regard, state practice and *opinio juris* as the constituent elements of customary international law will be examined in turn. Chapter 5 will not only consider whether the aforementioned requirements are fulfilled with regard to universal custom but will also evaluate whether these requirements are fulfilled on a regional level with respect to any of the world regions.

Moreover, in the light of the human rights era, in particular following the Universal Declaration of Human Rights of 1948,[87] Chap. 6 will assess whether the right to diplomatic asylum may be legitimately granted on humanitarian grounds[88] i.e. where the human rights of the person seeking diplomatic asylum risk being seriously breached without such sanctuary. Indeed, maintaining human rights is one

[85]The term general international law denotes international law on a universal level as opposed to international legal norms with a mere regional scope.

[86]Cf. Art. 38 (1) (a) ICJ Statute.

[87]The UDHR was adopted and proclaimed by General Assembly Resolution 217 A (III), Universal Declaration of Human Rights, 183rd Plenary Meeting, 10 December 1948.

[88]Cf. UN General Assembly, 29th Session, Sixth Committee, Summary Record of the 1505th Meeting, Agenda Item 105, Diplomatic Asylum, A/C.6/SR.1505, 25 November 1974, p. 241, para. 1. Gregory goes as far as to argue that where a right to diplomatic asylum has been exercised in modern times, this was only in the context of nations with governments so unstable that humanity has required the practice and it was this rather than law which justified it: Gregory (1905), p. 184. On this point, also see Foakes and Denza (2017), p. 234.

of the primary aims of the Latin American institution of asylum,[89] which encompasses the concept of diplomatic asylum. In particular, Chap. 6 will explore various principles and provisions of international human rights law in order to determine whether a state's right to grant diplomatic asylum on humanitarian grounds is founded either directly thereunder or by way of constituting a rule of customary international law status.

Finally, in the context of Chap. 7, a determination will be made as to whether general international law supports a right to diplomatic asylum. In this regard, the status quo will be examined and the mechanisms international law has at its disposal will be explored in order to propose a solution going forward, which would provide adequate clarification to states so as to prevent further disputes over the practice in the future. This chapter will also offer a future-orientated perspective of the development of both the practice of diplomatic asylum and indeed its prospective legal basis.

References

Accioly H (1961) Das Asylrecht. AdV 9(3):289–293

Ambos K (2012) Diplomatic asylum for Julian Assange? In: EJIL Blog. https://www.ejiltalk.org/diplomatic-asylum-for-julian-assange/. Last accessed 14 Dec 2020

Bhargava Ray S (2013) Optimal asylum. VJTL 46:1215–1265

Carrie H (1994) Das diplomatische Asyl im gegenwärtigen Völkerrecht. Dissertation, Heidelberg University, Nomos, Baden-Baden

Chisholm JT (2014) Chen Guangcheng and Julian Assange: the normative impact of international incidents on diplomatic asylum law. George Wash Int Law Rev 82(2):528–555

Cullen H, Burgess B (2015) Extradition from A to Z: Assange, Zentai and the challenge of interpreting international obligations. UWALR 39(2):208–238

Dahm G, Delbrück J, Wolfrum R (1989) Völkerrecht, vol I/1, 2nd edn. De Gruyter, Berlin/New York

Den Heijer M (2013) Diplomatic asylum and the Assange case. LJIL 26(2):399–425

Denza E (2016) Diplomatic law, Commentary on the Vienna Convention on Diplomatic Relations, 4th edn. Oxford University Press, Oxford

Dupuy PM (1976) La position française en matière d'asile diplomatique. AFDI 22:743–755

Duxbury A (2012) Assange and the law of diplomatic relations. In: ASILI 16 (32). https://www.asil.org/insights/volume/16/issue/32/assange-and-law-diplomatic-relations. Last accessed 14 Dec 2020

Evans AE (1951) The Colombian-Peruvian asylum case: termination of the judicial phase. AJIL 45 (4):755–762

Evans AE (1965) Reviewed work(s): El Asilo Diplomatico: Su Aspecto Antijuridico e Inhumano. by Roberto S. Corpen. AJIL 59(3):674–675

[89] Colombian-Peruvian Asylum Case (Colombia v Peru), Judgment of 20 November 1950, ICJ Reports 1950, No. 7, Dissenting Opinion by Judge M. Caicedo Castilla (translation), p. 359. Also see IACtHR, Advisory Opinion OC-25/18 of 30 May 2018 Requested by the Republic of Ecuador, The Institution of Asylum and its Recognition as a Human Right in the Inter-American System of Protection (Interpretation and Scope of Articles 5, 22.7 and 22.8 in Relation to Article 1(1) of the American Convention on Human Rights), p. 3 f.

Foakes J, Denza E (2017) Privileges and immunities of diplomatic missions. In: Roberts I (ed) Satow's diplomatic practice, 7th edn. Oxford University Press, Oxford, pp 222–245
Frank S (2014) Das diplomatische Asyl am Beispiel von Julian Assange, Studienarbeit, GRIN
García-Mora MR (1951) The Colombian-Peruvian asylum case and the doctrine of human rights. VLR 37(7):927–965
Gregory CN (1905) The privileges of ambassadors and foreign ministers. MLR 3(3):173–184
Happold M (2012) Julian Assange and Diplomatic Asylum. In: EJIL Blog. https://www.ejiltalk.org/julian-assange-and-diplomatic-asylum/. Last Accessed 22 Apr 2021
Happold M (2016) Julian Assange and the UN Working Group on Arbitrary Detention. In: EJIL Blog. https://www.ejiltalk.org/julian-assange-and-the-un-working-group-on-arbitrary-detention/. Last accessed 14 Dec 2020
Hobe S (2020) Einführung in das Völkerrecht, 11th edn. A. Francke Verlag, Tübingen
Kau M (2019) Der Staat und der Einzelne als Völkerrechtssubjekte. In: Vitzthum W, Proelß A (eds) Völkerrecht, 7th edn. DeGruyter, Berlin/Boston, pp 159–318
Kimminich O (1961) Asyl in Stützpunkten der UN Truppen. ZfP 8(3):235–240
Kitschenberg H (1965) Das diplomatische Asyl unter besonderer Berücksichtigung des Asylstreits zwischen Kolumbien und Peru. Dissertation, Universität zu Köln
Klepper I (2009) Diplomatisches Asyl, Zulässigkeit und Grenzen. Dissertation, Universität zu Köln, vol 4814, Peter Lang Verlag, Frankfurt am Main/Berlin/Bern/Brussels/New York/Oxford/Vienna
Kovács P, Ádány TV (2017) The non-customary practice of diplomatic asylum. In: Behrens P (ed) Diplomatic law in a new millennium. Oxford University Press, Oxford, pp 179–203
Kristiyati A (2013) Ecuador's decision to grant asylum to Julian Assange: the manifestation of human security. IJIL 10(3):217–230
Lacey HM (2011) Government secrets, national security and freedom of the press, the ability of the United States to prosecute Julian Assange. UMNSACLR 1:202–226
Lavender T (2014) Using the Julian Assange dispute to address international law's failure to address the right of diplomatic asylum. BJIL 39(1):443–486
Lazarus L (2016) The United Nations Working Group on Arbitrary Detention decision on Assange: 'ridiculous' or 'justifiable'? In: EJIL Blog. https://www.ejiltalk.org/the-united-nations-working-group-on-arbitrary-detention-decision-on-assange-ridiculous-or-justifiable/. Last accessed 14 Dec 2020
Marauhn T, Simon S (2012) Diplomatisches Asyl für Julian Assange. ZJS 5:593–601
McClanahan GV (1989) Diplomatic immunity, principles, practices, problems. Hurst and Company, London
McNair A (1956) International law opinions, vol II, peace. Cambridge University Press, Cambridge
Nur Kayacan D (2016) Julian Assange's Allegedly Illegal Detention by the United Kingdom and Sweden in the Ecuadorian Embassy in London. Master's Thesis, Europa Institut Saarland University
Puthikampol A (1990) The practice of diplomatic asylum: principles, recognition, solution. Research Paper, Victoria University of Wellington
Ronning CN (1965) Diplomatic asylum: legal norms and political reality in Latin American relations. Martinus Nijhoff, The Hague
Rubin AP (1990) Diplomatic asylum and Fang Lizhi. Diplomacy Statescraft 1(1):84–89
Schack H (2014) Zugriff auf Potentatengelder – zwischen Vollstreckungsimmunität und Opferschutz. In: Paulus AL, Dethloff N, Giegerich T et al (eds) Internationales, nationales und privates Recht: Hybridisierung der Rechtsordnungen – Immunität, Issue 46, BDGIR. C.F. Müller, Heidelberg, pp 377–397
Schiffbauer B (2013) Julian Assange und das Völkerrecht: Aktuelle Fragen zum Schutz für und durch diplomatische Missionen, COPIPSL, Books on Demand, Norderstedt
Sinha SP (1971) Asylum and international law. Martinus Nijhoff, The Hague
Stein T, Von Buttlar C, Kotzur M (2017) Völkerrecht, 14th edn. Verlag Franz Vahlen, Munich

Tawiah S (2013) Diplomatic asylum: are Julian Assange and Ecuador on firm legal grounds. CLJ 18:125–130
Thebes M (2012) The prospect of extraditing Julian Assange. NCJILCR 37(3):889–915
Tye H (2016) Does Julian Assange illustrate a gap in the law that should be codified? PLCJR 1:218–238
Urrutia-Aparicio C (1960) Diplomatic Asylum in Latin America. Dissertation, American University Guatemala, Editorial del Ministerio de Educación Pública "José de Pineda Ibarra"
Värk R (2012) Diplomatic asylum: theory, practice and the case of Julian Assange. Sisekaitseakadeemia Toimetised 11:240–259
von Arnauld A (2019) Völkerrecht, 4th edn. C.F. Müller, Heidelberg

Chapter 2
What Is Diplomatic Asylum?

It is imperative to establish a precise definition of the term diplomatic asylum before the practice's status under international law can be evaluated.

2.1 What Is Diplomatic Asylum?

There is controversy as to what practice, exactly, the concept of diplomatic asylum actually denotes. In order to define the term diplomatic asylum, it is first necessary to establish the bearer of any such right to claim asylum. This could be either the state[1] or the individual. Furthermore, in order to define the term diplomatic asylum, it is necessary to have defined the term asylum. Only then, can the more specific term of "diplomatic asylum" be defined. In doing so, both a narrow and a wider interpretation of the term will be explored. It is also necessary to distinguish diplomatic asylum from the following constellations:

(1) territorial asylum,
(2) political asylum,
(3) asylum using the diplomatic premises as a facilitation mechanism
(4) collective shelter.

[1]The state is defined by Art. 1 Montevideo Convention on the Rights and Duties of States as possessing the following: a permanent population, a defined territory, government and; capacity to enter into relations with the other states: Montevideo Convention on the Rights and Duties of States 1933, Adopted by the Seventh International Conference of American States in Montevideo on 26 December 1933, Entered into Force on 26 December 1934, LNTS Vol. No. 165, p. 19.

L. Hughes-Gerber, *Diplomatic Asylum*,
https://doi.org/10.1007/978-3-030-73046-8_2

2.1.1 *Right of a State*

It is important to note that when speaking of a right to diplomatic asylum, one is speaking of the right of a state[2] to grant such asylum to an individual and not of an individual's right to request such asylum from a host state.[3] Even if states have a general right to grant an individual diplomatic asylum, this would not automatically accord an individual the right to request such a right.[4] This is in line with states being the primary subjects of public international law, whilst individuals are only secondary subjects of public international law.[5] Nevertheless, some states would also understand a subjective individual right to be inherent in the term asylum.[6] This book will, however, focus on diplomatic asylum as a potential right of a state to grant such asylum to an individual. In any case, such a right must first be established before any corresponding individual right may develop.

In this context, it is furthermore important to note that international organisations may not grant diplomatic asylum.[7]

[2]Or indeed the Holy See with regard to the Vatican State: cf. Barberis (1985), p. 41.

[3]Addison Smith (1911), p. 201; Barberis (1985), p. 41; Shah (2007), para. 1. Cf. IACtHR, Advisory Opinion OC-25/18 of 30 May 2018 Requested by the Republic of Ecuador, The Institution of Asylum and its Recognition as a Human Right in the Inter-American System of Protection (Interpretation and Scope of Articles 5, 22.7 and 22.8 in Relation to Article 1(1) of the American Convention on Human Rights), p. 38, para. 108.

[4]Cf. Barberis (1985), p. 41. Cf. UN General Assembly, 21st Session, Sixth Committee, Summary Record of the 922nd Meeting, Agenda Item 85, Draft Declaration on the Right of Asylum, A/C.6, SR.922, 28 October 1966, p. 134, para. 38; UN General Assembly, 21st Session, Sixth Committee, Summary Record of the 923rd Meeting, Agenda Item 85, Draft Declaration on the Right of Asylum, A/C.6, SR.923, 31 October 1966, p. 140, para. 32.

[5]In this regard, the ILC has stated that "the individual may have rights under international law but remedies are few. Diplomatic protection conducted by a State at inter-State level remains an important remedy for the protection of persons whose human rights have been violated abroad:" Art. 1 ILC Draft Articles on Diplomatic Protection with Commentaries, Text adopted by the International Law Commission at its fifty-eighth session, in 2006, and submitted to the General Assembly as a part of the Commission's report covering the work of that session (A/61/10), p. 26.

[6]For example, Ecuador which describes asylum in all its forms as a "fundamental human right [which] creates obligations *erga omnes*:" Statement of the Government of the Republic of Ecuador on the asylum request of Julian Assange, News Release, No. 1. https://web.archive.org/web/20130615201655/http://www.mmrree.gob.ec/eng/2012/com042.asp. Last Accessed 14 Dec 2020. The breach of *erga omnes* obligations as obligations owed by states to the entire international community as a collective renders any state capable of invoking international state responsibility. Cf. Case Concerning the Barcelona Traction, Light and Power Company, Limited (New Application: 1962) (Belgium v Spain), Second Phase, Judgment of 5 February 1970, ICJ Reports 1970, No. 50, p. 31, paras 33 and 34.

[7]See for example Section 9 (b) of the Agreement between the United Nations and the United States Regarding the Headquarters of the United Nations 1947; cf. Barberis (1985), p. 41.

2.1.2 Asylum

Though, there is no universally recognised definition of the term asylum,[8] the concept is well established in international law and is generally held to denote:

> the protection which a State grants on its territory or in some other place under the control of certain of its organs, to a person who comes to seek it.[9]

This clearly emphasises the ordinary meaning of the term to denote territorial asylum, though the inclusion of the phrase "or in some other case under the control of certain of its organs" equally allows for diplomatic asylum to fall hereunder. Nevertheless, the term falls short of explicitly recognising other forms of asylum, in particular diplomatic asylum, as akin to territorial asylum. The voluntary nature of the discretion of a state to grant asylum stems from a state's territorial sovereignty,[10] entrenched in Art. 2 (1) UN Charter.

The term asylum has also been described as depicting:

> a place of refuge where one could be free from the reach of a pursuer.[11]

This idea of protection from a pursuer strongly correlates to the Institute of International Law's definition of asylum. The concepts of both refuge and protection also correlate with the idea of religious sanctuary.[12]

Though closely interlinked,[13] asylum is furthermore to be differentiated from refugee status.[14] Whilst asylum denotes an institution offering protection, the term

---

[8]Cf. O'Nions (2014), p. 1; Przetacznik (1983), p. 121.

[9]Art. 1, Institute of International Law (5th Commission), Resolutions Adopted at its Bath Session, Asylum in Public International Law (Excluding Neutral Asylum), Sept 1950, AJIL: 45(2): Supplement: Official Documents (Apr.1951): 15. This definition is recognised for example by: García Mora (1956), p. 1; Przetacznik (1983), p. 121; Weis (1966), p. 14. Addison Smith also emphasises this idea of protection: Addison Smith (1911), p. 199. Moreover, this definition correlates to that provided by the ICJ, specifically regarding diplomatic asylum and in the context of the Colombian-Peruvian asylum case: Colombian-Peruvian Asylum Case (Colombia v Peru), Judgment of 20 November 1950, ICJ Reports 1950, No. 7, p. 284: "Asylum protects the political offender against any measures of a manifestly extra-legal character which a government might take or attempt to take against its political opponents." Cf. IACtHR, Advisory Opinion OC-25/18 of 30 May 2018 Requested by the Republic of Ecuador, The Institution of Asylum and its Recognition as a Human Right in the Inter-American System of Protection (Interpretation and Scope of Articles 5, 22.7 and 22.8 in Relation to Article 1(1) of the American Convention on Human Rights), p. 25, para. 66.

[10]Cf. Art. 1 (1) UN Declaration on Territorial Asylum contained within General Assembly Resolution 2312 (XXII), 1631st Plenary Meeting, 14 December 1967; Gil-Bazo (2015), p. 7; Gilbert and Rüsch (2018), p. 813; Goodwin-Gill and McAdam (2007), p. 357; Sen (1988), p. 356. Cf. Kimminich (1961), p. 236.

[11]Boed (1994), p. 2.

[12]Cf. Chap. 3: Sect. 3.1.

[13]Goodwin-Gill and McAdam (2007), p. 357; Pastorino and Ippoliti (2019), p. 4.

[14]For further information on the distinction between asylum and refugee status, acknowledging that this distinction is at times blurred, see: O'Nions (2014), p. 1 f.

"refugee" can be accorded to a certain category of individuals seeking such protection or indeed may denote the content of the protection obligation owed.[15] Art. 1 (2) Convention Relating to the Status of Refugees 1951[16] defines refugees using the following three characteristics:

- persecution
- being outside of one's state of nationality
- the inability or lack of desire to seek protection from one's national state.

Therefore, the term "asylum" denotes the state of protection itself, whilst the term "refugee" generally refers to the subject of such protection. Though a degree of overlap between the terms asylum and refugee is inevitable, with refugees frequently seeking asylum, further elaboration on the rights of refugees is outside of the scope of this book.

There are three different types of asylum:

- diplomatic asylum
- territorial asylum
- political asylum.

Though the focus of this book is on the former, it is necessary to define all three terms in order to distinguish between them. The following three sections[17] will provide a definition as to each of the aforementioned terms.

2.1.3 *Diplomatic Asylum*

2.1.3.1 In a Narrow Sense

Once broken down into its component parts (diplomatic and asylum), a literal definition[18] of the concept of diplomatic asylum indicates:

- the extraterritorial granting of asylum (that is outside of a sovereign state's own territory)
- to persons

---

[15]Gil-Bazo (2015), pp. 3–4.

[16]Convention relating to the Status of Refugees 1951, Adopted by the United Nations Conference of Plenipotentiaries on the Status of Refugees and Stateless Persons in Geneva on 28 July 1951, Registered and Entered into Force on 22 April 1954, UNTS Vol. No. 89, p. 137.

[17]Cf. Chap. 2: Sects. 2.1.3–2.1.5.

[18]Cf. Art. 31 (1) VCLT.

- specifically in the context of the premises of the diplomatic mission (usually the embassy) or the residence of its staff[19]

This mission is located within the territory of the receiving state, which typically objects to such asylum[20] and may seek the criminal prosecution of the asylee. For this reason, diplomatic asylum is sometimes also known as extraterritorial or internal asylum[21] and is more controversial than the ordinary granting of territorial asylum as it necessarily conflicts with the host state's territorial sovereignty.[22]

There is no requirement in terms of the duration of a case of diplomatic asylum and it may be short-term, e.g. to fill an interim period before political asylum in the granting state can be facilitated, or longer-term, for example where this may not be possible due to resistance from the host state and thus a longer period of asylum may be required.

This narrow definition of the concept of diplomatic asylum limits the practice to the boundaries of the premises of a sovereign state's diplomatic mission.[23]

2.1.3.2 In a Broader Sense

However the idea of diplomatic asylum, in a broader sense, also denotes asylum granted in the context of a sending state's consulate,[24] as well as on board its ships in the territorial waters of another state, on board its aircraft or in the context of its military or para-military installations on foreign soil—i.e. premises under the

[19]This definition finds some support in the broad definition described by the report of the UN Secretary General on diplomatic asylum: UN General Assembly, Question of Diplomatic Asylum, Report of the Secretary-General, 2 September 1975, A/10139 (Part I), para. 1. The premises of the diplomatic mission are defined by Art. 1 (i) VCDR.

[20]Colombian-Peruvian Asylum Case (Colombia v Peru), Judgment of 20 November 1950, ICJ Reports 1950, No. 7, p. 274 f.

[21]Kitschenberg (1965), p. 1.

[22]UN General Assembly, 29th Session, Sixth Committee, Summary Record of the 1505th Meeting, Agenda Item 105, Diplomatic Asylum, A/C.6/SR.1505, 25 November 1974, p. 241, para. 6; Colombian-Peruvian Asylum Case (Colombia v Peru), Judgment of 20 November 1950, ICJ Reports 1950, No. 7, p. 275; Porcino (1976), p. 456; Reale (1938), p. 511; Also see: Dahm et al. (1989), p. 290; Kitschenberg (1965), pp. 5–6; Morgenstern (1948), pp. 236–261; Taylor (2019), p. 392.

[23]UN General Assembly, Question of Diplomatic Asylum, Report of the Secretary-General, 2 September 1975, A/10139 (Part I), para. 1.

[24]The issue of consular asylum is predominately governed by the legal regime of the Vienna Convention on Consular Relations 1963. Many of its provisions mirror those of the VCDR e.g. Art. 31 VCCR on the inviolability of the consular premises, Art. 55 VCCR providing that a sending state must respect the laws of the host state and that the consular premises may not be used in a manner incompatible with their functions. The consular functions, contained in Art. 5 VCCR, are, similar to the diplomatic functions, codified in Art. 3 VCDR, encompassing *inter alia* "helping and assisting nationals. . .of the sending state." For further information on the concept of consular asylum, see for example Ronning (1965), p. 125 f.

jurisdiction of the so-called sending state over which it is permitted to exercise authority.[25] State practice in the context of this wider interpretation of the term "diplomatic asylum" has been broader, encompassing states which largely reject the notion of asylum in the context of diplomatic premises.[26]

From this wider interpretation of the term, it is evident that diplomatic asylum denotes the *ad hoc* extension of a state's territorial sovereignty, permitting such a state to exceptionally exercise its own territorial authority in the territory of another state or indeed in the context of the global commons.[27] Such an extension of a state's sovereign and territorial rights would on the one hand appear to be inconsistent with the fundamental idea of a state's exclusive territorial sovereignty over its own jurisdiction[28] in that the sending state would exercise its territorial sovereignty over its embassy—part of the receiving state's legitimate territory.

However, such an exercise of a sovereign state's territorial rights being permissible within the context of its embassy could emanate from the historic notion that the premises of the diplomatic mission are to be regarded as being part of the territory of the sending state[29]—a notion that has long since been disregarded.[30] Indeed Art. 45 (a) VCDR now requires a receiving state to actively protect the mission's premises. This purpose would be entirely redundant if a sending state were

[25] UN General Assembly, Question of Diplomatic Asylum, Report of the Secretary-General, 2 September 1975, A/10139 (Part I), para. 1; Barberis (1985), p. 41; Greenburgh (1955), p. 103; Morgenstern (1948), p. 236; Reale (1938), p. 511; Ronning (1965), p. 7. For further examples, also see Moore (1892), p. 15 f. Cf. IACtHR, Advisory Opinion OC-25/18 of 30 May 2018 Requested by the Republic of Ecuador, The Institution of Asylum and its Recognition as a Human Right in the Inter-American System of Protection (Interpretation and Scope of Articles 5, 22.7 and 22.8 in Relation to Article 1(1) of the American Convention on Human Rights), p. 26, para. 67.

[26] With regard to the U.S. see e.g. Gregory (1905), p. 184; UN General Assembly, Question of Diplomatic Asylum, Report of the Secretary-General, 2 September 1975, A/10139 (Part I), para. 88. Also see: Chap. 3: Sects. 3.3.1 and 3.3.2.

[27] The high seas, the atmosphere, Antarctica and outer space are held to constitute global commons over which no state may exercise territorial sovereignty. Nevertheless, all states may exercise sovereign rights and benefit from the resources of such global commons.

[28] Emanating for example from Art. 2 (1) UN Charter, which provides for the sovereign equality of all UN members; see also Colombian-Peruvian Asylum Case (Colombia v Peru), Judgment of 20 November 1950, ICJ Reports 1950, No. 7, p. 274 f. Cf. UN General Assembly, 29th Session, Sixth Committee, Summary Record of the 1505th Meeting, Agenda Item 105, Diplomatic Asylum, A/C.6/SR.1505, 25 November 1974, p. 244, para. 22.

[29] Grotius described ambassadors as being, by way of a legal fiction, in the place of those who sent them [i.e. in the territory of the sending state]: Cited by Foakes and Denza (2017), p. 225 and by Denza (2016), Art. 22, p. 111.

[30] See for example Paust (1999), pp. 305–328 or Shaw (2017), p. 1015: "The premises remain under the general jurisdiction of the host state." States and scholars have now overwhelmingly abandoned this principle of extraterritoriality: UN General Assembly, Question of Diplomatic Asylum, Report of the Secretary-General, 2 September 1975, A/10139 (Part I), paras 13, 83, 139, 202, 221, 222, 302, 303, 304; Foakes and Denza (2017), p. 225; García-Mora (1951), pp. 934–935; Rafii (2014), p. 56. However, advocates of the extraterritoriality concept exist even up to the present day e.g. Kristiyati (2013), p. 229; Viveros Montoya (2017).

to be permitted to exercise unfettered extraterritorial jurisdiction over its embassies on foreign soil.

Moreover, diplomatic asylum may also be regarded as a form of internal asylum—i.e. asylum granted to an asylee within the territory of the state pursuing him/her.[31] This notion of internal asylum would also, for example, encompass consular asylum,[32] asylum on warships, military bases and military planes,[33] thus denoting a wider interpretation of the term diplomatic asylum.

2.1.3.3 Safe-Conduct

Diplomatic asylum generally terminates by way of the host state granting so-called safe-conduct to the asylee[34] and this may be regarded as the ultimate goal of diplomatic asylum.[35] Such safe-conduct is constituted by the diplomatic asylee being permitted to leave the mission premises, and subsequently the host state, without fear of arrest or persecution. From there, the asylee is then able to travel back to his/her home state or indeed take up political asylum in the state granting diplomatic asylum or in a third state. Vitally, the host state is under no obligation to grant such safe-conduct to a diplomatic asylee but equally the state granting asylum is under no obligation to alternatively terminate the asylum by surrendering the refugee.[36] This may lead to a stalemate in which the host state refuses to grant safe-conduct, whilst the granting state refuses to surrender the refugee.[37] In such situations, cases of diplomatic asylum may be longer in duration.

2.1.3.4 Diplomatic Protection

The concept of diplomatic asylum may be regarded as a form of diplomatic protection.[38] Diplomatic protection, the use of which dates back to the 1700s,[39] is one of the oldest rights belonging to a state in international law.[40] It is defined as:

[31] Jully (1951), p. 25; Kimminich (1961), p. 235; von Pollern (1980), p. 91.

[32] Kimminich (1961), p. 235. For further information on this concept, see for example Ronning (1965), p. 125 f.

[33] Von Pollern (1980), p. 91.

[34] Evans (1951), p. 760.

[35] Riveles (1989), p. 159.

[36] Evans (1951), p. 760.

[37] This is true for many long-term cases of diplomatic asylum e.g. that of Julian Assange. Such cases of a stalemate may also occur in cases in which the issue of qualification is disputed. Cf. Kau (2019), p. 198, para. 75a.

[38] Cf. Helfant (1947), p. 26 referring to, *inter alia,* asylum as constituting "humanitarian diplomatic protection." Also see Klepper (2009), p. 11 f.

[39] Cf. Dugard (2013), p. 1.

[40] Vermeer-Künzli (2006), p. 279.

> the invocation by a State, through diplomatic action or other means of peaceful settlement, of the responsibility of another State for an injury caused by an internationally wrongful act of that State to a natural or legal person that is a national of the former State with a view to the implementation of such responsibility.[41]

Such diplomatic protection works on the basis of injury to an individual being accorded to a state and regarded as injury to said state.[42] The injured state may then hold the state in question to account by way of diplomatic means.

Indeed, the practice of diplomatic protection denotes:

> a mechanism of international law that is still employed by States to secure just treatment for their nationals abroad.[43]

This is in line with states being the primary subjects of international law.[44]

Such diplomatic protection may generally only be exercised by the state of nationality,[45] save for in the context of stateless persons and refugees.[46] This does not correlate with the practice of diplomatic asylum, many cases of which depict a state granting asylum to individuals who are not its nationals.[47]

2.1.4 Territorial Asylum

It is also important to differentiate between diplomatic asylum and territorial asylum. The latter depicts the granting of a right to asylum upon the legitimate territory of the granting state: a concept therefore based entirely on the territorial sovereignty of the granting state and one which, thus, relies utterly upon the discretion of the granting

---

[41] Art. 1 Draft Articles on Diplomatic Protection, Text adopted by the International Law Commission at its fifty-eighth session, in 2006, and submitted to the General Assembly as a part of the Commission's report covering the work of that session (A/61/10). Cf. "By taking up the case of one of its subjects and by resorting to diplomatic action or international judicial proceedings on his behalf, a State is in reality asserting its own rights - its right to ensure, in the person of its subjects, respect for the rules of international law:" The Mavrommatis Palęstine Concessions (Greece v United Kingdom of Great Britain and Northern Ireland) Objection to the Jurisdiction of the Court, Judgment of 30 August 1924, Publications of the Permanent Court of International Justice, Series A, No. 2, p. 12.

[42] Cf. Art. 1 ILC Draft Articles on Diplomatic Protection with Commentaries 2006, p. 25; Vermeer-Künzli (2007), p. 37 f.

[43] Dugard (2013), p. 2.

[44] Cf. Art. 1 ILC Draft Articles on Diplomatic Protection with Commentaries 2006, p. 26.

[45] Cf. Art. 3 ILC Draft Articles on Diplomatic Protection 2006.

[46] Art. 8 ILC Draft Articles on Diplomatic Protection 2006. With regard to individuals with dual/multiple nationalities, several states may exercise diplomatic protection. Cf. Art. 6 and 7 ILC Draft Articles on Diplomatic Protection 2006.

[47] Cf. Chap. 7: Annex, Table 7.1.

state to accord an individual such a right.[48] This discretionary power of a state is also in line with the general concept of diplomatic protection, which denotes the exercise of a state-held right for the benefit of an individual.[49] A state has jurisdiction over the entirety of its territory[50] and thus the authority to grant refuge to individuals as it sees fit, ordinarily within the restraints of its own domestic legal system. As with diplomatic asylum, the decision of a state to grant an individual territorial asylum may be based on humanitarian, foreign policy or domestic policy considerations.[51]

Hence, the decision as to whether to grant a right to territorial asylum lies entirely within the domestic realm of the granting state. Thus, any intervention by a third state would, in public international law terms, necessarily constitute an illegitimate intervention into the domestic affairs of the granting state contrary to its sovereign equality under Art. 2 (1) UN Charter.[52] Consequently, any decision as to extradition also constitutes an example of a sovereign state exercising its territorial sovereignty over individuals within its domain.[53]

2.1.5 *Political Asylum*

It is also necessary to differentiate the concept of diplomatic asylum from that of political asylum. This concept has recently gained media attention due to Edward Snowden, who to the present day (April 2021) remains a political asylee resident in Russia, where he was recently granted permanent residence.[54]

Political asylum denotes the granting of territorial asylum by a sovereign state and is usually granted to persons sought for political reasons by the domestic authorities of either their state of nationality or of the state in which they reside at the point in time of being granted political asylum—hence the name political asylum. For this

---

[48]Colombian-Peruvian Asylum Case (Colombia v Peru), Judgment of 20 November 1950, ICJ Reports 1950, No. 7, p. 274; Kitschenberg (1965), p. 1; IACtHR, Advisory Opinion OC-25/18 of 30 May 2018 Requested by the Republic of Ecuador, The Institution of Asylum and its Recognition as a Human Right in the Inter-American System of Protection (Interpretation and Scope of Articles 5, 22.7 and 22.8 in Relation to Article 1(1) of the American Convention on Human Rights), p. 37, para. 104.

[49]Art. 1 ILC Draft Articles on Diplomatic Protection with Commentaries 2006, p. 26; Leys (2016), p. 2.

[50]Cf. Art. 2 (4) UN Charter preserving the territorial integrity of UN members.

[51]Evans (1963), p. 2.

[52]This prohibition is also contained within the Declaration on Principles of International Law concerning Friendly Relations and Co-operation among States in accordance with the Charter of the United Nations, which is annexed to General Assembly Resolution 2625 (XXV), 1883rd Plenary Meeting, 24 October 1970. Cf. Stein et al. (2017), pp. 221, 278.

[53]Colombian-Peruvian Asylum Case (Colombia v Peru), Judgment of 20 November 1950, ICJ Reports 1950, No. 7, p. 274. Cf. Borchard (1915), p. 48.

[54]CNN (22 October 2020), Edward Snowden gets permanent residency in Russia—lawyer.

reason, those accorded political asylum may also be referred to as political refugees.[55] Political asylum is to be regarded as a sub-category of territorial asylum.

Indeed, the concept of political asylum has also been discussed in relation to cases in which diplomatic asylum has been claimed or indeed granted. For example, Julian Assange requested political asylum from Ecuador,[56] which, had it been accepted, would have required Assange to reside in Ecuador. Indeed, had Assange been able to reach Ecuador, it is likely that Ecuador would, at the time, have granted him political (territorial) asylum. After all, he was eventually granted diplomatic asylum on the basis of him being sought for political offences.[57] This is generally also a prerequisite in the context of diplomatic asylum requests on the South American continent.[58]

In this context, unlike political asylum, diplomatic asylum constitutes a derogation from the sovereignty of the state in which the offence was committed[59] and a possible intervention into the domestic affairs of the host state.[60] Thus, its recognition depends upon the establishment of its legal basis.[61] The terms diplomatic and political asylum have also historically been used interchangeably, creating obvious confusion as to what is meant by each respective term.[62]

---

[55]This term is used for example by Schleifer (1980), p. 360.

[56]Statement of the Government of the Republic of Ecuador on the asylum request of Julian Assange, News Release. https://web.archive.org/web/20130615201655/http://www.mmrree.gob.ec/eng/2012/com042.asp. Last Accessed 14 Dec 2020.

[57]"The imputation of politic felonies is what backs up his request for asylum:" Statement of the Government of the Republic of Ecuador on the asylum request of Julian Assange, News Release. https://web.archive.org/web/20130615201655/http://www.mmrree.gob.ec/eng/2012/com042.asp. Last Accessed 14 Dec 2020.

[58]For example Art. 16 Treaty on International Penal Law 1889. Indeed, Greenburgh defines diplomatic asylum in general as asylum granted to those alleged to have committed political crimes: Greenburgh (1955), p. 103. Also see Barberis (1985), p. 41.

[59]UN General Assembly, 14th Session, Sixth Committee, Summary Record of the 608th Meeting, Agenda Item 55, Report of the International Law Commission on the work of its eleventh session, A/C.6/SR.608, 7 October 1959, p. 39, para. 17; Kitschenberg (1965), p. 5; Porcino (1976), p. 450; Riveles (1989), p. 158; Rossitto (1987), p. 113; Shah (2007), para. 1; Tye (2016), p. 219. This idea is also lent support by Reale who describes diplomatic asylum as a limitation of sovereignty: Reale (1938), p. 511. Also see Wallace and Janeczko (2013), p. 137 where diplomatic asylum is described as a restraint on sovereignty. Cf. Jurisdictional Immunities of the State (Germany v Italy: Greece Intervening), Judgment of 3 February 2012, ICJ Reports 2012, No. 143, pp. 123–124, para. 5 providing that a state has sovereignty over all persons and events in its territory.

[60]Klepper (2009), p. 11.

[61]Colombian-Peruvian Asylum Case (Colombia v Peru), Judgment of 20 November 1950, ICJ Reports 1950, No. 7, pp. 274–275; Kitschenberg (1965), p. 5.

[62]UN General Assembly, Question of Diplomatic Asylum, Report of the Secretary-General, 2 September 1975, A/10139 (Part I), para. 1. Cf. for example Kleiner (2010), p. 170.

2.1.6 *Using an Embassy as a Mechanism to Achieve Territorial Asylum*

Diplomatic asylum has to be further distinguished from claims of asylum in which the embassy is used by an individual as a mechanism in order to apply for territorial asylum in the host state. Typically, in such cases, the individual concerned will not be sought by the local authorities and the intention tends to be fast-tracking an asylum application rather than seeking protection.[63] This asylum mechanism lies outside of the remit of this book.

2.1.7 *Collective Shelter*

Diplomatic asylum has also been distinguished from the concept of collective shelter or mass asylum.[64] Foakes and Denza have held in this regard that such collective shelter is granted in order to "assert grievances" in line with an old rule of customary international law status emanating from Persia.[65] They distinguish such cases from asylum granted to an individual. This book will not distinguish between an individual right to diplomatic asylum and a right to collective shelter as both fulfil the above-mentioned definition of diplomatic asylum.

Where human rights considerations are at stake, diplomatic asylum has also been distinguished from the concept of temporary shelter.[66]

2.2 Summary

In summary, the term diplomatic asylum in a strict sense denotes the granting of extraterritorial asylum by a state in the context of its diplomatic premises. Historically this definition has been wider and has also included further extraterritorial premises under the jurisdiction of a so-called sending state, for example its consulates, ships, aircraft and military or para-military installations.

Diplomatic asylum must be distinguished both from territorial asylum, denoting a state granting asylum within its own legitimate territory, and political asylum—a sub-category of territorial asylum, denoting a state granting territorial asylum to an individual/group of individuals accused of political offences.

[63]For further information on this practice see: Noll (2005), pp. 542–573. Also see Ogg (2014), pp. 81–113.

[64]See Denza (2016), Art. 22, pp. 116–117; Foakes and Denza (2017), pp. 236–237.

[65]Foakes and Denza (2017), p. 236.

[66]Cf. Chap. 6: Sect. 6.2.7.

References

Addison Smith G (1911) Right of asylum. LQR 27(106):199–203
Barberis (1985) Asylum, diplomatic. In: Biglieri E, Prati G (eds) Encyclopedia of Public International Law, Published under the Auspices of the Max Planck Institute for Comparative Public Law and International Law under the Direction of Rudolf Bernhardt, 8: Human Rights and the Individual in International Law, International Economic Relations, North Holland. Elsevier Science Publishers B.V., Amsterdam, pp 40–42
Boed R (1994) The state of the right of asylum in international law. DJCIL 5(1):1–34
Borchard EM (1915) The diplomatic protection of citizens abroad or the law of international claims. The Banks Law Publishing Co., New York
Dahm G, Delbrück J, Wolfrum R (1989) Völkerrecht, vol I/1, 2nd edn. De Gruyter, Berlin/New York
Denza E (2016) Diplomatic law, Commentary on the Vienna Convention on Diplomatic Relations, 4th edn. Oxford University Press, Oxford
Dugard J (2013) Articles on diplomatic protection. UNALIL. http://legal.un.org/avl/pdf/ha/adp/adp_e.pdf. Last accessed 14 Dec 2020
Evans AE (1951) The Colombian-Peruvian asylum case: termination of the judicial phase. AJIL 45 (4):755–762
Evans AE (1963) Reflections upon the political offense in international practice. AJIL 57(1):1–24
Foakes J, Denza E (2017) Privileges and immunities of diplomatic missions. In: Roberts I (ed) Satow's diplomatic practice, 7th edn. Oxford University Press, Oxford, pp 222–245
García Mora MR (1956) International law and asylum as a human right. Public Affairs Press, Washington D. C.
García-Mora MR (1951) The Colombian-Peruvian asylum case and the doctrine of human rights. VLR 37(7):927–965
Gil-Bazo M (2015) Asylum as a general principle of international law. IJRL 27(1):3–28
Gilbert G, Rüsch AM (2018) International refugee and migration law. In: Evans MD (ed) International law, 5th edn. Oxford University Press, Oxford
Goodwin-Gill GS, McAdam J (2007) The refugee in international law, 3rd edn. Oxford University Press, Oxford/New York
Greenburgh RB (1955) Recent developments in the law of diplomatic asylum. Trans Grotius Soc 41:103–122. Problems of Public and Private International Law
Gregory CN (1905) The privileges of ambassadors and foreign ministers. MLR 3(3):173–184
Helfant H (1947) The Trujillo doctrine of the humanitarian diplomatic asylum. Editorial Offset Continente, Mexico
Jully L (1951) L'asile diplomatique devant la Cour internationale de Justice. Die Friedens-Warte 51:20–58
Kau M (2019) Der Staat und der Einzelne als Völkerrechtssubjekte. In: Vitzthum W, Proelß A (eds) Völkerrecht, 7th edn. DeGruyter, Berlin/Boston, pp 159–318
Kimminich O (1961) Asyl in Stützpunkten der UN Truppen. ZfP 8(3):235–240
Kitschenberg H (1965) Das diplomatische Asyl unter besonderer Berücksichtigung des Asylstreits zwischen Kolumbien und Peru. Dissertation, Universität zu Köln
Kleiner J (2010) Diplomatic practice, between tradition and innovation. World Scientific Publishing Company Limited, Hackensack/London
Klepper I (2009) Diplomatisches Asyl, Zulässigkeit und Grenzen. Dissertation, Universität zu Köln, vol 4814. Peter Lang Verlag, Frankfurt am Main/Berlin/Bern/Brussels/New York/Oxford/Vienna
Kristiyati A (2013) Ecuador's decision to grant asylum to Julian Assange: the manifestation of human security. IJIL 10(3):217–230
Leys D (2016) Diplomatic protection and individual rights: a complementary approach. HILJO 57. https://harvardilj.org/wp-content/uploads/sites/15/January-2016_Vol-57_Leys1.pdf. Last accessed 14 Dec 2020

Moore JB (1892) Asylum in legations and consulates and in vessels. PSQ 7(1):1–37
Morgenstern F (1948) Extra-territorial asylum. BYIL 25:236–261
Noll G (2005) Seeking asylum at embassies: a right to entry under international law. IJRL 17 (3):542–573
O'Nions H (2014) Asylum – a right denied, a critical analysis of European Asylum Policy. Ashgate Publishing, Farnham/Burlington
Ogg K (2014) Protection closer to home? A legal case for claiming asylum at embassies and consulates. RSQ 33(4):81–113
Pastorino AM, Ippoliti MR (2019) A propósito del Asilo Diplomático. Revista de la Facultad de Derecho 47:1–37. https://doi.org/10.22187/rfd2019n47a3
Paust JJ (1999) Non-extraterritoriality of "Special Territorial Jurisdiction" of the United States: forgotten history and the errors of Erdos. YJIL 24(1):305–328
Porcino P (1976) Toward codification of diplomatic asylum. NYUJILP 8:435–456
Przetacznik F (1983) Protection of officials of foreign states according to international law. Martinus Nijhoff Publishers, The Hague/Boston/London
Rafii M (2014) Diplomatenrecht. In: Schöbener B (ed) Völkerrecht, Lexikon zentraler Begriffe und Themen. C.F. Müller, Heidelberg, pp 52–61
Reale E (1938) Le droit d'asile, Collected Courses of the Hague Academy of International Law, vol 63. Nijhoff, Leiden/Boston, pp 469–601
Riveles S (1989) Diplomatic asylum as a human right: the case of the Durban Six. HRQ 11:139–159
Ronning CN (1965) Diplomatic asylum: legal norms and political reality in Latin American relations. Martinus Nijhoff, The Hague
Rossitto AM (1987) Diplomatic asylum in the United States and Latin America: a comparative analysis. BJIL 13:111–135
Schleifer N (1980) Territorial asylum in the Americas: practical considerations for relocation. IALR 12(2):359–380
Sen B (1988) A Diplomat's handbook of international law and practice, 3rd revised edition. Martinus Nijhoff, Dordrecht/Boston/London
Shah P (2007) Asylum, diplomatic. In: MPEPIL (Online). Oxford University Press. https://opil.ouplaw.com/view/10.1093/law:epil/9780199231690/law-9780199231690-e756. Last accessed 14 Dec 2020
Shaw MN (2017) International law, 8th edn. Cambridge University Press, Cambridge
Stein T, Von Buttlar C, Kotzur M (2017) Völkerrecht, 14th edn. Verlag Franz Vahlen, Munich
Taylor S (2019) Australia's diplomatic asylum initiative at the United Nations: comparing international law rhetoric with foreign policy practice. AJIA 73(4):376–396
Tye H (2016) Does Julian Assange illustrate a gap in the law that should be codified? PLCJR 1:218–238
Vermeer-Künzli A (2006) Restricting discretion: judicial review of diplomatic protection. NJIL 75:279–307
Vermeer-Künzli A (2007) As if: the legal fiction in diplomatic protection. EJIL 18(1):37–68
Viveros Montoya L (2017) Flat 3B: Assange, Ecuador and the right to asylum. In: The Law of Nations Blog. https://lawofnationsblog.com/2017/03/29/flat-3b-assange-ecuador-right-asylum/. Accessed 14 Dec 2020
von Pollern H (1980) Das moderne Asylrecht, Völkerrecht und Verfassungsrecht der Bundesrepublik Deutschland, Schriften zum Völkerrecht, Band 67. Duncker & Humblot, Berlin
Wallace RMM, Janeczko FAW (2013) The concept of asylum in international law. In: Islam R, Bhuiyan JH (eds) An introduction to international refugee law. Martinus Nijhoff Publishers, Leiden/Boston, pp 133–158
Weis P (1966) Territorial asylum. In: Lambert H (2016) International refugee law. Routledge, Taylor and Francis Group, Oxon/New York

Chapter 3
The History of the Practice in the Context of Diplomatic Law

The concept of asylum is an ancient notion, which can be traced as far back as Biblical times.[1] Indeed Reale describes it as being as old as humanity itself.[2] Moreover, the quintessential idea of asylum being accorded in the context of a diplomatic mission is, though not nearly so ancient, also not novel. Indeed, its origins can be traced at least as far back as the fifteenth century.[3] In its youth, nearly all of the practice was limited to Europe.[4]

In order to be able to fully understand the concept of diplomatic asylum today, it is imperative to analyse and understand its historical context. An appreciation of the evolution of diplomatic asylum is equally important. Such an appreciation is crucial in ascertaining the modern-day legality of the practice, particularly in the context of customary international law, for which a virtually uniform state practice element is

---

[1]Gil-Bazo (2015), pp. 17–18. Cf. UN General Assembly, 14th Session, Sixth Committee, Summary Record of the 602nd Meeting, Agenda Item 55, Report of the International Law Commission on the work of its eleventh session (A/4169, A/C.6/L.443, 444 and Add. 1, A/C.6//L.445) continued, A/C.6/SR.602, 28 September 1959, p. 10, para. 9; UN General Assembly, 21st Session, Sixth Committee, Summary Record of the 923rd Meeting, Agenda Item 85, Draft Declaration on the Right of Asylum, A/C.6, SR.923, 31 October 1966, p. 143, para. 54; IACtHR, Advisory Opinion OC-25/18 of 30 May 2018 Requested by the Republic of Ecuador, The Institution of Asylum and its Recognition as a Human Right in the Inter-American System of Protection (Interpretation and Scope of Articles 5, 22.7 and 22.8 in Relation to Article 1(1) of the American Convention on Human Rights), p. 27, para. 72. Though its establishment and codification in international law didn't come until much later: Scupin (2011), para. 23.

[2]Reale (1938), p. 473.

[3]UN General Assembly, Question of Diplomatic Asylum, Report of the Secretary-General, 2 September 1975, A/10139 (Part I), para. 2; Sinha (1971), p. 21. Also see Accioly (1961), p. 291 tracing the practice as far back as the Middle Ages.

[4]Cf. UN General Assembly, Question of Diplomatic Asylum, Report of the Secretary-General, 2 September 1975, A/10139 (Part I), paras 2–3; Shah (2007), para. 2; Tye (2016), p. 219.

L. Hughes-Gerber, *Diplomatic Asylum*,
https://doi.org/10.1007/978-3-030-73046-8_3

constitutive.[5] Such state practice can generally only emerge over the course of a significant period of time,[6] save for the concept of sporadic custom.[7] The following chapter will therefore detail the history of the practice of diplomatic asylum, from its inception to the present day, picking out key time periods and cases. This will enable a greater appreciation of the nature of the practice going forward, particularly with regard to its status under customary international law.

3.1 Foundations

The first origins of the notion of diplomatic asylum stem from the ambassador's dwelling becoming a permanent institution in the host state in the fifteenth and sixteenth centuries (culminating in the Congress of Westphalia in 1648)[8] and from the concept of this dwelling being regarded for the first time as inviolable.[9] Indeed this notion of diplomatic inviolability is thought to be one of the earliest principles of international law.[10]

Prior to this and in the context of ambassadors then being only temporarily resident in their respective receiving states, the idea of religious sanctuary being granted to persecuted persons was widespread.[11] Such religious sanctuary was

[5]North Sea Continental Shelf (Federal Republic of Germany v Denmark/Federal Republic of Germany v Netherlands), Judgment of 20 February 1969, ICJ Reports 1969, Nos 51 and 52, p. 43, para. 74. Cf. Legal Consequences of the Separation of the Chagos Archipelago from Mauritius in 1965, Advisory Opinion of 25 February 2019, ICJ Reports 2019, No. 169, p. 130, para. 142 recognising the importance of considering the evolution of a legal concept when determining custom.

[6]Though the passage of a short period of time does not preclude custom so long as its constituent elements are fulfilled: North Sea Continental Shelf (Federal Republic of Germany v Denmark/Federal Republic of Germany v Netherlands), Judgment of 20 February 1969, ICJ Reports 1969, Nos 51 and 52, p. 43, para. 74.

[7]See for example: Cheng (1997), p. 136 f.; Sharf (2014).

[8]Young (1964), p. 152. Cf. IACtHR, Advisory Opinion OC-25/18 of 30 May 2018 Requested by the Republic of Ecuador, The Institution of Asylum and its Recognition as a Human Right in the Inter-American System of Protection (Interpretation and Scope of Articles 5, 22.7 and 22.8 in Relation to Article 1(1) of the American Convention on Human Rights), p. 27, para. 75.

[9]Reale (1938), pp. 511–513; UN General Assembly, Question of Diplomatic Asylum, Report of the Secretary-General, 2 September 1975, A/10139 (Part I), para. 2. Though the widespread establishment of this principle of inviolability came about much later by the end of the eighteenth century: Foakes and Denza (2017), p. 225.

[10]Barker (2000), p. 161. Cf. Akinsanya (1989), p. 99; Denza (2016), p. 1; Fox (2017), p. 203; Subramanian (2017), p. 185.

[11]Chhabra (2015), p. 38; Dupuy (1976), p. 743; Jeffery (1985), p. 14; IACtHR, Advisory Opinion OC-25/18 of 30 May 2018 Requested by the Republic of Ecuador, The Institution of Asylum and its Recognition as a Human Right in the Inter-American System of Protection (Interpretation and Scope of Articles 5, 22.7 and 22.8 in Relation to Article 1(1) of the American Convention on Human Rights), p. 27, para. 73. For further information on this concept, see for example Ronning (1965), p. 214.

equally facilitated by the inviolability of the holy places providing the shelter: the reverence of which was based upon their status as places of God.[12] In time, the salience of religious sanctuary gave way to the concept of secular asylum.[13] This shift can be accorded to a change in attitude as some states, e.g. France, came to perceive the granting of religious sanctuary as a threat to their sovereignty.[14] This idea of religious sanctuary is thus less relevant nowadays at a time when individuals may be accorded a more established right to asylum by a state. It is important to note, however, that modern day examples of religious institutions shielding individuals from the domestic authorities do still persist.[15]

The newly emerged principle of the inviolability of the ambassador's dwelling place[16] was held to be an extension of the ambassador's established personal immunity—a functional necessity to guarantee his independence from the influence of the receiving state.[17] Hence, this dwelling place could therefore be used for the practical purpose of receiving persons sought by the territorial state, thus evading the imposition of its domestic jurisdiction. In this context, the diplomatic premises being utilised contrary to their intended purpose in order to enable an individual to circumvent the domestic (generally criminal) jurisdiction of the receiving state in which he resides is a tradition as old as the practice itself.[18] In the absence of an international legal framework, such as that we have come to know today, this earliest habituated form of the practice would have been without any sort of legal status or foundation,[19] cloaked within the inviolability of the ambassador's dwelling place and thus the exercise of which was left subject to his sole discretion.[20]

Indeed, a legal basis for the practice, were it to have been required, could have also been determined within the realm of the relevant sending state's domestic legal

[12]Sinha (1971), p. 5.

[13]IACtHR, Advisory Opinion OC-25/18 of 30 May 2018 Requested by the Republic of Ecuador, The Institution of Asylum and its Recognition as a Human Right in the Inter-American System of Protection (Interpretation and Scope of Articles 5, 22.7 and 22.8 in Relation to Article 1(1) of the American Convention on Human Rights), p. 27, paras 74–75.

[14]Rabben (2016), p. 222.

[15]For example the 1998 Église Saint-Jean de la Croix incident in Montréal, in which seventeen Chileans were granted sanctuary insofar as the Parish Council refused to evict them: for further information see Patsias and Williams (2013), p. 182 f. Also see Lippert (2005), p. 37 f.

[16]This principle is still valid up to the present day and is now reflected by Art. 28 (1) VCDR.

[17]UN General Assembly, Question of Diplomatic Asylum, Report of the Secretary-General, 2 September 1975, A/10139 (Part I), para. 2. Cf. League of Nations Committee of Experts for the Progressive Codification of International Law, Report to the Council of the League of Nations on the Questions Which Appear Ripe for International Regulation, Questionnaires Nos 1 to 7, Adopted by the Committee at its Third Session, held in March–April 1927, Geneva, 20 April 1927, p. 242.

[18]UN General Assembly, Question of Diplomatic Asylum, Report of the Secretary-General, 2 September 1975, A/10139 (Part I), para. 2.

[19]Evans describes the practice as having been "indulged in for a long time, with and without formal legal sanction": Evans (1952), p. 142.

[20]Cf. Greenburgh (1955), p. 119 providing that the discretion of a diplomatic officer to grant or refuse diplomatic asylum constitutes an established juridical principle.

provisions. Grotius described ambassadors as being, by way of a legal fiction, in the place of those who sent them (i.e. in the place of the sending state)[21] thus justifying the sending state's exceptional extension of its jurisdiction outside of its territory.

3.2 Continuation in Sixteenth and Seventeenth Centuries and Subsequent Fall from Favour

By the sixteenth century, the practice of diplomatic asylum was already widely recognised and accepted,[22] so too in the context of scholarly writings.[23] This spread of the practice may not only be accredited to the diminishment in salience of alternative establishments, such as church sanctuary,[24] but also to the imperfect nature of territorial sovereignty at the time.[25] Against the backdrop of a great increase in diplomatic intercourse in the sixteenth century,[26] the advancement of the practice was further facilitated by an increase in the scope of the premises enjoying immunity as these came to include the ambassador's carriage, neighbouring buildings and eventually the entire quarter.[27]

However, the infancy of the practice was not without its controversies. In some instances, an offender was forcibly removed from diplomatic premises by the local authorities, thus infringing the inviolability of these premises.[28] For example, in 1540 the Republic of Venice demanded the release of a number of magistrates who had been accused of high treason and were being sheltered by the French embassy in Venice. Despite the resistance of the French King, this demand was met.[29]

In Venice in 1554, a statute held that he who had taken refuge in the house of a diplomat would not be prosecuted and that his presence would be ignored as long as the offence in question was a common crime as opposed to, for example, treason or the theft of public funds.[30]

---

[21] Cited by Foakes and Denza (2017), p. 225 and by Denza (2016), Art. 22, p. 111.

[22] UN General Assembly, Question of Diplomatic Asylum, Report of the Secretary-General, 2 September 1975, A/10139 (Part I), para. 2; cf. Sinha (1971), p. 21. Cf. Den Heijer (2013), p. 401.

[23] See the historic authors cited by UN General Assembly, Question of Diplomatic Asylum, Report of the Secretary-General, 2 September 1975, A/10139 (Part I), para. 2; cf. Den Heijer (2013), p. 401; Sinha (1971), p. 22.

[24] Cf. Rabben (2016), p. 222.

[25] Den Heijer (2013), p. 401.

[26] Young (1964), pp. 145–146.

[27] UN General Assembly, Question of Diplomatic Asylum, Report of the Secretary-General, 2 September 1975, A/10139 (Part I), para. 2; Klepper (2009), p. 1; von Pollern (1980), p. 92.

[28] UN General Assembly, Question of Diplomatic Asylum, Report of the Secretary-General, 2 September 1975, A/10139 (Part I), para. 4. Cf. Klepper (2009), p. 2 arguing that in this period, the inviolability of the diplomatic premises was restricted.

[29] UN General Assembly, Question of Diplomatic Asylum, Report of the Secretary-General, 2 September 1975, A/10139 (Part I), para. 3.

[30] Reale (1938), p. 513.

In 1601 the practice was further legitimised by an arbitral award granted by Pope Clement VIII with regard to a dispute between France and Spain.[31] The dispute was caused by Spain storming the French embassy in Madrid in order to seize a number of Frenchmen, who had killed several Spanish soldiers and subsequently fled to the embassy.[32] Spain was repentant for having violated the inviolability of the mission premises but nevertheless refused to hand the prisoners back to France.[33] The Pope, finding in favour of France and facilitating the handover of the prisoners from Spain, provided the practice with a greater degree of legitimacy than ever before—i.e. papal legitimacy and recognition.

In 1609 the precedent laid down in the 1540 case was invoked by England in order to bring about the surrender of a chaplain being harboured by the Venetian ambassador in London.[34] In turn, the precedents of these cases came to provide a legal basis for the crime of treason being exempt from the type of crime for which individuals may be granted a right to diplomatic asylum by states.

In 1655, the French ambassador to Rome was sheltering a group of Neapolitan exiles and rebels in his residence. Due to the cost of housing the group, the ambassador arranged for their transport back to Naples. During transit, the asylees were captured from the ambassador's carriage and subsequently imprisoned. The French ambassador protested against the arrest and though the Pope took exception to diplomatic protection being granted to individuals held to be criminals by the Holy See, he duly released the prisoners—this came to be seen as a sign of the Pope's contrition.[35]

However, despite such recognition of the practice at the highest echelons of statecraft and despite it being widespread by the end of the seventeenth century,[36] the practice subsequently fell out of favour. This can be accorded to the so-called *franchise du quartier* (meaning freedom of the quarter), a quarter in which a property bore the flag of the ambassador thus rendering the entire quarter immune to domestic jurisdiction, coming to be grotesquely abused, in certain instances for commercial gain, for the purpose of harbouring criminals from the domestic jurisdiction of the receiving state.[37]

---

[31] UN General Assembly, Question of Diplomatic Asylum, Report of the Secretary-General, 2 September 1975, A/10139 (Part I), para. 4.

[32] UN General Assembly, Question of Diplomatic Asylum, Report of the Secretary-General, 2 September 1975, A/10139 (Part I), para. 4.

[33] UN General Assembly, Question of Diplomatic Asylum, Report of the Secretary-General, 2 September 1975, A/10139 (Part I), para. 4.

[34] UN General Assembly, Question of Diplomatic Asylum, Report of the Secretary-General, 2 September 1975, A/10139 (Part I), para. 3.

[35] For further information on this case see: Moore (1892), p. 7.

[36] Denza (2016), Art. 22, p. 111.

[37] Denza (2016), Art. 22, p. 111; Moore (1892), pp. 5–7; IACtHR, Advisory Opinion OC-25/18 of 30 May 2018 Requested by the Republic of Ecuador, The Institution of Asylum and its Recognition as a Human Right in the Inter-American System of Protection (Interpretation and Scope of Articles 5, 22.7 and 22.8 in Relation to Article 1(1) of the American Convention on Human Rights), p. 27, para. 76. See also Klepper (2009), p. 1.

3.3 Revival in the Eighteenth and Nineteenth Centuries

The practice was, however, not destined to remain dormant for long. In 1726 the Duke of Ripperda, Finance and Foreign Affairs Minister for Philip V of Spain, was granted asylum "against the insults he dreaded from the people of Madrid"[38] at the house of the English ambassador in Madrid.[39] Ripperda had unsuccessfully tried to obtain asylum at the Dutch embassy and was only permitted to remain at the British embassy upon assuring the ambassador that he neither came in disgrace, nor had he been accused of any crime.[40] The Spanish Government, however, concerned at having discovered that Ripperda had important papers on his person, posed the question to the Council of Castile as to whether Ripperda could be seized.[41] The Council found in favour of the Spanish Government holding:

> It would "operate to the subversion and utter ruin [of sovereigns] if persons who had been intrusted with the finances, the power and the secrets of the state, were, when violating the duties of their office, allowed to take shelter under a privilege which had been granted to the houses of ambassadors in favour only of ordinary offenders."[42]

It is important to note the distinction made here between Ripperda, accused of breaching the obligations of his political office, and so-called "ordinary offenders." On the basis of the Council of Castile's decision, the Spanish then proceeded to seize Ripperda from the ambassador's residence, hereby creating heightened friction between Spain and Britain, which opposed Spain's actions on the basis that it wasn't given the opportunity to surrender Ripperda voluntarily.[43] The decision of the Council of Castile was also affirmed in scholarly writings.[44]

Following this, in 1747 asylum was once again granted by the British to a Russian national with his domicile in Sweden, Christopher Springer. Springer had been convicted of high treason and before sentencing managed to escape to the embassy to which he gained entry under false pretences, posing as a courier.[45] Britain refused to surrender Springer and Sweden in turn surrounded the diplomatic premises, searching all those who entered, in addition to putting a tail on the ministerial carriage.[46] The case ended up severing diplomatic relations between Britain and Sweden when, upon the asylee being surrendered due to mounting international

---

[38]Ripperda (1744), p. 174.

[39]Ripperda (1744), p. 131 f. Also see Addison Smith (1911), p. 201.

[40]Moore (1906), p. 765.

[41]Moore (1906), p. 765.

[42]Cited by Vattel (1797), p. 496, § 118.

[43]Moore (1906), p. 765.

[44]Vattel held that "nothing could be said on this... with greater truth and judgment:" Vattel (1797), p. 496, § 118. Phillimore held that "Spain was not guilty of any violation of international law:" Cited by Moore (1906), pp. 765–766.

[45]For further information on this case see: Moore (1906), p. 766. Also see Addison Smith (1911), p. 201.

[46]Moore (1906), p. 766.

pressure and the subsequent redress requested by Britain not being delivered, both states recalled their ambassadors.[47]

In regard to the practice, prominent Swiss legal scholar Vattel posed the question:

> Can he *[an ambassador]* take advantage of the privilege, in order to convert his house into an asylum, to afford shelter and protection to the enemies of the prince, and to malefactors of any kind. . .[48]

It is apparent herewith that even in the eighteenth century, the nature of the practice as functioning contrary to the purpose of diplomatic immunity was recognised. The phrase "take advantage of the privilege" also indicates that even at this stage, diplomatic asylum was regarded as an abuse of such privileges and immunities. Moreover, the inclusion of so-called ordinary offences was affirmed by Vattel when he held:

> I grant, indeed, that when there is question only of certain ordinary transgressions, and these committed by persons who often prove to be rather unfortunate than criminal, and whole punishment is of no great importance to the peace of society, the house of an ambassador may well serve as an asylum for such offenders.[49]

This is interesting as it directly opposes modern-day diplomatic asylum practice in Latin America, which specifically excludes ordinary offenders from its scope.[50] Furthermore, Vattel reaffirmed that highly political crimes, such as treason, were exempt from the practice.

In 1858 a right to diplomatic asylum was granted by France to former Venezuelan president, José Tadeo Monagas Burgos.[51] Threats by Venezuela to storm the embassy in order to retrieve General Burgos prompted Britain and France to commence a blockade of Venezuela's ports until the latter agreed to grant the asylee safe passage out of the country.[52] This case is particularly interesting not only because it involves two European states granting diplomatic protection to an individual against the wishes of the Latin American territorial state. More interesting in this case is that it also depicts a third state, in this instance Britain, joining the sending state in both exerting political pressure upon the receiving state and in affording diplomatic protection to the diplomatic asylee in order ultimately to compel the receiving state to permit the asylee safe passage out of the country, thus enabling the realisation of political asylum elsewhere. At least under modern international law, Britain's conduct here would indisputably amount to an

---

[47] Moore (1906), p. 766.

[48] Vattel (1797), p. 495, § 118.

[49] Vattel (1797), p. 495, § 118. The exclusion of such offences later came to constitute a fundamental feature of diplomatic asylum: cf. e.g. Addison Smith (1911), p. 200; Yearbook of the International Law Commission, 1957, 394th Meeting, 3 May 1957, p. 55, para. 53.

[50] Cf. Chap. 4: Sect. 4.2 and Chap. 5: Sects. 5.3.4 and 5.4.1.1.

[51] Rudolph and Rudolph (1971), p. 116.

[52] Esquirol (2012), p. 559.

illegitimate intervention into the domestic affairs of Venezuela pursuant to Art. 2 (1) UN Charter.

Moreover, this is not the only nineteenth (and early twentieth) century example of France granting a right to diplomatic asylum. It later did so in the following states in the years specified:

- Greece 1862
- Turkey 1867
- Chile 1858 and 1892
- Paraguay 1898
- Peru 1865 and 1913
- Haiti 1876, 1878, 1890, 1908 and 1915.[53]

The prevalence of Latin American states depicting the receiving state in this regard cannot fail to go unnoticed. Furthermore, Latin American states themselves began granting individuals a right to diplomatic asylum from the middle of the nineteenth century.[54]

The practice of diplomatic asylum was also permitted in 1899 by the U.S. in Haiti, when a Haitian, Ulrick Duvivier, gained access to the U.S. embassy in Port-au-Prince. Duvivier was then seized by force by the Haitian authorities, prompting the U.S. to demand his return.[55] In this regard, the wording of the reaction of the U.S. State Department would at least imply the preclusion of diplomatic asylum for ordinary offences:

> If newspaper telegrams correctly state Duvivier case *[sic] [,]* your remonstrance against violation and demand for refugee's return were rightly made. He should be sheltered against all but strictly regular legal process.[56]

This is in direct contrast to Vattel and is in line with modern-day Latin American practice.[57]

It is important to note that the U.S. also distinguished between the violation of the immunity of a diplomatic residence and the right to grant asylum to Duvivier:

---

[53]Dupuy (1976), p. 745.

[54]See UN General Assembly, Question of Diplomatic Asylum, Report of the Secretary-General, 2 September 1975, A/10139 (Part I), para. 1; IACtHR, Advisory Opinion OC-25/18 of 30 May 2018 Requested by the Republic of Ecuador, The Institution of Asylum and its Recognition as a Human Right in the Inter-American System of Protection (Interpretation and Scope of Articles 5, 22.7 and 22.8 in Relation to Article 1(1) of the American Convention on Human Rights), p. 27, para. 78. For further detail on Latin American practice in the twentieth and twenty-first centuries, see Chap. 3: Sects. 3.4 and 3.7 respectively.

[55]See: U.S. Department of State, Papers Relating to the Foreign Relations of the United States, Docs. 364 and 365, Mr Powell to Mr Hay, Telegram/Legation of the United States, Port au Prince, 2 August 1899.

[56]U.S. Department of State, Papers Relating to the Foreign Relations of the United States, Doc. 366, Mr Adee to Mr Powell, Department of State, Washington, 3 August 1899.

[57]Cf. Chap. 3: Sect. 3.4 and Chap. 5: Sect. 5.3.4.

> Such an invasion of your domicile is, however, to be carefully distinguished from the collateral question of your right or power to afford to a native of the country immunity from the pursuit of the territorial authorities by claiming for him so-called "asylum." The Department has uniformly discountenanced the assertion by its diplomatic agents of the claims of right of asylum. In holding, as it has repeatedly done, that its agents are not competent, under international law, to harbor an accused criminal from the pursuit of law it has also held that the pursuit must be shown to be orderly and regular. It could, under no circumstances, admit that mere arbitrary force can be exerted by local agents to effect the capture of any person within the minister's dwelling.[58]

In this statement, whilst the U.S. denies a legal right to diplomatic asylum in its diplomatic residence, it equally stresses that local authorities must pursue individuals in an "orderly" and "regular" manner and rejects the arbitrary use of force with regard to individuals residing in said premises. The violation of the premises' immunity is also stressed through the use of the phrase "invasion of your domicile".

It is important to note at this stage that by the nineteenth century, reliance on the concept of extraterritoriality, which provided a convenient legal basis for a claim to diplomatic asylum, had waned.[59]

3.3.1 Asylum on Warships

During the nineteenth century, there are also multiple examples of individuals being granted asylum by various states whilst on board ships.[60] In particular, the practice in the context of warships, or so-called men-of-war,[61] may be justified by the idea of the role of warships as "floating portions of the flag state."[62]

---

[58]U.S. Department of State, Papers Relating to the Foreign Relations of the United States, Doc. 367, Mr Adee to Mr Powell, Department of State, Washington, 3 August 1899.

[59]U.S. Department of State, Papers Relating to Foreign Affairs, Doc. 460, Memorandum relative to diplomatic asylum (Translation), Department of Foreign Relations, Lima, 29 January 1867; Denza (2016), Art. 22, p. 111; Farhangi (1986), pp. 1521–1522; Kau (2019), p. 197, para. 74; Maginnis (2002), p. 994. Cf. League of Nations Committee of Experts for the Progressive Codification of International Law, Report to the Council of the League of Nations on the Questions Which Appear Ripe for International Regulation, Questionnaires Nos 1 to 7, Adopted by the Committee at its Third Session, held in March–April 1927, Geneva, 20 April 1927, p. 243; IACtHR, Advisory Opinion OC-25/18 of 30 May 2018 Requested by the Republic of Ecuador, The Institution of Asylum and its Recognition as a Human Right in the Inter-American System of Protection (Interpretation and Scope of Articles 5, 22.7 and 22.8 in Relation to Article 1(1) of the American Convention on Human Rights), p. 27, para. 75; Kimminich (1961), p. 236. Though it is important to note that advocates of the extraterritoriality concept exist to the present day e.g. Kristiyati (2013), p. 229; Viveros Montoya (2017). Nevertheless, international law does not generally prohibit the notion of extraterritoriality: cf. Skogly (2006), p. 23 f.

[60]Cf. Accioly (1961), p. 293 holding that asylum on warships has been granted by states which do not recognise the concept of diplomatic asylum when such warships are in foreign waters.

[61]Used, for example, by Lauterpacht (1955), p. 852 f.; and Moore (1906), p. 847 f.

[62]Lauterpacht (1955), p. 853; Rader (1971), p. 189.

For example, in April 1831 the U.S. flagged warship *St. Louis* granted the Vice-President of Peru and General Miller temporary shelter on board upon the condition that they would not remain any longer than was necessary to protect them from the ongoing mob violence.[63]

Moreover in August 1848, the Duke of Parma (Charles II), owing to the fact that his life was in danger, was granted asylum by the British flagged Hecate.[64] Furthermore, in that very same month, *HMS Bulldog* was sent to Civitavecchia due to the eventuality of it becoming necessary for the Pope to take refuge there.[65]

The following year, in 1849, Vice-Admiral W. Parker noted in his communication to Captain Martin:

> You cannot, however, err in receiving for protection any individuals whose lives or freedom may be endangered, for any act purely political...[66]

This underlines the legitimacy of granting asylum (and thus diplomatic protection) to individuals in the context of ships/warships in cases in which they are sought for political reasons. This passage also indicates that even as early as the nineteenth century, diplomatic asylum was already being granted on the basis of humanitarian considerations.

This was followed up by communication from the British Foreign Office, which went further in stating:

> His Lordship *[Viscount Palmerston]* is of *[the]* opinion that it would not be right to receive and harbour on board a British ship of war any person flying from justice on a criminal charge...But a British man-of-war has always and everywhere been considered a safe place of refuge for persons of whatever country or party who have sought shelter under the British flag from persecution on account of their political conduct and opinions; and this protection has been equally afforded, whether the refugee was escaping from the arbitrary acts of a monarchical Government, or from the lawless violence of a revolutionary Committee.[67]

Here, the distinction between political acts and ordinary (criminal) offences is highlighted once again—asylum in the context of warships also only being permissible in the former case. This statement also highlights that the British did not view diplomatic asylum in the context of warships to be reserved only for situations of political disturbance akin to revolution. Moreover, this passage, through the use of

---

[63]Moore (1906), p. 849.

[64]Moore (1906), p. 849.

[65]Recounted by Matsumoto-Best (2003), p. 100.

[66]Communication of Sir W. Parker (Vice-Admiral) to Captain Martin, 18 July 1849, Report of the Commissioners, Minutes of the Evidence, and Appendix, with General Index of Minutes of Evidence and Appendix, Presented to both Houses of Parliament by Command of her Majesty, George Edward Eyre and William Spottiswoode, London, 1876, p. 155.

[67]Communication of Mr Addington of the Foreign Office to the Admiralty, 4 August 1849, Report of the Commissioners, Minutes of the Evidence, and Appendix, with General Index of Minutes of Evidence and Appendix, Presented to both Houses of Parliament by Command of her Majesty, George Edward Eyre and William Spottiswoode, London, 1876, p. 155.

the words "persecution" and "lawless violence", would seem to indicate a British willingness to grant diplomatic asylum on the basis of humanitarian considerations.

Of course, such asylum cases also emerge in the midst of a revolutionary context. For example, in 1862, the Greek royal couple, King Otho and his wife Amelia, took refuge on board *HMS Scylla* in the midst of the revolution unfolding around them.[68] In the light of this, several others were sheltered on a French vessel, *Zénobie*.[69] In this very same year, in the city of New Orleans in the U.S., three Spanish warships sheltered various persons on board, among them citizens of the U.S. who were at the time required to have a pass to leave the country, in order to transport them to Cuba. The Spanish government affirmed that such warships may grant asylum to political offenders, whilst the U.S. objected to the transport from a U.S. port of any persons not belonging to the civil, military or naval service of the ship's flag state. In particular, it took issue with the transport of its own citizens.[70]

The civil war in Chile in 1891 also gave further occasion for refuge to be granted to Chilean nationals aboard both German and American warships.[71]

Moreover, on 13th March 1894, a group of insurgents were granted asylum by the Portuguese flagged vessels, *Mindello* and *Alfonso de Albuquerque*, which ultimately triggered the suspension of diplomatic relations between Brazil and Portugal by Brazil on the basis that it held the insurgents to be pirates (and thus common criminals) as opposed to political offenders, as argued by Portugal.[72]

The more restrictive U.S. position was followed up in 1896 by its Navy Regulations,[73] Art. 288 of which held:

> The right of asylum for political or other refugees has no foundation in international law. In countries, however, where frequent insurrections occur, and constant instability of government exists, local usage sanctions the granting of asylum, but even in the waters of such countries*[,]* officers should refuse all applications for asylum except when required by the interests of humanity in extreme or exceptional cases, such as the pursuit of a refugee by a mob. Officers must not directly or indirectly invite refugees to accept asylum.

In this passage, diplomatic asylum for political offenders is explicitly rejected. However, the legal status of the practice in the region of Latin America is recognised. It is also interesting to note that as early as the nineteenth century, humanitarian considerations played a role in a state accepting requests for diplomatic asylum in this context.[74]

---

[68]Baird (1863), p. 246. Also see Addison Smith (1911), p. 200.

[69]UN General Assembly, Question of Diplomatic Asylum, Report of the Secretary-General, 2 September 1975, A/10139 (Part I), para. 17.

[70]For further information on this case, see Moore (1906), pp. 849–850.

[71]Moore (1906), pp. 851–852.

[72]See: Note of the Portuguese Delegation to the Brazilian Government in: U.S. Department of State, Papers Relating to the Foreign Relations of the United States, 1894, Brazil, Doc. 56, Mr Thompson to Mr Gresham. Also see Gomes dos Santos Júnior (2014), pp. 134–157.

[73]Regulations, Government of the Navy, United States, 1896, Government Printing Office, Washington, 1896.

[74]For further information on the concept of diplomatic asylum based upon human rights considerations, see Chap. 6.

3.3.2 *Asylum on (Merchant) Ships*

In contrast to warships, practice with regard to asylum on merchant ships is much more limited.[75] This can be explained by merchant vessels, unlike warships, being very much subject to the territorial jurisdiction of the state in whose waters/port they reside.[76] However, this does not exclude the possibility of state practice in this regard as there have nevertheless been several attempts by flag states to exercise such a right.

For example, in 1840 a French vessel, *L'Ocean*, upon docking at Valencia, boarded a former Spanish Minister, M. Sotelo, who was facing prosecution in Spain for political offences. Upon the vessel's subsequent inspection in the port of Alicante, Spanish officials seized Soleto and duly imprisoned him. *L'Ocean's* captain argued, to no avail, that he was permitted to grant such an extraterritorial right to asylum under the laws of his flag. Subsequent diplomatic communications between the two states ultimately affirmed the decision of the Spanish authorities.[77]

Moreover, in April 1849, Terrence Bellew McManus, who was sought for his role in the 1848 rebellion, was seized by the British police from the American flagged ship *N.D. Chase* in waters near Spike Island, Ireland.[78] Both McManus himself and the captain of the ship objected to the arrest, holding it to be contrary to international law as they believed McManus was under the jurisdiction of the flag state, the U.S., whilst on board its vessel. Nevertheless McManus appeared before a Magistrate, was imprisoned and, upon his original death sentence being commuted to transportation, he was sent to Van Diemen's Land[79] later that year.[80] In its response, the U.S. government distinguished between the legality of the arrest in the event that it had occurred within British territorial waters and the illegality of the practice as constituting a breach of the U.S. flag-holder's sovereignty if it were to have occurred upon the high seas.[81] Given the lack of evidence to the contrary, the arrest was assumed to have taken place whilst the vessel was still within British territorial waters[82]—hence the U.S. did not officially challenge the British authorities'

[75]Cf. League of Nations Committee of Experts for the Progressive Codification of International Law, Report to the Council of the League of Nations on the Questions Which Appear Ripe for International Regulation, Questionnaires Nos 1 to 7, Adopted by the Committee at its Third Session, held in March–April 1927, Geneva, 20 April 1927, p. 56 rejecting this notion of asylum.

[76]Moore (1906), p. 855.

[77]Moore (1906), p. 856.

[78]At the time Ireland was part of the United Kingdom of Great Britain and Ireland, which existed until 1912.

[79]Modern day Tasmania.

[80]For further information on this case see: Document written and signed by Terence Bellew McManus, 5 April 1849, Particulars of Arrest, NLI Catalogue. http://catalogue.nli.ie/Record/vtls000584764. Last Accessed 14 Dec 2020.

[81]See Letter of James Buchanan to Mr Jordan, Washington, 23 January 1849 in: Moore (1909), pp. 291–292.

[82]Moore (1906), p. 856.

decision. This position of the U.S. government was further upheld with regard to the arrest of passengers of a French mail steamer by Haitian authorities.[83] An American mail steamer later also provided asylum to a Nicaraguan fugitive.[84]

For the purposes of this work, the practice of flag states seeking to exercise diplomatic protection over transit passengers of their merchant ships after they have disembarked will not be explored. Such an attempt to exercise territorial jurisdiction extraterritorially in order to circumvent the criminal justice of the territorial state demonstrates a flagrant breach of the port state's territorial sovereignty contrary to Art. 2 (1) UN Charter. Moreover, a legal basis for such diplomatic protection emanating from a flag state's jurisdiction over its vessels cannot extend to disembarked passengers even if such passengers plan to re-board the ship.[85]

3.4 Notable Twentieth Century Practice

By the twentieth century, the practice of states according individuals an extraterritorial right to asylum within the context of their diplomatic premises was no longer as prevalent as it once was:

> The right of asylum which at one time was generally recognised in Europe has long since been abandoned there, and it is now held that the immunity of the mission premises from local jurisdiction extends only to the minister, his suite and household.[86]

Indeed, the practice had historically been so abused that the immunity which had once extended to the entire *franchise du quartier* came to be drastically restricted in scope in an attempt to stem the flow of such asylum cases.[87] Consequently although the practice continued to be facilitated by European states, these states came to be motivated rather by political or altruistic considerations than the conviction that the practice was legally binding.

This, however, isn't to say that there are few examples of states granting such a right. Table 7.1[88] depicts many such examples. For example, in 1915 former Haitian President Jean Vilbrun Guillaume Sam took refuge in the French embassy in Port-au-Prince, Haiti.[89] Despite being granted diplomatic protection by France, Sam was nevertheless seized from the embassy by rebels and then killed. His body parts were

---

[83]Moore (1906), p. 867 f.

[84]UN General Assembly, Question of Diplomatic Asylum, Report of the Secretary-General, 2 September 1975, A/10139 (Part I), para. 88.

[85]For further information on this practice, see Moore (1906), p. 865 f.

[86]Foster (1906), p. 165. Also see Colombian-Peruvian Asylum Case (Colombia v Peru), Counter-Memorial Submitted by the Government of the Republic of Peru, 21 March 1950, p. 121.

[87]Cf. Shah (2007), para. 4.

[88]See Chap. 7: Annex.

[89]Also see Chap. 7: Annex, Table 7.1, Case No. 1.

later paraded around the city.[90] This case therefore constitutes a rare example of the inviolability of the diplomatic premises being violated in order to remove a diplomatic asylee. Ultimately this event signalled the beginning of a nineteen-year period in which the U.S. governed Haiti.[91] Indeed, this case, and others like it,[92] depicts that by the twentieth century, perceptions of the practice had evolved to such a degree that it had become largely reserved for political disturbances where life was in danger.[93] This strongly correlates with the development of the practice in the context of warships.

In the context of the twentieth century, the practice of diplomatic asylum played a vital role in many Latin American states' struggle for independence. Furthermore, it played an equally important role in protecting lives in the context of the Spanish Civil war.[94] It also protected many lives of citizens fleeing from the German Democratic Republic.[95] Table 7.1 depicts many cases in which incumbent politicians forced out of office by revolution were granted refuge by other states in order to spare their lives.[96] It also depicts cases in which political circumstances forced individuals to seek temporary refuge, in some cases as a prelude to ultimate exile.[97] The following section will detail selected historical practice firstly from Spain and then from various Latin American states. The latter will be catalogued according to the receiving state (and generally also the state of nationality of the asylee) and then detailed chronologically.

This practice has been selected in order to, in the first instance, depict an example of the extensive use of the practice in times of crisis and, in the second, in order to illustrate the widespread nature of the practice and convey its common features in Latin America. This will assist with assessing the presence of regional custom in Latin America later on.[98] The practice of the other regions of the world, Asia, Europe, Northern America, Oceania and Africa, will be analysed in the context of Chap. 5, in which state practice will be analysed.[99] The focus on the region of Latin

[90] See: The American Conservative (1 April 2010), Haitian-Building.

[91] IBP (2013), p. 60.

[92] See Chap. 7: Annex, Table 7.1.

[93] Gilbert notes that "In those countries in which the government is stable and enduring and the local law dominant, the privilege is seldom called in question, but has fallen into 'innocuous desuetude,' simply because there has been no necessity for its exercise. . .:" Gilbert (1901), p. 118. Cf. Colombian-Peruvian Asylum Case (Colombia v Peru), Counter-Memorial Submitted by the Government of the Republic of Peru, 21 March 1950, p. 121.

[94] Cf. Chap. 7: Annex, Table 7.1, Case Nos 9–38. Also see Chap. 3: Sect. 3.4.1.

[95] Cf. Chap. 7: Annex, Table 7.1, Case Nos 92–98, 100–103. For more information on diplomatic asylum granted to citizens of the GDR, see in particular Chap. 5: Sect. 5.3.3.6.

[96] Cf. for example Chap. 7: Annex, Table 7.1, Case Nos 46, 48, 50, 51, 59, 113, 152, 168, 180.

[97] Cf. for example Chap. 7: Annex, Table 7.1, Case Nos 2–8, 42, 44–50, 59–60, 65, 67–76, 80, 86–87, 104–105, 107, 133, 138–139, 141, 152, 161, 168, 171, 178, 187, 198–201.

[98] Cf. Chap. 5: Sects. 5.3.4; 5.4.1.1; 5.4.3; 5.5.

[99] Cf. Chap. 5: Sect. 5.3.

America in this historical context owes to the particularity of the history of the practice in the region.

3.4.1 Spain: Diplomatic Asylum in the Context of the Spanish Civil War[100]

The practice of diplomatic asylum played a vital role as a mechanism for protecting human life during the Spanish civil war.[101] Indeed, Table 7.1 provides for thirty cases, many of which involve multiple asylees and ranging from just a couple of individuals to a case in which 2000 persons were granted diplomatic protection by a diplomatic mission at one time, connected to the Spanish civil war.[102]

These cases also involve sending states from three continents, South America, Europe and Asia (in the case of Turkey, the majority of the territory of which lies in Asia). The move was led by Latin American embassies[103] and was criticised by the Spanish government, which held such a use of the right to asylum to be abusive.[104] While details on the individual cases are rather sparse, it is clear that the practice, which can also be regarded as a case of collective shelter,[105] was both widespread and motivated by welfare considerations.[106] Many asylees were also ultimately granted safe-conduct.

3.4.2 Argentina

3.4.2.1 Juan Domingo Perón[107]

Argentinian President Juan Domingo Perón was ousted from power by a military coup in September 1955. He was granted diplomatic asylum by Paraguay's diplomatic mission in Buenos Aires. Whilst it is unclear exactly how long Perón remained

[100]Cf. Chap. 7: Annex, Table 7.1, Case Nos 9–38.

[101]Cf. Moral Roncal (2013), p. 97.

[102]Cf. Chap. 7: Annex, Table 7.1, Case Nos. 9–38.

[103]Moral Roncal (2013), p. 97.

[104]Sinha (1971), p. 34. Cf. Kimminich (1962), p. 141 providing that this even led to a severance of diplomatic relations between Spain and Peru.

[105]Cf. Chap. 2: Sect. 2.1.7. The total number of persons granted shelter is estimated to be around 11,000: Moral Roncal (2013), p. 97.

[106]Moral Roncal (2013), p. 97 f. For further information on diplomatic asylum motivated by humanitarian considerations, see Chap. 6.

[107]Cf. Chap. 7: Annex, Table 7.1, Case No. 51.

in the embassy, it is known that he was transferred from the embassy to a Paraguayan warship.

This case therefore depicts an interesting example of diplomatic asylum in its narrowest sense, in the context of mission premises, being utilised in combination with diplomatic asylum in a wider sense, to include naval asylum, in order ultimately to facilitate political asylum. Whilst Perón would subsequently remain in exile for sixteen years, he eventually did return to Argentina and later became President again in 1973.[108]

3.4.2.2 Rodolfo Puiggrós and His Wife[109]

Former University of Buenos Aires rector, Dr Rodolfo Puiggrós and his wife, Delia, had strong links to the Peronist left-wing movement. Following the assassinations of leading left-wing Peronists, Puiggrós and his wife entered the Mexican embassy in Buenos Aires on 23rd September 1974.

This case may, therefore, be considered as a case in which the granting of diplomatic asylum was motivated by human rights considerations.[110] It is not clear exactly how long the couple spent in the embassy.[111]

3.4.2.3 Héctor Cámpora[112]

Former President of Argentina Héctor Cámpora returned to Argentina in 1975 to an oppressive political climate. Following the military coup of 24th March 1976, he sought refuge in the Mexican embassy in Buenos Aires where he remained for three and a half years. Héctor Cámpora left the embassy in late 1979 due to bad health and then lived in exile in Mexico.[113]

This case is therefore indicative of diplomatic asylum being granted to a former high-ranking politician—a common theme to the history of the practice in the context of Latin America. This case is also indicative of the use of the practice in the midst of political tension.

[108]See Hedges (2011), p. 168; MercoPress (12 September 2013), Argentina thanks Paraguay for granting General Peron asylum in 1955.

[109]Cf. Chap. 7: Annex, Table 7.1, Case No. 74.

[110]For further information on diplomatic asylum motivated by humanitarian considerations, see Chap. 6.

[111]See The New York Times (25 September 1974), Argentines Given Embassy Refuge.

[112]Cf. Chap. 7: Annex, Table 7.1, Case No. 75.

[113]See Kohut and Vilella (2010), p. 99; The Washington Post (21 December 1979), Historically Mexico Has Been a Haven for Political Exiles; UPI (19 December 1980), Former Argentine President Hector Campora, who paved the way...

3.4.2.4 Juan Abal Medina[114]

Following the very same military coup that caused Cámpora to seek asylum, Peronist leader Juan Abal Medina secretly entered the Mexican embassy in Buenos Aires on 29th April 1976. His wife, disguised as a nurse, managed to trick the guards into opening the gates to the heavily guarded embassy. Medina was to remain in the embassy for over six years, breaking the Latin American record at the time. He was eventually granted safe-conduct and permitted to leave the country.[115]

This case is thus indicative of diplomatic asylum being granted in the context of political unrest—another common feature to the practice in the context of Latin America. Moreover, this case depicts diplomatic asylum being granted for a longer duration than is typical. Nevertheless, the case still resulted in the asylee being granted safe-conduct.

3.4.2.5 Summary

Twentieth century state practice in Argentina therefore depicts a number of common features:

- diplomatic asylum being granted to key political figures
- in the context of political unrest.

3.4.3 Bolivia[116]

Hugo Céspedes was a Retired General, Former Defence Minister and Head of the Bolivian Army Academy. When army cadets rebelled, Céspedes was accused of having instigated the rebellion. Whilst those who participated in the rebellion itself were arrested and tried in military court, in March 1981 Céspedes obtained diplomatic asylum in the Brazilian embassy of La Paz, Bolivia. It is not clear how long Céspedes remained there or when he left.[117] This practice in Bolivia depicts a further example of diplomatic asylum being granted in the context of political instability.

---

[114]Cf. Chap. 7: Annex, Table 7.1, Case No. 76.

[115]See UPI (3 September 1981), Peronist holds Latin American record for asylum; UPI (25 May 1982), Argentina increases pressure on U.S. over Falklands.

[116]Cf. Chap. 7: Annex, Table 7.1, Case No. 86.

[117]See UPI (21 March 1981), CBS' 60 Minutes influences coup attempt.

3.4.4 *Chile*[118]

In the months following the 1973 *coup d'état* in Chile, several embassies accepted vast numbers of refugees, including members of the former government, and granted them diplomatic asylum. Canada, Venezuela, Panama, Italy and Mexico all accepted diplomatic asylees and most of the individuals concerned were granted safe-conduct from the embassy and subsequently transported out of the country by the new Chilean government.[119] The Swedish embassy is also particularly noted as having saved Chileans from the Pinochet regime,[120] whilst Austalia notably assisted in helping to facilitate other states granting diplomatic asylum.[121] These cases, depicting state practice in Chile in the twentieth century, constitute notable examples of diplomatic asylum being granted based upon human rights considerations.[122] They also constitute examples of asylum being granted in the context of political unrest.

3.4.5 *Colombia*

3.4.5.1 Alfonso López Pumarejo and Dr. Carlos Lleras Restrepo[123]

Former Colombian President Alfonso López Pumarejo and Dr. Carlos Lleras Restrepo, both of who were leaders of the opposition liberal party, were granted asylum by the Venezuelan embassy in Bogota, Colombia on approximately 12th September 1952.[124] It is not clear how long the duo remained in the embassy or when they left. This case depicts a further example of diplomatic asylum being granted in the context of political instability.

---

[118]Cf. Chap. 7: Annex, Table 7.1, Case Nos 67–73.

[119]See Bassuener (2013), p. 429; Dembinski (1988), p. 249; Kovács and Ádány (2017), p. 182; The Independent (3 March 2016), Chile honours Italian diplomats whose 'Schindler's List' saved 750 lives during Augusto Pinochet's brutal regime; China Daily (7 October 2002), Serra faces election struggle against workers' champion Lula.

[120]Ensalaco (2000), p. 31; The Independent (3 March 2016), Chile honours Italian diplomats whose 'Schindler's List' saved 750 lives during Augusto Pinochet's brutal regime.

[121]Taylor (2019), p. 380.

[122]For further information on diplomatic asylum motivated by humanitarian considerations, see Chap. 6.

[123]Cf. Chap. 7: Annex, Table 7.1, Case No. 49.

[124]The New York Times (13 September 1952), 2 Colombian Liberal Chiefs Get Asylum in Venezuelan Embassy; Take Refuge in Venezuelan Embassy EMBASSY ASYLUM FOR 2 COLOMBIANS.

3.4.5.2 Gabriel García Márquez[125]

Colombian author, Gabriel García Márquez, who would later go on to win the Nobel prize in literature, sought asylum in Mexico's embassy in Bogota, Colombia on 26th March 1981. Márquez alleged that he feared arrest. The Colombian government denied this allegation, arguing that the left-wing author sought to publicly shame Colombia. Márquez's asylum was, however, short-lived as he was permitted to leave the embassy to take up political asylum in Mexico later that day.[126] This case constitutes both an example of diplomatic asylum being used as a means of interim relief against alleged political oppression and also of diplomatic asylum being used as a gateway to political asylum.

3.4.5.3 Summary

Like state practice in Argentina, Bolivia and Chile,[127] Colombian state practice also depicts diplomatic asylum being granted in the context of political unrest.

3.4.6 Costa Rica[128]

Following a *coup d'état* in January 1917, which saw Costa Rican President Alfredo González Flores ousted from power by Federico Tinoco, several members of the González family sought refuge in the U.S. legation in San José. On 17th May 1917, Domingo González, his six sons and three daughters entered the U.S. legation fearing immediate arrest or even execution.[129] Costa Rica permitted the group to leave a week later on 25th May 1917.[130] This case, indicative of state practice in Costa Rica in the twentieth century, also constitutes an example of diplomatic asylum being granted in the context of political instability—in this case to the family of the ousted president. Furthermore, it also arguably depicts an example of

[125]Cf. Chap. 7: Annex, Table 7.1, Case No. 87.

[126]See UPI (26 March 1981), Gabriel Garcia Marquez, Colombia's best-known novelist, sought political asylum...

[127]Cf. Chap. 3: Sects. 3.4.2–3.4.4.

[128]Cf. Chap. 7: Annex, Table 7.1, Case No. 2.

[129]U.S. Department of State, Foreign Relations of the United States, Papers Relating to the Foreign Relations of the United States, With the Address of the President to Congress December 4, 1917, Doc. 399, 17 May 1917.

[130]U.S. Department of State, Foreign Relations of the United States, Papers Relating to the Foreign Relations of the United States, With the Address of the President to Congress December 4, 1917, Doc. 404, Chargé Johnson to the Secretary of State, Telegram, 25 May 1917.

diplomatic asylum motivated by humanitarian considerations as the family feared for their lives.[131]

3.4.7 *Cuba*

3.4.7.1 Mario G. Menocal, His Nephew, Martín Menocal, and (Pedro) Martínez Fraga[132]

Following the Cuban government's arrest of several individuals for alleged revolutionary activity, former Cuban President and leader of the opposition, Mario G. Menocal, his nephew, Martín Menocal, and (Pedro) Martínez Fraga feared they were in imminent danger of arrest and personal injury from government forces. They entered the Brazilian embassy in Havana, Cuba on 24th May 1932. The trio were granted diplomatic asylum by Brazil based on it being a contracting state to the Havana Convention 1928.[133] The case caused a diplomatic stand-off between Brazil and Cuba, the government forces of which initially surrounded the embassy building. An agreement was reached in July 1932 by which the trio were granted safe-conduct to depart to Europe—with Cuba agreeing to let them pass without hindrance in exchange for Brazil agreeing that General Menocal would not pose an obstacle to Cuban peace and would reside in Europe for at least a year.[134] As above, this case depicts an example of diplomatic asylum being granted in the context of political instability and motivated by humanitarian considerations. Moreover, it also constitutes an example of diplomatic asylum being granted to a former president.

3.4.7.2 October 1932[135]

The assassination of Senate President Clemente Vázquez Bello on 28th September 1932 by members of the opposition set into motion a chain of events that was to cause great political unrest in Cuba. Police raids, arrests, tortures and killings targeted both students and members of the opposition.[136] These assassinations led to a widespread feeling of insecurity, which in turn caused many to seek shelter within the premises of diplomatic missions. Whilst the U.S. delegation turned away requests, the Spanish, Mexican, Uruguayan and Colombian legations all admitted

[131]For further information on diplomatic asylum motivated by humanitarian considerations, see Chap. 6.

[132]Cf. Chap. 7: Annex, Table 7.1, Case Nos 3 and 4.

[133]For further information on this convention, see Chap. 4: Sect. 4.2.2.4.

[134]See U.S. Department of State, Foreign Relations of the United States Diplomatic Papers, 1932, The American Republics, Vol. V, Cuba, Political Unrest in Cuba, Doc. 602.

[135]Cf. Chap. 7: Annex, Table 7.1, Case Nos 5–8.

[136]Suchlicki (2002), p. 92.

individuals and granted them temporary asylum. Cuban President Machado was indignant that so many legations had granted asylum to the refugees, who he argued intended rather to embarrass the government.

Though it is not known how long the refugees resided within the diplomatic premises, it was noted by the U.S. State Department that only one individual was granted safe-conduct and thus permitted to leave Cuba.[137]

This case also depicts an example of diplomatic asylum being granted in the context of political instability. Furthermore, it depicts a rare example, in the context of Latin America, of safe-conduct for the large part being refused.

3.4.7.3 Carlos Prío Socarrás[138]

Carlos Prío Socarrás was President of Cuba from 1948 until 10th March 1952 when he was deposed by a military coup. On the very same day, Socarrás sought asylum in the Mexican embassy in Havana. He remained there for three days after which he was granted safe-conduct and permitted to travel to Mexico.[139] This case therefore depicts a further example of a former president being granted diplomatic asylum as a means of protection following a forceful regime change.

3.4.7.4 Manuel Urrutia[140]

Manuel Urrutia was the first President of Cuba following the revolution in 1959. Though he took office in January 1959 at Castro's request, Urrutia was accused of treason six months later, prompting a threatening crowd to gather around the Presidential palace. Urrutia was able to slip away in disguise and enter the Venezuelan embassy, which granted him diplomatic asylum.[141] Though it is not known exactly how long Urrutia spent under the protection of the Venezuelan legation, he is known to have also spent time being sheltered by the Mexican legation before being granted safe-conduct in the form of passage to the U.S.[142]

This case depicts another example of diplomatic asylum being granted to a former president following the regime being overthrown. Notably, this case depicts an interesting example of several states extending diplomatic protection to the same individual prior to safe-conduct being granted.

---

[137]See U.S. Department of State, Foreign Relations of the United States Diplomatic Papers, 1932, The American Republics, Vol. V, Cuba, Political Unrest in Cuba, Doc. 608.

[138]Cf. Chap. 7: Annex, Table 7.1, Case No. 48.

[139]See Leonard (2004), p. 16.

[140]Cf. Chap. 7: Annex, Table 7.1, Case No. 59.

[141]Cuzán (1999), p. 185; The New York Times (6 July 1981), Manuel Urrutia; Was Foe of Castro.

[142]The New York Times (6 July 1981), Manuel Urrutia; Was Foe of Castro.

3.4.7.5 Olga Morgan[143]

Olga Morgan was married to American William Morgan, who came to Cuba in 1957 in order to help overthrow the government of Fulgencio Batista. The Morgans were united in their opposition to the Cuban government, particularly the later Castro regime. Eventually both were arrested in October 1960 for providing anti-Castro guerrillas with weaponry. William Morgan was later executed by firing squad. His wife managed to escape and entered the Brazilian embassy in Havana on 4th January 1961, asking for asylum. She remained there for three months before leaving and going into hiding. Morgan was, however, arrested and imprisoned in March 1961. She was eventually freed in 1972 and left Cuba for the U.S. as part of the Mariel Cuban Exodus.[144]

This case depicts another example of diplomatic asylum being granted in the midst of political tension—in this case to an opponent of the regime. Human rights considerations may well have also motivated the decision to grant asylum to Morgan in this case, particularly in the light of her husband's later execution.

3.4.7.6 The Mariel Cuban Exodus[145]

A series of escapes by discontented Cubans into Latin American embassies in Havana, which commenced in 1979, eventually came to culminate in the famous Mariel exodus. On 14th May 1979, twelve Cuban refugees tried to gain entry to Venezuela's embassy, with several being wounded in the process. Later, several groups of refugees successfully gained entry to Venezuela's embassy in order to request diplomatic asylum. On 21st January 1980, two separate groups of Cubans attempted to gain entry to the Peruvian and Venezuelan embassies in an escape attempt which met resistance, resulting in a fatality and multiple injuries.

Another attempt on 1st April 1980 saw a further fatality (a guard) and injuries. Peru refused to surrender the refugees to Cuban authorities, prompting Castro to declare that Cuba would no longer protect the Peruvian embassy, thus withdrawing Cuban security forces from outside the embassy. Within hours, 10,000 Cubans had gathered at the embassy requesting diplomatic asylum.

Cuba responded by obstructing access to the embassy, whilst Peru called on the international community for assistance in homing the refugees. Venezuela, Ecuador, Costa Rica and the U.S. all agreed to take refugees. Several groups of refugees leaving the embassy bound for various Latin American countries were met with violent resistance from orchestrated mobs. Castro then publicly declared that any person(s) wanting to leave Cuba could do so via boat from the Northern port of

---

[143] Cf. Chap. 7: Annex, Table 7.1, Case No. 60.

[144] See Chap. 3: Sect. 3.4.7.6; Toledo Blade (5 March 2002), An Escape from Cuba: Olga comes home to Toledo.

[145] Cf. Chap. 7: Annex, Table 7.1, Case No. 83.

Mariel, Cuba. In total approximately 125,000 Cubans left Cuba from Mariel, bound for Florida, U.S.[146]

As human rights considerations also played a predominant role in this case, it may be seen as a case in which diplomatic asylum was granted based on such considerations. Moreover, civil unrest is a further identifying theme of this case. This case may also be regarded as one in which multiple states provided collective shelter.

3.4.7.7 July 1990[147]

In the context of the Cuban revolution, a number of Cuban asylum seekers sought refuge in European embassies in July 1990. Whilst the duration those staying in the Belgian, Czechoslovakian, Italian and Swiss embassies did not exceed the end of July, some of those in the Spanish embassy remained there until 4th September 1990. As Cuba refused to grant the diplomatic asylees safe-conduct, they remained in Havana upon leaving the embassy.[148] These cases again depict the use of the practice in the context of political unrest and also depict mass use of the practice.

3.4.7.8 Arturo Sandoval, His Wife and Son[149]

Renowned Cuban jazz musician Arturo Sandoval became disillusioned with the governing Castro regime and began to make plans to defect. Upon his wife and son being permitted to join him abroad, the trio seized the opportunity and requested diplomatic asylum in the U.S. embassy in Rome, Italy in July 1990. Their request was granted and a matter of days later they travelled to the U.S., where they were granted permanent residency.[150]

This case depicts the use of the practice to facilitate defection, a theme later common to cases involving North Korean nationals.[151]

3.4.7.9 Alina Fernández Revuelta[152]

Alina Fernández Revuelta, the daughter of Fidel Castro, was a long-time critic of his regime. On 20th December 1993, Fernández Revuelta arrived at the U.S. embassy in Madrid, Spain and requested asylum.

---

[146] See Dupes Hawk et al. (2014), pp. 29–30; Global Security, Mariel Boatlift. https://www.globalsecurity.org/military/ops/mariel-boatlift.htm. Last accessed 14 Dec 2020.

[147] Cf. Chap. 7: Annex, Table 7.1, Case Nos 129–132.

[148] See The New York Times (12 September 1990), Spanish-Cuban Asylum Battle Ends, Bitterly.

[149] Cf. Chap. 7: Annex, Table 7.1, Case No. 133.

[150] See Los Angeles Times (23 April 1997), Trumpeter Arturo Sandoval Is Denied U.S. Citizenship.

[151] See Chap. 5: Sect. 5.3.2.5.

[152] Cf. Chap. 7: Annex, Table 7.1, Case No. 139.

Fernández Revuelta's case thus depicts a clear case of diplomatic asylum being used as a gateway to political asylum to a defector of the governing regime. Fernández Revuelta was granted asylum and arrived in Atlanta, U.S. the following day.[153]

3.4.7.10 Twenty-one Cuban Asylum Seekers[154]

On 27th February 2002 a bus carrying Cuban asylum seekers forcibly entered the diplomatic premises of Mexico. This reportedly followed rumours that Mexico was offering asylum to Cubans. Though it is rare that attempts to penetrate an embassy result in asylum being granted, this case constitutes a rare such example of asylum being granted to the individuals concerned. It is not clear exactly how long the group remained in the embassy though this is reported as being longer than a few days.[155] This case also depicts the use of the practice to facilitate defection.

3.4.7.11 Summary

Twentieth century practice in Cuba is also indicative of diplomatic asylum being granted in the midst of political unrest, in many cases to key political figures and in several cases motivated by human rights considerations. Several cases also depict diplomatic asylum being granted to groups and several depict diplomatic asylum being used as a means of defection.

3.4.8 Guatemala

3.4.8.1 Juan José Arévalo Bermejo[156]

In 1944, Presidential nominee Juan José Arévalo Bermejo returned to Guatemala from Argentina to commence his campaign on 3rd September 1944. His campaign, however, was fraught with interference and oppression from the government, which led Arévalo Bermejo to seek asylum in the Mexican embassy of Guatemala City on 18th October 1944.[157] It is unclear exactly how long Arévalo Bermejo remained at the embassy, though he went on to win the election and officially took office as

[153]See Los Angeles Times (23 December 1993), Fidel Castro's Daughter Gets U.S. Asylum: Defection: Longtime critic of the Cuban dictator flees island. She is now in Atlanta.

[154]Cf. Chap. 7: Annex, Table 7.1, Case No. 147.

[155]See The New York Times (1 March 2002), Cubans Set on Asylum Crash a Bus into Embassy.

[156]Cf. Chap. 7: Annex, Table 7.1, Case No. 42.

[157]Fry (2018), p. 50.

President of Guatemala in March 1945. This case also depicts the use of the practice in the midst of political instability, in this case to a prospective presidential candidate.

3.4.8.2 Jacobo Árbenz Guzmán and Family[158]

President Jacobo Árbenz Guzmán's government was overthrown on 18th June 1954. Árbenz Guzmán subsequently resigned on 27th June 1954 and together with his family immediately took up diplomatic asylum within the premises of Mexico's diplomatic mission in Guatemala.[159] Árbenz Guzmán and his family spent 73 days in the Mexican embassy in the company of another 300 persons also seeking asylum.[160] Following this, the family were eventually able to take up political asylum in Mexico.

This case depicts both the use of diplomatic asylum as a gateway to political asylum and also the use of the practice to protect a former president following forceful regime change. This case may also be regarded as one of collective shelter.

3.4.8.3 Francisco Bobadilla Palomo[161]

Following the government of President Fernando Romeo Lucas García being overthrown in April 1982, agriculture minister Francisco Bobdilla Palomo sought asylum in the Brazilian embassy in Guatemala City due to embezzlement charges against him. He remained there until late August 1982, when upon being refused safe-conduct to Brazil, he left the embassy with his wife and disappeared.[162] Once again, this case depicts the use of the practice to protect a member of the outgoing governmental regime from its successor.

3.4.8.4 Summary

State practice in Guatemala in the twentieth century also depicts diplomatic asylum being used as a tool to protect key political figures in the context of political unrest and/or tension.

---

[158]Cf. Chap. 7: Annex, Table 7.1, Case No. 50.

[159]Garcia Ferreira (2008), p. 61 f.

[160]Garcia Ferreira (2008), p. 62.

[161]Cf. Chap. 7: Annex, Table 7.1, Case No. 89.

[162]UPI (31 August 1983), Five members of council quit in protest.

3.4.9 *Haiti*

3.4.9.1 Twenty-two Opponents of the Governing Regime[163]

In May 1963, twenty-two opponents of the governing Duvalier regime were granted diplomatic asylum in the diplomatic premises of the Dominican Republic.[164] Duvalier sent the police into the embassy. This case depicts a rare example of the inviolability of the mission premises being breached, as well as a more frequent example of diplomatic asylum being granted to a regime's political opponents. Such cases are, in particular, often motivated by the risk of a breach to the fundamental human rights of the individual concerned.

3.4.9.2 Leon Veillard[165]

In the late 1960s, Leon Veillard, a trained attorney and a captain in the Haitian army, was accused of plotting to overthrow President Francois Duvalier and was sentenced to death along with twenty others, eighteen of which were executed by firing squad. Veillard entered the Brazilian embassy in Port-au-Prince, Haiti and remained there for eight months.[166] This case thus depicts an example of the use of the practice motivated by human rights considerations.[167] Political considerations are also likely to have motivated the granting state's decision.

3.4.9.3 Albert Pierre, Gener Crotin, Edner Pageotte et al[168]

Following the departure of President Francois Duvalier on 7th February 1986, many of his supporters felt that their lives were in danger. Six officials from Duvailer's former government were granted diplomatic asylum by the Brazilian embassy in Port-au-Prince, Haiti in February 1986. Though several of the asylees were subsequently granted political asylum in Brazil, at least one voluntarily renounced his asylum as he felt his life was no longer at risk.[169] This case also a further example of human rights considerations playing a role. It furthermore evidences part of the former executive being shielded from the new governing regime.

---

[163] Cf. Chap. 7: Annex, Table 7.1, Case No. 62.

[164] Die Zeit (24 May 1963), Tyrann mit sanften Augen; Kitschenberg (1965), Einleitung.

[165] Cf. Chap. 7: Annex, Table 7.1, Case No. 65.

[166] See Orlando Sentinel (28 December 1991), He Raises His Voice for Haiti.

[167] For further information on diplomatic asylum motivated by humanitarian considerations, see Chap. 6.

[168] Cf. Chap. 7: Annex, Table 7.1, Case No. 107.

[169] See UPI (24 February 1986), Former Duvalier Supporters said to flee Haiti.

3.4.9.4 Franck Romain[170]

Franck Romain, a former Haitian mayor accused of involvement in a church massacre, sought asylum in the mission premises of the Dominican Republic on 17th September 1989.[171] Romain remained in the mission premises until January of the following year.[172] This case constitutes a rare example of diplomatic asylum being granted to an individual alleged to have committed common crimes, in this case grave crimes. It therefore depicts a deviation from the general rules governing the right to diplomatic asylum in Latin America.[173]

3.4.9.5 Prosper Avril[174]

Following a police raid of his home and the arrest of his daughter, the former Haitian President, Prosper Avril, sought refuge in the Colombian embassy in Port au Prince Haiti on 7th November 1995.[175] Though it is not known how long Avril remained in the embassy, he is noted as still being there at the end of 1995.[176] This case depicts an example of diplomatic asylum being granted in the context of political instability to a former president.

3.4.9.6 Summary

Twentieth century state practice from Haiti also depicts asylum being granted to key political figures in the context of political instability. Several cases also show human rights considerations motivating the granting state's decision.

---

[170] Cf. Chap. 7: Annex, Table 7.1, Case No. 110.

[171] AP (21 January 1989), Former Mayor Franck Romain Indicted for Massacre.

[172] OAS, Inter-American Commission on Human Rights, Annual Report of the Inter-American Commission on Human Rights 1988–1989, 18 September 1989; Haiti, Doc. 10, OEA/Ser.L/V/II.76. Available at: http://www.cidh.org/annualrep/88.89eng/chap.4c.htm. Last Accessed 14 Dec 2020.

[173] Cf. Chap. 4: Sect. 4.2; Chap. 5: Sect. 5.3.4.

[174] Cf. Chap. 7: Annex, Table 7.1, Case No. 141.

[175] Stotzky (1997), p. 162; U.S. Department of State, Country Reports on Human Rights Practices for 1995, Vols 8 to 15, 1 March 1996, p. 445.

[176] U.S. Department of State, Country Reports on Human Rights Practices for 1995, Vols 8 to 15, 1 March 1996, p. 370.

3.4.10 Nicaragua

3.4.10.1 Leonardo Argüello Barreto, His Wife and Eleven Officers; Captain Francisco (Panchito) Aguirre Baca and His Brother Horacio[177]

President of Nicaragua Leonardo Argüello Barreto was overthrown in a *coup d'état* in May 1947. He, his wife and eleven officers were subsequently granted diplomatic asylum by the Mexican embassy in Managua, Nicaragua. Captain of the National Guard Francisco (Panchito) Aguirre Baca and his brother Horacio were granted diplomatic protection by Panama and were soon transported from the embassy to be taken abroad.[178] This case depicts a further example of diplomatic asylum being granted to a former president, a member of his family and eleven officers, following a forceful regime change.

3.4.10.2 Sergio Ramírez Mercado[179]

Following failed talks to achieve a resolution to the political crisis, negotiator Sergio Ramírez Mercado sought refuge in the Mexican embassy in Managua in September 1978. He remained there until a pre-Christmas amnesty secured his release.[180] This case depicts a further example of diplomatic asylum being granted in the context of political instability.

3.4.10.3 Lt. Roberto Granera[181]

Lt. Roberto Granera was a military doctor who, disillusioned with the Sandinista regime, sought asylum in the Venezuelan mission's premises of Nicaragua in 1985. It is unclear how long Granera remained in the embassy.[182] This case depicts an example of diplomatic asylum being granted based upon disillusionment with the governing political regime.

---

[177]Cf. Chap. 7: Annex, Table 7.1, Case Nos 45 and 46.

[178]See U.S. Department of State, Foreign Relations of the United States Diplomatic Papers, 1947, The American Republics, Vol. VIII, Nicaragua, Political Upheaval in Nicaragua: United States policies of nonintervention and nonrecognition, Doc. 731.

[179]Cf. Chap. 7: Annex, Table 7.1, Case No. 80.

[180]The New York Times (16 July 1979), Sergio Ramirez Mercado.

[181]Cf. Chap. 7: Annex, Table 7.1, Case No. 104.

[182]See Behrens (2014), p. 331, Fn. 70.

3.4.10.4 José Efrén Martínez Mondragón (and Nine Other Persons)[183]

José Efrén Martínez Mondragón was a task force commander of the anti-Sandinista resistance in Nicaragua, who upon becoming disillusioned with the resistance movement entered the Mexican embassy in Tegucigalpa, Honduras with nine others in March 1985, seeking political asylum in Mexico. Again, this case poses another example of diplomatic asylum being used as a gateway to political asylum. Although the Honduran government initially resisted Mexican attempts to obtain safe-conduct for Martínez Mondragón, he was eventually permitted to leave the country for Mexico though he returned to Nicaragua a short time after.[184]

3.4.10.5 Summary

Twentieth century state practice in Nicaragua shows diplomatic asylum being granted to a number of former presidents. As is the case for other Latin American states,[185] political upheaval is a consistent theme. Interestingly, several cases in Nicaragua depict diplomatic asylum being utiltised as a gateway in an attempt to ultimately secure political asylum.

3.4.11 Panama[186]

In December 1989, the U.S. invaded Panama in order to depose ruler Manuel Noriega. Following the invasion, Noriega and several of his associates went into hiding, seeking refuge in diplomatic premises across Panama City. Whilst Noriega himself sought refuge at the Apostolic Nunciature of the Holy See, akin to an embassy, his associates were given asylum by Peru, Cuba and Mexico.

In the face of intense international pressure and unusual extraction methods, Noriega remained in the Apostolic Nunciature of the Holy See until 3rd January 1990, when he surrendered to the U.S. authorities. His associates remained in their respective embassies until 11th May 1990.[187] This case, constitutive of twentieth century state practice in Panama, depicts yet another example of diplomatic asylum being granted to a former ruler to shield him from the repercussions of a regime change.

---

[183] Cf. Chap. 7: Annex, Table 7.1, Case No. 105.

[184] See The Washington Post (8 May 1985), A Defecting Nicaraguan Contra's Tale.

[185] Cf. Chap. 3: Sects. 3.4.2–3.4.9.

[186] Cf. Chap. 7: Annex, Table 7.1, Case No. 113.

[187] See UPI (11 May 1991), Former Noriega associates allowed to leave country; BBC News (30 May 2017), Music torture: How heavy metal broke Manuel Noriega; The Telegraph (30 May 2017), How Panama's military dictator Manuel Noriega was defeated by rock'n'roll.

3.4.12 *Paraguay*[188]

In Paraguay in 1947, author Augusto Roa Basto's previous writings, critical of military governments, forced him to seek sanctuary in Brazil's diplomatic mission in Asunción. He sheltered here until he was able to leave to take up exile in Argentina.[189] This case, constitutive of twentieth century state practice in Paraguay, depicts an example of diplomatic asylum being granted to a critic of the governing regime.

3.4.13 *Peru*

3.4.13.1 Haya de la Torre[190]

Perhaps the most renowned case of diplomatic asylum, certainly in terms of international jurisprudence, is that of Peruvian politician, Víctor Raúl Haya de la Torre. On 3rd October 1948, a military rebellion broke out in Peru. A day later, Peru's President issued a decree according responsibility for the rebellion to the American People's Revolutionary Alliance. The very next day, a note of denunciation was issued for Haya de la Torre, the leader of said party, for the crime of military rebellion. Judicial proceedings were instituted against him on 11th October 1948. In the light of these events, Haya de la Torre sought asylum in the Colombian embassy in Lima on 3rd January 1949:[191]

> The Colombian Ambassador granted the protection sought by Mr. Haya de la Torre, who presented himself as a political refugee.[192]

The use of the term "political refugee" is important as a person accused of a so-called common crime would be unable to claim diplomatic asylum under the doctrine of diplomatic asylum in Latin America.[193]

Colombia then proceeded to inform Peru that it had granted Haya de la Torre asylum and to request the guarantee of his safe passage from the embassy, in line

---

[188] Cf. Chap. 7: Annex, Table 7.1, Case No. 44.

[189] Roa Bastos, Augusto, Encyclopedia of World Biography, Encylopedia.com. https://www.encyclopedia.com/history/encyclopedias-almanacs-transcripts-and-maps/roa-bastos-augusto. Last Accessed 14 Dec 2020.

[190] Cf. Chap. 7: Annex, Table 7.1, Case No. 47.

[191] For further information pertaining to the facts of the case, see Colombian-Peruvian Asylum Case (Colombia v Peru), Judgment of 20 November 1950, ICJ Reports 1950, No. 7, p. 272 f.

[192] Colombian-Peruvian Asylum Case (Colombia v Peru), Application Instituting Proceedings by the Republic of Colombia Against Peru, 15 October 1949, p. 9, para. 7.

[193] Cf. Chap. 4: Sect. 4.2; Chap. 5: Sects. 5.3.4 and 5.4.1.1.

with his rights under the Havana Convention on Asylum of 1928.[194] Peru refused to grant this request.[195] Following the unsuccessful exchange of further diplomatic notes between the two states,[196] Colombia proceeded to submit the dispute to the International Court of Justice.

Colombian-Peruvian Asylum Case

In delivering its judgment on the dispute, the ICJ considered not only both states' obligations under the aforementioned Havana Convention on Asylum,[197] but also their obligations under the Bolivian Agreement on Extradition of 1911,[198] general rules of international law, customary international law, the unique juridical nature of the institution of asylum in America and subsequent state practice.[199] The application posed the following questions to the court:

> First question - Within the limits of the obligations resulting in particular from the Bolivarian Agreement on Extradition of July 18th 1911 and the Convention on Asylum of February 20th 1928, both in force between Colombia and Peru and in general from American international law, was Colombia competent, as the country granting asylum, to qualify the offence for the purposes of said asylum?
>
> Second question - In the specific case under consideration, was Peru, as the territorial State, bound to give the guaranties necessary for the departure of the refugee from the country, with due regard to the inviolability of his person?[200]

Not only did Peru and Colombia disagree on the legitimacy of Haya de la Torre's right to diplomatic asylum and thus in turn on the legitimacy of Colombia's request regarding his safe passage out of Peru, they also disagreed upon the right to qualify Haya de la Torre's alleged offence. Colombia argued that as the state granting asylum, it also had the right to qualify Haya de la Torre's alleged offence as political in nature (as opposed to an ordinary offence which would have meant Haya de la Torre was ineligible for diplomatic asylum), thus rendering him an eligible recipient of diplomatic asylum according to international law, in particular Art. 1 Havana

[194] Colombian-Peruvian Asylum Case (Colombia v Peru), Application Instituting Proceedings by the Republic of Colombia Against Peru, 15 October 1949, p. 9, paras 8 and 9.

[195] Colombian-Peruvian Asylum Case (Colombia v Peru), Application Instituting Proceedings by the Republic of Colombia Against Peru, 15 October 1949, p. 9, para. 10.

[196] See Colombian-Peruvian Asylum Case (Colombia v Peru), Application Instituting Proceedings by the Republic of Colombia Against Peru, 15 October 1949, p. 9, paras 11–13.

[197] Cf. Chap. 4: Sect. 4.2.2.4.

[198] Cf. Chap. 4: Sect. 4.2.2.3.

[199] Colombian-Peruvian Asylum Case (Colombia v Peru), Application Instituting Proceedings by the Republic of Colombia Against Peru, 15 October 1949, p. 10, para. 16.

[200] Colombian-Peruvian Asylum Case (Colombia v Peru), Application Instituting Proceedings by the Republic of Colombia Against Peru, 15 October 1949, p. 11, para. 19.

Convention on Asylum.[201] In this regard, scholar García-Mora holds that to deny a state the right of qualification is tantamount to rejecting the doctrine of asylum altogether.[202]

By way of a counterclaim, Peru also requested the court to declare the grant and/or maintenance of Haya de la Torre's right to asylum to be in violation of the Havana Convention on Asylum.[203]

Pertaining to the first question, the issue of qualification, the ICJ held:

> These considerations show that the alleged right of unilateral and definitive qualification cannot be regarded as recognized by implication in the Havana Convention. Moreover, this Convention, in pursuance of the desire expressed in its preamble of "fixing the rules" which the Governments of the States of America must observe for the granting of asylum, was concluded with the manifest intention of preventing the abuses which had arisen in the previous practice, by limiting the grant of asylum.[204]

This passage, though silent on explicitly according the right of qualification to one state or the other under the Havana Convention, would imply that in order to prevent the abuse which had in the past occurred, the right to diplomatic asylum under the Havana Convention is to be interpreted narrowly.

Furthermore, in considering whether definitive unilateral qualification of a right to diplomatic asylum for Haya de la Torre could find its basis in customary international law, albeit regional custom, the Court was clear in apportioning the burden of proof upon the state seeking to establish the custom—in this instance Colombia:

> The Party which relies on a custom of this kind must prove that this custom is established in such a manner that it has become binding on the other Party.[205]

This is consistent with the jurisprudence of the PCIJ/ICJ, both preceding and succeeding this judgment, holding that the party seeking to make an assertion bears the burden of proof of doing so.[206]

---

[201]Judge M. Caicedo Castilla agreed in his dissenting opinion: Colombian-Peruvian Asylum Case (Colombia v Peru), Judgment of 20 November 1950, ICJ Reports 1950, No. 7, Dissenting Opinion by Judge M. Caicedo Castilla (translation), pp. 360, 364.

[202]García-Mora (1951), p. 930. In this vein, Kau also argues that qualification falls to the state granting asylum: Cf. Kau (2019), p. 198, para. 75a.

[203]Colombian-Peruvian Asylum Case (Colombia v Peru), Judgment of 20 November 1950, ICJ Reports 1950, No. 7, p. 271.

[204]Colombian-Peruvian Asylum Case (Colombia v Peru), Judgment of 20 November 1950, ICJ Reports 1950, No. 7, p. 275.

[205]Colombian-Peruvian Asylum Case (Colombia v Peru), Judgment of 20 November 1950, ICJ Reports 1950, No. 7, p. 276.

[206]Cf. The Mavrommatis Jerusalem Concessions (Greece v United Kingdom of Great Britain and Northern Ireland), Judgment of 26th March 1925, Publications of the Permanent Court of International Justice, Series A, No. 5, p. 44; Legal Status of Eastern Greenland (Denmark v Norway), Judgment of 5 April 1933, Publications of the Permanent Court of International Justice, Series A/B, No. 53, p. 49; Case Concerning Military and Paramilitary Activities in and against Nicaragua (Nicaragua v United States of America), Jurisdiction of the Court and Admissibility of the

In the case at hand, the Court found that Colombia failed to establish uniform and consistent usage with regard to the qualification of a right to diplomatic asylum.[207] Moreover, the Court held that even if such a custom existed, it would not be binding upon Peru:

> The Court cannot therefore find that the Colombian Government has proved the existence of such a custom. But even if it could be supposed that such a custom existed between certain Latin-American States only, it could not be invoked against Peru which, far from having by its attitude adhered to it, has, on the contrary, repudiated it by refraining from ratifying the Montevideo Conventions of 1933 and 1939, which were the first to include a rule concerning the qualification of the offence in matters of diplomatic asylum.[208]

This passage introduces the notion of regional custom i.e. customary international law rules applicable only to a certain geographical region, in this case Latin America.[209] It has also been interpreted by some authors as evidence that Peru, at least at the time of the judgment, constituted a persistent objector with regard to the regional custom of diplomatic asylum.[210]

With regard to the second question, the ICJ held that as Peru had contested the legality of Haya de la Torre's right to asylum, Colombia was therefore not entitled to request that Peru guarantee Haya de la Torre's safe passage from the country.[211] The Court also provided a helpful definition of the grant of asylum, holding it to be ongoing for as long as the asylee remains in the diplomatic premises:

> The grant of asylum is not an instantaneous act which terminates with the admission, at a given moment, of a refugee to an embassy or a legation. Any grant of asylum results in, and in consequence logically implies, a state of protection; the asylum is granted as long as the continued presence of the refugee in the embassy prolongs this protection.[212]

Application, Judgment of 26 November 1984, No. 70, p. 437, para. 101; Case Concerning Application of the Convention on the Prevention and Punishment of the Crime of Genocide (Bosnia and Herzegovina v Serbia and Montenegro), Judgment of 26 February 2007, ICJ Reports 2007, No. 91, p. 128, para, 204; Case Concerning Sovereignty over Pedra Branca/Pulau Batu Puteh, Middle Rocks and South Ledge (Malaysia/Singapore), Judgment of 23 May 2008, ICJ Reports 2008, No. 130, p. 31, para. 45; Maritime Delimitation in the Black Sea (Romania v Ukraine), Judgment of 3 February 2009, ICJ Reports 2009, No. 132, p. 86, para. 68; Case Concerning Pulp Mills on the River Uruguay (Argentina v Uruguay), Judgment of 20 April 2010, ICJ Reports 2010, No. 135, p. 71, para. 162; Case Concerning Ahmadou Sadio Diallo (Republic of Guinea v Democratic Republic of the Congo), Judgment of 30 November 2010, ICJ Reports 2010, No. 103, p. 660; Application of the Interim Accord of 13 September (The Former Yugoslav Republic of Macedonia v Greece), Judgment of 5 December 2011, ICJ Reports 2011, No. 142, p. 668, para. 72. Also see Tomka and Proulx (2015), p. 16.

[207] Colombian-Peruvian Asylum Case (Colombia v Peru), Judgment of 20 November 1950, ICJ Reports 1950, No. 7, p. 277 f.

[208] Colombian-Peruvian Asylum Case (Colombia v Peru), Judgment of 20 November 1950, ICJ Reports 1950, No. 7, pp. 277–278.

[209] Cf. Chap. 5: Sect. 5.2.

[210] See e.g. Dörr (2018), p. 549; Mendelson (1998), p. 228; von Arnauld (2019), p. 109, para. 254.

[211] Colombian-Peruvian Asylum Case (Colombia v Peru), Judgment of 20 November 1950, ICJ Reports 1950, No. 7, p. 279.

[212] Colombian-Peruvian Asylum Case (Colombia v Peru), Judgment of 20 November 1950, ICJ Reports 1950, No. 7, p. 281.

Therefore, a diplomatic asylee need only remain in the diplomatic premises in order to continue to benefit from the state of protection generated by the asylum granted.

The use of the term "state of protection" is interesting here as its usage correlates with the use of the term "under (diplomatic) protection" to describe the status of a diplomatic asylee. This latter term was used with regard to multiple cases detailed in Table 7.1, for example that of Andry Rajoelina in March 2009 who was held to be under UN protection[213] or that of an aide to Jang Song Thaek in December 2013.[214]

The Court also held that Peru had, however, not proven that Haya de la Torre's alleged crime, military rebellion, was a so-called common crime,[215] which would have exempted Haya de la Torre from being eligible for diplomatic asylum under Art. 1 Havana Convention.[216] On this basis, the Court dismissed Peru's counterclaim regarding the second question.[217] The Court also considered whether the case of Haya de la Torre could be deemed to be an "urgent case," as required by Art. 2 Havana Convention. Here, the Court gave a clear statement that the practice of diplomatic asylum being used in order to circumvent justice is contrary, at least, to the Havana Convention:

> In principle, therefore, asylum cannot be opposed to the operation of justice. An exception to this rule can occur only if, in the guise of justice, arbitrary action is substituted for the rule of law. Such would be the case if the administration of justice were corrupted by measures clearly prompted by political aims. Asylum protects the political offender against any measures of a manifestly extra-legal character which a government might take or attempt to take against its political opponents.[218]

This passage is interesting as it depicts the Court recognising that diplomatic asylum may frustrate the ordinary course of justice i.e. the receiving state's ability to enforce its own justice system within its jurisdiction. For this reason, the scope of the practice was held to be very limited.

In 1950, the Court thus viewed diplomatic asylum as only being permissible where justice is no longer subject to the rule of law,[219] but instead to arbitrariness in situations in which a government perverts the justice system in order to eliminate its

---

[213]Cf. Chap. 7: Annex, Table 7.1, Case No. 177.

[214]Cf. Chap. 7: Annex, Table 7.1, Case No. 190.

[215]Colombian-Peruvian Asylum Case (Colombia v Peru), Judgment of 20 November 1950, ICJ Reports 1950, No. 7, p. 281 f.

[216]Cf. Chap. 4: Sect. 4.2.2.4.

[217]Colombian-Peruvian Asylum Case (Colombia v Peru), Judgment of 20 November 1950, ICJ Reports 1950, No. 7, p. 282. In the form of a counterclaim, Peru had asked the Court to declare Colombia granting asylum to Haya de la Torre, or at least the maintenance of said asylum, to be contrary to the Havana Convention.

[218]Colombian-Peruvian Asylum Case (Colombia v Peru), Judgment of 20 November 1950, ICJ Reports 1950, No. 7, p. 284.

[219]For further information on the rule of law see Crawford (2003), p. 3 f.

political rivals. In the case at hand, the Court held that such an "urgent case" was not constituted and that the continuation of the asylum therefore did not comply with the provisions of the Havana Convention.[220] The Court failed, however, to provide examples of such "urgent cases" and this definition has therefore been left open to interpretation.

Though the Court in this instance ultimately held Colombia granting diplomatic asylum to Haya de la Torre to be contrary to the Havana Convention, it fell short of both rebuking such a right in general and of ordering Colombia to surrender Haya de la Torre to the Peruvian authorities. The Court did however provide some useful guidance on the right to diplomatic asylum, generally holding a territorial state to be often guided by considerations of convenience or political expediency rather than by a legal obligation.[221] It also held the Latin American institution of asylum to owe its development to extra-legal developments.[222]

In conclusion, the Court rejected the first submission on the basis that Colombia could not qualify the nature of the alleged offence in such a way as to be binding on Peru. Furthermore, the Court rejected the second submission, and Peru's counter-claim on the basis of the asylum granted to Haya de la Torre not being in line with Art. 1 and Art. 2 of the Havana Convention.[223]

Request for Interpretation of the Asylum Case

However, on the very same day as the Colombian-Peruvian Asylum Case judgment was delivered, Colombia once again instituted proceedings by requesting that the Court interpret the judgment, which in its view "contains gaps of such a nature as to render its execution impossible."[224] In doing so, Colombia posed to the Court the following three questions:

> First - Must the Judgment of November 20th, 1950, be interpreted in the sense that the qualification made by the Colombian Ambassador of the offence attributed to M. Haya de la Torre, was correct, and that, consequently, it is necessary to recognize that the above-mentioned qualification, in so far as it has been confirmed by the Court, has legal effect?
>
> Second - Must the Judgment of November 20th, 1950, be interpreted in the sense that the Government of Peru is not entitled to demand the surrender of the political refugee M. Haya

[220]Colombian-Peruvian Asylum Case (Colombia v Peru), Judgment of 20 November 1950, ICJ Reports 1950, No. 7, p. 287. On these provisions see Chap. 4: Sect. 4.2.2.4.

[221]Colombian-Peruvian Asylum Case (Colombia v Peru), Judgment of 20 November 1950, ICJ Reports 1950, No. 7, p. 286.

[222]Colombian-Peruvian Asylum Case (Colombia v Peru), Judgment of 20 November 1950, ICJ Reports 1950, No. 7, p. 286.

[223]Colombian-Peruvian Asylum Case (Colombia v Peru), Judgment of 20 November 1950, ICJ Reports 1950, No. 7, p. 288.

[224]Request for Interpretation of the Judgment of November 20th 1950 in the Asylum Case (Colombia v Peru), Institution of Proceedings by the Republic of Colombia, 20 November 1950, p. 466.

de la Torre, and that, consequently, the Government of Colombia is not bound to surrender him even in the event of this surrender being requested?

Third- Or, on the contrary, does the Court's decision on the counter-claim of Peru imply that Colombia is bound to surrender the refugee Víctor Raúl Haya de la Torre to the Peruvian authorities, even if the latter do not so demand, in spite of the fact that he is a political offender and not a common criminal, and that the only convention applicable to the present case does not order the surrender of political offenders?[225]

The questions posed to the Court therefore concerned the legal effect of the Colombian qualification of the offence; whether the judgment should be interpreted as such that Peru is not permitted to request the surrender of Haya de la Torre and thus that Colombia is under no obligation to surrender him and; whether the judgment should be interpreted as such so as to require Colombia to surrender the diplomatic asylee.

On 27th November 1950, the Court then responded by delivering a second judgment, Request for Interpretation of the Judgment of 20 November 1950, in which it declared Colombia's request to be inadmissible.[226] This inadmissibility resulted from the three questions posed by Colombia in its request for interpretation being outside of the scope of the submissions originally submitted by Colombia in its original application and therefore outside of the scope of the Colombian-Peruvian Asylum Case judgment.[227]

Haya de la Torre Case

Following both judgments, Peru once again requested that Colombia surrender Haya de la Torre to its authorities.[228] Colombia held that the Court's judgment in both the Colombian-Peruvian Asylum Case and in Request for Interpretation of the Judgment of 20 November 1950 in the Asylum Case did not impose upon Colombia a legal obligation to surrender Haya de la Torre to Peru.[229] On 13th December 1950, Colombia, therefore, once again lodged an application instituting proceedings before

[225]Request for Interpretation of the Judgment of November 20th 1950 in the Asylum Case (Colombia v Peru), Institution of Proceedings by the Republic of Colombia, 20 November 1950, pp. 468–469.

[226]Request for Interpretation of the Judgment of November 20th 1950 in the Asylum Case (Colombia v Peru), Judgment of 27 November 1950, ICJ Reports 1950, No. 13, p. 404.

[227]Request for Interpretation of the Judgment of November 20th 1950 in the Asylum Case (Colombia v Peru), Judgment of 27 November 1950, ICJ Reports 1950, No. 13, pp. 402–403.

[228]Haya de la Torre Case (Colombia v Peru), Application Instituting Proceedings by the Republic of Colombia, 13 December 1950, p. 7.

[229]Haya de la Torre Case (Colombia v Peru), Application Instituting Proceedings by the Republic of Colombia, 13 December 1950, pp. 7–8.

the Court.[230] In doing so, its principal claim centred around the following concrete question:

> Whether Colombia is, or is not, bound to deliver to the Government of Peru M. Víctor Raúl Haya de la Torre, a refugee in the Colombian Embassy at Lima.[231]

This question is of course the central theme to all three applications and in order to answer it, the Court would have to decide upon the legitimacy of Haya de la Torre's claim to diplomatic asylum.

In the alternative, and in the event of its principal claim being dismissed, it asked the Court to decide the following question:

> ...To adjudge and declare whether, in accordance with the law in force between the Parties and particularly American international law, the Government of Colombia is, or is not, bound to deliver M. Víctor Raul Haya de la Torre to the Government of Peru.[232]

Indeed, this question is in fact a regurgitation of Colombia's principal claim, with the exception of the specification that the question is to be determined by the law in force between the parties and "American international law". The latter can be understood as a reference to regional custom.[233]

Interestingly this case also saw an intervention from Cuba, which delivered a statement in support of the institution of diplomatic asylum.[234] This statement called for the Court to declare Peru to have a legal obligation to facilitate the safe-conduct of Haya de la Torre from Colombia's embassy in Peru.[235] Peru argued this intervention by Cuba to be inadmissible.[236] The Court, however, held Cuba's intervention to be admissible and permitted it to participate in the public hearings.[237]

In its short judgment, the Court upheld its judgments in Colombian-Peruvian Asylum Case and Request for Interpretation of the Asylum Case by holding that it would be outside of the Court's judicial function to determine the manner in which the parties should execute the court's judgment in Columbian-Peruvian Asylum

[230] See Haya de la Torre Case (Colombia v Peru), Application Instituting Proceedings by the Republic of Colombia, 13 December 1950.

[231] Haya de la Torre Case (Colombia v Peru), Application Instituting Proceedings by the Republic of Colombia, 13 December 1950, p. 9.

[232] Haya de la Torre Case (Colombia v Peru), Application Instituting Proceedings by the Republic of Colombia, 13 December 1950, p. 10.

[233] Cf. Chap. 5: Sect. 5.2.

[234] Haya de la Torre Case (Colombia v Peru), Application Instituting Proceedings by the Republic of Colombia, 13 December 1950.

[235] See Haya de la Torre Case (Colombia v Peru), Declaration of Intervention by the Government of Cuba, 13 March 1951, pp. 117–121.

[236] Haya de la Torre Case (Colombia v Peru), Judgment of 13 June 1951, ICJ Reports 1951, No. 14, p. 74.

[237] Haya de la Torre Case (Colombia v Peru), Judgment of 13 June 1951, ICJ Reports 1951, No. 14, p. 75.

Case i.e. to determine the manner in which the asylum should terminate.[238] The Court also held that the Court was not in a position to state whether or not Colombia was legally obliged to hand over Haya de la Torre to the Peruvian authorities as this question had not been submitted to the Court at the time of the previous judgments.[239] Regarding Colombia's second alternative submission that the Court declare that Colombia is not bound to deliver Haya de la Torre to the Peruvian authorities under the law in force between the parties and American international law, the Court made the following statement on diplomatic asylum under the Havana Convention in general:

> According to the Havana Convention, diplomatic asylum is a provisional measure for the temporary protection of political offenders. Even if regularly granted it cannot be prolonged indefinitely, but must be terminated as soon as possible... The Court finds that the Convention does not give a complete answer to the question of the manner in which an asylum shall be terminated.[240]

In this passage, the Court defines diplomatic asylum as a provisional measure. Such a provisional measure has the purpose of protection and is international law's equivalent to an interim injunction.[241] The Court also stresses the temporary nature of diplomatic asylum. This is consistent with the practice of diplomatic asylum under Latin American treaty law.[242]

Moreover, the Court clearly stresses that diplomatic asylum under the Havana Convention should continue only for as long as is necessary to protect the political offender.[243] Nevertheless, the Convention does not provide for how such asylum should end i.e. whether or not this is with the safe-conduct of the asylee from the embassy premises. The Court left this determination to the parties:

> The silence of the Convention implies that it was intended to leave the adjustment of the consequences of this situation to decisions inspired by considerations of convenience or of simple political expediency. To infer from this silence that there is an obligation to surrender a person to whom asylum has been irregularly granted would be to disregard both the role of these extra-legal factors in the development of asylum in Latin America, and the spirit of the Havana Convention itself.[244]

---

[238]Haya de la Torre Case (Colombia v Peru), Judgment of 13 June 1951, ICJ Reports 1951, No. 14, p. 79.

[239]Haya de la Torre Case (Colombia v Peru), Judgment of 13 June 1951, ICJ Reports 1951, No. 14, p. 79.

[240]Haya de la Torre Case (Colombia v Peru), Judgment of 13 June 1951, ICJ Reports 1951, No. 14, p. 80.

[241]On provisional measures see e.g. Gill (ed.) (2003), p. 79 f.

[242]Cf. Chap. 4: Sect. 4.2.

[243]Cf. This corresponds to the urgency requirement reflected by Latin American treaty law in general. See Chap. 4: Sect. 4.2.2.

[244]Haya de la Torre Case (Colombia v Peru), Judgment of 13 June 1951, ICJ Reports 1951, No. 14, p. 81.

This passage thus refers the resolution of diplomatic asylum cases under the Havana Convention to the diplomacy of the parties. Moreover, the political undertone of the development of diplomatic asylum in Latin America is also recognised.

The Court then went on to refer back to its earlier judgment in the Colombian-Peruvian Asylum Case, stressing that asylum cannot oppose the operation of justice.[245]

The Court ultimately came to what some may argue to be a somewhat contradictory conclusion:

> The Court has thus arrived at the conclusion that the asylum must cease, but that the Government of Colombia is under no obligation to bring this about by surrendering the refugee to the Peruvian authorities. There is no contradiction between these two findings, since surrender is not the only way of terminating asylum. . . It *[the Court]* is unable to give any practical advice as to the various courses which might be followed with a view to terminating the asylum, since, by doing so, it would depart from its judicial function. But it can be assumed that the Parties, now that their mutual legal relations have been made clear, will be able to find a practical and satisfactory solution by seeking guidance from those considerations of courtesy and good-neighbourliness which, in matters of asylum, have always held a prominent place in the relations between the Latin-American republics.[246]

The Court therefore neither ruled that Colombia was obliged to surrender Haya de la Torre to the Peruvian authorities, nor that Peru was obliged to grant him safe-conduct to facilitate his departure from Peru. Instead, it referred the resolution of the dispute to the parties' own diplomacy. In doing so, the Court adopted a rather hands-off approach, refusing to guide the parties in any way as to how the asylum should terminate for fear of exceeding its judicial function. Thus, the Court failed to decide for one side of the dispute or the other.

An agreement between Colombia and Peru was eventually reached and Haya de la Torre left Colombia's Lima embassy on 6th April 1954[247] in order to take up exile abroad.

3.4.13.2 Alan García[248]

Against the backdrop of the then sitting Peruvian President, Fujimori, suspending the Constitution, dissolving the Senate and House of Deputies and taking legislative power, former Peruvian President Alan García filed a petition with the Inter-

[245]Haya de la Torre Case (Colombia v Peru), Judgment of 13 June 1951, ICJ Reports 1951, No. 14, p. 81.

[246]Haya de la Torre Case (Colombia v Peru), Judgment of 13 June 1951, ICJ Reports 1951, No. 14, pp. 82–83.

[247]U.S. Department of State, Foreign Relations of the United States, 1949, The United Nations; The Western Hemisphere, Vol. II, Doc. 475, 20 December 1949.

[248]Cf. Chap. 7: Annex, Table 7.1, Case No. 138.

American Petition on Human Rights on 15th April 1992.[249] This petition alleged violations of rights protected by the American Convention on Human Rights[250] with regard to García and his family—namely a threat to García's life and personal safety, the house arrest of his wife and removal of personal family documents.[251] This event prompted García to go into hiding.

The Inter-American Commission on Human Rights instituted proceedings, which the Government of Peru responded to in May 1992 refuting the facts put forward by the petitioner and alleging that García's sole aim was to create scandal for the purpose of political partisan.[252] García entered the Colombian embassy in Lima on 31st May 1992 and requested diplomatic asylum.[253] He remained there until 2nd June 1992 when he was permitted to exit the embassy in order to take up political asylum in Colombia.[254]

This case, therefore, constitutes a further example of a former president being granted diplomatic asylum. In this case, human rights considerations also played a key role. Interestingly, only recently García was again granted asylum by Uruguay in the context of the ambassador's residence.[255]

3.4.13.3 Summary

Twentieth century state practice in Peru also depicts the use of the practice to protect key political figures at times of political upheaval. The case of Haya de la Torre, and the three-stage dispute before the ICJ initiated by his case, also raised the issues as to which state should be permitted to qualify the offence and whether or not a receiving state is obliged to grant safe conduct.

---

[249] See OAS, Inter-American Commission on Human Rights, Report Number 1/95, Case 11.006, Peru, 7 February 1995. Available at: https://www.cidh.oas.org/annualrep/94eng/Peru11006.htm. Last Accessed 14 Dec 2020.

[250] American Convention on Human Rights 1969, Adopted in San José, Costa Rica at the Inter-American Specialized Conference on Human Rights on 22 November 1969, Entered into Force on 18 July 1978, UNTS Vol. No. 1144, p. 123.

[251] Cf. OAS, Inter-American Commission on Human Rights, Report Number 1/95, Case 11.006, Peru, 7 February 1995. Available at: https://www.cidh.oas.org/annualrep/94eng/Peru11006.htm. Last Accessed 14 Dec 2020.

[252] OAS, Inter-American Commission on Human Rights, Report Number 1/95, Case 11.006, Peru, 7 February 1995. Available at: https://www.cidh.oas.org/annualrep/94eng/Peru11006.htm. Last Accessed 14 Dec 2020.

[253] Los Angeles Times (2 June 1992), WORLD IN BRIEF: COLOMBIA: Peru's Ex-President Is Granted Asylum; Los Angeles Times (3 June 1992), Ex-Peruvian President Garcia Arrives in Colombia for Asylum.

[254] Los Angeles Times (3 June 1992), Ex-Peruvian President Garcia Arrives in Colombia for Asylum.

[255] Al Jazeera (18 November 2018), Ex-Peru president seeks Uruguay asylum following travel ban.

3.4.14 *Venezuela*[256]

On 1st October 1961 five military prisoners, originally arrested for "crimes against the security of the state,"[257] killed one and injured two more persons in order to escape from a military hospital. They then took up diplomatic asylum in the Peruvian diplomatic mission in Caracas, Venezuela in order to escape prosecution.

Venezuelan authorities entered the embassy in an attempt to retrieve the fugitives. Venezuela eventually withdrew and Peru asserted that Venezuela had violated its embassy's inviolability. It then proceeded to request safe-conduct for the asylees, which Venezuela refused to grant on the basis of the crimes committed being common crimes. A tense period of relations between the two states followed, after which the prisoners were eventually granted safe-conduct in March 1962.[258]

The case is interesting in terms of the history of diplomatic asylum for several reasons: firstly it represents a rare example of asylum being granted to a common criminal—the murder/injury-related offences had been committed directly before the asylees took up diplomatic asylum (though their original offence of crimes against the security of the state may well have been classified as political in nature); secondly it represents an even rarer example of the right to diplomatic asylum being disregarded by a state, which recognises the principle, through the invasion of the embassy by territorial authorities.[259]

3.5 ILC Attempts to Codify the Issue

In the light of such a wealth of cases, the International Law Commission has long sought to address the question of diplomatic asylum. Indeed, prior to this, the need to codify the issue had already been recognised by the League of Nations in the context of determining the extent of privileges and immunities.[260] The need generally to codify the right to asylum in order to stay true to developments in international law was then recognised by the memorandum of the Secretary-General with regard to the

[256]Cf. Chap. 7: Annex, Table 7.1, Case No. 61.

[257]Whiteman (1968), p. 494.

[258]Whiteman (1968), pp. 494–495; also see Rossitto (1987), p. 130 f.

[259]Such an invasion is contrary to Art. 22 (1) VCDR.

[260]Cf. League of Nations Committee of Experts for the Progressive Codification of International Law, Report to the Council of the League of Nations on the Questions Which Appear Ripe for International Regulation, Questionnaires Nos 1 to 7, Adopted by the Committee at its Third Session, held in March–April 1927, Geneva, 20 April 1927, p. 76.

Survey of International Law in Relation to the Work of Codification of the International Law Commission[261] in 1949.[262]

The topic of diplomatic asylum was discussed at the sixth meeting of the International Law Commission, where it was proposed that the codification of the right of political asylum should be placed on the agenda of the first session of the Commission. Following discussion, the Chairman decided that the right to asylum would be included in the list of topics to be retained.[263]

In the course of deliberating the Draft Declaration on the Rights and Duties of States, three members of the Commission suggested including an article on the right to asylum in the Declaration. This would read as follows:

> Every State has the right to accord asylum to persons of any nationality who request it in consequence of persecutions for offences which the State according asylum deems to have a political character. The State of which the refugee is a national has the duty to respect the asylum accorded and may not consider it an unfriendly act.[264]

The draft article reaffirms the practice of asylum as excluding ordinary offences. Interestingly, it also provides for an obligation of the asylee's national state to respect the asylum and not to consider it an unfriendly act. In the case of diplomatic asylum, the diplomatic asylee's state of nationality may of course also depict the receiving state, however this is not necessarily the case.

In justifying the inclusion of the right, particular emphasis, and indeed praise, was placed upon Latin American practice.[265] Asylum was also described as:

> one of the noblest creations of customary international law.[266]

A British member of the ILC, James Leslie Brierly, however, requested that the text of the article be amended in such a way so as to expressly exclude embassies and legations as places of asylum, given the non-recognition of European states, in particular the UK, of such practice.[267] Following further discussion, the first sentence of the proposed article was adopted, whilst the second sentence was

---

[261] Survey of International Law in relation to the Work of Codification of the International Law Commission, United Nations Publication, Sales No: 1948. V. 1.

[262] See Survey of International Law in Relation to the Work of Codification of the International Law Commission: Preparatory work within the purview of article 18, paragraph 1, of the Statute of the International Law Commission - Memorandum submitted by the Secretary-General, Doc. A/CN.4/1/Rev.1, 10 February 1949, United Nations Publications, Sales No.: 1948.V.1(1), pp. 50–51.

[263] Yearbook of the International Law Commission, 1949, 6th Meeting, 20 April 1949, pp. 47–48, paras 5–13.

[264] Yearbook of the International Law Commission, 1949, 16th Meeting, 5 May 1949, p. 125, para. 67.

[265] Yearbook of the International Law Commission, 1949, 16th Meeting, 5 May 1949, pp. 125–126, paras 67 and 72.

[266] Yearbook of the International Law Commission, 1949, 16th Meeting, 5 May 1949, p. 126, para. 73.

[267] Yearbook of the International Law Commission, 1949, 16th Meeting, 5 May 1949, p. 127, para. 85.

rejected.[268] National states were therefore free not to recognise the asylum granted to their nationals. Moreover, in line with the fundamental principle of state sovereignty,[269] all states were free to consider another state granting asylum to be an unfriendly act.

The topic was rejected again in the course of the ILC's 383rd meeting on 24th April 1957[270] and then raised again in the course of the ILC's 394th Meeting on 9th May 1957 when discussing the draft text of the codification of the rules of diplomatic intercourse and immunities, a rudimentary form of the later Vienna Convention on Diplomatic Relations.[271] In this regard, the British ILC Member, Sir Gerald Fitzmaurice, suggested the following text be included in Art. 12 of the draft convention:

> c) A new paragraph 3, to read:
>
> Except to the extent recognized by any established local usage, or to save life or prevent grave physical injury in the face of an immediate threat or emergency, the premises of a mission shall not be used for giving shelter to persons charged with offences under the local law, not being charges preferred on political grounds.
>
> Alternative text:
>
> Persons taking shelter in mission premises must be expelled upon a demand made in proper form by the competent local authorities showing that the person concerned is charged with an offence under the local law, except in the case of charges preferred on political grounds.[272]

In this first draft text, codifying a prohibition on diplomatic asylum, a clear exception is made for the region of Latin America and for cases where serious human rights are at stake. Furthermore, the caveat excluding "charges preferred on political grounds" correlates with the historical use of diplomatic asylum as protecting asylees accused of political and not ordinary crimes. The second draft text gives rise to a positive obligation for a sending state to surrender a diplomatic asylee, however, interestingly, it does not prohibit asylum from being granted in the first place.

The Soviet Union's ILC Member Grigory Tunkin followed this up with the following suggestion:

> Such inviolability of the premises of the mission shall not however confer the right forcibly to detain therein any person whomsoever or to grant asylum therein to persons in respect of whom a warrant for arrest or detention has been issued by the competent State authorities.[273]

---

[268] Yearbook of the International Law Commission, 1949, 16th Meeting, 5 May 1949, p. 128, paras 107–110.

[269] Cf. Art. 2 (1) UN Charter.

[270] See Yearbook of the International Law Commission, 1957, 383rd Meeting, 24 April 1957, p. 2, para. 7.

[271] Yearbook of the International Law Commission, 1957, 394th Meeting, 3 May 1957, p. 54 f.

[272] Yearbook of the International Law Commission, 1957, 394th Meeting, 3 May 1957, p. 54, para. 33.

[273] Yearbook of the International Law Commission, 1957, 394th Meeting, 3 May 1957, p. 54, para. 34.

The need to prevent the privilege of the embassy's inviolability from being abused and the susceptibility of the mission premises to being used as such was also recognised by Tunkin.[274] The superior importance, however, of maintaining the inviolability of the mission's premises was also recognised in the course of this session.[275] The absolute nature of this principle even in the face of abuse was further reiterated using the example of Brazil seeking to trace the source of a yellow fever epidemic to another mission's diplomatic premises, its efforts were however frustrated without the consent of the head of the mission.[276] It was then ultimately held that the question of asylum should not be dealt with at this session.[277]

The question of asylum was mentioned again in debating the draft codification of the rules regarding diplomatic intercourse and immunities in the 411th meeting on 5th June 1957.[278] Here, it was proposed that the following paragraph be included in Art. 27 of the draft convention, with regard to the premises of the mission:

> The premises of the mission shall be used solely for the performance of the functions recognized as normal and legitimate under the provisions herein laid down or other rules of general international law and any special agreements in force between the sending and the receiving States.[279]

This provision strongly correlates to Art. 41 (3) VCDR, protecting the mission premises from use inconsistent with the functions of the mission.[280] The clause "such special agreements in force between the sending and the receiving states" was included in order to respect diplomatic asylum as a legitimate use of the diplomatic premises for those (Latin American) states which had subscribed to the relevant conventions.[281]

In the course of the 428th meeting, a discussion took place as to whether or not a legal basis for diplomatic asylum was treaty based, though as the question of asylum was to be left aside, this discussion was held to be immaterial.[282]

---

[274] Yearbook of the International Law Commission, 1957, 394th Meeting, 3 May 1957, p. 54, para. 38.

[275] Yearbook of the International Law Commission, 1957, 394th Meeting, 3 May 1957, pp. 54 and 56, paras 38 and 63.

[276] Yearbook of the International Law Commission, 1957, 394th Meeting, 3 May 1957, p. 56, para. 64. See also Yearbook of the International Law Commission, 1957, 395th Meeting, 10 May 1957, p. 58, paras 13 and 14 for a similar discussion regarding a kidnapping in the Chinese embassy in London.

[277] Yearbook of the International Law Commission, 1957, 394th Meeting, 3 May 1957, pp. 54–57, paras 41–43, 57 and 72.

[278] Yearbook of the International Law Commission, 1957, 411th Meeting, 5 June 1957, p. 143 f.

[279] Yearbook of the International Law Commission, 1957, 411th Meeting, 5 June 1957, p. 143, para. 55.

[280] Cf. Art. 3 VCDR. See Chap. 4: Sect. 4.1.4.

[281] Cf. Chap. 4: Sect. 4.2.2.

[282] Yearbook of the International Law Commission, 1957, 428th Meeting, 27 June 1957, p. 220 f., para. 82 f.

In General Assembly Resolution 1400 (XIV) of 21st November 1959, the General Assembly requested that the International Law Commission codify the rules and principles relating to the right of asylum. The Resolution reads:

> The General Assembly
>
> Considering that it is desirable to standardize the application of the principles and rules relating to the right of asylum,
>
> Recalling that the International Law Commission at its first session included the right of asylum in the provisional list of topics of international law selected for codification,
>
> Requests the International Law Commission, as soon as it considers it advisable, to undertake the codification of the principle and rules of international law relating to the right of asylum.[283]

Here, the General Assembly recognised the immediate need for the right to asylum to be codified in order for its application to be standardised. Reference is also made to the ILC at its very first session identifying the right to asylum as a topic ripe for codification. Such codification has yet to take place.

On 15th December 1975, upon the recommendation of the ILC, the General Assembly adopted a resolution in which it was decided that the question of diplomatic asylum should be dealt with at a future session of the General Assembly.[284] In 1977, the ILC then decided that the right to asylum in general did not require further active consideration at that time.[285] Since then, the issue of asylum in general has only been discussed peripherally in the context of other items on the programme.

Owing to the divergent interpretations of the right to asylum, in particular whether or not it encompasses a right to diplomatic asylum and if so what such a right would look like, the issue of diplomatic asylum returning to the agenda of the ILC would appear unlikely.[286]

Indeed, the issue of asylum in general continues to polarise public opinion in the twenty-first century, most recently with regard to the refugee crisis in Europe.[287]

---

[283] General Assembly Resolution 1400 (XIV), Codification of the Principles and Rules of International Law Relating to the Right of Diplomatic Asylum, 842nd Plenary Meeting, 21 November 1959.

[284] General Assembly Resolution 3497 on the question of diplomatic asylum, 15 December 1975.

[285] Yearbook of the International Law Commission, 1977, 29th session, 9 May–29 July 1977, p. 129, para. 109.

[286] In this regard, the IACtHR has held that this is due to states being reluctant to adopt a positivist approach to the issue: IACtHR, Advisory Opinion OC-25/18 of 30 May 2018 Requested by the Republic of Ecuador, The Institution of Asylum and its Recognition as a Human Right in the Inter-American System of Protection (Interpretation and Scope of Articles 5, 22.7 and 22.8 in Relation to Article 1(1) of the American Convention on Human Rights), p. 41, para. 116.

[287] For further information, see Trix (2019).

3.6 The Vienna Convention on Diplomatic Relations

There was no suggestion to explicitly include the question of asylum in the Vienna Convention on Diplomatic Relations at the Vienna Conference.[288] This owes to a lack of consensus on the issue.[289] Therefore asylum continues to be governed by the more general provisions contained in Art. 22 VCDR (the inviolability of the mission premises),[290] Art. 41 (1) VCDR (the duty of persons enjoying immunities to respect the laws and regulations of the receiving state and not to interfere in its internal affairs)[291] and Art. 41 (3) VCDR (providing that the mission premises may not be used in a manner incompatible with the functions of the mission).[292] These provisions will be explored in greater detail in the course of Chap. 4 on International Treaty Law.

Moreover, the question of diplomatic asylum may be governed by customary international law.[293] Indeed, the Preamble to the VCDR, in affirming that questions not expressly covered by the VCDR may be governed by custom, provides for this possibility.[294]

The decision not to address diplomatic asylum explicitly in the Vienna Convention on Diplomatic Relations has ultimately led to a lack of clarity as to exactly what the convention permits and prohibits with regard to diplomatic asylum.[295]

3.7 Diplomatic Asylum in Latin America in the Twenty-first Century

Cases of diplomatic asylum being granted to individuals continue right up to the present day.[296] In this context, the prevalence of Latin American states as the granting state[297] in the midst of political unrest in the receiving state are continuous themes.

In the following sections, selected twenty-first century practice will again be detailed according to the receiving state (and generally also the state of nationality of the asylee) in order to depict the use, extent and characteristics of the practice in the

---

[288]Denza (2016), Art. 22, p. 115.

[289]Cf. Chap. 3: Sect. 3.5; Chap. 5: Sects. 5.4 and 5.5.

[290]Cf. Chap. 4: Sect. 4.1.2.

[291]Cf. Chap. 4: Sect. 4.1.3.

[292]Cf. Chap. 4: Sect. 4.1.4.

[293]Cf. Chap. 5.

[294]Cf. Värk (2012), p. 251; also see Tye (2016), p. 221.

[295]This issue will be evaluated in detail in the context of Chap. 4: Sects. 4.1.2–4.1.4.

[296]Cf. Annex, 1 Table 7.1.

[297]Though the same can also be said of European states. See Chap. 7: Annex, Table 7.1.

context of Latin America. Such practice will again assist in evaluating the presence of regional custom binding Latin America.[298] Corresponding practice for the regions of Europe, Northern America, Oceania, Africa and Asia will be examined in the context of Chap. 5 in order to evaluate the presence of a customary international law rule.[299]

3.7.1 *Bolivia*[300]

Roger Pinto was a Senator belonging to Bolivia's right-wing opposition bloc. After accusing the government of corruption and having been sentenced to twelve months in prison himself for corruption, Pinto and his family sought asylum in Brazil's embassy in La Paz, Bolivia in 2012. Pinto remained in the embassy for 452 days, after which he was secretly transported from the embassy to Brazil. This triggered a diplomatic crisis between Bolivia and Brazil, the former of which accused the latter of a smear campaign against its Presidency and maintained that it continued to pursue Pinto on the basis of criminal charges.[301]

This case, constitutive of state practice in Bolivia in the early twenty-first century, depicts an example of diplomatic asylum being utilised in the context of political instability, in this case to a government critic belonging to the opposition. There is a degree of correlation with state practice in Bolivia in the twentieth century,[302] as in both cases Brazil constitutes the granting state and both cases see asylum being granted to a perceived government opponent.

3.7.2 *Ecuador*[303]

Ecuadorian President Lucio Gutiérrez Borbúa was ousted from power by a vote of Congress in April 2005. After his way to the airport was blocked by protesters, Gutiérrez Borbúa sought asylum in Brazil's embassy in Quito. Gutiérrez Borbúa remained there for only four days before taking up political asylum in Brazil.[304]

---

[298] Cf. Chap. 5: Sects. 5.2, 5.3.4, 5.4.1.1 and 5.4.2.4.

[299] Cf. Chap. 5: Sects. 5.3.1, 5.3.2, 5.3.3, 5.3.5, 5.3.6.

[300] Cf. Chap. 7: Annex, Table 7.1, Case No. 187.

[301] See The Guardian (27 August 2013), Brazil foreign minister loses job in diplomatic fiasco over Bolivian senator; The Independent (28 August 2013), Diplomatic war erupts after Bolivian senator flees to Brazil.

[302] Cf. Chap. 3: Sect. 3.4.3.

[303] Cf. Chap. 7: Annex, Table 7.1, Case No. 168.

[304] ABC News (24 April 2005), Ecuador's former president leaves country for Brazil: report.

This case, constitutive of state practice in Ecuador in the early twenty-first century, depicts an example of a former president being granted diplomatic asylum as a gateway to political asylum.

3.7.3 *Honduras*[305]

Honduran President Manuel Zelaya planned a controversial referendum on the introduction of a fourth ballot box. Upon his orders not being carried out, he fired the chief of the military causing friction with the Supreme Court and Congress, both of which held this dismissal to be illegal. The Supreme Court then issued an order for President Zelaya to be detained on 28th June 2009, following which he was captured by the military and taken into exile to Costa Rica.

On this very same day, Zelaya's daughter, who was seven months pregnant at the time, and her child entered the Republic of China's embassy in Honduras. The Republic of China's decision to provide the pair with diplomatic protection was said to have been motivated by human rights considerations. They remained there until 10th July 2009.[306]

Zelaya returned to Honduras to lobby for his reinstatement on 21st September 2009. He arrived at the Brazilian embassy in Tegucigalpa. His return sparked widespread protests in Honduras. Zelaya's telephone connection, electricity and water were all cut off in an attempt to lure him out of the embassy.[307] A stalemate emerged. Diplomatic relations between the two states became strained and Honduras instituted proceedings against Brazil before the ICJ on 28th October 2009 in order to compel Brazil to hand over Zelaya.[308] However, following the election of new President Porfirio Lobo on 27th January 2010, a deal was negotiated under which Zelaya was permitted to leave the embassy to take up exile in the Dominican Republic.[309] Proceedings before the ICJ were thus discontinued and the case removed from the list.[310]

These cases, constitutive of state practice in Honduras in the early twenty-first century, therefore, depict diplomatic asylum being granted to a former president in

---

305 Cf. Chap. 7: Annex, Table 7.1, Case Nos. 179 and 180.

306 See Taiwan Today (30 September 2009), Deposed Honduran leader's daughter granted asylum. Cf. Chap. 7: Annex, Table 7.1, Case No. 179.

307 See The Guardian (25 June 2009), Manuel Zelaya undergoes strange siege inside Brazilian embassy.

308 See Certain Questions concerning Diplomatic Relations (Honduras v Brazil) Application Instituting Proceedings by the Republic of Honduras against the Federative Republic of Brazil, 28 October 2009.

309 See Reuters (27 January 2010), Honduras' Zelaya leaves Brazilian embassy. Cf. Chap. 7: Annex, Table 7.1, Case No. 180.

310 See Certain Questions concerning Diplomatic Relations (Honduras v Brazil), Order of 12 May 2010, No. 147, ICJ Reports 2010, pp. 303–305.

the midst of political instability and of human rights considerations motivating the granting of diplomatic asylum in the case of Zelaya's daughter. The fact that this case also ended up before the ICJ depicts that even in Latin America, where at least a treaty (and arguably also a customary based) right to diplomatic asylum is undisputed,[311] there is discrepancy as to its legal parameters.

3.7.4 Peru

3.7.4.1 Alberto Pizango[312]

Indigenous Peruvian leader Alberto Pizango requested asylum in Nicaragua's embassy in Lima, Peru after an arrest warrant was issued for him on 6th June 2009 for sedition charges related to anti-government protests in the Amazon.[313] Pizango remained in the embassy until 17th June 2009 when he was granted safe-conduct to take up political asylum in Nicaragua.[314] Peru, however, stressed that this safe-conduct did not preclude it from seeking Pizango's extradition at a later date. Upon his return to Peru a year later, Pizango was arrested and detained in relation to the sedition charges.[315]

3.7.4.2 Alan García[316]

Following allegations of corruption, former Peruvian President Alan García entered the Uruguayan ambassador's residence in Lima, Peru on 17th November 2018. He remained there for several weeks, whilst Uruguay considered his request for political asylum. This request was, however, denied by Uruguay and García left the embassy around 3rd December 2018.[317] Interestingly, this was the second time García had been granted diplomatic asylum.[318]

---

[311] Cf. Chap. 4: Sect. 4.2 and Chap. 5: Sect. 5.5.
[312] Cf. Chap. 7: Annex, Table 7.1, Case No. 178.
[313] The Guardian (9 June 2009), Peruvian indigenous leader seeks asylum in Nicaragua's embassy.
[314] Andean Air Mail and Peruvian Times (17 June 2009), Indigenous leader Alberto Pizango granted safe passage from Peru to Nicaragua.
[315] See BBC News (28 May 2010), Peru indigenous leader Pizango freed on bail.
[316] Cf. Chap. 7: Annex, Table 7.1, Case No. 203.
[317] BBC News (3 December 2018), Peru corruption: Ex-President Alan García denied asylum.
[318] Cf. Chap. 7: Annex, Table 7.1, Case No. 138.

3.7.4.3 Conclusion

These cases, constitutive of state practice in Peru in the early twenty-first century, depict examples of diplomatic asylum being granted to both a government critic and a former president respectively. This also correlates to a degree with state practice in Peru in the twentieth century[319] in that asylum being sought by key political figures is a recurrent theme.

3.7.5 *Venezuela*

3.7.5.1 Pedro Carmona[320]

Pedro Carmona, a Venezuelan businessman, sought diplomatic asylum in May 2002 following a failed coup attempt during which he briefly replaced President Hugo Chávez. Carmona fled to the Colombian ambassador's personal residence in Caracas. He was subsequently granted political asylum in Colombia.[321]

This case also demonstrates an example of diplomatic asylum being used to protect the instigator of a failed coup attempt.

3.7.5.2 Carlos Ortega[322]

On 14th March 2003, Costa Rica granted diplomatic asylum to the leader of a failed strike, Carlos Ortega, which had intended to oust Venezuelan President Chávez.[323] It is not known how long Ortega remained within the embassy, though he later took up political asylum in Costa Rica.[324] This case constitutes another example of diplomatic asylum being granted in the context of political instability, in this case to the instigator of an attempt to usurp the sitting president.

3.7.5.3 Nixon Moreno[325]

Nixon Moreno, a student leader and opponent of the government, sought diplomatic asylum in the Vatican's diplomatic mission in Caracas, Venezuela in 2007. The

[319]Cf. Chap. 3: Sect. 3.4.13.
[320]Cf. Chap. 7: Annex, Table 7.1, Case No. 152.
[321]See BBC News (27 May 2002), Venezuelan Coup Leader Given Asylum.
[322]Cf. Chap. 7: Annex, Table 7.1, Case No. 161.
[323]Deseret News (15 March 2003), Venezuelan strike leader given asylum.
[324]The Washington Post (2 March 2005), World in Brief.
[325]Cf. Chap. 7: Annex, Table 7.1, Case No. 171.

government had accused him of promoting violence. Moreno remained there for fifteen months before being granted political asylum in June 2008.[326]

This case thus provides an example both of diplomatic asylum being used as a gateway to political asylum and also of diplomatic asylum being granted to a government critic.

3.7.5.4 Roberto Enríquez and Eduardo Vetancourt[327]

Roberto Enríquez and Eduardo Vetancourt, party members of the COPEI, the Venezuelan opposition, were accused of rebellion, treason and plotting to overthrow the government and consequently entered the Chilean ambassador's residence in Caracas on 5th April 2017, asking for protection. Chile described the situation as humanitarian in nature. It is not known how long the pair spent under Chilean diplomatic protection, though Chile did express a willingness to grant political asylum to at least one of the duo.[328]

This case depicts an example both of diplomatic asylum being granted to opponents of the government and also of a case in which human rights considerations played a role.

3.7.5.5 Venezuelan Judges[329]

Venezuelan Supreme Court Judges Beatriz Ruiz Marín, Zuleima Del Valle González, Elenis Rodríguez Martínez, José Fernando Núñez Sifontes and Luis Manuel Marcano Salazar, all of whom were appointed to the Supreme Court by the opposition-controlled National Assembly following the pro-government party having lost its majority, entered the Chilean embassy in Caracas in August 2017 citing political persecution from President Maduro's administration as their motivation.[330] All five of the group arrived in Chile via Colombia on 19th October 2017, where they were granted political asylum for a two-year period.[331] The diplomatic mission of Panama in Caracas also granted diplomatic protection to a further two

[326]Country Reports on Human Rights Practices for 2008, Vol. I, Report Submitted to the Committee on Foreign Relations US Senate and the Committee on Foreign Affairs US House of Representatives by the Department of State in Accordance with Sections 116(d) and 502B(b) of the Foreign Assistance Act of 1961, U.S. Government Printing Office, Washington 2010, p. 2781.

[327]Cf. Chap. 7: Annex, Table 7.1, Case No. 198.

[328]For further information see Reuters (6 April 2017), Chile says will give Venezuelan politician asylum if requested.

[329]Cf. Chap. 7: Annex, Table 7.1, Case Nos 199 and 200.

[330]Cf. Chap. 7: Annex, Table 7.1, Case No. 199.

[331]See EFE (19 October 2017), Venezuelan judges granted asylum by Chile arrive in Santiago.

Venezuelan judges, Magistrates Gustavo Sosa Izaguirre and Manuel Antonio Espinoza Melet. It is not clear how long the duo remained in the embassy.[332]

These cases demonstrate examples of perceived opponents of the government regime being protected by means of diplomatic asylum.

3.7.5.6 Freddy Guevara[333]

Venezuelan member of Congress and opposition leader Freddy Guevara entered the Chilean ambassador's residence in Caracas on 4th November 2017 fearing that he would be tried on a charge of instigating violence after the authorities surrounded his house and sought to rescind his congressional immunity.[334] Guevara remained in the embassy for nearly three years and left upon being pardoned in September 2020.[335]

This case therefore depicts a case of diplomatic asylum being granted to an opposition leader.

3.7.5.7 Guaido Supporters[336]

In April 2019, Brazil granted refuge to at least twenty-five armed Guaido supporters in Caracas, Venezuela.[337] In May 2019, Panama also granted such refuge to eighteen national guardsmen who had responded to Guaido's call.[338] In that very same month, Américo de Grazia, Mariela Magallanes and five others were granted diplomatic asylum in the Italian embassy,[339] whilst on 14th May 2019 National Assembly member and member of the opposition Franco Manuel Casella was granted diplomatic protection in the diplomatic premises of Mexico in Caracas.[340] Casella remained there for four months.[341]

---

[332]See Panama Today (4 August 2017), Panama grants asylum to two Venezuelans magistrates seeking protection. Cf. Chap. 7: Annex, Table 7.1, Case No. 200.

[333]Cf. Chap. 7: Annex, Table 7.1, Case No. 201.

[334]See Reuters (5 November 2017), Venezuela opposition leader Guevara seeks refuge in Chile ambassador's home.

[335]RTL Today (10 September 2020), Maduro opponent exits Chilean embassy in Caracas.

[336]Cf. Chap. 7: Annex, Table 7.1, Case Nos 204, 207, 208, 209.

[337]RT (30 April 2019), Coup fizzles? Guaido's mentor takes refuge in Chilean embassy as 25 military seek asylum in Brazil's.

[338]The Japan Times (13 May 2019), Maduro's foes fill foreign embassies in Caracas as Venezuela crisis deepens.

[339]El Pitazo (9 May 2019), Américo De Grazia se refugia en la embajada de Italia.

[340]Rappler (15 May 2019), Mexico gives 'protection' to Venezuelan opposition lawmaker.

[341]Effecto Cocuyo (20 September 2019), Diputado Casella abandona residencia diplomática de México en Caracas.

While it is unclear how long the other groups remained in the embassy, it is likely that they were granted diplomatic asylum based upon human rights considerations in the light of increasing civil and political unrest in Venezuela.[342]

3.7.5.8 Leopoldo López and His Wife[343]

In April 2019, the Chilean embassy in Caracas, Venezuela granted diplomatic asylum to prominent opposition figure Leopoldo López, his wife, Lilian Tintori, and their daughter. López was then granted diplomatic protection by the Spanish ambassador's residence, where he remained for approximately 18 months.[344] As above,[345] the decision was likely motivated by human rights considerations in the light of political instability in Venezuela.

The case also depicts the use of the practice to protect a key political opposition figure.[346]

3.7.5.9 Summary

Early twenty-first century practice in Venezuela depicts diplomatic asylum being granted to opponents of the government regime and to key political figures. In several cases, human rights considerations also played a role and diplomatic asylum was used as a gateway to achieve political asylum.

3.8 Conclusion

The practice of diplomatic asylum boasts a longstanding history, dating from its origins in the fifteenth and sixteenth centuries right through to the twenty-first century. Certain trends are readily identifiable, particularly in the context of Latin American practice:

---

[342] RT (30 April 2019), Coup fizzles? Guaido's mentor takes refuge in Chilean embassy as 25 military seek asylum in Brazil's; The Japan Times (13 May 2019), Maduro's foes fill foreign embassies in Caracas as Venezuela crisis deepens; El Pitazo (9 May 2019), Américo De Grazia se refugia en la embajada de Italia; Rappler (15 May 2019), Mexico gives 'protection' to Venezuelan opposition lawmaker; Effecto Cocuyo (20 September 2019), Diputado Casella abandona residencia diplomática de México en Caracas.

[343] Cf. Chap. 7: Annex, Table 7.1, Case No. 205.

[344] RT (30 April 2019), Coup fizzles? Guaido's mentor takes refuge in Chilean embassy as 25 military seek asylum in Brazil's; BBC News (24 October 2020), Venezuela opposition figure Leopoldo López leaves Spanish embassy.

[345] See Chap. 3: Sect. 3.7.5.7.

[346] RT (30 April 2019), Coup fizzles? Guaido's mentor takes refuge in Chilean embassy as 25 military seek asylum in Brazil's.

- The broader historical use of the practice, to include asylum in the context of warships and even merchant ships
- the use of the practice in times of revolution or political instability e.g. the recent twenty-first century practice in Venezuela in the midst of a political crisis,[347]
- the practice frequently being motivated by human rights considerations
- Safe conduct being facilitated by the receiving state
- Reliance upon the Latin American treaty framework[348]
- Diplomatic asylum frequently being used as a gateway to political asylum
- the prevalence of the practice in Latin America[349] and
- the emergence of the practice as reserved for political offenders as opposed to common criminals.

Moreover, Latin American practice depicts a trend in the use of the practice in order to protect key political figures e.g. from the political opposition or from deposed governments. The issue of qualification has created difficulties where the host and sending states purport to classify the offence differently. This issue was of particular relevance in the Haya de la Torre dispute.

In Sects. 3.4 and 3.7,[350] a number of twentieth and twenty-first century diplomatic asylum cases have been illustrated. This includes those from the Spanish civil war, which are of historical significance in depicting the use of the practice in revolutionary periods, and those from the region of Latin America, which are of significance as Latin America is the only region in the world with an established treaty and customary law right to diplomatic asylum.[351] Whilst this practice is clearly indicative of the aforementioned trends, several cases also depict diplomatic asylum being used as a tool to protect the fundamental human rights of the individual(s) concerned.[352]

Latin American state practice on the issue of diplomatic asylum can be described as both lengthy and coherent. Whether or not it suffices to constitute state practice and whether or not is accompanied by *opinio juris* so as to give rise to customary international law will be examined in the context of Chap. 5.[353]

The International Court of Justice has been confronted with the issue of diplomatic asylum on four occasions,[354] of which the three-stage dispute surrounding

[347]Cf. Chap. 3, Sect. 3.7.5.

[348]Cf. Chap. 4: Sect. 4.2.

[349]Cf. Chap. 5: Sect. 5.3.4.

[350]Cf. Chap. 3: Sects. 3.4 and 3.7.

[351]Cf. Chap. 4: Sect. 4.2 and Chap. 5: Sect. 5.3.4.

[352]Cf. Chap. 6.

[353]Cf. Chap. 5: Sects. 5.3.4, 5.4.1.1 and 5.4.2.4.

[354]Cf. Colombian-Peruvian Asylum Case (Colombia v Peru), Judgment of 20 November 1950, ICJ Reports 1950, No. 7; Request for Interpretation of the Judgment of November 20th 1950 in the Asylum Case (Colombia v Peru), Judgment of 27 November 1950, ICJ Reports 1950, No. 13; Haya de la Torre Case (Colombia v Peru), Judgment of 13 June 1951, ICJ Reports 1951, No. 14 and Certain Questions concerning Diplomatic Relations (Honduras v Brazil) Application Instituting Proceedings by the Republic of Honduras against the Federative Republic of Brazil, 28 October 2009; Certain Questions concerning Diplomatic Relations (Honduras v Brazil), Order of 12 May 2010, No. 147, ICJ Reports 2010, pp. 303–305.

Haya de la Torre has contributed significantly to debate surrounding the issue. The jurisprudence has, however, failed to clarify the status of the topic under general international law. Though a more recent application regarding diplomatic asylum, which was filed by Honduras in 2009, was eventually discontinued and the case removed from the list, the application reaffirms that the issue of diplomatic asylum and in particular its legal basis and parameters continue to be unclear, even in the context of Latin America, in which at least a treaty-based right is undisputed.

The International Law Commission has also sought to codify the issue on several occasions, though until the present day these attempts have remained unsuccessful owing to the divergent interpretations of the right to asylum within the commission. These unsuccessful attempts to codify the right to diplomatic asylum do not of course preclude the existence of a customary law rule in favour of the practice.[355]

In summary, the history of the practice of diplomatic asylum is lengthy. Diplomatic asylum has proven itself to be an invaluable mechanism for individual protection historically, for example in the context of the Spanish Civil War but also in more recent times such as in the context of a political crisis in Venezuela. Furthermore, diplomatic asylum cases in the context of the region of Latin America depict a number of common characteristics, which may prove to be indicative of the regional right's legal parameters under treaty[356] and custom.[357]

References

Accioly H (1961) Das Asylrecht. AdV 9(3):289–293

Addison Smith G (1911) Right of asylum. LQR 27(106):199–203

Akinsanya AA (1989) Reflections on the inviolability of diplomatic premises and diplomatic bags, Pakistan Horizon 42(3/4):98–120

Baird HM (1863) The two Greek revolutions of 1862. MQR XLV 4th Series XV:227–249. Carlton and Porter, New York

Barker JC (2000) International law and international relations, international relations for the 21st century. Continuum, London/New York

Bassuener K (2013) The fall and rise of Chilean democracy: 1973–1989. In: Kinsman J, Bassuener K (eds) A Diplomat's handbook for democracy development support, 3rd edn. Centre for International Governance Innovation, Waterloo (Canada), pp 417–431

Behrens P (2014) The law of diplomatic asylum – a contextual approach. MJIL 35:319–367

Cheng B (1997) Studies in international space law. Clarendon Press, Oxford

Chhabra S (2015) Diplomatic asylum: a necessary evil to the protection of human rights. IJLLJS 4 (2):36–56

Crawford J (2003) International law and the rule of law, the James Crawford Biennial Lecture Series on international law. ALR 24:3–12

Cuzán AG (1999) Fidel Castro: A Machiavellian Prince? Proc ASCE 9:178–191

[355]Cf. Chap. 5.

[356]Cf. Chap. 4.

[357]Cf. Chap. 5.

Dembinski L (1988) The modern law of diplomacy, external missions of states and international organizations. Martinus Nijhoff Publishers, Dordrecht/Boston/Lancaster/Unitar
Den Heijer M (2013) Diplomatic asylum and the Assange case. LJIL 26(2):399–425
Denza E (2016) Diplomatic law, Commentary on the Vienna Convention on Diplomatic Relations, 4th edn. Oxford University Press, Oxford
Dörr O (2018) Weitere Rechtsquellen des Völkerrechts. In: Ipsen K (ed) Völkerrecht, 7th edn. C.H. Beck, Munich, pp 536–559
Dupes Hawk K, Villella R, Leyva de Varona A, Cifers K (2014) Florida and the Mariel Boatlift of 1980, the first twenty days. The University of Alabama Press, Tuscaloosa
Dupuy PM (1976) La position française en matière d'asile diplomatique. AFDI 22:743–755
Ensalaco M (2000) Chile under Pinochet, recovering the truth. University of Pennsylvania Press, Philadelphia
Esquirol JL (2012) Latin America. In: Fassbender B, Peters A, Peter S, Högger D (eds) The Oxford handbook of the history of international law, 1st edn. Oxford University Press, Oxford, pp 553–577
Evans AE (1952) The Colombian-Peruvian asylum case: the practice of diplomatic asylum. APSR 46(1):142–157
Farhangi LS (1986) Insuring against abuse of diplomatic immunity. SLR 38(6):1517–1547
Foakes J, Denza E (2017) Privileges and immunities of diplomatic missions. In: Roberts I (ed) Satow's diplomatic practice, 7th edn. Oxford University Press, Oxford, pp 222–245
Foster JW (1906) The practice of diplomacy as illustrated in the foreign relations of the United States. Houghton, Mifflin and Company, Boston/New York
Fox H (2017) Privileges and immunities of the state, the head of state, state officials, and state agencies. In: Roberts I (ed) Satow's diplomatic practice, 7th edn. Oxford University Press, Oxford, pp 199–221
Fry MF (2018) Historical dictionary of Guatemala. Rowman and Littlefield, Lanham/London
Garcia Ferreira R (2008) The CIA and Jacobo Arbenz: history of a disinformation campaign. J Third World Stud XXV(2):59–81
García-Mora MR (1951) The Colombian-Peruvian asylum case and the doctrine of human rights. VLR 37(7):927–965
Gil-Bazo M (2015) Asylum as a general principle of international law. IJRL 27(1):3–28
Gilbert B (1901) The right of asylum in the legations of the United States in Central and South America. HLR 15(2):118–139
Gill TD (ed) (2003) Rosenne's The World Court: what it is and how it works, 6th revised edition. Brill, Leiden
Gomes dos Santos Júnior JJ (2014) Entre barcos e telegramas: a crise do asilo diplomático depois do fim da Revolta da Armada (1894). Antíteses 7(13):134–157
Greenburgh RB (1955) Recent developments in the law of diplomatic asylum. Trans Grotius Soc 41:103–122. Problems of Public and Private International Law
Hedges J (2011) Argentina: a modern history. I.B. Tauris, London/New York
International Business Publications (2013) Haiti, constitution and citizenship laws handbook. Strategic Information and Developments International Business Publications, Washington D.C
Jeffery AJ (1985) Diplomatic asylum: its problems and potential as a means of protecting human rights. SAJHR 1:10–30
Kau M (2019) Der Staat und der Einzelne als Völkerrechtssubjekte. In: Vitzthum W, Proelß A (eds) Völkerrecht, 7th edn. DeGruyter, Berlin/Boston, pp 159–318
Kimminich O (1961) Asyl in Stützpunkten der UN Truppen. ZfP 8(3):235–240
Kimminich O (1962) Völkerrechtsfragen der expolitischen Betätigung. AdV 10(2):132–165
Kitschenberg H (1965) Das diplomatische Asyl unter besonderer Berücksichtigung des Asylstreits zwischen Kolumbien und Peru. Dissertation, Universität zu Köln
Klepper I (2009) Diplomatisches Asyl, Zulässigkeit und Grenzen. Dissertation, Universität zu Köln, vol 4814. Peter Lang Verlag, Frankfurt am Main/Berlin/Bern/Brussels/New York/Oxford/Vienna

Kohut D, Vilella O (2010) Historical dictionary of the "dirty wars," 2nd edn. Historical Dictionaries of War, Revolution, and Civil Unrest, No. 40. The Scarecrow Press Inc., Lanham/Toronto/Plymouth

Kovács P, Ádány TV (2017) The non-customary practice of diplomatic asylum. In: Behrens P (ed) Diplomatic law in a new millennium. Oxford University Press, Oxford, pp 179–203

Kristiyati A (2013) Ecuador's decision to grant asylum to Julian Assange: the manifestation of human security. IJIL 10(3):217–230

Lauterpacht H (ed) (1955) Oppenheim's international law, vol I, Peace, 8th edn. Longman's, Green and Co., London/New York/Toronto

Leonard TM (2004) Fidel Castro: a biography. Greenwood Press, Westport, Connecticut/London

Lippert RK (2005) Sanctuary, sovereignty, sacrifice, Canadian sanctuary incidents, power, and law. UBC Press, Vancouver/Toronto

Maginnis VL (2002) Limiting diplomatic immunity: lessons learned from the 1946 Convention on the Privileges and Immunities of the United Nations. BJIL 28(3):989–1023

Matsumoto-Best S (2003) Britain and the papacy in the age of revolution, 1846–1851. The Boydell Press, Suffolk

Mendelson MH (1998) The formation of customary international law. Collected Courses of the Hague Academy of International Law, vol 272, pp 155–410

Moore JB (1892) Asylum in legations and consulates and in vessels. PSQ 7(1):1–37

Moore JB (1906) A digest of international law, as embodied in diplomatic discussions, treaties and other international agreements, international awards, the decisions of municipal courts and the writings of jurists, vol II. Washington Government Printing Office, Washington

Moore JB (ed) (1909) The works of James Buchanan, comprising his speeches, state papers and private correspondence, vol VIII, 1848–1853. J.B. Lippincott Company, Philadelphia and London

Moral Roncal AM (2013) An analysis of foreign diplomatic aid to the catholic clergy during the Spanish Civil War (1936–1939). Religions 4:96–115

Patsias C, Williams N (2013) Religious sanctuary in France and Canada. In: Lippert RK, Rehaag S (eds) Sanctuary practices in international perspectives, migration, citizenship and social movements. Routledge, Oxon/New York

Rabben L (2016) Sanctuary and asylum, a social and political history. University of Washington Press, Seattle and London

Rader RM (1971) Alien Crewmen: The United States Asylum Policy. CILJ 4(2):167–209

Reale E (1938) Le droit d'asile. Collected Courses of the Hague Academy of International Law, vol 63. Nijhoff, Leiden/Boston, pp 469–601

Ripperda JW (1744) Memoirs of the Duke de Ripperda, 3rd edn. Daniel Brown, London

Ronning CN (1965) Diplomatic asylum: legal norms and political reality in Latin American relations. Martinus Nijhoff, The Hague

Rossitto AM (1987) Diplomatic asylum in the United States and Latin America: a comparative analysis. BJIL 13:111–135

Rudolph DK, Rudolph GA (1971) Historical dictionary of Venezuela. The Scarecrow Press Inc., Metuchen

Scupin H (2011) History of international law, 1815 to World War I. In: MPEPIL (Online). Oxford University Press. https://opil.ouplaw.com/view/10.1093/law:epil/9780199231690/law-9780199231690-e708?rskey=jGFeIe&result=1&prd=MPIL. Last accessed 14 Dec 2020

Shah P (2007) Asylum, diplomatic. In: MPEPIL (Online). Oxford University Press. https://opil.ouplaw.com/view/10.1093/law:epil/9780199231690/law-9780199231690-e756. Last accessed 14 Dec 2020

Sharf MP (2014) Accelerated formation of customary international law. Case Western Reserve University School of Law Faculty Publications, Paper 1167

Sinha SP (1971) Asylum and international law. Martinus Nijhoff, The Hague

Skogly S (2006) Beyond national borders: states' human rights obligations in international cooperation. Intersentia, Antwerpen/Oxford

Stotzky IP (1997) Silencing the Guns in Haiti: the promise of deliberative democracy. The University of Chicago Press, Chicago/London

Subramanian SR (2017) Abuse of diplomatic privileges and the duty to respect the local laws and regulations under the Vienna Conventions: the recent Indian experience. CJGG 3:182–233

Suchlicki J (2002) Cuba: from Columbus to Castro and beyond, 5th edn. Potomac Books Inc., Washington D.C.

Taylor S (2019) Australia's diplomatic asylum initiative at the United Nations: comparing international law rhetoric with foreign policy practice. AJIA 73(4):376–396

Tomka P, Proulx V (2015) The evidentiary practice of the World Court. NUS Faculty Working Paper Series 010:1–24

Trix F (2019) Europe and the refugee crisis: local responses to migrants. I.B. Tauris, Bloomsbury Academic Publishing, London/Oxford/New York/New Delhi/Sydney

Tye H (2016) Does Julian Assange illustrate a gap in the law that should be codified? PLCJR 1:218–238

Värk R (2012) Diplomatic asylum: theory, practice and the case of Julian Assange. Sisekaitseakadeemia Toimetised 11:240–259

Vattel E (1797) The law of nations, or, principles of the law of nature, applied to the conduct and affairs of nations and sovereigns, a new edition. G.G. and J. Robinson, London

Viveros Montoya L (2017) Flat 3B: Assange, Ecuador and the right to asylum. In: The Law of Nations Blog. https://lawofnationsblog.com/2017/03/29/flat-3b-assange-ecuador-right-asylum/. Last accessed 14 Dec 2020

von Arnauld A (2019) Völkerrecht, 4th edn. C.F. Müller, Heidelberg

von Pollern H (1980) Das moderne Asylrecht, Völkerrecht und Verfassungsrecht der Bundesrepublik Deutschland, Schriften zum Völkerrecht, Band 67. Duncker & Humblot, Berlin

Whiteman MM (1968) Digest of international law, vol 6. Department of State Publication 8350, U.S. Government Printing Office, Washington D.C.

Young E (1964) The development of the law of diplomatic relations. BYIL 40:141–182

Chapter 4
International Treaty Law

It is necessary to examine international treaty law, as a primary source of international law listed in Art. 38 (1) ICJ Statute, in order to establish whether it may provide a legal basis for the practice of diplomatic asylum. Art. 2 (1) (a) Vienna Convention on the Law of Treaties[1] provides a definition of such international treaties, which may be either bilateral or multilateral in nature and may be universal or regional in scope.

4.1 Universal Treaty Law

For the purposes of this book, universal treaty law is to be understood as treaty law with a global scope, for example the UN Charter or the Vienna Convention on the Law of Treaties. This is in contrast to regional treaty law with a solely regional scope, for example the European Convention on Human Rights, the African Charter on Human and Peoples' Rights or the Montevideo Convention on Political Asylum.[2]

A legal basis for the practice of diplomatic asylum akin to that of territorial asylum will first be evaluated;[3] the permissibility of a legal basis for diplomatic asylum under the VCDR will then be assessed.[4]

[1] Vienna Convention on the Law of Treaties 1969, Adopted in Vienna on 23 May 1969, Entered into Force on 27 January 1980, UNTS Vol. No. 1155, p. 331.

[2] Cf. Chap. 4: Sect. 4.2.2.5.

[3] Cf. Chap. 4: Sect. 4.1.1.

[4] Cf. Chap. 4: Sect. 4.1.2.

L. Hughes-Gerber, *Diplomatic Asylum*,
https://doi.org/10.1007/978-3-030-73046-8_4

4.1.1 *Akin to Territorial Asylum*

4.1.1.1 Art. 2 (1) and (4) UN Charter

One possible justification for diplomatic asylum is that, like its counterpart, territorial asylum, it also derives its legal basis from the territorial sovereignty of states, protected under Art. 2 (1) and (4) UN Charter.[5] This provides:

> Article 2
>
> The Organization and its Members, in pursuit of the Purposes stated in Article 1, shall act in accordance with the following Principles.
>
> 1. The Organization is based on the principle of the sovereign equality of all its Members.
>
> [...]
>
> 4. All Members shall refrain in their international relations from the threat or use of force against the territorial integrity or political independence of any state, or in any other manner inconsistent with the Purposes of the United Nations.

By virtue of this principle, no state may exercise authority over another and all states must respect the territorial jurisdiction of other states.

In line with this principle of territorial jurisdiction, any decision by a sovereign state to grant territorial asylum therefore entails an ordinary exercise of state sovereignty.[6] It can thus not be challenged by any other sovereign state without the former's territorial sovereignty being compromised. Of course, the application of this principle to the issue of diplomatic asylum would presuppose that the diplomatic premises constitute the legitimate territory of the sending state in line with the

[5]This principle is also protected by customary international law: cf. for example General Assembly Resolution 2131 (XX), Declaration on the Inadmissibility of Intervention and Interference in the Domestic Affairs of States and the Protection of Their Independence and Sovereignty, 1408th Plenary Meeting, 21 December 1965; General Assembly Resolution 2625 (XXV), Declaration on Principles of International Law concerning Friendly Relations and Co-operation among States in accordance with the Charter of the United Nations, 1883rd Plenary Meeting, 24 October 1970; General Assembly Resolution 36/103, Declaration on the Inadmissibility of Intervention and Interference in the Internal Affairs of States, 91st Plenary Meeting, 9 December 1981; International Law Commission, Report on the second part of its seventeenth session and on its eighteenth session, Monaco (3–28 January 1966), Document A/6309/Rev.l, Yearbook of the International Law Commission 1966, Vol. II, p. 267; The Corfu Channel Case (United Kingdom of Great Britain and Northern Ireland v Albania), Merits, Judgment of 9 April 1949, ICJ Reports 1949, No. 1, p. 35; Case Concerning Military and Paramilitary Activities in and against Nicaragua (Nicaragua v United States of America), Merits, Judgment of 27 June 1986, No. 70, p. 111, para. 212; Corten (2011), p. 88; Stein et al. (2017), p. 237; Valta (2019), p. 114.

[6]Addison Smith (1911), p. 199; Den Heijer (2011), p. 116. Also see UN General Assembly, 21st Session, Sixth Committee, Summary Record of the 922nd Meeting, Agenda Item 85, Draft Declaration on the Right of Asylum, A/C.6, SR.922, 28 October 1966, pp. 132–133, paras 33 and 40; UN General Assembly, 21st Session, Sixth Committee, Summary Record of the 923rd Meeting, Agenda Item 85, Draft Declaration on the Right of Asylum, A/C.6, SR.923, 31 October 1966, p. 143, para. 55.

principle of extraterritoriality[7]—a notion that has long been disregarded and come to be considered as a legal fiction.[8] In fact, the application of this principle would undermine the purpose of the mission's premises inviolability, which is to facilitate the full effectiveness of the work of the mission.[9]

4.1.1.2 The UN Declaration on Territorial Asylum

The UN Declaration on Territorial Asylum, though not a treaty, was adopted unanimously by the General Assembly on 14th December 1967.[10] In the framework of a General Assembly Resolution, it does not produce legally binding effect but can be regarded as a soft law instrument.[11] The declaration protects the right of a state to grant asylum, and so too the asylee's right to enjoy said asylum, which must be respected by other states:

> Article 1
>
> 1. Asylum granted by a State, in the exercise of its sovereignty, to persons entitled to invoke article 14 of the Universal Declaration of Human Rights, including persons struggling against colonialism, shall be respected by all other States.
>
> [...]
>
> 3. It shall rest with the State granting asylum to evaluate the grounds for the grant of asylum.
>
> [...]
> Article 3
>
> 1. No person referred to in article 1, paragraph 1, shall be subjected to measures such as rejection at the frontier or, if he has already entered the territory in which he seeks asylum, expulsion or compulsory return to any State where he may be subjected to persecution.
>
> [...]

---

[7] Grotius described ambassadors as being, by way of a legal fiction, in the place of those who sent them [i.e. in the territory of the sending state]: Cited by Foakes and Denza (2017), p. 225 and by Denza (2016), Art. 22, p. 111.

[8] UN General Assembly, 29th Session, Sixth Committee, Summary Record of the 1505th Meeting, Agenda Item 105, Diplomatic Asylum, A/C.6/SR.1505, 25 November 1974, pp. 242, 244 paras 7 and 23; Colombian-Peruvian Asylum Case (Colombia v Peru), Counter-Memorial Submitted by the Government of the Republic of Peru, 21 March 1950, p. 121; Colombian-Peruvian Asylum Case (Colombia v Peru), Judgment of 20 November 1950, ICJ Reports 1950, No. 7, Dissenting Opinion by Judge Azevedo (translation), p. 339; Denza (2016), Art. 22, p. 111; Hathaway (2005), p. 173; García-Mora (1951), p. 934; Jönsson and Hall (2005), p. 63; Kitschenberg (1965), p. 6; Maginnis (2002), p. 994; Ronning (1965), p. 6; Urrutia-Aparicio (1960), p. 50.

[9] Preamble to the VCDR; cf. Falconi Puig (2017), p. 174.

[10] UN Declaration on Territorial Asylum contained within General Assembly Resolution 2312 (XXII), 1631st Plenary Meeting, 14 December 1967.

[11] Cf. for example Fomerand (2014), p. 206; Wallace (2014), p. 421. Whilst soft law instruments are not legally binding *per se*, they typically contain standards of conduct, which are generally adhered to.

These provisions affirm the right to grant territorial asylum as depicting the exercise of state sovereignty.[12] Reference is also made to the UDHR, linking granting asylum to human rights considerations.[13] Furthermore, the discretion to assess the circumstances surrounding the asylum case and to decide whether to grant asylum are also held to fall within the discretion of the granting state. Art. 3 grants the asylee protection from being refused entry to the territory and from expulsion.

The declaration, however, cannot be held to be applicable to diplomatic asylum as in both its title and its Preamble, it clearly restricts its scope to territorial asylum only.[14] Therefore, the application of this declaration to the issue of diplomatic asylum would be impermissible. Even if the declaration could be held applicable to the issue of diplomatic asylum, its status as a soft law instrument prevents the imposition of an effective legal enforcement mechanism. Thus, compliance would anyway be subject to state discretion.

4.1.1.3 Conclusion

A legal basis for diplomatic asylum can therefore not be found in either Art. 2 UN Charter or in the UN Declaration on Territorial Asylum.

4.1.2 Art. 22 Vienna Convention on Diplomatic Relations

Art. 22 Vienna Convention on Diplomatic Relations[15] codifies a very old principle of diplomatic law, namely the inviolability of mission premises. This principle has been described by the ICJ as having "fundamental character".[16] The article provides:

ARTICLE 22

1. The premises of the mission shall be inviolable. The agents of the receiving State may not enter them, except with the consent of the head of the mission.
2. The receiving State is under a special duty to take all appropriate steps to protect the premises of the mission against any intrusion or damage and to prevent any disturbance of the peace of the mission or impairment of its dignity.

---

[12] Cf. Colombian-Peruvian Asylum Case (Colombia v Peru), Judgment of 20 November 1950, ICJ Reports 1950, No. 7, p. 274; Kitschenberg (1965), p. 1.

[13] Cf. Chapter 6 concerning diplomatic asylum on the basis of humanitarian considerations.

[14] "States should base themselves in their practices relating to territorial asylum on the following principles...": Preamble, UN Declaration on Territorial Asylum contained within General Assembly Resolution 2312 (XXII), 1631st Plenary Meeting, 14 December 1967.

[15] As of April 2021, the VCDR has 192 state parties and can therefore be regarded as a universal treaty.

[16] Case Concerning United States Diplomatic and Consular Staff in Tehran (United States of America v Iran), Judgment of 24 May 1980, ICJ Reports 1980, No. 64, p. 40, para. 86.

3. The premises of the mission, their furnishings and other property thereon and the means of transport of the mission shall be immune from search, requisition, attachment or execution.

This article in essence protects the mission premises from any intrusion or interference by the receiving state. It not only imposes upon the host state a negative obligation not to enter the mission premises save for with the permission of the head of the mission (1), but also provides the host state with a positive obligation to protect the mission premises from third party interference (2). Paragraph (3) provides a degree of clarity as to the scope of paragraph (1), holding that mission premises, their contents and diplomatic vehicles are immune from search requisition, attachment or execution. Though a literal interpretation of Art. 22 VCDR does not explicitly provide for a right to diplomatic asylum,[17] in protecting the immunity of diplomatic premises from the jurisdiction of the host state, it facilitates the practice, which would otherwise not be possible outside of the sending state's legitimate territory.[18]

Furthermore, a systematic interpretation of Art. 22 VCDR would not be consistent with the practice of diplomatic asylum.[19] Neither is diplomatic asylum consistent with a teleological interpretation[20] of Art. 22 VCDR, given that the fundamental principle of the VCDR is to facilitate the functionality of the diplomatic mission.[21] Diplomatic asylum, in practice, only hinders the efficient functioning of the mission, *inter alia* due to a necessary restriction in the use of the mission premises as a result of the asylum. Of course, cases of territorial asylum may equally provoke a deterioration in bilateral diplomatic relations.

Whilst considering its longstanding history,[22] a historical interpretation of the provision may be consistent with the practice of diplomatic asylum, recourse to this method of interpretation is only permissible in cases in which the aforementioned methods produce ambiguous or unreasonable results.[23] This is not the case. Consequently Art. 22 VCDR does not provide a legal basis for the practice of diplomatic asylum.

Nevertheless, in the context of the Columbian-Peruvian Asylum case, Judge Read described the institution of asylum as being founded upon the immunity of the diplomatic mission irrespective of whether the theory of extraterritoriality is

[17]Cf. Richtsteig (2010), Art. 22, p. 47; von Pollern (1980), p. 95.

[18]Cf. Yearbook of the International Law Commission, 1957, 394th Meeting, 3 May 1957, p. 56, para. 58. Also see McClanahan (1989), p. 54; von Pollern (1980), p. 95. Cf. Klepper (2009), p. 81.

[19]Cf. Chap. 4: Sects. 4.1.3 and 4.1.4. On systematic interpretation see Art. 31 (1) VCLT. Also see Lo (2017), p. 196 f.

[20]Cf. Art. 31 (1) VCLT; South West Africa Cases (Ethiopia v South Africa; Liberia v South Africa), Second Phase, Judgment of 18 July 1966, ICJ Reports 1966, Nos 46 and 47, p. 48, para. 91.

[21]Cf. Preamble to the VCDR; Akinsanya (1989), p. 99.

[22]Cf. Chapter 3.

[23]Cf. Art. 32 VCLT.

accepted or rejected.[24] Aust describes diplomatic asylum, save for in the context of Latin America, as an abuse of the inviolability of the diplomatic premises.[25] Indeed, whilst the diplomatic asylee remains in the diplomatic premises and therefore under the protection of the diplomatic mission, the host state is prevented from initiating any proceedings against him/her.[26] This was particularly apparent in the case of Julian Assange, with Sweden ceasing to pursue an investigaton into rape allegations made against him whilst he remained in the embassy,[27] the charges against Assange in the U.S. also only became public knowledge once Assange had left the embassy.[28]

Importantly, Art. 22 VCDR does not provide for any exceptions to the inviolability of the mission premises and is therefore generally held to be absolute.[29] For

---

[24]Colombian-Peruvian Asylum Case (Colombia v Peru), Judgment of 20 November 1950, ICJ Reports 1950, No. 7, Dissenting Opinion by Judge Read, p. 317. Diplomatic asylum has also been described both as "an aspect of the inviolability of diplomatic premises" and as a "mere by-product" thereof: UN General Assembly, 29th Session, Sixth Committee, Summary Record of the 1505th Meeting, Agenda Item 105, Diplomatic Asylum, A/C.6/SR.1505, 25 November 1974, pp. 242–243, paras 7 and 17. Cf. McClanahan (1989), p. 54.

[25]Aust (2010), p. 170. Cf. Yearbook of the International Law Commission, 1957, 394th Meeting, 3 May 1957, p. 54, para. 38. See also Dahm et al. (1989), p. 291; Oelfke et al. (2018), Art. 41, p. 337. Also see Evans (1951), p. 761 referring to diplomatic asylum as a misuse of diplomatic immunity. Cf. League of Nations Committee of Experts for the Progressive Codification of International Law, Report to the Council of the League of Nations on the Questions Which Appear Ripe for International Regulation, Questionnaires Nos 1 to 7, Adopted by the Committee at its Third Session, held in March–April 1927, Geneva, 20 April 1927, p. 243. On the problem of abuse of diplomatic status in general, see for example Bolewski (2005), p. 537 f.

[26]Cf. League of Nations Committee of Experts for the Progressive Codification of International Law, Report to the Council of the League of Nations on the Questions Which Appear Ripe for International Regulation, Questionnaires Nos 1 to 7, Adopted by the Committee at its Third Session, held in March–April 1927, Geneva, 20 April 1927, p. 84.

[27]Swedish Prosecution Authority, Press Release, The investigation against Julian Assange is discontinued, 19 May 2017. https://via.tt.se/pressmeddelande/the-investigation-against-julian-assange-is-discontinued?publisherId=3235541&releaseId=3252727. Last Accessed 14 Dec 2020. Also see The Guardian (19 May 2017), Swedish prosecutors drop Julian Assange rape investigation.

[28]The indictment remained sealed until April 2019 when Assange left the embassy, though it predates this event: see The United States District Court for the Eastern District of Virginia, Alexandria Division, United States of America v Julian Paul Assange, 6 March 2018.

[29]Akinsanya (1989), p. 113; Aust (2010), p. 115; Barker (1996), p. 72; cf. Cameron (1985), p. 611; Denza (2016), Art. 22, p. 115; Herdegen (1986), p. 739; Oelfke et al. (2018), Art. 22, p. 135. See also Yearbook of the International Law Commission, 1957, 394th Meeting, 3 May 1957, pp. 54, 56, paras 38, 63–64; IACtHR, Advisory Opinion OC-25/18 of 30 May 2018 Requested by the Republic of Ecuador, The Institution of Asylum and its Recognition as a Human Right in the Inter-American System of Protection (Interpretation and Scope of Articles 5, 22.7 and 22.8 in Relation to Article 1 (1) of the American Convention on Human Rights), p. 38, para. 106. Interestingly, the ICJ has, however, held Art. 22 VCDR to be subject to exceptions regarding the inviolability of the members of the diplomatic mission in that such persons may be temporarily arrested by police in order to prevent the commission of further crimes: Case Concerning United States Diplomatic and Consular Staff in Tehran (United States of America v Iran), Judgment of 24 May 1980, ICJ Reports 1980, No. 64, p. 40, para. 86. Akinsanya also holds that entry to the diplomatic premises could be justified

this reason, the article is controversial.[30] In practice, this means that even if a case of diplomatic asylum has no basis in law, the mission premises remain inviolable.[31] Capone holds that this guarantee of the mission's integrity has the potential to conflict with Art. 41 (1) VCDR's obligation for a sending state not to interfere in the internal affairs of the host state.[32]

Thus, even if one goes as far as to consider the practice of diplomatic asylum to be an internationally wrongful act under Art. 2, 3 ILC Draft Articles on the Responsibility of States for Internationally Wrongful Acts 2001,[33] the mission premises would still maintain their inviolability. In this respect, Crawford holds that although there is no right for a state to grant asylum, once an asylee has been accepted by a diplomatic mission, he cannot be retrieved, compelling the receiving state to resort to diplomacy.[34] Crucially, Art. 50 (2) lit. b ILC Draft Articles on the Responsibility of States for Internationally Wrongful Acts 2001 also explicitly prohibits states from infringing the inviolability of diplomatic premises in their exercise of countermeasures. Though the ILC Draft Articles were not initiated in the form of a formally

in an extreme case of abuse. When exactly such an extreme case of abuse would be constituted is unclear, see: Akinsanya (1989), p. 113. Some clarification as to the nature of Art. 22 VCDR has been provided by Judge Gaja: "Article 22, paragraph 3, of the Vienna Convention. . . does not grant total immunity to the building. It only refers to forcible measures that interfere with the use of the building for the diplomatic mission:" Immunities and Criminal Proceedings (Equatorial Guinea v France), Judgment of 6 June 2018, No. 163, Declaration by Judge Gaja.

[30]Chatterjee (2007), p. 190. Also see Capone (2016), p. 226. Cf. Judge Donoghue: "Despite their importance to the functioning of diplomacy, the immunity and inviolability of diplomatic personnel and missions exist in uneasy tension with other interests of States and private parties:" Immunities and Criminal Proceedings (Equatorial Guinea v France), Judgment of 6 June 2018, No. 163, Dissenting Opinion by Judge Donoghue, p. 5, para. 17. The controversy surrounding the absolute inviolability of embassies and consular premises was recently highlighted by the killing of Saudi Arabian journalist Jamal Khashoggi in the Saudi Arabian consulate in October 2018. See ABC News (10 October 2018), Jamal Khashoggi, Does diplomatic immunity make it possible to get away with murder? Another historic example is the killing of PC Yvonne Fletcher (and the wounding of several other bystanders) by stray bullets shot from the Libyan embassy in London. See: International Business Times (20 November 2015), PC Yvonne Fletcher: Was Britain right to 'allow murderer to walk free' under diplomatic immunity? In a similar vein, the immunity of diplomatic personnel and their spouses has recently caused controversy in the UK following the death of a teenage motorcyclist, who was hit by the car of a U.S. agent's (the status of the husband in relation to diplomatic immunity is also disputed) wife travelling on the wrong side of the road: cf. BBC News (5 October 2019), Harry Dunn crash: Mum appeals for US suspect's return.

[31]Yearbook of the International Law Commission, 1957, 394th Meeting, 3 May 1957, p. 56, para. 55; Jeffery (1985), p. 19; Marauhn and Simon (2012), p. 598. Cf. Ronning (1965), p. 22; Stein et al. (2017), p. 278.

[32]Capone (2016), p. 223.

[33]The ILC's Draft Articles on State Responsibility have dominated the law of state responsibility since their inception in 2001. They depict in part a codification of existing customary international law and in part its progressive development. Cf. Caron (2012), p. 872. The draft articles therefore constitute an example of the ILC acting in its dual function.

[34]Crawford (2019), p. 389.

legally binding document, the articles were taken note of by the General Assembly and annexed to Resolution 56/83 of 12 December 2001. In practice, they have also been widely used[35] and may, at least in part, be regarded as reflecting customary international law.[36]

4.1.3 Art 41 (1) Vienna Convention on Diplomatic Relations

According to Crawford, the issue of diplomatic asylum under the Vienna Convention on Diplomatic Relations depends upon the joint application of the aforementioned Art. 22 VCDR, together with Art. 41 (1) VCDR.[37] This provides:

> Article 41
>
> 1. Without prejudice to their privileges and immunities, it is the duty of all persons enjoying such privileges and immunities to respect the laws and regulations of the receiving State. They also have a duty not to interfere in the internal affairs of that State.

This provision obliges diplomats of the sending state to comply with local law and not to interfere in the domestic affairs of the receiving state.

As a diplomatic asylee is by nature being sought by the domestic authorities of the receiving state, granting diplomatic asylum *prima facie* constitutes interference in the internal affairs of the receiving state and thus an unlawful breach of Art. 41 (1) VCDR.[38] Indeed, Behrens describes diplomatic asylum as being subject to

---

[35] Cf. for example Noble Ventures, Inc. v Romania, ICSID Case No. ARB/01/11, Award of 12 October 2005, para. 69; Jan de Nul N.V. and Dredging International N.V. v. Arab Republic of Egypt, ICSID Case No. ARB/04/13, Decision on Jurisdiction of 16 June 2006, para. 89; Saipem S.p.A. v. The People's Republic of Bangladesh, ICSID Case No. ARB/05/07, Decision on Jurisdiction and Recommendation on Provisional Measures of 21 March 2007, para. 148; also see Crawford (2012), p. 2; Crawford (2019), p. 524.

[36] Cf. for example Noble Ventures, Inc. v Romania, ICSID Case No. ARB/01/11, Award of 12 October 2005, para. 69; Jan de Nul N.V. and Dredging International N.V. v. Arab Republic of Egypt, ICSID Case No. ARB/04/13, Decision on Jurisdiction of 16 June 2006, para. 89; Saipem S.p.A. v. The People's Republic of Bangladesh, ICSID Case No. ARB/05/07, Decision on Jurisdiction and Recommendation on Provisional Measures of 21 March 2007, para. 148; Caron (2012), p. 872. Also see Olleson (2007). On the point of attribution, see Case Concerning Application of the Convention on the Prevention and Punishment of the Crime of Genocide (Bosnia and Herzegovina v Serbia and Montenegro), Judgment of 26 February 2007, ICJ Reports 2007, No. 91, p. 209, para. 401. On attribution of the conduct of a state organ, see Difference Relating to Immunity from Legal Process of a Special Rapporteur of the Commission on Human Rights, Advisory Opinion of 29 April 1999, ICJ Reports 1999, No. 100, p. 87, para. 62.

[37] Crawford (2019), p. 389. Cf. Shah (2007), para. 8.

[38] On this point, see Kau (2019), p. 198, para. 75a; Rossitto (1987), p. 116, Fn. 51. Cf. Kleiner (2010), p. 181.

allegations of interference.[39] Moreover in Colombian-Peruvian Asylum Case, the Court found that diplomatic asylum depicts an intervention into affairs solely within the remit of the receiving state.[40] In this respect, it is important to note that the diplomatic duty of non-interference and the protection of human rights may come into conflict.[41]

Importantly, however, the Vienna Convention on Diplomatic Relations does not contain any sanction provision to compel diplomats to uphold Art. 41 (1) VCDR.[42] Indeed, Farhangi describes this provision itself as "unenforceable."[43] The unenforceable nature of this provision, coupled with the absolute nature of Art. 22 VCDR, contributes to the facilitation of the practice of diplomatic asylum even without an explicit legal basis. Moreover the inclusion of the term "without prejudice to their privileges and immunities" in Art. 41 (1) VCDR makes clear that even where Art. 41 (1) VCDR is breached by a sending state's diplomatic representatives, the obligation of the host state to respect said person's privileges and immunities remains unaffected.[44]

4.1.4 Art. 41 (3) Vienna Convention on Diplomatic Relations

Art. 41 (3) Vienna Convention on Diplomatic Relations is also of relevance to the question of diplomatic asylum under universal treaty law.[45] This article covers the manner[46] in which the mission premises may be used[47] and provides:

> 3. The premises of the mission must not be used in any way incompatible with the functions of the mission as laid down in the present Convention or by other rules of general

---

[39]Behrens (2016), p. 31. Also see Foreign Ministry Spokesperson Liu Weimin's Remarks on Chen Guangcheng's Entering the US Embassy in China, 2nd May 2012 regarding the Chen Guangcheng case.

[40]Colombian-Peruvian Asylum Case (Colombia v Peru), Judgment of 20 November 1950, ICJ Reports 1950, No. 7, p. 275.

[41]Denza (2016), Art. 41, p. 378.

[42]Ross (2011), p. 182. Indeed, Capone holds that it "sets the stage for international disputes without providing a clear mechanism for resolution:" Capone (2016), p. 223. Also see Mugunthan.

[43]Farhangi (1986), p. 1522.

[44]Cf. Farhangi (1986), p. 1519 providing that due to immunity, diplomats cannot be compelled to adhere to local laws.

[45]Indeed, this provision has been understood to constitute indirect recognition of the practice, see Nur Kayacan (2016), p. 5.

[46]This article has been described as a "general limitation:" Relocation of the United States Embassy to Jerusalem (Palestine v United States of America), Application Instituting Proceedings by the State of Palestine Against the United States of America, 28 September 2018 p. 11, para. 48.

[47]This sentiment is also echoed by Art. 1 (i) VCDR, which defines the mission premises *inter alia* as buildings used for the purposes of the mission.

international law or by any special agreements in place between the sending and the receiving State.

This is in line with the predominant idea of the functional necessity of diplomatic immunity in order to facilitate the functionality of the mission.[48] Moreover, this article aims to prevent abuses of the inviolability of the diplomatic premises from occurring by limiting the usage of said premises. In this regard, Denza refers to legal conduct that falls outside the remit of the ordinary functions of the mission, for example commercial activity, which therefore may either cause offence to the receiving state or constitute abuse of the mission status.[49]

The reference by Art. 41 (3) to the functions of the mission relates to Art. 3 VCDR, which codifies said functions:

1. The functions of a diplomatic mission consist, inter alia, in:
   a) Representing the sending State in the receiving State;
   b) Protecting in the receiving State the interests of the sending State and of its nationals, within the limits permitted by international law;
   c) Negotiating with the Government of the receiving State;
   d) Ascertaining by all lawful means conditions and developments in the receiving State, and reporting thereon to the Government of the sending State;
   e) Promoting friendly relations between the sending State and the receiving State, and developing their economic, cultural and scientific relations.

3. Nothing in the present Charter shall be construed as preventing the performance of consular functions by a diplomatic mission.

The majority of these functions, e.g. representation, protection of the sending state's interests, negotiation and promoting friendly relations, are closely interwoven with the nature of diplomacy.

It would be difficult to surmise, however, that granting diplomatic asylum could fall under any of these functions.[50] Protection by the receiving state of its nationals is, though remote, at least a possibility. A study of Table 7.1, however, would indicate that most cases of diplomatic asylum do not involve a sending state protecting its own national but rather a foreign national. It is, furthermore, important

---

[48]Cf. Preamble to the VCDR; Farhangi (1986), pp. 1521–1522.

[49]Denza (2016), Art. 41, p. 384.

[50]Cf. Executive Order No. 5956, Unsanctioned Asylum, Herbert Hoover, White House, 1 December 1932, CDILR 2:104 providing that the affording of asylum does not fall within the purposes of a diplomatic mission. Though this document predates the VCDR, it is relevant to the purposes of the mission under customary international law. Also see UN General Assembly, 29th Session, Sixth Committee, Summary Record of the 1505th Meeting, Agenda Item 105, Diplomatic Asylum, A/C.6/SR.1505, 25 November 1974, p. 244, para. 23. Cf. Klepper (2009), p. 82; Richtsteig (2010), Art. 22 and 41, pp. 47 and 101; von Arnauld (2019), pp. 257–258, para. 586; von Pollern (1980), p. 95.

to note, that the list of functions contained within Art. 3 VCDR is not intended to be exhaustive,[51] though it is almost complete.[52] Whilst the harbouring of asylees indisputably does not fall within the list of mission purposes contained within Art. 3 VCDR,[53] equally the VCDR does not contain any provision prohibiting the mission premises from being used specifically in this way.[54]

Furthermore, the non-exhaustive nature of Art. 3 VCDR allows for the possibility of further functions of the diplomatic mission to develop over time in line with a dynamic interpretation of the provision.[55]

In contrast, diplomatic asylum may even be regarded as directly violating the purposes of the diplomatic mission in that it may be regarded by the receiving state as an unfriendly act, which may provoke a deterioration in bilateral diplomatic relations.

In the light of divergent attitudes to diplomatic asylum, a function of the diplomatic premises permitting them to be utilised for the purpose of sheltering diplomatic asylees cannot be ascertained in the context of general international law.

Moreover, granting diplomatic asylum hereunder would be contrary to the purposes of the Vienna Convention on Diplomatic Relations, which stresses the maintenance of friendly relations between states.[56]

In this regard, diplomatic asylum can be differentiated from the concept of consular asylum,[57] governed by the legal regime of the Vienna Convention on

---

[51] Jeffery (1985), p. 18; Rafii (2014), p. 54. Also see UN General Assembly, 29th Session, Sixth Committee, Summary Record of the 1505th Meeting, Agenda Item 105, Diplomatic Asylum, A/C.6/SR.1505, 25 November 1974, p. 242, para. 7, which holds that Art. 3 VCDR was deliberately left open to provide for the possibility of diplomatic asylum. See also the wording of Relocation of the United States Embassy to Jerusalem (Palestine v United States of America), Application Instituting Proceedings by the State of Palestine Against the United States of America, 28 September 2018, p. 11, para. 44: "…whether or not these functions are mentioned in the article."

[52] Kempen and Hillgruber (2012), p. 178. Additional functions may emerge from customary international law: cf. Richtsteig (2010), Art. 41, p. 101.

[53] Yearbook of the International Law Commission, 1957, 394th Meeting, 3 May 1957, p. 55, para. 45; Happold (2012); Klepper (2009), pp. 82–83; Rossitto (1987), p. 116; von Pollern (1980), p. 95. Cf. Yearbook of the International Law Commission, 1957, 411th Meeting, 5 June 1957, p. 144, para. 63 in which it is held that under certain special agreements (the various conventions on diplomatic asylum), diplomatic asylum may constitute a legitimate use of the mission premises.

[54] Porcino (1976), p. 447 f. In this vein, Status vis-à-vis the Host State of a Diplomatic Envoy to the United Nations (Commonwealth of Dominica v Switzerland), Application Instituting Proceedings by the Commonwealth of Dominica Against Switzerland, No. 134, 26 April 2006, p. 4, para. 28 holds: "At the moment, there is a grey area of international law with respect to the powers and duties of a host State vis-à-vis a sending State and its envoys…"

[55] On dynamic interpretation cf. Legal Consequences for States of the Continued Presence of South Africa in Namibia (South West Africa) notwithstanding Security Council Resolution 276 (1970), Advisory Opinion of 21 June 1971, No. 53, p. 31, para. 53.

[56] See Preamble to the VCDR; also see Relocation of the United States Embassy to Jerusalem (Palestine v United States of America), Application Instituting Proceedings by the State of Palestine Against the United States of America, 28 September 2018, p. 9, para. 36.

[57] For further information on this concept, see for example Ronning (1965), p. 125 f.

Consular Relations.[58] Art. 5 VCCR regulates the consular functions. Art. 5 (e) VCCR provides "helping and assisting nationals. . .of the sending state" to be a consular function, whilst Art. 3 (b) VCDR refers to "protecting. . .the interests of the sending state and its nationals, within the limits permitted by international law." This would leave open the question of whether the sending state granting asylum to its own national(s) fulfils this consular function. Further analysis of the concept of consular asylum specifically is, however, outside of the remit of this book.

On the issue, as to whether diplomatic asylum should be included in the Draft Declaration on Human Rights in accordance with Uruguayan and Bolivian proposals, the Soviet delegate to the United Nations held in the context of the Third Committee on the UN General Assembly:

> The sole purpose of embassies and legations was to permit Governments to transact business with one another.[59]

This is consistent with the main functions of the diplomatic mission as provided for by Art. 3 VCDR.

Indeed, Denza holds that any case of a state granting diplomatic asylum, the circumstances of which are not covered by customary international law or special agreements, constitutes a breach of Art. 41 (3) VCDR.[60] This is because diplomatic asylum in such cases constitutes a use of the diplomatic premises incompatible with its functions. Denza thus rejects a legal basis for diplomatic asylum within universal treaty law.[61]

Interestingly, in the context of Latin America, granting diplomatic asylum to political offenders has been held to fall within the realm of ordinary diplomatic functions.[62] However, even if one rejects this argument, diplomatic asylum in the context of Latin America does not constitute a breach of Art. 41 (3) VCDR because the provision itself specifically provides for the existence of further functions of the diplomatic mission compatible with, for example, regional treaty or customary law.[63] Moreover, the Preamble to the VCDR specifically provides for customary

[58]Vienna Convention on Consular Relations 1963, Adopted in Vienna on 24 April 1963, Entered into Force on 19 March 1967, UNTS Vol. No. 596, p. 261.

[59]UN General Assembly, 3rd Session, Third Committee, 122nd Meeting, 4 November 1948, Draft International Declaration of Human Rights, p. 342.

[60]Denza (2016), Art. 41, pp. 384–385. See also Oelfke et al. (2018), Art. 41, p. 337. Cf. IACtHR, Advisory Opinion OC-25/18 of 30 May 2018 Requested by the Republic of Ecuador, The Institution of Asylum and its Recognition as a Human Right in the Inter-American System of Protection (Interpretation and Scope of Articles 5, 22.7 and 22.8 in Relation to Article 1(1) of the American Convention on Human Rights), p. 37, para. 105.

[61]Also see Kimminich (1961), p. 236.

[62]Colombian-Peruvian Asylum Case (Colombia v Peru), Judgment of 20 November 1950, ICJ Reports 1950, No. 7, Dissenting Opinion by Judge Read, p. 317.

[63]Denza (2016), Art. 41, p. 384.

international law continuing to govern questions—such as diplomatic asylum—not expressly provided for in the VCDR.[64]

Importantly, even though diplomatic asylum on a universal level as a demonstrable unfriendly act constitutes a breach of Art. 41 (3) VCDR, the absolute nature of Art. 22 VCDR, providing for the inviolability of the mission premises, prevents the receiving state from retrieving the asylee by entering the embassy.[65] In practice, this means that receiving states cannot compel granting states to terminate the asylum. Thus, an interesting legal lacuna arises in which it is impermissible under universal treaty law to grant an individual diplomatic asylum, nevertheless the very same legal regime facilitates this impermissible practice and prevents a receiving state from taking effective action to bring it to an end. In effect, a receiving state is therefore often forced to resort to diplomacy.[66]

4.1.5 *Conclusion*

Following an analysis of relevant universal treaty law provisions, in particular the VCDR, a legal basis for the practice of diplomatic asylum could not be found. Indeed, the practice of diplomatic asylum in general constitutes a breach of Art. 41 (1) and (3) VCDR as the practice constitutes both an effort to circumvent the laws and regulations of the receiving state and a use of the diplomatic premises incompatible with its functions.

4.2 Regional Treaty Law: Latin America

Having established that universal treaty law does not provide for a legal basis for the practice of diplomatic asylum,[67] it is necessary to analyse regional treaty law to ascertain whether it provides a legal basis for the practice. In this regard, the regional treaty law of Latin America will be analysed owing to it being the only region of the world with an established treaty law regime governing the issue of diplomatic

[64]Cf. Chap. 5: Sects. 5.3.4, 5.4.1.1, 5.4.2.4 and 5.5.

[65]Cf. Chap. 4: Sect. 4.1.2.; Art. 40 ILC Draft Articles on Diplomatic Intercourse and Immunities with Commentaries 1958, Text adopted by the International Law Commission at its tenth session, in 1958, and submitted to the General Assembly as a part of the Commission's report covering the work of that session, Yearbook of the International Law Commission, 1958, Vol. II, p. 104, para. 4; Oelfke et al. (2018), Art. 41, p. 337. See also: Foakes and Denza (2017), p. 226; von Arnauld (2019), p. 259, para. 288.

[66]Cf. Crawford (2019), p. 389.

[67]Cf. Chap. 4: Sect. 4.1.

asylum. If evidence of regional treaty law is established, it will then be necessary to demonstrate the extent to which such treaty law may bind non-parties.[68]

Diplomatic asylum has been a practice particularly prevalent on the Latin American continent since the middle of the nineteenth Century due to the historical frequency of revolution and armed struggles.[69] Greenburgh also accords the rise of the practice to the "geo-physical composition" of Latin America.[70] Indeed the right to asylum has saved many lives in the region—both those of ordinary people but in particular those of prominent political figures.[71] In stark contrast to Europe, such a Latin American claim for diplomatic asylum may arguably also base itself upon the exterritoriality of the premises, with the diplomatic premises being considered as legitimate territory of the sending state.[72]

Though some may consider diplomatic asylum in the context of Latin America to conflict with the equally important Latin American principle of non-intervention,[73] this principle of exterritoriality renders diplomatic asylum to constitute neither an unlawful intervention on the part of the sending state, nor a limitation of the receiving state's sovereignty.[74] The notion of reciprocity further prevents the practice from being considered as contrary to the fundamental principle of non-intervention.[75]

---

[68]Cf. Chap. 4: Sect. 4.2.3.

[69]Colombian-Peruvian Asylum Case (Colombia v Peru), Judgment of 20 November 1950, ICJ Reports 1950, No. 7, Dissenting Opinion by Judge Álvarez (translation), p. 292; Colombian-Peruvian Asylum Case (Colombia v Peru), Judgment of 20 November 1950, ICJ Reports 1950, No. 7, Dissenting Opinion by Judge Badawi Pasha (translation), pp. 309, 312; Colombian-Peruvian Asylum Case (Colombia v Peru), Judgment of 20 November 1950, ICJ Reports 1950, No. 7, Dissenting Opinion by Judge Read, p. 317; Colombian-Peruvian Asylum Case (Colombia v Peru), Judgment of 20 November 1950, ICJ Reports 1950, No. 7, Dissenting Opinion by Judge Azevedo (translation), p. 333; UN General Assembly, 14th Session, Sixth Committee, Summary Record of the 608th Meeting, Agenda Item 55, Report of the International Law Commission on the work of its eleventh session, A/C.6/SR.608, 7 October 1959, p. 39, para. 17; Baumann (1973), p. 56; Clinton Nolan (1934), p. 176; Pradier-Fodéré (1881), p. 91. Cf. UN General Assembly, 21st Session, Sixth Committee, Summary Record of the 922nd Meeting, Agenda Item 85, Draft Declaration on the Right of Asylum, A/C.6, SR.922, 28 October 1966, p. 130, para. 15; For further information on this concept, see for example Ronning (1965), p. 218. Cf. Kitschenberg (1965), Einleitung.

[70]Greenburgh (1955), pp. 107–108.

[71]Grugel and Quijada (1990), p. 355. Also see Monasterio. Cf. Chap. 3: Sects. 3.4.2–3.4.14, 3.7. Also see Chap. 7: Annex, Table 7.1.

[72]Colombian-Peruvian Asylum Case (Colombia v Peru), Judgment of 20 November 1950, ICJ Reports 1950, No. 7, Dissenting Opinion by Judge Álvarez (translation), p. 292.

[73]Esquirol (2012), p. 559.

[74]Colombian-Peruvian Asylum Case (Colombia v Peru), Judgment of 20 November 1950, ICJ Reports 1950, No. 7, Dissenting Opinion by Judge Álvarez (translation), p. 292.

[75]Colombian-Peruvian Asylum Case (Colombia v Peru), Judgment of 20 November 1950, ICJ Reports 1950, No. 7, Dissenting Opinion by Judge Azevedo (translation), p. 343.

In line with the practice's development,[76] diplomatic asylum has traditionally been reserved for political offenders in cases of urgency. Examples of diplomatic asylum in Latin America date back to as early as 1850.[77]

4.2.1 *Founding Principles*

Before examining the relevant Latin American treaties, several sets of rules will be examined, which were drafted by delegations to Latin American states and came to form the basis of later treaty law.

4.2.1.1 Rules of Lima 1865

The Rules of Lima emerged following a case in which asylum was granted to the Peruvian General Canseco in May 1865 by the U.S. minister in Peru. Canseco was charged with conspiracy and remained in the U.S. delegation for nearly 4 months after which he proceeded to drum up support for his cause and invade Lima.[78] Serious discord followed, prompting the diplomatic corps to agree upon the following rules governing asylum on 19th May 1865:

> (1) that apart from inhibitions in their instructions or in conventional stipulations, there were limits to the privilege of asylum which the prudence of diplomatic agents ought to counsel;
> (2) that the diplomatic corps adopted the instructions given by Brazil to its minister, according to which asylum was to be conceded with the greatest reserve, and only for such time as was necessary in order that the fugitive should secure his safety in another manner - an end which it was the duty of the diplomatic agent to do all in his power to accomplish.[79]

These rules already display several key characteristics of the modern regional treaty law regime:

- that asylum should only be granted in exceptional cases
- that the asylum should endure only for so long as is necessary.
- The rules were to apply only to political offences subject to the approval of the accredited governments.[80]

---

[76]See Chap. 3.

[77]UN General Assembly, Question of Diplomatic Asylum, Report of the Secretary-General, 2 September 1975, A/10139 (Part I), para. 12.

[78]Clinton Nolan (1934), p. 176.

[79]UN General Assembly, Question of Diplomatic Asylum, Report of the Secretary-General, 2 September 1975, A/10139 (Part I), para. 27.

[80]As cited by UN General Assembly, Question of Diplomatic Asylum, Report of the Secretary-General, 2 September 1975, A/10139 (Part I), para. 27.

These Rules of Lima constitute the first attempt to set clear limits to the practice of diplomatic asylum in treaty-like form. The Peruvian government, however, failed to accept the rules.[81] Their relevance to the modern treaty law regime is, therefore, very limited.

4.2.1.2 Rules of La Paz 1898

In December 1898 the U.S. Minister drew up the following set of rules governing diplomatic asylum, which were approved by both the Brazilian and French legations:

> Every person asking asylum must be received first in the outer or waiting room of the legation, and there state his name, official capacity, if any, residence, and reasons for demanding refuge; also if his life is threatened by mob violence or is in active danger from any attack.
>
> If, according to the joint rules laid down by the committee composed of the Brazilian, American, and French ministers, he shall be adjudged eligible for protection, he must subscribe to the following rules in writing:
>
> First. To agree that the authorities shall be at once notified of his place of refuge.
>
> Second. To hold no communication with any outside person, and to receive no visitors except by permission of the authority quoted above.
>
> Third. To agree not to leave the legation without permission of the resident minister.
>
> Fourth. To hold himself as virtually the prisoner-guest of the minister in whose legation he is.
>
> Fifth. To agree to peaceably yield himself to the proper authorities when so demanded by them and requested by his host.
>
> Sixth. To quietly depart when so requested by the minister, should the authorities not demand his person after a reasonable time has elapsed.[82]

These rules are rather formal compared to their modern-day counterparts e.g. the provision that the would-be asylee be received first in the outer waiting room and that he/she should provide pre-specified information. Moreover, the rules provide for strict stipulations to which the diplomatic asylee is subject, with he/she being obliged to formally consent by providing a written declaration. The stipulations that asylees should have no communication with the outside world, receive guests only with the permission of the sending state's authorities, be the prisoner-guest of the minister of the legation and leave peacefully if so required drastically contrast to modern-day practice, depicted for example by the Assange case, which saw Assange accused of

[81] Moore (1906), p. 836.

[82] As cited by Moore (1906), p. 784.

interference in other states' affairs,[83] receive many visitors,[84] frequently at odds with Ecuador[85] and protest his eventual removal from the embassy.[86]

In the Rules of La Paz, some modern-day features of diplomatic asylum on the South American continent can also already be identified e.g. the humanitarian theme in the face of political unrest, the reservation of the practice for urgent cases and the restrictive conditions under which the practice is permitted.[87] Furthermore, the drafting of the rules by the U.S. legation and the approval of both the French and Brazilian legations depict that interpretations as to the permissibility of diplomatic asylum in the context of Latin America, Northern America and Europe were, at least in the nineteenth century, not that far apart.

4.2.1.3 The Rules of Asunción 1922

The Rules of Asunción were adopted by the following eleven states' diplomatic missions to Paraguay in 1922: Argentina, Bolivia, Brazil, Cuba, France, Germany, Peru, Spain, the United Kingdom, the U.S. and Uruguay.[88] It is interesting to see several Western European states, France, Germany, Spain and the UK, adopting these otherwise Latin American rules, indicating that at least in 1922, European and Latin American principles governing diplomatic asylum were not that far apart.

The Rules of Asunción provide:

> Any person who, invoking reasons of a political character, seeks asylum in the residence of a foreign legation, shall set forth the facts which have led him to ask for this asylum; and the chief of the legation shall be the one to judge such facts.

---

[83]Cf. BBC News (19 October 2016), Wikileaks: Is Julian Assange interfering in US election?; The Times (17 July 2019), Julian Assange 'helped Russia from Ecuadorian embassy.'

[84]Cf. The Guardian (18 May 2018), Assange's guest list: the RT reporters, hackers and film-makers who visited embassy; El País (9 October 2019), Russian and US visitors, targets for the Spanish firm that spied on Julian Assange.

[85]See The Guardian (15 May 2018), How Julian Assange became an unwelcome guest in Ecuador's embassy; The Guardian (16 October 2018), Ecuador tells Assange to avoid political activity online—and feed the cat; The Guardian (19 October 2018), Julian Assange launches legal action against Ecuador; The Guardian (24 October 2018), Ecuador says Assange must sort out own issues with Britain; The Guardian, (29 October 2018), Assange must follow new Ecuador embassy rules, says judge; The Telegraph (6 December 2018), Julian Assange rejects UK-Ecuador deal for him to leave the embassy; The Guardian (11 April 2019), The seven-year itch: Assange's awkward stay in the embassy.

[86]Cf. The Arab American News (4 November 2019), Julian Assange forcibly removed from Ecuadorian embassy, arrested in London.

[87]Cf. The wording of the fourth rule of the Rules of La Paz: "To hold himself as virtually the prisoner-guest of the minister in whose legation he is."

[88]UN General Assembly, Question of Diplomatic Asylum, Report of the Secretary-General, 2 September 1975, A/10139 (Part I), para. 30.

Once asylum is granted, the person to whom it is granted shall promise, in writing, upon his word of honour:

1. To refrain from all participation in political questions.
2. To receive no visits without prior consent of the foreign representative, who will reserve the right to be present in the conversations.
3. To maintain no written communications without prior censure of the chief of the legation.
4. Not to leave the legation without the consent and authorization of the head of the same; failure to keep this promise will mean the loss of the right to renewed refuge within the legation.
5. To submit to the decisions of the head of the mission, concerning the termination of the asylum or leaving the country, with the guarantees which he may deem proper.

These principles shall be observed provided they are not contradicted by instructions received by each head of mission.[89]

Here, the reservation of the practice for political offences is affirmed. Moreover, the asylee is required to put forward his/her reasons for seeking asylum, which are to be assessed by the head of the diplomatic mission. This implies that the issue of qualification of the alleged offence also falls to the head of the diplomatic mission as representative of the sending state.

Like the Rules of La Paz before them, these rules also place specific obligations on the asylee e.g. not to engage in political activity or leave the mission premises without permission. Such a prohibition on engaging in political activity is relevant due to the practice's reservation for political offences.[90] The restrictive nature of the obligations placed upon the diplomatic asylee may be seen as testament to the difficulty of achieving a consensus between Latin American, Northern American and European states on the issue of diplomatic asylum by the early twentieth century. Still, the consensus achieved on the issue contrasts dramatically from such states' modern-day positions on the issue of diplomatic asylum nearly 100 years later.[91]

4.2.2 Treaties

Relevant Latin American treaties, more specifically their provisions explicitly pertinent to the issue of diplomatic asylum, will now be analysed in order to determine the extent to which they provide a legal basis for the practice of diplomatic asylum. These treaties will be detailed chronologically.

---

[89] As cited by the UN General Assembly, Question of Diplomatic Asylum, Report of the Secretary-General, 2 September 1975, A/10139 (Part I), para. 30.

[90] García-Mora (1951), p. 933.

[91] Cf. Chap. 5: Sects. 5.4.1.1, 5.4.2.3 and 5.4.2.5.

4.2.2.1 The Treaty on International Penal Law 1889[92]

Initiated by Argentina and Uruguay and further agreed upon by Bolivia, Paraguay and Peru, the Treaty on International Penal Law was adopted by the First South American Congress on Private International Law[93] in Montevideo on 23rd January 1889. As its title suggests, the treaty primarily regulates international criminal law. Art. 17, however, governs the right to diplomatic asylum. It provides:

> Such persons as may be charged with non-political offenses and seek refuge in a legation, shall be surrendered to the local authorities by the head of the said legation, at the request of the Ministry of Foreign Relations, or of his own motion.
>
> Said asylum shall be respected with regard to political offenders, but the head of the legation shall be bound to give immediate notice to the government of the State to which he is accredited; and the said government shall have the power to demand that the offender be sent away from the national territory in the shortest possible time.
>
> The head of the legation shall, in his turn, have the right to require proper guarantees for the exit of the refugee without any injury to the inviolability of his person.
>
> The same rule shall be applicable to the refugees on board a man-of-war anchored in the territorial waters of the State.

The treaty followed two incidents of diplomatic asylum.[94]

The following key principles of the concept of Latin American diplomatic asylum were either reaffirmed or established by this article: reservation for political offences, a notice requirement, the duration being as short as possible and the guarantee of safe-conduct. It is interesting also to note that this provision applied in equal measure to warships. Provision is furthermore explicitly made for the surrender of those accused of non-political offences. This correlates to modern-day Latin American treaty law.[95]

Though many of these key principles would remain common themes to diplomatic asylum going forward, this treaty was limited from providing a formal legal basis thereto, even on a regional level, due to its small number—five—of state

---

[92]Adopted by the First South American Congress on Private International Law in Montevideo on 23 January 1889, OAS Official Records, OEA/Ser.X/7, Treaty Series No. 34. For further information on this treaty, also see IACtHR, Advisory Opinion OC-25/18 of 30 May 2018 Requested by the Republic of Ecuador, The Institution of Asylum and its Recognition as a Human Right in the Inter-American System of Protection (Interpretation and Scope of Articles 5, 22.7 and 22.8 in Relation to Article 1(1) of the American Convention on Human Rights), p. 29, paras 81–82.

[93]Private International Law, also known as the Conflict of Laws, governs the relationship between individuals and corporations. This is in contrast to Public International Law, governing the relationship between states. Further elaboration on Private International Law is outside of the remit of this work.

[94]IACtHR, Advisory Opinion OC-25/18 of 30 May 2018 Requested by the Republic of Ecuador, The Institution of Asylum and its Recognition as a Human Right in the Inter-American System of Protection (Interpretation and Scope of Articles 5, 22.7 and 22.8 in Relation to Article 1(1) of the American Convention on Human Rights), p. 29, para. 81.

[95]Cf. Chap. 4: Sects. 4.2.2.4–4.2.2.7.

parties. This also meant that its impact was greatly limited. It did, however, pave the way for later treaty law.

4.2.2.2 Treaty of Peace and Friendship 1907[96]

Though the Treaty of Peace and Friendship between Costa Rica, El Salvador, Guatemala, Honduras and Nicaragua was primarily a friendship treaty[97] and is also no longer in force,[98] it is worthy of mention as it contained a provision pertaining to the right of asylum. This provision, Art. X, provided for an inviolable right to asylum on board merchant ships of any nationality for political offences. It read:

> The Governments of the contracting Republics bind themselves to respect the inviolability of the right of asylum aboard the merchant vessels of whatsoever nationality anchored in their ports. Therefore, only persons accused of common crimes can be taken from them after due legal procedure and by order of the competent judge. Those prosecuted on account of political crimes or common crimes in connexion with political ones can only be taken therefrom in case they have embarked in a port of the State which claims them, during their stay in its jurisdictional waters, and after the requirements hereinbefore set forth in the case of common crimes have been fulfilled.[99]

This provision is interesting as it grants an explicit right to asylum on board merchant ships, a practice which has been granted very restrictively historically speaking.[100] The content of this right also correlates to some degree with the right to diplomatic asylum regionally in that the practice is reserved for political offenders.

No correlation can be identified between this rule and the historical practice, of which there is a very limited state practice, of asylum on merchant ships save for the exemption of transit passengers.[101]

4.2.2.3 The Bolivarian Agreement on Extradition 1911[102]

Though the Bolivarian Agreement on Extradition of 1911 between Bolivia, Colombia, Ecuador, Peru and Venezuela primarily relates to extradition rules, it is important to mention as it not only provides for a specific exception with regard to asylum

[96]Treaty of Peace and Friendship 1907, Adopted at the Conference in Peace in Washington on 20 December 1907, Ceased to Have Effect (following Nicaraguan denouncement) in 1920.

[97]For the background to the treaty, see Leonard (2012), p. 155.

[98]It ceased to have effect following Nicaraguan denouncement in 1920.

[99]As cited by the UN General Assembly, Question of Diplomatic Asylum, Report of the Secretary-General, 2 September 1975, A/10139 (Part I), para. 32.

[100]Cf. Chap. 3: Sect. 3.3.2.

[101]See Chap. 3: Sect. 3.3.2.

[102]Bolivarian Agreement on Extradition 1911, Adopted in Caracas on 18 July 1911 at the Bolivarian Congress, Entered into Force on 18 July 1911.

but it also came to play a major role in the Colombian-Peruvian Asylum Case. Art. 18 of the Agreement provides:

> Aside from the stipulations of the present Agreement, the signatory States recognize the institution of asylum in conformity with the principles of International Law.

The purpose of the provision was to exempt the institution of asylum from the general rules of extradition outlined in the agreement.[103] Hence, an individual legitimately granted asylum, be it diplomatic or territorial, by the member states to the convention could not be subject to an extradition request. This is important as it provides vital protection for the asylee. This ties in with the humanitarian nature of diplomatic asylum in Latin America.

The wording of the provision also depicts that already in 1911, Latin American states considered asylum as an institution.

4.2.2.4 Convention on Asylum 1928[104]

The Convention on Asylum was signed at the Sixth International Conference of American States in Havana on 20th February 1928. It has been ratified by the following states: Brazil, Colombia, Costa Rica, Cuba, Dominican Republic, Ecuador, El Salvador, Guatemala, Haiti, Honduras, Mexico, Nicaragua, Panama, Paraguay, Peru, Uruguay. The five following states have signed but never ratified the convention: Argentina, Bolivia, Chile, the U.S. and Venezuela. The status of the U.S. as a signatory to an otherwise Latin American convention is interesting, particularly as the U.S. has traditionally rejected the notion of diplomatic asylum.[105] Though the convention is not legally binding upon the U.S. owing to its lack of ratification,[106] its status as a signatory state shows that even in the early twentieth Century, the American understanding of diplomatic asylum wasn't that far apart from that of Latin American states.

Boasting 16 state parties, the convention itself enjoys the highest number of state parties compared to the other Latin American treaties regulating diplomatic asylum. Importantly, the Convention on Asylum applies to the majority of Latin American states. The convention's Preamble reflects its purpose:

> The Governments of the States of America, being desirous of fixing the rules they must observe for the granting of asylum, in their mutual relations have agreed to establish them in a Convention…

[103] García-Mora (1951), p. 932.

[104] Convention on Asylum 1928, Adopted in Havana on 20 February 1928 at the Sixth International Conference of American States, Entered in Force on 21 May 1929, OAS Official Records, OEA/Ser.X/I. Treaty Series 34.

[105] Cf. Chap. 5: Sect. 5.4.2.5.

[106] Though a signatory state is obliged to refrain from conduct which would defeat the object and purpose of a treaty: cf. Art. 18 (a) VCLT.

The convention therefore aimed to streamline the existing practice.

Art. 1 of the Convention forbids the signatory states from granting asylum to anyone accused or condemned of common crimes. This correlates strongly with the Latin American practice being reserved for political offences. Importantly, however, the convention does not provide a definition for either category of offence, nor does it accord the unilateral right to qualify the offence to either state.[107]

Art. 2 of the Convention outlines the right to diplomatic asylum and indeed its conditions and limitations. It provides:

> Asylum granted to political offenders in legations, warships, military camps or military aircraft, shall be respected to the extent in which allowed, as a right or through humanitarian toleration, by the usages, the conventions or the laws of the country in which granted and in accordance with the following provisions:
>
> First: Asylum may not be granted except in urgent cases and for the period of time strictly indispensable for the person who has sought asylum to ensure in some other way his safety.
>
> Second: Immediately upon granting asylum, the diplomatic agent, commander of a warship, or military camp or aircraft, shall report the fact to the Minister of Foreign Relations of the State of the person who has secured asylum, or to the local administrative authority, if the act occurred outside the capital.
>
> Third: The Government of the State may require that the refugee be sent out of the national territory within the shortest time possible; and the diplomatic agent of the country who has granted asylum may in turn require the guaranties necessary for the departure of the refugee with due regard to the inviolability of his person, from the country.
>
> Fourth: Refugees shall not be landed in any point of the national territory nor in any place too near thereto.
>
> Fifth: While enjoying asylum, refugees shall not be allowed to perform acts contrary to the public peace.
>
> Sixth: States are under no obligation to defray expenses incurred by one granting asylum.

Through the inclusion of warships, military camps and military aircraft, in addition to legations, the Convention on Asylum embraces a broad definition of the term diplomatic asylum. The article, further, refers to the humanitarian foundation of the asylum institution. This is interesting as it again reaffirms that asylum in the context of Latin America is motivated by humanitarian considerations though curiously it refers to diplomatic asylum as being either a right or a "humanitarian toleration", thus implying that—even in the context of Latin America—states which do not recognise such a right may also tolerate the practice for humanitarian reasons.[108]

The Convention on Asylum also outlines six conditions for the exercise of asylum. The first provides that diplomatic asylum, in the context of the convention, is reserved for urgent cases and only for the period of time necessary to ensure the

---

[107] IACtHR, Advisory Opinion OC-25/18 of 30 May 2018 Requested by the Republic of Ecuador, The Institution of Asylum and its Recognition as a Human Right in the Inter-American System of Protection (Interpretation and Scope of Articles 5, 22.7 and 22.8 in Relation to Article 1(1) of the American Convention on Human Rights), p. 30, para. 83.

[108] Cf. Chap. 6.

safety of the asylee. The convention is the first to use the term "urgent cases." [109] However, even as early as the Rules of Lima, the theme of necessity in the length of the asylum was apparent, thus depicting a sense of urgency.[110]

In line with earlier principles, the convention also provides for a notification requirement,[111] a stipulation that the asylum should endure for the shortest time possible[112] and a requirement that asylees should not conduct themselves contrary to public peace.[113] Moreover, asylees should be kept away from the receiving state's territory and there is no obligation for asylum costs to be compensated—both of which constitute new requirements in the context of Latin American treaty law.

The obligations afforded to states under the convention were expounded in the course of the Columbian-Peruvian Asylum Case, in particular the question as to whether the convention conveyed upon the sending state a right to unilaterally qualify the alleged offence of the asylee in such a way so as to be binding on the receiving state.[114] The Court answered this question in the negative with regard to Colombia and Peru.[115]

4.2.2.5 Montevideo Convention on Political Asylum 1933[116]

The Montevideo Convention on Political Asylum was signed on 26th December 1933 at the 7th International Conference of American States. The following 14 states are state parties to the convention: Brazil, Chile, Colombia, Costa Rica, Cuba, Ecuador, El Salvador, Guatemala, Honduras, Mexico, Nicaragua, Panama, Paraguay, Peru. Both the Dominican Republic and Haiti were initially state parties to the convention but later denounced their membership. Argentina and Uruguay have signed but never ratified the convention. The U.S. made the following statement with regard to the convention:

[109] Cf. Colombian-Peruvian Asylum Case (Colombia v Peru), Judgment of 20 November 1950, ICJ Reports 1950, No. 7, Dissenting Opinion by Judge Badawi Pasha (translation), p. 303.

[110] Cf. Chap. 4: Sect. 4.2.1.1.

[111] Cf. Rules of La Paz 1898; The Treaty on International Penal Law 1889.

[112] Cf. Rules of Lima 1865; The Treaty on International Penal Law 1889.

[113] Cf. Rules of La Paz 1898; Rules of Asunción 1922.

[114] Colombian-Peruvian Asylum Case (Colombia v Peru), Application Instituting Proceedings by the Republic of Colombia Against Peru, 15 October 1949, p. 11, para. 19.

[115] Colombian-Peruvian Asylum Case (Colombia v Peru), Judgment of 20 November 1950, ICJ Reports 1950, No. 7, p. 277 f.

[116] Convention on Political Asylum 1933, Adopted by the Organisation of American States in Montevideo on 26 December 1933 at the Seventh International Conference of American States, Entered into Force on 28 March 1935, OAS Treaty Series No. 34.

> Since the United States of America does not recognize or subscribe to, as part of international law, the doctrine of asylum, the delegation of the United States of America refrains from signing the present Convention on Political Asylum.[117]

This is interesting as it indicates a shift in the American attitude to diplomatic asylum in the years between 1928, when the U.S. signed the Convention on Asylum, and 1933, when the U.S. did not sign the Convention on Political Asylum.

Though the convention is titled "The Convention on Political Asylum," it in fact regulates the practice of diplomatic asylum when accorded its broadest meaning. The title is thus indicative of the interchangeable language used when defining the practice.[118]

In the Preamble, reference is made to the earlier Havana Convention on Asylum of 1928:

> ...Wishing to conclude a Convention on Political Asylum, to define the terms of the one signed at Havana...

This suggests a degree of discrepancy in the interpretation of the Havana Convention's terms.

Art. 1 of the Montevideo Convention then goes on to explicitly replace the same provision from the Havana Convention on Asylum, which held that the practice of diplomatic asylum was not applicable to so-called common crimes, [119] providing:

> In place of Article 1 of the Convention of Havana on Right of Asylum [*sic*], of February 20, 1928, the following is substituted: 'It shall not be lawful for the States to grant asylum in legations, warships, military camps, or airships to those accused of common offenses who may have been duly prosecuted or who may have been sentenced by ordinary courts of justice, nor to deserters of land or sea forces. The persons referred to in the preceding paragraph who find refuge in some of the above-mentioned places shall be surrendered as soon as requested by the local government'.

This provision is lengthier and provides further specifications when compared to its predecessor. It also reaffirms the Latin American diplomatic asylum practice as excluding common crimes—a core principle of diplomatic asylum in the context of Latin America. Deserters from the armed forces are also exempted from the practice under the Montevideo Convention though interestingly only land and sea, and not air, forces are expressly provided for in the convention.

Art. 2 of the Montevideo Convention deals with the qualification of the alleged offence and provides:

> The judgment of political delinquency concerns the State which offers asylum.

This provision accords the right to unilateral qualification of the offence to the state granting asylum i.e. the sending state. This means that the granting state may

[117] UNHCR, Refworld, Organisation of American States, Convention on Political Asylum, Signatories and Ratifications. Available at: http://www.refworld.org/cgi-bin/texis/vtx/rwmain/opendocpdf.pdf?reldoc=y&docid=51d3f62f4. Last Accessed 15 Dec 2020.

[118] See Chap. 2: Sect. 2.1.5.

[119] See Chap. 4: Sect. 4.2.2.4.

qualify the alleged offence as political or non-political in nature, thus creating the risk of abuse of the practice in that a sending state may opt to categorise an offence as political in nature in order to enable the individual in question to benefit from the mechanism of diplomatic asylum.[120] With regard to the issue of qualification, it is important to note that the Montevideo Convention was not critically examined in the course of the Colombian-Peruvian Asylum Case as Peru didn't ratify the convention until 1960[121] and thus could not have been held to be bound by its provisions in 1949.[122]

Art. 3 of the Montevideo Convention also outlines several conditions for the exercise of the right to diplomatic asylum:

> Political asylum, as an institution of humanitarian character, is not subject to reciprocity. Any man may resort to its protection, whatever his nationality, without prejudice to the obligations accepted by the State to which he belongs; however, the States that do not recognize political asylum, except with limitations and peculiarities, can exercise it in foreign countries only in the manner and within the limits recognized by said countries.

This provision constitutes the first treaty provision making reference to the humanitarian character of the practice. Furthermore, it provides that would-be asylees shall not be discriminated against on the basis of their nationality or on the basis of their national state's domestic law. The practice not being underpinned by the principle of reciprocity renders an individual free to claim diplomatic asylum even where his/her national state would not accord such a right. Moreover, states which only recognise a limited right to diplomatic asylum may only grant such a right to the extent which it is recognised by a receiving state.

The principal significance of this treaty is in paving the way for the later Convention on Diplomatic Asylum 1954.[123]

4.2.2.6 Treaty on Political Asylum and Refuge 1939[124]

The Treaty on Political Asylum and Refuge was signed in Montevideo on 4th August 1939 by the following six states: Peru, Argentina, Uruguay, Bolivia, Paraguay and Chile. The treaty was, however, only ever ratified by Paraguay and Uruguay and its significance in evidencing a general Latin American practice on diplomatic asylum is therefore much limited. The Treaty on Political Asylum and

[120]Cf. Ronning (1965), p. 186 describing qualification of the offence as subject to the intuition of the diplomatic representative.

[121]See UNHCR, Refworld, Organisation of American States, Convention on Political Asylum, Signatories and Ratifications. Available at: http://www.refworld.org/cgi-bin/texis/vtx/rwmain/opendocpdf.pdf?reldoc=y&docid=51d3f62f4. Last Accessed 15 Dec 2020.

[122]Cf. Art. 11 and 28 VCLT.

[123]Jeffery (1985), p. 17.

[124]Treaty on Political Asylum and Refuge 1939, Adopted in Montevideo on 4 August 1939, Entered into Force on 29 December 1954, AJIL 37(3), Supplement: Official Documents, July 1943, pp. 99–103.

Refuge emerged in the context of diplomatic asylum taking on new forms and with greater intensity during the Spanish Civil War[125]—resulting in a revival of the practice's significance.[126] The treaty constitutes a comprehensive attempt to regulate the issue of diplomatic asylum from its inception until its termination, and indeed the various methods of termination.

In its Preamble, the treaty makes reference to the International Treaty on Penal Law 1889 and acknowledges the need for elaboration thereof in the light of "new situations which have arisen." This is a direct reference to its context and the use of the practice during the Spanish Civil War.

Art. 1 of the Treaty on Political Asylum and Refuge affirms the non-discrimination principle introduced by the Montevideo Convention of 1933 and embellishes it, providing:

> The State which grants asylum does not thereby incur an obligation to admit the refugees into its territory, except in cases where they are not given admission by other States.

Hence, the state granting diplomatic asylum has no subsequent obligation to grant the asylee territorial political asylum, should the asylee succeed in being permitted to leave the territory of the receiving state. This raises the question as to where indeed safe-conduct should lead an asylee to if no state is required to grant him/her territorial asylum. An asylee may in such cases be left in limbo with no possibility to return his/her previous state of residence (and possibly also of nationality) and no established right to asylum elsewhere.

Art. 2 Treaty on Political Asylum and Refuge establishes the conditions for asylum under the convention providing:

> Asylum may be granted only in embassies, legations, men-of-war, military camps or military airplanes, and exclusively to persons pursued for political reasons or offenses, or under circumstances involving concurrent political offenses, which do not legally permit of extradition. The chiefs of mission may also receive refugees in their residences, in cases where the former do not live on the premises of the embassies or legations.

As has become a recurrent theme to Latin American Treaty Law, the broader definition of diplomatic asylum is reaffirmed by this provision. It furthermore provides that the head of the mission's residence may also serve as a place of refuge, additional to the mission premises. This is the first such treaty provision, though its inclusion strongly correlates with the historical development of the practice to include an ambassador's dwelling place.[127] The reservation of the practice for individuals accused of political offences is also reaffirmed by this provision, as well as the prohibition on extradition in such cases. The explicit inclusion of ambassadors' residences as places of asylum ties in with the practice's origins.

---

[125] Cf. Chap. 3: Sect. 3.4.1 and Chapter 7: Annex, Table 7.1, Case Nos 9-38.

[126] UN General Assembly, Question of Diplomatic Asylum, Report of the Secretary-General, 2 September 1975, A/10139 (Part I), para. 63.

[127] See Chap. 3: Sects. 3.1 and 3.2.

Art. 3 Treaty on Political Asylum provides for several exceptions to the practice of diplomatic asylum and upholds the unilateral classification provision of the Montevideo Convention on Political Asylum 1933. The provision holds:

> Asylum shall not be granted to persons accused of political offenses, who shall have been indicted or condemned previously for common offenses, by the ordinary tribunals.
>
> The determination of the causes which induce the asylum appertains to the State which grants it.
>
> Asylum may not be granted to deserters from the sea-, land-, or air forces, except when the act is clearly of a political character.

The first paragraph upholds that the practice of not granting diplomatic asylum to ordinary offenders is in line with the practice's development and history up to 1939. However, this provision goes further than previous provisions, holding that diplomatic asylum cannot be granted to political offenders, who have been convicted of common crimes in the past. Furthermore, deserters from the armed forces are also generally exempt from the provision's scope. The article thus restricts the scope of the practice rather significantly. Moreover, the provision also accords the sending state the right to qualify the offence by permitting it to determine the causes which induce the asylum. Again, this margin of discretion granted to sending states is of course subject to abuse.

Art. 4 Treaty on Political Asylum and Refuge provides for a notification requirement, similar in nature to that of the 1928 Convention on Asylum. It does, however, provide that this notification requirement does not apply "when grave circumstances materially impede such communication or make it dangerous to the safety of the refugees."

Art. 5 provides for certain conditions with which the asylee must comply:

> While the asylum continues, the refugees shall not be permitted to commit acts which may disturb the public tranquillity or may tend toward participation in, or influence upon, political activities. The diplomatic agents or military commanders shall require of the refugees information as to their personal history, and a promise not to enter into external communications without the express intervention of the former. This promise shall be in writing and signed; and if the refugees should refuse to accept, or should violate, any of these conditions, the diplomatic agent or commander shall immediately terminate the asylum...

This provision in part constitutes a reaffirmation of Art. 2 (6) Convention on Asylum 1928,[128] though it is more specific and imposes additional conditions upon the asylee. These conditions also strongly correlate to those codified in the Rules of La Paz and the Rules of Asunción.[129] They underline that diplomatic asylum in the context of Latin America is not an unfettered right bestowed upon a diplomatic asylee, but is in fact subject to conditions with which the asylee is expected to comply. This ties in with modern day practice with regard to the practice, with Julian Assange for example being accused of not complying with the conditions of his asylum due *inter alia* to alleged hacking and intervention into the foreign affairs of

[128] See Chap. 4: Sect. 4.2.2.4.

[129] Cf. Chap. 4: Sects. 4.2.1.2 and 4.2.1.3.

other states[130]—ultimately resulting in his asylum being terminated. Should the asylee fail to comply, this provision also holds that the diplomatic agent is to put an end to the asylum without delay. Again, this ties in with modern day practice, with the termination of Assange's asylum being ascribed to this very reasoning.[131]

Art. 6 Treaty on Political Asylum and Refuge holds that a receiving state may demand that an asylee is removed from its territory as soon as possible. It furthermore provides that a sending state may request the safe-conduct of the asylee from the receiving state "with due regard for the inviolability of the latter's [*the asylee's*] person." The article further holds that where such safe-conduct is not guaranteed by the host state in the first instance, the asylee's exit from the embassy will not take place straight away. This provision further reaffirms that it is only permissible for the asylum to endure for as long as is necessary. Moreover, it underlines that there is no obligation placed on a receiving state to permit an individual safe-conduct.

Art. 7 Treaty on Political Asylum and Refuge holds that an asylee should neither return to the host state after his/her safe-conduct from the mission premises has taken place, nor is such an asylee entitled to subsequent asylum in the diplomatic premises of the sending state where the reason for said asylum no longer exists. This provision essentially prevents the asylee from becoming a burden upon the receiving state, albeit at the same time raising the legitimate question as to where the asylee should go.

Art. 8 Treaty on Political Asylum and Refuge holds that where diplomatic premises are insufficient in capacity to hold diplomatic asylees, "the diplomatic agents or military commanders may provide other places, under the protection of their flag, for the safety and lodging of the said refuge." The article does not specify further or provide examples as to the places of refuge envisaged under the article. Nevertheless, this article constitutes an example of Latin American states embracing the broader definition of diplomatic asylum, to include other places under the protection of the sending (flag) state.[132] Art. 9 of the Treaty, however, restricts the scope of Art. 8 by exempting "men-of-war or military airplanes temporarily located in dry-docks or workshops for repairs" from providing such places of refuge. This provision, therefore, restricts the scope of the right to diplomatic asylum.

Art. 10 Treaty on Political Asylum and Refuge governs the situation in which a severance of diplomatic relations between the sending and the host states has taken place. It holds:

> If in a case of severance of relations, the diplomatic representative who has granted the asylum should have to leave the territory of the country where he is located, he shall depart from it accompanied by the refugees; or, if this should be impossible for some reason not dependent upon the choice of the refugees or of the diplomatic agent, he may deliver them to

[130]The Guardian (2 April 2019), Julian Assange has 'repeatedly violated' asylum terms, Ecuador's president says.

[131]Cf. The Financial Times (11 April 2019), Julian Assange faces extradition to US after arrest in London.

[132]For further information on diplomatic asylum in the context of warships and merchant ships, see Chap. 3: Sects. 3.3.1 and 3.3.2.

> the agent of a third State, with the guaranties specified in this treaty. Such delivery shall be effected by the transfer of the said refugees to the premises of the diplomatic mission which shall have accepted the charge in question, or by leaving the refugees on the premises where the archives of the departing diplomatic mission are kept; and these premises shall remain under the direct protection of the diplomatic agent to whom that function has been intrusted. In either case, the local Ministry for Foreign Affairs shall be duly advised, in conformity with the provisions of Article 4.

This very comprehensive provision, which has the protection of the asylee at its core, ensures that where diplomatic relations are discontinued between the two states, an act which may be initiated by the host state in an attempt to compel the expulsion of the asylee, the status of the asylee remains respected i.e. he/she will not be surrendered to the territorial authorities. In such cases, all diplomatic personnel are required to leave the host state within a reasonable timeframe,[133] taking with them any asylees whose place of refuge becomes defunct. In certain cases where the departure of the asylee with the mission personnel isn't possible, this may entail the appointment of a third state to grant protection to asylees in the premises of its diplomatic mission.[134] Alternatively, the asylee may stay on the premises of the archives of the mission under the protection of the diplomatic agent. A notification requirement is also in place with regard to the host state. This provision ultimately guards against a receiving state severing diplomatic relations in order to compel the sending state to hand over the asylee by ensuring the safe-conduct of the asylee in such cases.

Art. 11 Treaty on Political Asylum and Refuge, which also provides for the inviolability of the asylum granted, follows treaty law that has gone before it[135] but goes further by imposing on sending states an obligation to ensure asylees do not conduct themselves contrary to the "public peace." This also correlates with earlier obligations placed on the diplomatic asylee by both the Rules of La Paz and the Rules of Asunción.[136]

Art. 12 then goes on to provide that asylees may not form groups with the objective of public disturbance and that any such groups will be disbanded. Art. 11 further holds that it is the responsibility of the state granting the asylum to determine the reason(s) behind it and that granting diplomatic asylum does not entitle the diplomatic asylee to territorial asylum in the granting state. This is a notion earlier reflected by Art. 1 of the same treaty.

[133]This principle is now reflected by Art. 9 VCDR.

[134]This custodial function of a third state is reflected on the universal level by Art. 45 (b) and (c) VCDR, albeit referring to the protection of the mission premises and its interests, rather than to asylees.

[135]This being the Convention on Asylum 1928: see Chap. 4: Sect. 4.2.2.4.

[136]Cf. Chap. 4: Sects. 4.2.1.2 and 4.2.1.3.

4.2.2.7 Convention on Diplomatic Asylum (Caracas) 1954[137]

The Convention on Diplomatic Asylum was signed at the Tenth Inter-American Conference in Caracas on 28th March 1954. Argentina, Brazil, Costa Rica, Dominican Republic, Ecuador, El Salvador, Guatemala, Haiti, Mexico, Panama, Paraguay, Peru, Uruguay and Venezuela are the fourteen state parties to the convention. Furthermore, the following six states, Bolivia, Chile, Colombia, Cuba, Honduras and Nicaragua, have also signed, but never ratified, the convention. The Convention on Diplomatic Asylum followed the three-step jurisprudence relating to the diplomatic asylum case of Haya de la Torre.

Art. 1 Convention on Diplomatic Asylum regulates the places in which asylum can and cannot be granted:

> Asylum granted in legations, war vessels, and military camps or aircraft, to persons being sought for political reasons or for political offenses shall be respected by the territorial State in accordance with the provisions of this Convention.
>
> For the purposes of this Convention, a legation is any seat of a regular diplomatic mission, the residence of chiefs of mission, and the premises provided by them for the dwelling places of asylees when the number of the latter exceeds the normal capacity of the buildings.
>
> War vessels or military aircraft that may be temporarily in shipyards, arsenals, or shops for repair may not constitute a place of asylum.

Here, the term "legation" is defined so as to include the residence of the heads of the diplomatic mission. The "political offence" component remains key to this convention. Again, a broad definition of diplomatic asylum is invoked, though the exemptions introduced by Art. 9 Treaty on Political Asylum and Refuge 1939 are also upheld here. Furthermore, Art. 1 Convention on Diplomatic Asylum also goes further than its predecessor, the Treaty on Political Asylum and Refuge,[138] in implying an obligation of the receiving state to provide the sending state with further premises in the event that there are too many diplomatic asylees to be housed in the diplomatic premises and the ambassador's dwelling place.

Art. 2 Convention on Diplomatic Asylum protects a state's sovereign right to grant asylum, as well as its right to refuse an asylum request and indeed its right to not disclose its reasons for doing so. This underlines that the right to grant diplomatic asylum is to be exercised subject to the discretion of a sovereign state. An individual therefore has no claim to such an asylum right.

Art. 3 reaffirms that the practice is reserved for political offences and that deserters of the armed forces are generally exempt from being eligible. This is in line with previous conventions and founding principles such as the Rules of Asunción, the Treaty on International Penal Law, the Treaty of Peace and

---

[137]Convention on Diplomatic Asylum 1954, Adopted in Caracas on 28 March 1954, Entered into Force on 29 December 1954, Registered by the Organisation of American States on 23 October 1986, UNTS Vol. No. 24377, p. 105.

[138]See Chap. 4: Sect. 4.2.2.6.

Friendship, the Convention on Asylum, the Montevideo Convention on Political Asylum and the Treaty on Political Asylum and Refuge.[139]

Art. 4 Convention on Diplomatic Asylum provides that it falls to the state granting asylum to qualify the offence as political or non-political in nature.[140] This convention, like the Montevideo Convention on Political Asylum before it,[141] provides clear guidance as to the issue of qualification—avoiding further disputes over this issue such as that which arose in the context of the Colombian-Peruvian Asylum Case.[142] Nevertheless, this article is still of course subject to the risk of being abused by a sending state.

Art. 5 codifies and reaffirms the urgency requirement, the condition of diplomatic asylum only being permissible for as long as is necessary, and that safe-conduct should be granted by the host state. The latter is specified in further detail than in previous treaties:

> to the end that his life, liberty, or personal integrity may not be endangered, or that the asylee's safety is ensured in some other way.

Therefore, safe-conduct must not endanger the asylee. All of these aforementioned principles have by now become key features of the right to diplomatic asylum.[143]

Art. 6 Convention on Diplomatic Asylum provides a definition of the term "urgent cases" holding:

> Urgent cases are understood to be those, among others, in which the individual is being sought by persons or mobs over whom the authorities have lost control, or by the authorities themselves, and is in danger of being deprived of his life or liberty because of political persecution and cannot, without risk, ensure his safety in any other way.

This definition strongly correlates with the historical evolution of diplomatic asylum in Latin America.[144] Of particular note is that diplomatic asylum must be the asylee's last resort. This conveys the notion that even in the context of Latin America, sending states are reluctant to restrict a host state's sovereignty by way of granting an individual diplomatic asylum unless it is absolutely necessary.

---

[139] Cf. Chap. 4: Sects. 4.2.1.3, 4.2.2.1–4.2.2.2 and 4.2.2.4–4.2.2.6.

[140] For further information on offences which may not be considered political, see IACtHR, Advisory Opinion OC-25/18 of 30 May 2018 Requested by the Republic of Ecuador, The Institution of Asylum and its Recognition as a Human Right in the Inter-American System of Protection (Interpretation and Scope of Articles 5, 22.7 and 22.8 in Relation to Article 1(1) of the American Convention on Human Rights), pp. 32–33, para. 81.

[141] See Chap. 4: Sect. 4.2.2.5.

[142] See Chap. 3: Sect. 3.4.13.1.1.

[143] The urgency requirement was previously contained within the Rules of Lima and the Convention on Asylum; the necessity of the shortest possible duration requirement was previously reflected in the Rules of Lima, the Treaty on International Penal Law and the Convention on Asylum; and safe-conduct was previously codified by the Treaty on International Penal Law, the Convention on Asylum and the Treaty on Political Asylum and Refuge.

[144] Cf. Chapter 3.

Art. 7 provides that it is the responsibility of the granting state to decide the degree of urgency to be accorded to the case. As with previous conventions according the right of qualification to the sending state and as depicted by the case of Haya de la Torre,[145] leaving the issue of qualification, be it of the offence or of the urgency of the case, to the discretion of the sending state carries a risk of abuse.

Art. 8 and 9 Convention on Diplomatic Asylum provide for a notification obligation of the sending state (Art. 8), which is to be considered by the host state (Art. 9) in deciding whether to immediately request the safe-conduct of the asylee. Art. 11 holds that the host state may at any time request the expulsion of the asylee from its territory, hereby ensuring his/her safe-conduct. Equally, the sending state may also at any time request the safe-conduct of the refugee to outside of the host state's territory (Art. 12). These provisions aim to strike a balance between the rights of the sending and receiving states, both of which are to remain informed and entitled to request safe-conduct.

Art. 13–17 Convention on Diplomatic Asylum regulate further stipulations relating to the safe-conduct of the asylee. These provisions have at their core the protection of the fundamental human rights of the asylee. Herein, it is also reaffirmed that the granting state is not obliged to provide the asylee with subsequent territorial asylum.

Art. 18 reaffirms the obligation of the sending state to prevent the asylee from acting in a manner contrary to the public peace, though the convention provides that this obligation falls specifically upon the individual official. It also includes a prohibition on the asylee interfering in the political affairs of the host state. Again, these obligations, to which the asylee is subject, are consistent with previous conventions and principles.[146] Once again, they underline that diplomatic asylum in the context of Latin America is not an unfettered right.

Art. 19 Convention on Diplomatic Asylum re-establishes the rules governing a termination of diplomatic relations between the two states,[147] though in this instance the rules are simplified. Nevertheless, the essence of this rule is still the maintenance of the asylum. Furthermore, in the case of a third state being required to step in to preserve the asylum, state parties to this treaty are favoured.

Finally, Art. 20 Convention on Diplomatic Asylum, as the convention's last substantive provision, reasserts the practice's lack of reciprocity and the non-discrimination principle.[148] The latter has the protection of the asylee's rights at its core.

The Convention on Diplomatic Asylum 1954 is to be regarded as one of the most important treaties in the context of Latin American treaty law relating to diplomatic asylum. It is indeed the only treaty to specifically and exclusively regulate

[145] Cf. Chap. 3: Sect. 3.4.13.1.

[146] Cf. Rules of La Paz, Rules of Asunción and Art. 2 Convention on Asylum.

[147] Established by Art. 10 Treaty on Political Asylum and Refuge. See Chap. 4: Sect. 4.2.2.6.

[148] Thus upholding Art. 3 Montevideo Convention on Political Asylum. See Chap. 4: Sect. 4.2.2.5.

diplomatic asylum.[149] Moreover, it has widespread participation and reaffirms most of the key principles common to the practice. These are specifically: the practice being reserved for political offenders, the urgency requirement, the length of the asylum only being permissible for as long as necessary, safe-conduct, the right of qualification being accorded to the granting state, the lack of reciprocity and the non-discrimination principle.

4.2.3 Applicability of Regional Treaty Law on a Universal Level

Latin American regional treaty law can, of course, not be held to create binding legal obligations for third states.[150] Art. 34 VCLT clearly states that a third state cannot be bound by a treaty without its consent.[151] This body of Latin American treaty law has also not had a strong influence on the diplomatic asylum doctrine under general international law, under which no legal basis for the right to diplomatic asylum could be identified.[152] Arguably, such treaty law can, however, even be held to be indicative of (Latin) American international law.[153] That is international law common to the region in question.[154] However, in the light of Art. 34 VCLT, this Latin American treaty law framework can only be held to be constitutive of Latin American international law.

Latin American practice generally, however, offers little assistance on the issue of interpreting its regional treaty law.[155] Indeed, in many cases in which diplomatic asylum is granted in the context of Latin America, political considerations take precedent over legal issues in the sense that Latin American states rarely question whether or not the receiving state is obliged to respect the asylum granted.[156]

In summary, Latin American treaty law can only be held to be applicable to the region in question and can, at best, only be held to be reflective of Latin American practice with regard to diplomatic asylum.

---

[149]Jeffery (1985), pp. 17–18. Cf. Chap. 4: Sects. 4.2.2.1–4.2.2.6.

[150]Cf. Art. 34 VCLT. This principle was also upheld by the ICJ in Colombian-Peruvian Asylum Case (Colombia v Peru), Judgment of 20 November 1950, ICJ Reports 1950, No. 7, p. 276. This would also be contrary to the fundamental notion of state sovereignty: cf. Art. 2 (1) UN Charter.

[151]Cf. Art. 35 VCLT: Such consent has to be express.

[152]Jeffery (1985), p. 16. Cf. Ronning (1965), p. 22. Nevetheless Kitschenberg hails Latin American treaty law as a development in public international law: Kitschenberg (1965), Einleitung.

[153]The question as to whether American international law includes not just Latin America but also the U.S is controversial.: cf. Esquirol (2012), pp. 563–564. Also see Colombian-Peruvian Asylum Case (Colombia v Peru), Judgment of 20 November 1950, ICJ Reports 1950, No. 7, Dissenting Opinion by Judge Álvarez (translation), p. 292 f.; Ronning (1965), p. 22.

[154]Cf. Chap. 5: Sect. 5.2.

[155]Ronning (1965), p. 59.

[156]Cf. Ronning (1965), p. 66. Also see Chap. 3: Sects. 3.4.2–3.4.14, 3.7.1–3.7.5.

4.2.4 Conclusion

In the light of no corresponding regional treaty framework existing for the other world regions, the above section has detailed the established regional treaty framework of diplomatic asylum in Latin America. This treaty framework both encompasses the fundamental principles established by the Rules of Lima, La Paz and Asunción, all of which interestingly depict states outside and inside Latin America achieving a consensus on the issue of diplomatic asylum, and the treaties themselves, which depict only Latin American states. This displays the progression of the Latin American concept of diplomatic asylum from an issue capable of achieving multi-continental consensus to a distinctly Latin American idea.

Not all of the treaties detailed above can be considered to evidence modern Latin American Treaty Law with regard to the practice: the Treaty on International Penal Law 1889 and the Bolivarian Agreement on Extradition have only five state parties (of a total of twenty modern-day Latin American states); the Treaty of Peace and Friendship 1907 is no longer in force and the Treaty on Political Asylum and Refuge 1939 has only two state parties.

Nevertheless, the rules codified by Latin American treaty law, in particular, the Convention on Asylum 1928 (sixteen state parties), the Montevideo Convention on Political Asylum 1933 (fourteen state parties) and the Convention on Diplomatic Asylum 1954 (fourteen state parties), are of course binding for state parties thereto.[157] They detail certain key characteristics of a Latin American treaty-based right to diplomatic asylum, including the requirement of urgency and necessity, the right to qualification being accorded to the sending state, the right being subject to certain conditions to be fulfilled by the asylee, the principle of non-reciprocity and the right being reserved for individuals accused of political offences.

Latin American treaty law cannot be held to bind states universally as they have not consented to be bound thereto. Furthermore, whether or not a universal right to diplomatic asylum, if it is found to exist in the context of customary international law,[158] would in any way resemble the established regional treaty-based right remains to be seen.

References

Addison Smith G (1911) Right of asylum. LRQ 27(106):199–203

Akinsanya AA (1989) Reflections on the inviolability of diplomatic premises and diplomatic bags. Pakistan Horizon 42(3/4):98–120

Aust A (2010) Handbook of international law, 2nd edn. Cambridge University Press, Cambridge

Barker JC (1996) The abuse of diplomatic privileges and immunities: a necessary evil? Dartmouth, Aldershot

[157]By virtue of Art. 11 f. and Art. 26 VCLT.

[158]See Chap. 5.

Baumann CE (1973) The diplomatic kidnappings: a revolutionary tactic of urban terrorism. Martinus Nijhoff, The Hague
Behrens P (2016) Diplomatic interference and the law. Hart Publishing, Oxford
Bolewski W (2005) Völkerrechtliches Instrument und Gefahren seines Missbrauchs. AdV 43 (4):537–553
Cameron I (1985) First report of the foreign affairs committee of the House of Commons. ICLQ 34 (3):610–620
Capone D (2016) Diplomatic asylum: a new path forward. NCJIL 41:221–247
Caron DD (2012) The ILC articles on state responsibility: the paradoxical relationship between form and authority. AJIL 96:857–873
Chatterjee C (2007) International law and diplomacy. Routledge, London
Clinton-Nolan L (1934) Limitations upon the right of diplomatic Asylum in Peru, 1867. World Aff 97(3):176–178
Corten O (2011) Territorial integrity narrowly interpreted: reasserting the classical inter- state paradigm of international law. LJIL 24:87–94
Crawford J (2012) Articles on responsibility of states for internationally wrongful acts, United Nations audiovisual library of international law. https://legal.un.org/avl/pdf/ha/rsiwa/rsiwa_e.pdf . Last Accessed 15 Dec 2020
Crawford J (2019) Brownlie's principles of public international law, 9th edn. Oxford University Press, Oxford
Dahm G, Delbrück J, Wolfrum R (1989) Völkerrecht, vol I/1, 2nd edn. De Gruyter, Berlin
Den Heijer M (2011) Europe and extraterritorial asylum, Dissertation. Leiden University, Leiden
Denza E (2016) Diplomatic law, Commentary on the Vienna Convention on Diplomatic Relations, 4th edn. Oxford University Press, Oxford
Esquirol JL (2012) Latin America. In: Fassbender B, Peters A, Peter S, Högger D (eds) The Oxford handbook of the history of international law, 1st edn. Oxford University Press, Oxford, pp 553–577
Evans AE (1951) The Colombian-Peruvian asylum case: termination of the judicial phase. AJIL 45 (4):755–762
Falconi Puig JE (2017) Contemporary developments relating to the inviolability of mission premises. In: Behrens P (ed) Diplomatic law in a new millennium. Oxford University Press, Oxford, pp 172–178
Farhangi LS (1986) Insuring against abuse of diplomatic immunity. SLR 38(6):1517–1547
Foakes J, Denza E (2017) Privileges and immunities of diplomatic missions. In: Roberts I (ed) Satow's diplomatic practice, 7th edn. Oxford University Press, Oxford, pp 222–245
Fomerand J (2014) Historical dictionary of human rights. Rowman and Littlefield, Lanham
García-Mora MR (1951) The Colombian-Peruvian Asylum Case and the doctrine of Human Rights. VLR 37(7):927–965
Greenburgh RB (1955) Recent developments in the law of diplomatic asylum. Trans Grotius Soc 41:103–122, Problems of Public and Private International Law
Grugel J, Quijada M (1990) Chile, Spain and Latin America: the right of asylum at the onset of the Second World War. JLAS 22(2):353–374
Happold M (2012) Julian assange and diplomatic Asylum, In: EJIL Blog. https://www.ejiltalk.org/julian-assange-and-diplomatic-asylum/ Last Accessed 15 Dec 2020
Hathaway JC (2005) The rights of refugees under international law. Cambridge University Press, Cambridge
Herdegen M (1986) The abuse of diplomatic privileges and countermeasures not covered by the Vienna Convention on diplomatic relations, some observations in the light of recent British experience. ZaöRV 46:734–757
Jeffery AJ (1985) Diplomatic Asylum: its problems and potential as a means of protecting Human Rights. SAJHR 1:10–30
Jönsson C, Hall M (2005) Essence of diplomacy, studies in diplomacy and international relations. Palgrave MacMillan, Hampshire/New York

Kau M (2019) Der Staat und der Einzelne als Völkerrechtssubjekte. In: Vitzthum W, Proelß A (eds) Völkerrecht, 7th edn. DeGruyter, Berlin, pp 159–318
Kempen B, Hillgruber C (2012) Völkerrecht, 2nd edition, JuS Schriftenreihe. C.H. Beck, Munich
Kimminich O (1961) Asyl in Stützpunkten der UN Truppen. ZfP 8(3):235–240
Kitschenberg H (1965) Das diplomatische Asyl unter besonderer Berücksichtigung des Asylstreits zwischen Kolumbien und Peru, Dissertation. Universität zu Köln, Köln
Kleiner J (2010) Diplomatic practice, between tradition and innovation. World Scientific Publishing Company Limited, Hackensack
Klepper I (2009) Diplomatisches Asyl, Zulässigkeit und Grenzen, Dissertation, Universität zu Köln, vol 4814. Peter Lang Verlag, Frankfurt am Main
Leonard TM (2012) Central American Conference, Washington, 1907. In: Leonard TM, Buchenau J, Longley K, Mount GS (eds) Encyclopedia of U.S. - Latin American relations, vol 1. Sage/CQ Press Publications, Los Angeles/London, p 155
Lo C (2017) Treaty interpretation under the Vienna Convention on the Law of Treaties, a new round of codification. Springer, Singapore
Maginnis VL (2002) Limiting diplomatic immunity: lessons learned from the 1946 Convention on the privileges and immunities of the United Nations. BJIL 28(3):989–1023
Marauhn T, Simon S (2012) Diplomatisches Asyl für Julian Assange. ZJS 5:593–601
McClanahan GV (1989) Diplomatic immunity, principles, practices, problems. Hurst and Company, London
Monasterio LO Guatemalan Refugees in Mexico: A Happy Ending. OAS Department of International Legal Affairs. http://www.oas.org/juridico/english/ortize.html. Last Accessed 15 Dec 2020
Moore JB (1906) A digest of international law, as embodied in diplomatic discussions, treaties and other international agreements, international awards, the decisions of municipal courts and the writings of jurists, vol II. Washington Government Printing Office, Washington
Mugunthan S Diplomatic immunity in the context of International Human Rights. Legal Service India. http://www.legalserviceindia.com/articles/dhuman.htm . Last Accessed 15 Dec 2020
Nur Kayacan D (2016) Julian Assange's allegedly illegal detention by the United Kingdom and Sweden in the Ecuadorian Embassy in London, Master's Thesis. Europa Institut Saarland University, Saarbrücken
Oelfke C, Pröpstl T, Raasch H, Wagner N (2018) Vienna Convention on diplomatic relations of 18 April 1961, Commentaries on practical application. Berliner Wissenschaftsverlag, Berlin
Olleson S (2007) The impact of the ILC's articles on responsibility of states for internationally wrongful acts, British Institute of International and Comparative Law. https://www.biicl.org/files/3107_impactofthearticlesonstate_responsibilitypreliminarydraftfinal.pdf. Last Accessed 15 Dec 2020
Porcino P (1976) Toward codification of diplomatic Asylum. NYUJILP 8:435–456
Pradier-Fodéré P (1881) Cours de droit diplomatique a l'usage des agents politiques du ministère des affaires étrangères des états européens et américains, vol II. G. Pedone-Lauriel, Paris
Rafii M (2014) Diplomatenrecht. In: Schöbener B (ed) Völkerrecht, Lexikon zentraler Begriffe und Themen. C.F. Müller, Heidelberg, pp 52–61
Richtsteig M (2010) Wiener Übereinkommen über diplomatische und konsularische Beziehungen, Entstehungsgeschichte, Kommentierung, Praxis, 2nd edn. Nomos, Baden-Baden
Ronning CN (1965) Diplomatic Asylum: legal norms and political reality in Latin American relations. Martinus Nijhoff, The Hague
Ross MS (2011) Rethinking diplomatic immunity: a review of remedial approaches to address the abuses of diplomatic privileges and immunities. Am Univ Int Law Rev 4(3):173–205
Rossitto AM (1987) Diplomatic Asylum in the United States and Latin America: a comparative analysis. BJIL 13:111–135
Shah P (2007) Asylum, diplomatic. In: MPEPIL (Online). Oxford University Press, Oxford. https://opil.ouplaw.com/view/10.1093/law:epil/9780199231690/law-9780199231690-e756. Last Accessed 15 Dec 2020

Stein T, Von Buttlar C, Kotzur M (2017) Völkerrecht, 14th edn. Verlag Franz Vahlen, Munich
Urrutia-Aparicio C (1960) Diplomatic Asylum in Latin America, Dissertation, American University Guatemala, Editorial del Ministerio de Educación Pública "José de Pineda Ibarra"
Valta M (2019) Staatenbezogene Wirtschaftssanktionen zwischen Souveränität und Menschenrechten, Jus Publicum, Beiträge zum Öffentlichen Recht, Band 283. Mohr Siebeck, Tübingen
von Arnauld A (2019) Völkerrecht, 4th edn. C.F. Müller, Heidelberg
von Pollern H (1980) Das moderne Asylrecht, Völkerrecht und Verfassungsrecht der Bundesrepublik Deutschland, Schriften zum Völkerrecht, Band 67. Duncker & Humblot, Berlin
Wallace RMM (2014) The principle of non-refoulement in international refugee law. In: Chetail V, Bauloz C (eds) Research handbook on international law and migration, Research handbooks on international law. Edward Elgar Publishing Limited, Cheltenham, pp 417–438

Chapter 5
Customary International Law

Having established that international treaty law does not provide a universal legal basis for the practice of diplomatic asylum,[1] it is necessary to analyse customary international law in order to determine whether a legal basis for diplomatic asylum finds its legal roots here. Such a legal basis could exist in the context of customary international law with a universal[2] or regional[3] scope.

5.1 What Is Customary International Law?

The concepts of customary international law and regional custom will first be defined. Secondly, state practice from the following six regions, Africa,[4] Asia,[5] Europe,[6] Latin America,[7] Northern America[8] and Oceania,[9] will be examined in turn in order to determine the extent to which it fulfils the state practice requirement of customary international law. A determination will also be made as to whether regional state practice, which could give rise to regional custom, exists in any of the six regions in question. Then *opinio juris* in favour of the practice, as well as evidence of states rebuking the practice, will be analysed in order to determine

[1]Cf. Chapter 4.
[2]Cf. Chap. 5: Sect. 5.1.
[3]Cf. Chap. 5: Sect. 5.2.
[4]Cf. Chap. 5: Sect. 5.3.1.
[5]Cf. Chap. 5: Sect. 5.3.2.
[6]Cf. Chap. 5: Sect. 5.3.3.
[7]Cf. Chap. 5: Sect. 5.3.4.
[8]Cf. Chap. 5: Sect. 5.3.5.
[9]Cf. Chap. 5: Sect. 5.3.6.

L. Hughes-Gerber, *Diplomatic Asylum*,
https://doi.org/10.1007/978-3-030-73046-8_5

whether a right to diplomatic asylum in international law is constituted regionally or universally.

Unlike treaty law, for which various core principles are codified by the VCLT, customary international law is by nature far less tangible and thus its existence is difficult to determine.[10] It is defined by Art. 38 (1) (b) ICJ Statute as "evidence of a general practice accepted by law." However, even the ICJ has seldom revealed its methodology for deducing the existence of custom,[11] though it has described custom as:

> ...a set of customary rules whose presence in the opinio juris of States can be tested by induction based on the analysis of a sufficiently extensive and convincing practice, and not by deduction from preconceived ideas.[12]

Hence, the ICJ in establishing the formation of customary international law requires the determination of the following objective criteria, (state) practice and *opinio juris*.

In 2000, the International Law Association's Committee on the Formation of Customary (General) International Law adopted the following definition of custom:

> (i) Subject to the Sections which follow, a rule of customary international law is one which is created and sustained by the constant and uniform practice of States and other subjects of international law in or impinging upon their international legal relations, in circumstances which give rise to a legitimate expectation of similar conduct in the future.
>
> (ii) If a sufficiently extensive and representative number of States participate in such a practice in a consistent manner, the resulting rule is one of "general customary international law". Subject to Section 15, such a rule is binding on all States.

---

[10] ILA, London Conference 2000, Committee on the Formation of Customary (General) International Law, Final Report of the Committee, Statement of Principles Applicable to the Formation of General Customary International Law, p. 2. Cf. von Arnauld (2019), p. 110, para. 259. Also see ILC Draft conclusions on identification of customary international law, with commentaries, Adopted by the International Law Commission at its seventieth session, in 2018, and submitted to the General Assembly as a part of the Commission's report covering the work of that session (A/73/10), p. 123.

[11] Talmon (2015), p. 418.

[12] Case Concerning Delimitation of the Maritime Boundary in the Gulf of Maine Area (Canada/ United States of America), Judgment of 12 October 1984, ICJ Reports 1984, No. 67, p. 299, para. 111. Emphasis added. The elements of (state) practice and *opinio juris* have been recognised by various ICJ jurisprudence e.g. Case Concerning the Continental Shelf (Libyan Arab Jamahiriya/ Malta), Judgment of 3 June 1985, ICJ Reports 1985, No. 68, p. 29; para. 27 (later reaffirmed by Legality of the Threat or Use of Nuclear Weapons, Advisory Opinion of 8 July 1996, ICJ Reports 1996, No. 95, p. 253, para. 64); Case Concerning Military and Paramilitary Activities in and against Nicaragua (Nicaragua v United States of America), Merits, Judgment of 27 June 1986, No. 70, pp. 97–98, para. 184; Jurisdictional Immunities of the State (Germany v Italy: Greece Intervening), Judgment of 3 February 2012, ICJ Reports 2012, No. 143, p. 122, para. 55. Even the PCIJ recognised the elements of customary international law, though not by name, when deliberating over whether or not a rule could be held to have customary international law status. Here *opinio juris* was referred to as "being conscious of having a duty:" The Case of the S.S. "Lotus" (France v Turkey), Judgment of 7 September 1927, Publications of the Permanent Court of International Justice, Series A, No. 10, p. 28.

(iii) Where a rule of general customary international law exists, for any particular State to be bound by that rule it is not necessary to prove either that State's consent to it or its belief in the rule's obligatory or (as the case may be) permissive character.[13]

This definition places the emphasis strongly on state practice, with *opinio juris* not even being mentioned. In recent years, however, the emphasis has been placed increasingly less on state practice.[14] Indeed Cheng goes so far as to hold that custom has in reality only one constitutive element, *opinio juris*.[15] The focus has very much shifted to interpretative law-finding methods.[16]

Examples of customary international law norms include maritime delimitation,[17] natural prolongation regarding the law of the sea,[18] fishery zones and preferential fishing rights,[19] exhaustion of local remedies before instituting international proceedings,[20] the methods for establishing, presenting and settling an international claim,[21] the right to send warships through international straits[22] and termination of a treaty on account of a change of circumstances.[23]

Before customary international law with regard to diplomatic asylum can be examined in its constituent parts, state practice and *opinio juris,* in order to establish whether its requirements are fulfilled, it is first necessary to define the constituent elements of customary international law.

[13] ILA, London Conference 2000, Committee on the Formation of Customary (General) International Law, Final Report of the Committee, Statement of Principles Applicable to the Formation of General Customary International Law, p. 8. Emphasis added.

[14] Bradley and Goldsmith (1997), p. 839; Peterson (2008), p. 503.

[15] Cheng (1997), p. 138.

[16] Peterson (2008), p. 503.

[17] Case Concerning Delimitation of the Maritime Boundary in the Gulf of Maine Area (Canada/United States of America), Judgment of 12 October 1984, ICJ Reports 1984, No. 67, p. 300, para. 113.

[18] Case Concerning the Continental Shelf (Tunisia/Libyan Arab Jamahiriya), Judgment of 24 February 1982, ICJ Reports 1982, No. 63, p. 46, para. 43.

[19] Fisheries Jurisdiction Case (Federal Republic of Germany v Iceland), Merits, Judgment of 25 July 1974, ICJ Reports 1974, No. 56, p. 192, para. 44; Fisheries Jurisdiction Case (United Kingdom of Great Britain and Northern Ireland v Iceland), Merits, Judgment of 25 July 1974, ICJ Reports 1974, No. 55, p. 23, para. 52.

[20] Interhandel Case (Switzerland v United States of America), Preliminary Objections, Judgment of 21 March 1959, ICJ Reports 1959, No. 34, p. 27.

[21] Reparation for Injuries Suffered in the Service of the United Nations, Advisory Opinion of 11 April 1949, ICJ Reports 1949, No. 4, p. 177.

[22] The Case of the S.S. "Lotus" (France v Turkey), Judgment of 7 September 1927, Publications of the Permanent Court of International Justice, Series A, No. 10, p. 28.

[23] Fisheries Jurisdiction Case (Federal Republic of Germany v Iceland), Jurisdiction of the Court, Judgment of 2 February 1973, ICJ Reports 1973, No. 56, p. 63, para. 36; Fisheries Jurisdiction Case (United Kingdom of Great Britain and Northern Ireland v Iceland), Jurisdiction of the Court, Judgment of 2 February 1973, ICJ Reports 1973, No. 55, p. 18, para. 36.

5.1.1 State Practice

Though state practice is the more straightforward of the two requirements constituting customary international law, the term is vague and Art. 38 (1) (b) ICJ Statute provides no definition or qualification of the term.

ICJ jurisprudence has, however, been more fruitful in providing various guidance as to what kind of state practice, and indeed to what extent, is required for customary international law. The North Sea Continental Shelf Case held that state practice must be "virtually uniform."[24] In this regard, the Case Concerning Military and Paramilitary Activities in and against Nicaragua Merits judgment held:

> The Court does not consider that, for a rule to be established as customary, the corresponding practice must be in absolutely rigorous conformity with the rule. In order to deduce the existence of customary rules, the Court deems it sufficient that the conduct of States should, in general, be consistent with such rules, and that instances of State conduct inconsistent with a given rule should generally have been treated as breaches of that rule, not as indications of the recognition of a new rule.[25]

Therefore, for a rule to be considered customary in nature, the standard required is not absolute uniformity but instead general consistency. State conduct opposing such a rule is possible only insofar as such conduct is regarded as a breach of this rule, rather than evidence of a newly forming rule.[26]

Moreover, the passage of a certain amount of time is not necessary to constitute custom so long as its requirements are fulfilled.[27] The North Sea Continental Shelf case also introduced the concept of so-called "specially-affected states" i.e. states,

---

[24]North Sea Continental Shelf (Federal Republic of Germany v Denmark/Federal Republic of Germany v Netherlands), Judgment of 20 February 1969, ICJ Reports 1969, Nos 51 and 52, p. 43, para. 74.

[25]Case Concerning Military and Paramilitary Activities in and against Nicaragua (Nicaragua v United States of America), Merits, Judgment of 27 June 1986, No. 70, p. 98, para. 186. Cf. Case Concerning Delimitation of the Maritime Boundary in the Gulf of Maine Area (Canada/United States of America), Judgment of 12 October 1984, ICJ Reports 1984, No. 67, p. 299, para. 111 speaking of a "sufficiently extensive and convincing practice..." Also see Fisheries Jurisdiction Case (United Kingdom of Great Britain and Northern Ireland v Iceland), Merits, Judgment of 25 July 1974, ICJ Reports 1974, No. 55, p. 39, para. 79 and Fisheries Jurisdiction Case (Federal Republic of Germany v Iceland), Merits, Judgment of 25 July 1974, ICJ Reports 1974, No. 56, p. 212, para. 77 providing that rules governing fisheries jurisdiction still evolving in the light of varied and opposing state practice have not yet become customary international law.

[26]ILC Draft conclusions on identification of customary international law, with commentaries, Adopted by the International Law Commission at its seventieth session, in 2018, and submitted to the General Assembly as a part of the Commission's report covering the work of that session (A/73/10), p. 137.

[27]North Sea Continental Shelf (Federal Republic of Germany v Denmark/Federal Republic of Germany v Netherlands), Judgment of 20 February 1969, ICJ Reports 1969, Nos 51 and 52, p. 43, para. 74. Also see ILC Draft conclusions on identification of customary international law, with commentaries, Adopted by the International Law Commission at its seventieth session, in 2018, and submitted to the General Assembly as a part of the Commission's report covering the work of that session (A/73/10), p. 136.

the interests of which are specially affected rendering their state practice weightier than that of states less affected by the issue in question.[28] A criticism of customary international law in this regard is that in practice, larger more powerful states tend to act as specially affected states in that their practice is rendered weightier in the formation of customary international law.[29]

State practice can stem from acts of the executive, legislature or judiciary of a state.[30] Importantly, omissions may also constitute state practice.[31] There is, however, controversy among international lawyers as to which state acts can specifically give rise to state practice.[32]

5.1.1.1 ICJ Jurisprudence

From the definition of the ILA and the jurisprudence of the ICJ, one can surmise that state practice must be common to a significant number of states in order to create a rule of customary international law.[33] Exactly how many states are required is, however, controversial.[34] Indeed, the ILC has rejected to establish an absolute quantitative standard to quantify state practice,[35] though the practice of the ICJ can be examined in this respect.

---

[28]North Sea Continental Shelf (Federal Republic of Germany v Denmark/Federal Republic of Germany v Netherlands), Judgment of 20 February 1969, ICJ Reports 1969, Nos 51 and 52, pp. 42–43, paras 73–74. Also see ILC Draft conclusions on identification of customary international law, with commentaries, Adopted by the International Law Commission at its seventieth session, in 2018, and submitted to the General Assembly as a part of the Commission's report covering the work of that session (A/73/10), p. 136.

[29]Cf. Danilenko (1993), p. 96. In this regard, it has also been questioned whether in practice only larger more powerful states possess sovereignty: see Krüger (1957), p. 1.

[30]Cf. Jurisdictional Immunities of the State (Germany v Italy: Greece Intervening), Judgment of 3 February 2012, ICJ Reports 2012, No. 143, p. 123, para. 55; ILC Draft conclusions on identification of customary international law, with commentaries, Adopted by the International Law Commission at its seventieth session, in 2018, and submitted to the General Assembly as a part of the Commission's report covering the work of that session (A/73/10), p. 134.

[31]Da Rocha et al. (2013), p. 189.

[32]Cf. Peterson (2008), pp. 502–503. For further information on the forms of practice which can suffice to fulfil the state practice requirement see ILC Draft conclusions on identification of customary international law, with commentaries, Adopted by the International Law Commission at its seventieth session, in 2018, and submitted to the General Assembly as a part of the Commission's report covering the work of that session (A/73/10), p. 133 f.

[33]Weisburd (2009), p. 302.

[34]Cf. Peterson (2008), p. 502.

[35]ILC Draft conclusions on identification of customary international law, with commentaries, Adopted by the International Law Commission at its seventieth session, in 2018, and submitted to the General Assembly as a part of the Commission's report covering the work of that session (A/73/10), p. 136. In this regard, the ILC however held its draft conclusions to "aim to offer clear guidance without being overly prescriptive:" ILC Draft conclusions on identification of customary international law, with commentaries, Adopted by the International Law Commission at its seventieth session, in 2018, and submitted to the General Assembly as a part of the Commission's report covering the work of that session (A/73/10), p. 123.

The ICJ has tended not to quantify state practice but has at times held the number of states in favour of a norm or the number of state parties to a treaty to be declaratory in value with regard to the formation of customary international law.[36] For example, in Legal Consequences of the Separation of the Chagos Archipelago from Mauritius in 1965, the ICJ held that eighty-nine states voting in favour of a resolution on self-determination, with no states contesting the existence of such a right and nine states abstaining due to the time period required for implementation, rendered the resolution declaratory in character with regard to the formation of a customary international law norm on self-determination.[37] Similarly in Case Concerning the Territorial Dispute,[38] Legality of the Use by a State of Nuclear Weapons in Armed Conflict,[39] the LaGrand Case[40] and Case Concerning Armed Activities on the Territory of the Congo (New Application: 2002,[41] the Court held that rules contained in the VCLT were declaratory of their customary international law status.[42] In this vein, in both Case Concerning the Continental Shelf (Libyan Arab Jamahiriya/ Malta)[43] and Case Concerning Maritime Delimitation and Territorial Questions between Qatar and Bahrain,[44] the ICJ held that rules pertaining to maritime rights of a coastal state and the continental shelf respectively, both of which were contained in the UNCLOS,[45] were reflective of customary international law.[46] Moreover, in

---

[36]Cf. Case Concerning the Continental Shelf (Libyan Arab Jamahiriya/Malta), Judgment of 3 June 1985, ICJ Reports 1985, No. 68, p. 29, para. 27: "...multilateral conventions may have an important role to play in recording and defining rules deriving from custom[.]".

[37]Legal Consequences of the Separation of the Chagos Archipelago from Mauritius in 1965, Advisory Opinion of 25 February 2019, ICJ Reports 2019, No. 169, p. 132, para. 152.

[38]Case Concerning the Territorial Dispute (Libyan Arab Jamahiriya/Chad), Judgment of 3 February 1994, ICJ Reports 1994, No. 83, p. 21, para. 41.

[39]Legality of the Use by a State of Nuclear Weapons in Armed Conflict, Advisory Opinion of 8 July 1996, ICJ Reports 1996, p. 75.

[40]LaGrand Case (Germany v United States of America), Judgment of 27 June 2001, ICJ Reports 2001, No. 104, p. 501, para. 99.

[41]Case Concerning Armed Activities on the Territory of the Congo (New Application: 2002) (Democratic Republic of the Congo v Rwanda), Jurisdiction of the Court and Admissibility of the Application, Judgment of 3 February 2006, ICJ Reports 2006, No. 126, pp. 51–52, para. 125.

[42]This is also an example of overlapping treaty and customary law norms. As of April 2021, the VCLT has 116 state parties. At the time of the Case Concerning Armed Activities on the Territory of the Congo (New Application: 2002 judgment in February 2006, it had 105; at the time of the LaGrand Case judgment in June 2001, it had 104; at the time of the Legality of the Use by a State of Nuclear Weapons in Armed Conflict advisory opinion in July 1996, it had 91; and at the time of the Case Concerning the Territorial Dispute judgment in February 1994, it had 87.

[43]Case Concerning the Continental Shelf (Libyan Arab Jamahiriya/Malta), Judgment of 3 June 1985, ICJ Reports 1985, No. 68, p. 55, para. 77.

[44]Case Concerning Maritime Delimitation and Territorial Questions between Qatar and Bahrain (Qatar v Bahrain), Merits, Judgment of 16 March 2001, ICJ Reports 2001, No. 87, p. 97, para. 185.

[45]United Nations Convention on the Law of the Sea, Adopted in Montego Bay on 10 December 1982, Entered into Force on 16 November 1994, UNTS Vol. No. 1833, p. 3.

[46]As of April 2021, the UNCLOS has 168 state parties. At the time of the Case Concerning Maritime Delimitation and Territorial Questions between Qatar and Bahrain judgment in March

Case Concerning the Arrest Warrant of 11 April 2000, the ICJ also held that rules contained in the VCDR[47] and the VCCR[48] were reflective of custom.[49]

In such cases, the ICJ effectively held that the number of state parties to a treaty may be indicative of a rule's customary law status, where such a rule is reflected by a treaty provision in said treaty.[50]

Former ICJ Judge Shahabuddeen has furthermore stated that new ICJ jurisprudence can also influence the development of state practice.[51] Similarly, resolutions of the General Assembly may also inspire new customary international law practices.[52]

5.1.1.2 Conclusion

Whilst the jurisprudence of the ICJ provides far from clear guidance as to exactly how much state practice is required for the formation of customary international law, of the aforementioned cases referencing customary international law, the vast majority refer to at least 87 member states in favour of a practice, displayed either through state practice or through treaty ratification, as being declaratory of custom. In line with this rationale, as there are currently 195 sovereign states,[53] the quantitative benchmark for the formation of customary international law with a universal scope would be approximately half of all state parties being in favour of such a norm,[54]

2001, the Convention had 135 state parties. At the time of the Case Concerning the Continental Shelf (Libyan Arab Jamahiriya/Malta) judgment in June 1985, the UNCLOS had only a handful of state parties and had yet to enter into force.

[47] As of April 2021, the VCDR has 192 state parties. At the time of the judgment in February 2002, the Convention had 180 state parties.

[48] As of April 2021, the VCCR has 180 state parties. At the time of the judgment in February 2002, it had 167.

[49] Case Concerning the Arrest Warrant of 11 April 2000 (Democratic Republic of the Congo v Belgium), Judgment of 14 February 2002, ICJ Reports 2002, No. 121, p. 21, para. 52.

[50] Cf. Conclusion 11 ILC Draft conclusions on identification of customary international law, with commentaries, Adopted by the International Law Commission at its seventieth session, in 2018, and submitted to the General Assembly as a part of the Commission's report covering the work of that session (A/73/10), p. 143 f.

[51] Shahabuddeen (1996), p. 209. Cf. Case Concerning Delimitation of the Maritime Boundary in the Gulf of Maine Area (Canada/United States of America), Judgment of 12 October 1984, ICJ Reports 1984, No. 67, p. 293, para. 91 stating that the North Sea Continental Shelf Case has greatly contributed to the formation of customary international law in the field.

[52] Voyiakis (2011), p. 209.

[53] The 193 member states of the United Nations, plus the two observer states.

[54] Though 87 is 45% of 195, this calculation takes account of the fact that the number of states has increased in the time since these judgments/advisory opinions.

accounting also for the qualitative guidance of the ILC in this respect providing that in order to be general, practice must be widespread, representative and consistent.[55]

5.1.2 *Opinio Juris*

Opinio juris is less tangible and more difficult to identify or even to define.[56] Cassese defines it as "the conviction that. . .practice reflects to, or amounts to, law."[57] The ILC similarly defines this element as "accepted as law."[58] How to evidence this conviction is, however, far from straightforward.

The question as to whether *opinio juris* is constitutive or merely declaratory in value for the formation of customary international law is also controversial. The constitutive theory, for example, holds that a state is required to consent before it becomes bound by a rule of customary international law status.[59] On the other hand, from the perspective of the declaratory view, the requirement itself has been held to be contradictory, as it requires evidence of a conviction that a practice is legally binding before it actually strictly becomes legally binding i.e. states must believe themselves to be bound by a rule before the *opinio juris* element is actually constituted and therefore before states are actually bound by said rule.[60]

Examples of *opinio juris* include a consensus among scholarly writings or in the context of international/national jurisprudence.[61] Further examples include express statements by states,[62] oral pleadings before international

[55]Cf. Conclusion 8 ILC Draft conclusions on identification of customary international law, with commentaries, Adopted by the International Law Commission at its seventieth session, in 2018, and submitted to the General Assembly as a part of the Commission's report covering the work of that session (A/73/10), p. 135 f.

[56]See e.g. Crawford et al. (2013), p. 10; Kammerhofer (2004), p. 532 f.

[57]Cassese (2005), p. 156.

[58]International Law Commission, Report of the work of the sixty-sixth session (5 May–6 June and 7 July–8 August 2014), General Assembly Official Records, sixty-ninth session, Supplement No. 10 (A/69/10), p. 242, para. 145. Cf. Roberts and Sivakumaran (2018), p. 92.

[59]Kammerhofer (2004), p. 533. This view is also in line with the fundamental principle of state sovereignty, codified in Art. 2 (1) UN Charter.

[60]Cf. Elias (1995), pp. 502–503; Roberts and Sivakumaran (2018), p. 96.

[61]Crawford (2019), p. 24.

[62]Jurisdictional Immunities of the State (Germany v Italy: Greece Intervening), Judgment of 3 February 2012, ICJ Reports 2012, No. 143, p. 123, para. 55; Dumberry (2016), p. 310; Cf. Conclusion 10 ILC Draft conclusions on identification of customary international law, with commentaries, Adopted by the International Law Commission at its seventieth session, in 2018, and submitted to the General Assembly as a part of the Commission's report covering the work of that session (A/73/10), p. 140.

courts,[63] diplomatic correspondence[64] and resolutions of international organisations.[65]

The ICJ has defined *opinio juris* in the context of the North Sea Continental Shelf Cases, holding:

> Not only must the acts concerned amount to a settled practice, but they must also be such, or be carried out in such a way, as to be evidence of a belief that this practice is rendered obligatory by the existence of a rule of law requiring it... The States concerned must therefore feel that they are conforming to what amounts to a legal obligation.[66]

Therefore, state conduct must not only be sufficiently consistent, general and uniform to fulfil the state practice requirement, but it must also occur based upon a notion that there is a legal obligation compelling the state to act in this way.[67]

Paradoxically, state practice itself may also provide evidence of *opinio juris*.[68]

---

[63] Crawford et al. (2013), p. 10.

[64] Cf. Conclusion 10 ILC Draft conclusions on identification of customary international law, with commentaries, Adopted by the International Law Commission at its seventieth session, in 2018, and submitted to the General Assembly as a part of the Commission's report covering the work of that session (A/73/10), p. 140.

[65] International Law Commission, Report of the work of the sixty-sixth session (5 May–6 June and 7 July–8 August 2014), General Assembly Official Records, sixty-ninth session, Supplement No. 10 (A/69/10), p. 246, para. 171.

[66] North Sea Continental Shelf (Federal Republic of Germany v Denmark/Federal Republic of Germany v Netherlands), Judgment of 20 February 1969, ICJ Reports 1969, Nos 51 and 52, p. 44, para. 77.

[67] Cf. Conclusion 9 ILC Draft conclusions on identification of customary international law, with commentaries, Adopted by the International Law Commission at its seventieth session, in 2018, and submitted to the General Assembly as a part of the Commission's report covering the work of that session (A/73/10), p. 138 f.

[68] Cf. North Sea Continental Shelf (Federal Republic of Germany v Denmark/Federal Republic of Germany v Netherlands), Judgment of 20 February 1969, ICJ Reports 1969, Nos 51 and 52, p. 44, para. 77; Fisheries Jurisdiction Case (United Kingdom of Great Britain and Northern Ireland v Iceland), Merits, Judgment of 25 July 1974, ICJ Reports 1974, No. 55, p. 26, para. 58; Case Concerning Delimitation of the Maritime Boundary in the Gulf of Maine Area (Canada/United States of America), Judgment of 12 October 1984, ICJ Reports 1984, No. 67, p. 299, para. 111; Case Concerning the Continental Shelf (Libyan Arab Jamahiriya/Malta), Judgment of 3 June 1985, ICJ Reports 1985, No. 68, p. 38, para. 44; Case Concerning Military and Paramilitary Activities in and against Nicaragua (Nicaragua v United States of America), Merits, Judgment of 27 June 1986, No. 70, p. 98, para. 184; Legality of the Threat or Use of Nuclear Weapons, Advisory Opinion of 8 July 1996, ICJ Reports 1996, No. 95, p. 254, para. 67. Also see Lepard (2010), pp. 133–134. Akehurst holds that in order to give rise to customary international law, *opinio juris* can only be inferred from state practice where a state is claiming the conduct in question is permissible and not when claiming the conduct in question is required or prohibited, where express approval is required: Akehurst (1975), p. 53.

5.2 Regional Custom

Regional, special or local custom[69] may be defined as rules of customary international law with a purely regional scope. The practice of regional custom has a longstanding history.[70] Regional custom exists in contrast to universal or general custom, which has a universal scope. In this regard, the ICJ has distinguished between such rules with a solely regional impact and the application of general rules regionally.[71] Thus, regional custom denotes a norm legally binding only for a particular region. Examples of such regional custom include agricultural rights,[72] rights of passage[73] or land-related rights such as those applicable in a boundary dispute.[74]

In contrast, general customary international law rules may be applied regionally. As an example, a state may terminate a regional treaty due to a fundamental change in circumstances. Though the treaty is regional in scope, the customary international law norm permitting the treaty termination is a rule of general international law applied to the region in question.

In Colombian-Peruvian Asylum Case, Colombia argued the existence of such a local custom providing for a right to diplomatic asylum common to Latin American states,[75] the existence of which the Court argued had not been proven.[76] However, in Case Concerning the Rights of Nationals of the United States of America in

---

[69]This requires the practice of a minimum of two states to be constituted: Case Concerning Right of Passage Over Indian Territory (Portugal v India), Merits, Judgment of 12 April 1960, ICJ Reports 1960, No. 32, p. 39. Cf. Case Concerning the Rights of Nationals of the United States of America in Morocco (France v United States of America), Judgment of 27 August 1952, ICJ Reports 1952, No. 11, p. 200. For further information on regional custom, see D'Amato (1969), p. 211 f. Also see Conclusion 16 ILC Draft conclusions on identification of customary international law, with commentaries, Adopted by the International Law Commission at its seventieth session, in 2018, and submitted to the General Assembly as a part of the Commission's report covering the work of that session (A/73/10), p. 155 f.

[70]Cf. D'Amato (1969), p. 213.

[71]Cf. Case Concerning the Frontier Dispute (Burkina Faso/Republic of Mali), Judgment of 22 December 1986, ICJ Reports 1986, No. 69, p. 565, para. 21. Cf. Case Concerning Right of Passage Over Indian Territory (Portugal v India), Merits, Judgment of 12 April 1960, ICJ Reports 1960, No. 32, p. 11 f.

[72]Cf. Case Concerning the Frontier Dispute (Burkina Faso/Republic of Mali), Judgment of 22 December 1986, ICJ Reports 1986, No. 69, p. 617, para. 116.

[73]Cf. Case Concerning Right of Passage Over Indian Territory (Portugal v India), Merits, Judgment of 12 April 1960, ICJ Reports 1960, No. 32, p. 44.

[74]D'Amato (1969), p. 211.

[75]Colombian-Peruvian Asylum Case (Colombia v Peru), Judgment of 20 November 1950, ICJ Reports 1950, No. 7, p. 276 f.

[76]Colombian-Peruvian Asylum Case (Colombia v Peru), Judgment of 20 November 1950, ICJ Reports 1950, No. 7, p. 277.

Morocco, the ICJ referred to diplomatic asylum as an example of such a local custom.[77]

The requirements of regional custom are the same as those for universal customary international law, with the state practice and *opinio juris* required being limited to the region in question, and with the requirements being stricter particularly with regard to consistency of practice.[78] Regional custom is to be regarded as distinct from universal custom and the presence of a rule of regional customary international law status cannot alone influence the development of universal custom, save for the requirements of universal custom being met. Equally, many regional customs, e.g. rules applicable in a bilateral boundary dispute, are by their very nature not applicable universally.

5.3 State Practice with Regard to the Practice of Diplomatic Asylum

Having defined the requirements of customary international law,[79] it is necessary to establish whether these requirements are fulfilled with regard to the practice of diplomatic asylum. The requirements will be analysed in turn, starting with state practice. Various state practice from all six major continents will be examined, with assistance from Table 7.1,[80] in order ultimately to conclude whether universal or regional state practice in favour of the practice exists.

5.3.1 Africa

There is no significant state practice from the African continent to support a right to diplomatic asylum. Indeed, Table 7.1 provides for only four cases in which an

---

[77]Case Concerning the Rights of Nationals of the United States of America in Morocco (France v United States of America), Judgment of 27 August 1952, ICJ Reports 1952, No. 11, p. 200. Cf. D'Amato (1969), p. 212; Roberts and Sivakumaran (2018), p. 97; ILC Draft conclusions on identification of customary international law, with commentaries, Adopted by the International Law Commission at its seventieth session, in 2018, and submitted to the General Assembly as a part of the Commission's report covering the work of that session (A/73/10), p. 155.

[78]ILC Draft conclusions on identification of customary international law, with commentaries, Adopted by the International Law Commission at its seventieth session, in 2018, and submitted to the General Assembly as a part of the Commission's report covering the work of that session (A/73/10), p. 156.

[79]Cf. Chap. 5: Sect. 5.1.

[80]It is important to note at thie stage that Table 7.1 is not intended to be an exhaustive list of twentieth/twenty-first Century diplomatic asylum cases, with further unreported cases being very much assumed. It is therefore important to consider that the actual extent of the respective state practice detailed hereunder may in fact be far greater.

African state depicted the state granting the asylum: those of Algeria and Egypt granting diplomatic asylum to a number of Albanian asylum seekers in July 1990,[81] that of Nigeria granting diplomatic asylum to 1800 people in around August 1990[82] and that of Malian Amadou Toumani Toure, who was granted asylum for a 2-day period in the diplomatic premises of Senegal in April 2012.[83] Due to the isolated nature of these cases, depicting only four African states and with no African state granting diplomatic asylum on more than one occasion, the state practice requirement of regional customary international law cannot be held to be fulfilled with regard to African states, of which there are 54.

Though of course, the African continent found itself in the throes of colonialism up until the middle of the twentieth century, with most modern-day African states not yet being 70 years old, the sparsity of state practice in Africa is nevertheless notable.

5.3.2 Asia

Asian state practice with regard to a right of diplomatic asylum is somewhat more fruitful. Table 7.1 provides for a total of 25 twentieth/twenty-first century cases in which an Asian state depicted the state granting a right to diplomatic asylum. The majority of these cases also depict isolated incidents in which a state exceptionally recognised a right to diplomatic asylum: i.e. the asylum granted to Iraqi Sharif Ali bin al-Hussein and family by Saudi Arabia in 1958;[84] to a number of Albanian asylum seekers by China in July 1990;[85] to seven North Korean Asylum Seekers by Thailand in June 2005;[86] to Honduran Xiomara Hortensia Zelaya and her 5-year-old child by Taiwan from June—July 2009,[87] to Iranian Shahram Amiri by

[81] The New York Times (4 July 1990), Evolution in Europe; Albanians Take Refuge in Embassies; The Washington Post (4 July 1990), Albanians Seek Asylum in Embassies. Cf. Chap. 7: Annex, Table 7.1, Case Nos 121 and 126.

[82] The New York Times (11 August 1990), 5 Nations Moving Troops to Liberia. Cf. Chap. 7: Annex, Table 7.1, Case No. 135.

[83] BBC News (18 April 2012), Mali's Amadou Toumani Toure in Senegal's embassy; BBC News (20 April 2012), Mali's ex-leader Amadou Toumani Toure flees to Senegal. Cf. Chap. 7: Annex, Table 7.1, Case No. 185.

[84] See: The New York Times (2 April 2001), London Journal; If Iraq Ever Needs a King, Here's a Dapper Hopeful; The New York Times (28 January 2005), The King Is Dead (Has Been for 46 Years) but Two Iraqis Hope: Long Live the King! Cf. Chap. 7: Annex, Table 7.1, Case No. 56.

[85] The New York Times (4 July 1990), Evolution in Europe; Albanians Take Refuge in Embassies; The Washington Post (4 July 1990), Albanians Seek Asylum in Embassies. Cf. Chap. 7: Annex, Table 7.1, Case No. 124.

[86] See Reuters (11 July 2007), Four North Koreans enter Danish embassy in Hanoi. Cf. Chap. 7: Annex, Table 7.1, Case No. 170.

[87] See Taiwan Today (30 September 2009), Deposed Honduran leader's daughter granted asylum. Cf. Chap. 7: Annex, Table 7.1, Case No. 179.

Iran/Pakistan[88] in July 2010[89] and to Malidivian Mohamed Nasheed by India in February 2013.[90] Vietnam rejected to grant a right of diplomatic asylum to North Korean Kim Ryen-hi in March 2016.[91]

However, several Asian states have granted a right to diplomatic asylum on multiple occasions, warranting a closer analysis of their practice. Table 7.1 provides for the following states as having recognised a right to diplomatic asylum on two separate occasions: Indonesia, North Korea and Japan. Turkey, the state practice of which will be evaluated hereunder owing to the majority of its territory being situated within the continent of Asia, has granted a right to diplomatic asylum on four occasions detailed by Table 7.1. South Korea, however, has granted a right to diplomatic asylum on eight separate occasions recorded by Table 7.1. The state practice of these states will thus be examined in turn in the following sections.

5.3.2.1 Indonesia

Indonesia recognised a right to diplomatic asylum in favour of Filipino Alfredo B. Saulo in November 1958[92] and in favour of Laotian Kong Le in 1966.[93] Both cases occurred in a short timeframe, now over 50 years ago.

5.3.2.2 North Korea

North Korea granted asylum to its own diplomat O Nam Chol from 1982 to 1983[94] and to its own citizens Hyon Kwang Song, Kim Uk Il and Ri Ji U in February/March

[88] Amiri sought refuge in the Iranian interest section of the Pakistani diplomatic mission in Washington D.C: The Guardian (14 July 2010), Iranian nuclear scientist Shahram Amiri heads home.

[89] The Guardian (14 July 2010), Iranian nuclear scientist Shahram Amiri heads home. Cf. Chap. 7: Annex, Table 7.1, Case No. 182.

[90] See The Hindu (23 February 2013), Nasheed leaves Indian embassy after 'deal'. Cf. Chap. 7: Annex, Table 7.1, Case No. 189.

[91] As Ms Ryen-hi was not immediately expelled from the diplomatic premises, this constitutes a case of *de facto* diplomatic asylum: see The New York Times (7 March 2016), North Korean Defector in South Seeks Vietnam's Help to Return Home. Cf. Chap. 7: Annex, Table 7.1, Case No. 195.

[92] Balbastro (1959), p. 350 f. Also see: Official Gazette (14 November 1958), Statement: President Garcia at his regular weekly press conference; The Official Gazette (17 November 1958), Official Week in Review: November 9 - November 15, 1958. Cf. Chap. 7: Annex, Table 7.1, Case No. 57.

[93] See for example Scott (1989), p. 162. Cf. Chap. 7: Annex, Table 7.1, Case No. 64.

[94] See Farhangi (1986), p. 1525. For further information on Chol's stay, also see The New York Times (9 December 1982), U.S. Stand on Envoy Backed by U.N. Aide; The New York Times (22 July 1983), U.S. Threatens to Expel Envoy in Assault Case, The New York Times (29 July 1983), The Region; Korean Diplomat Heads for Home. Cf. Chap. 7: Annex, Table 7.1, Case No. 91.

2017.[95] Both cases involve North Korea granting refuge to its own citizens and thus depict North Korea extending diplomatic protection to them. Such cases are not typical diplomatic asylum cases, with most cases depicting a sending state granting diplomatic protection to non-nationals.[96]

5.3.2.3 Japan

Japan granted a right to diplomatic asylum to five North Korean asylum seekers in May 2002[97] and then again to a further 29 North Korean asylum seekers in September 2004.[98] In these cases, asylum was granted to nationals of one state in a short time frame. Both cases therefore depict atypical cases, in which asylum was granted in exceptional circumstances, though this characteristic of course remains a key feature of the right to diplomatic asylum in Latin America.[99] Owing to the political climate in North Korea at the time, both cases are in any case likely to have been motivated rather by political considerations than a conviction relating to the legally binding nature of the practice on the part of Japan.

5.3.2.4 Turkey

Turkey[100] has, according to Table 7.1, recognised a right to diplomatic asylum on four separate occasions. Turkey granted diplomatic asylum to 923 (presumably all Spanish) asylees in the context of the Spanish civil war in the years between 1936 and 1939.[101] It also recognised a right to diplomatic asylum in favour of Hungarian Miklós Kállay in 1944,[102] in favour of 32 Albanian asylum seekers in July 1990[103]

---

[95] The Telegraph (22 February 2017), Exclusive: North Korean suspects in Kim Jong-nam murder 'hiding' in Pyongyang's embassy in Kuala Lumpur; The Seattle Times (31 March 2017), Malaysia interviewed, cleared 3 N. Koreans before they left. Cf. Chap. 7: Annex, Table 7.1, Case No. 197.

[96] Cf. Chap. 7: Annex, Table 7.1.

[97] Chicago Tribune (10 May 2002), Beijing defends raid to seize N. Koreans; The New York Times (10 May 2002), Japan Protests China's Arrest of Koreans at Consulate. Cf. Chap. 7: Annex, Table 7.1, Case No. 151.

[98] Jeffries (2006), pp. 101–102. Cf. Chap. 7: Annex, Table 7.1, Case No. 159.

[99] Cf. Chap. 3: 3.4.2–3.4.14, 3.7.1–3.7.5; Chap. 4: 4.2.

[100] Though its territory is split across the continents of Europe and Asia, for the purposes of this book, Turkey has been categorised as an Asian state owing to the vast majority of its territory being situated upon the Asian continent.

[101] Cited by Moral Roncal (2013), p. 101. Cf. Chap. 7: Annex, Table 7.1, Case No. 33.

[102] See Kovács and Ádány (2017), p. 185; Vági et al. (2013), p. 149. Cf. Chap. 7: Annex, Table 7.1, Case No. 39.

[103] The New York Times (4 July 1990), Evolution in Europe; Albanians Take Refuge in Embassies; The Washington Post (4 July 1990), Albanians Seek Asylum in Embassies: at least twenty-six of the thirty-two were granted safe-conduct. Cf. Chap. 7: Annex, Table 7.1, Case No. 120.

and in favour of Malaysian Anwar Ibrahim in June 2008.[104] Turkish state practice, of which cases two and three are separated by 64 years of inactivity, is therefore somewhat sporadic.

5.3.2.5 South Korea

The Asian state with the most state practice according to Table 7.1 is South Korea, which granted a right to diplomatic asylum on eight separate occasions: on 23/24 May 2002,[105] on 27 May 2002,[106] from June to September 2002,[107] from September to October 2002,[108] in October 2003,[109] on 15 November 2004,[110] in December 2013[111] and in July 2016.[112] On all of these occasions, asylum was granted to North Korean citizens. For this reason, South Korean practice is also atypical in the sense that it has only granted asylum to nationals of one state. Furthermore, the decision to grant diplomatic asylum was almost certainly motivated by domestic legal and political considerations[113] as opposed to a notion of international legal obligation.

---

[104]Reuters (30 June 2008), Malaysia's Anwar leaves Turkish embassy. Cf. Chap. 7: Annex, Table 7.1, Case No. 175.

[105]Chicago Tribune (29 May 2002), China tells S. Korea to give up migrants. Cf. Chap. 7: Annex, Table 7.1, Case No. 154.

[106]Chicago Tribune (29 May 2002), China tells S. Korea to give up migrants. Cf. Chap. 7: Annex, Table 7.1, Case No. 155.

[107]Chicago Tribune (12 September 2002), 36 defectors arrive near Seoul; Human Rights Watch, The Invisible Exodus: North Koreans in the People's Republic of China, A Human Rights Watch Report, November 2002, Vol. 14, No. 8 (C), p. 3, Fn. 3. Cf. Chap. 7: Annex, Table 7.1, Case No. 156.

[108]Chicago Tribune (13 October 2002), Koreans reach Seoul from China via Philippines. Cf. Chap. 7: Annex, Table 7.1, Case No. 158.

[109]Chicago Tribune (7 October 2003), S. Korea Embassy shuts to clear out defectors. Cf. Chap. 7: Annex, Table 7.1, Case No. 162.

[110]Jeffries (2006), p. 100. Cf. Chap. 7: Annex, Table 7.1, Case No. 165.

[111]Reuters (6 December 2013), Aide to North Korean leader's ousted uncle seeks asylum in South: media. Cf. Chap. 7: Annex, Table 7.1, Case No. 190.

[112]BBC News (28 July 2016), North Korean 'seeks asylum at S Korean consulate in Hong Kong'; The Telegraph (28 July 2016), North Korean defector seeks asylum at South Korean consulate in Hong Kong. Cf. Chap. 7: Annex, Table 7.1, Case No. 196.

[113]Art. 4 (2) North Korean Refugees Protection and Settlement Support Act (Last Amended by Act 15432, Mar. 13, 2018), Statutes of the Republic of Korea, provides that "The Republic of Korea shall make all of its diplomatic efforts to protect and support residents escaping from North Korea who are staying in foreign countries." Art. 3 of the South Korean Constitution (Constitution of the Republic of Korea, 12 July 1948, Amended Eight Times Subsequently, 29 October 1987, Ministry of Government Legislation, Ref. 20669, 2010) furthermore provides "The territory of the Republic of Korea shall consist of the Korean peninsula and its adjacent islands", thus in defining its own territory, South Korea also purports to encompass North Korea. Thus under this legislation, North Koreans may be regarded as South Korean citizens: Ryu (2016), p. 2. Also see Choi (2018), p. 80: "South Korea seeks to accommodate all who flee the North and so grants citizenship to North Koreans entering South Korea."

5.3.2.6 Conclusion

State practice recorded by Table 7.1 in Asia depicts thirteen states, out of a total of 48 Asian states, having granted a right to diplomatic asylum on 25 occasions in the twentieth and twenty-first centuries. Asian state practice is therefore not extensive in terms of the number of granting states or the number of cases. Measured against the aforementioned high threshold of consistent practice required for regional custom,[114] this falls far short of the consistent practice required to bind the entire continent.

With regard to several states, for example Japan, North Korea and South Korea, Asian state practice is atypical in the sense that asylum was granted to nationals of only one state (in the case of North Korea its own) in some cases in a short timeframe. It is also not general in that there are few common features. Whilst several Asian states have—unusually—granted diplomatic asylum to nationals of only one state, others have deviated from this trend. Moreover, whilst several cases were likely motivated by political considerations, others saw human rights considerations play a central role.

Furthermore, Asian state practice lacks consistency in that there are gaps between cases, for example no Asian case predates the 1930s and none took place in the 1970s, and these are disproportionately dispersed, with twelve of the 25 cases having taken place in the twenty-first century.

Due to a lack of extensive, general and consistent usage, the state practice requirement for regional custom cannot be held to be fulfilled with regard to Asian states. Even if the state practice requirement was constituted, the motivation of many Asian states being exclusively political rather than a sense of legal obligation underscores that *opinio juris* is in any case lacking.

5.3.3 Europe

European state practice with regard to the right of diplomatic asylum is more fruitful still, with Table 7.1 providing for 75 such cases having occurred in the twentieth/twenty-first Centuries. Europe is therefore the region with the most state practice recorded by Table 7.1.[115]

Several of these cases, i.e. the grant of asylum to: 137 (presumably all Spanish) asylees by Austria,[116] 900 (presumably all Spanish) asylees by Norway in the

[114]Cf. Chap. 5: Sect. 5.2.

[115]It is worth stating again at this point that Table 7.1 is not intended to be exhaustive, with the existence of further cases being strongly assumed. The greater accessibility of European cases to a European author compared to cases from other regions is of course also a factor.

[116]Cited by Moral Roncal (2013), p. 101.Cf. Chap. 7: Annex, Table 7.1, Case No. 17.

context of the Spanish civil war in the years 1936–1939,[117] to a number of Albanian asylum seekers by Bulgaria in July 1990[118] and to Bissau-Guinean João Bernardo Vieira by Portugal from May–June 1999,[119] depict isolated incidents.

The practice of several other European states is, however, more regular and therefore must be examined in greater detail in order to determine whether or not it fulfils the state practice requirement of customary international law. These states are as follows: France (Table 7.1 contains eleven cases in which it depicts the granting state), Spain (Table 7.1 contains four cases in which it depicts the granting state), Hungary (Table 7.1 contains four cases in which it depicts the granting state), Yugoslavia[120] (Table 7.1 contains two cases in which it depicts the granting state), Switzerland (Table 7.1 contains four cases in which it depicts the granting state), Germany (Table 7.1 contains fifteen cases in which it depicts the granting state), Belgium (Table 7.1 contains three cases in which it depicts the granting state), The Netherlands (Table 7.1 contains two cases in which it depicts the granting state), Romania (Table 7.1 contains two cases in which it depicts the granting state), The Holy See (Table 7.1 contains three cases in which it depicts the granting state), Italy (Table 7.1 contains five cases in which it depicts the granting state), United Kingdom (Table 7.1 contains four cases in which it depicts the granting state), Sweden (Table 7.1 contains three cases in which it depicts the granting state), Poland (Table 7.1 contains two cases in which it depicts the granting state), Czechoslovakia[121] (Table 7.1 contains three cases in which it depicts the granting state), Greece (Table 7.1 contains two cases in which it depicts the granting state) and Denmark (Table 7.1 contains two cases in which it depicts the granting state).

The practice of each of these states will be analysed in turn in the following sections. Following this and in the context of determining *opinio juris*, European states embracing and rejecting the concept of diplomatic asylum will be detailed in order to facilitate a conclusion as to whether the right of diplomatic asylum finds foundation in customary international law for the region of Europe.[122]

---

[117] Cited by Moral Roncal (2013), p. 101. Cf. Chap. 7: Annex, Table 7.1, Case No. 31.

[118] The New York Times (4 July 1990), Evolution in Europe; Albanians Take Refuge in Embassies; The Washington Post (4 July 1990), Albanians Seek Asylum in Embassies. Cf. Chap. 7: Annex, Table 7.1, Case No. 123.

[119] BBC News (13 May 1999), Portugal says ex-president safe; BBC News (6 June 1999), Ousted Bissau president leaves country. Cf. Chap. 7: Annex, Table 7.1, Case No. 144.

[120] Though Yugoslavia ceased to be a state in the early 1990s, its state practice is still important in establishing whether or not state practice in favour of a right to diplomatic asylum exists for the European region. This could prove important in determining the presence of regional custom. Moreover, successor states continue to be bound by existing customary international law: cf. Aust (2010), p. 366. On the historical application of this principle, see Rudolf (1976), p. 6 f.

[121] Though Czechoslovakia ceased to be a state in 1992, its state practice is also still important in establishing whether or not state practice in favour of a right to diplomatic asylum exists for the European region. This could also prove important in determining the presence of regional custom. Moreover, successor states continue to be bound by existing customary international law: cf. Aust (2010), p. 366.

[122] Cf. Chap. 5: Sects. 5.4.1.2 and 5.4.2.3.

5.3.3.1 France

Though France has declared that it does not recognise the principle of diplomatic asylum,[123] it has nevertheless granted such a right on multiple occasions, with Table 7.1 providing for eleven such occasions. Firstly, France granted diplomatic asylum in the aforementioned case of Haitian Jean Vilbrun Guillaume Sam in July 1915.[124] In the context of the Spanish civil war breaking out in 1936, France also granted diplomatic asylum to Spaniard José Ungría Jiménez until April 1937[125] and to a total of 900 (presumably all Spanish) asylees in the years 1936–1939.[126]

Moreover, asylum was granted by France to a Soviet citizen of Armenian descent from July to October 1978.[127] Soon afterwards, France granted asylum in its diplomatic premises to Liberian Adolphus Tolbert from April to June 1980[128] and then to Ange-Félix Patassé of the Central African Republic in April 1982.[129] In July 1990, asylum was granted to a number of Albanian asylum seekers in Tirana, Albania.[130] From October 1990 to August 1991, asylum was also granted by France to Lebanese Michel Aoun[131] and then in 2002 to Ivorian Alassane Ouattara.[132] In December 2004, France also granted diplomatic asylum to four North Korean asylum seekers in Vietnam.[133] Moreover, as recently as March 2009, France granted asylum in its diplomatic premises to Madagascan Andry Rajoelina.[134] It is interesting to note that three of these ten cases depict France granting asylum to nationals of its former colonies in Africa.[135] These cases can thus also be regarded as atypical cases in which a colonial state grants diplomatic protection in the form of diplomatic asylum to citizens of its former colonies, with France being the only state to do so. Whether this observation is significant for the formation of customary

---

[123] Dupuy (1976), p. 747.

[124] The American Conservative (1 April 2010), Haitian-Building; IBP (2013), p. 60. See Chap. 3: 3.4. Cf. Chap. 7: Annex, Table 7.1, Case No. 1.

[125] Romero Salvadó (2013), p. 332. Cf. Chap. 7: Annex, Table 7.1, Case No. 37.

[126] Cited by Moral Roncal (2013), p. 101. Cf. Chap. 7: Annex, Table 7.1, Case No. 32.

[127] Dembinski (1988), p. 249. Cf. Chap. 7: Annex, Table 7.1, Case No. 79.

[128] Dembinski (1988), p. 249. Cf. Chap. 7: Annex, Table 7.1, Case No. 84.

[129] East and Thomas (2003), p. 97. Cf. Chap. 7: Annex, Table 7.1, Case No. 90.

[130] The New York Times (4 July 1990), Evolution in Europe; Albanians Take Refuge in Embassies; The Washington Post (4 July 1990), Albanians Seek Asylum in Embassies. Cf. Chap. 7: Annex, Table 7.1, Case No. 127.

[131] The New York Times (30 August 1991), Lebanese General Is Spirited to France. Cf. Chap. 7: Annex, Table 7.1, Case No. 136.

[132] BBC News (22 September 2002), France sends troops to Ivory Coast. Cf. Chap. 7: Annex, Table 7.1, Case No. 146.

[133] Reuters (11 July 2007), Four North Koreans enter Danish embassy in Hanoi. Cf. Chap. 7: Annex, Table 7.1, Case No. 166.

[134] France24 (9 March 2009), Opposition leader leaves French embassy. Cf. Chap. 7: Annex, Table 7.1, Case No. 177.

[135] Ivory Coast, Madagascar and Central African Republic are all former French colonies.

international law is unclear i.e. whether France, owing to its former colonial ties to the asylees' state of nationality, felt that it had a legal obligation to grant them diplomatic protection, this being the *opinio juris* element of customary international law. Indeed, for a great many diplomatic asylum cases, deducing the motivation behind a state granting diplomatic asylum has proven difficult.

5.3.3.2 Spain

Though there is historic evidence of Spain supporting a right of diplomatic asylum,[136] Table 7.1 details only four examples of Spain granting a right to diplomatic asylum in the twentieth and twenty-first centuries. In the first, asylum was granted in October 1932 to Cubans Gabriel and Mario Menocal y Moreno.[137] In the second, Spain granted diplomatic asylum to at least eighteen Cuban asylum seekers in Havana from July to September 2002.[138] In the third, Spain granted diplomatic asylum to 25 North Korean asylum seekers in Beijing in March 2002.[139] In the fourth, Spain granted diplomatic asylum to Venezuelan opposition figure Leopoldo López and his wife Lilian Tintori in the ambassador's residence from April 2019 to October 2020.[140]

The first two of these cases are separated by nearly 60 years of inactivity and depict asylum being granted to nationals of one state. In the fourth case, the duo are also noted as being of Spanish descent, which renders possible that they also possessed Spanish citizenship and Spain was therefore extending diplomatic protection to its own citizens.[141] This case may therefore constitute an atypical case.

[136]See the willingness of the Chilean representative to cite Spanish cases up to 1931 in the 96th Session of the Council of the League of Nations, First Meeting (Private), 21 January 1937, League of Nations Official Journal, February 1937, p. 68. Also see Colombian-Peruvian Asylum Case (Colombia v Peru), Judgment of 20 November 1950, ICJ Reports 1950, No. 7, Dissenting Opinion by Judge Azevedo (translation), p. 337, which argues that Spain is bound to accept the Latin American custom due to its status as their mother-country. Cf. Bailey (1955), p. 83 stating that "the granting of diplomatic asylum to political refugees has long been a common practice in Spain."

[137]U.S. Department of State, Foreign Relations of the United States Diplomatic Papers, 1932, The American Republics, Vol. V, Cuba, Political Unrest in Cuba, Doc. 608. For further details on the case, also see Chap. 3: 3.4.7.1. Cf. Chap. 7: Annex, Table 7.1, Case No. 7.

[138]The New York Times (12 September 1990), Spanish-Cuban Asylum Battle Ends, Bitterly. Cf. Annex, Table 7.1, Case No. 134.

[139]BBC News (13 May 2002), Japan-China refugees row deepens; Chicago Tribune (15 March 2002), North Korean defectors leave Beijing. See also: Human Rights Watch, The Invisible Exodus: North Koreans in the People's Republic of China, A Human Rights Watch Report, November 2002, Vol. 14, No. 8 (C), p. 3, Fn. 3. Cf. Chap. 7: Annex, Table 7.1, Case No. 148.

[140]RT (30 April 2019), Coup fizzles? Guaido's mentor takes refuge in Chilean embassy as 25 military seek asylum in Brazil's; The Guardian (25 October 2020), Leopoldo López flees Venezuela vowing to continue fighting Maduro regime. Cf. Chap. 7: Annex, Table 7.1, Case No. 205. Also see Payendeh and Saake (2019).

[141]Cf. RT (30 April 2019), Coup fizzles? Guaido's mentor takes refuge in Chilean embassy as 25 military seek asylum in Brazil's.

Humanitarian considerations may have also played a role in Spain's decision to grant asylum in all four cases, rather than a sense of legal conviction.

5.3.3.3 Hungary

Table 7.1 details four instances in which Hungary has granted diplomatic asylum: to eighteen (presumably all Spanish) asylees in the years 1936 to 1939 in the context of the Spanish civil war,[142] to twelve people of the Hungarian minority from Romania from September 1988 to February 1989,[143] to four Albanian asylum seekers in July 1990[144] and to former Macedonian Prime Minister Nikola Gruevski in November 2018.[145] Hungarian state practice is therefore rather sparse and depicts asylum being granted to other European nationals—in all four cases to nationals of different states.

5.3.3.4 Yugoslavia[146]

Table 7.1 details two occasions upon which Yugoslavia granted diplomatic asylum: to 21 (presumably all Spanish) asylees in the context of the Spanish civil war in the years 1936–1939[147] and to Hungarian Imre Nagy in November 1956.[148] These two cases were likely both motivated by humanitarian considerations rather than a sense of legal conviction.

It is important to note that there is no evidence of state practice for the modern-day states of Serbia, Montenegro, Croatia, Slovenia, Bosnia and Herzegovina, Macedonia and Kosovo.

5.3.3.5 Switzerland

Table 7.1 also contains four cases in which Switzerland granted a right to diplomatic asylum: to 85 (presumably all Spanish) asylees in the context of the Spanish civil

[142] Cited by Moral Roncal (2013), p. 101. Cf. Chap. 7: Annex, Table 7.1, Case No. 10.

[143] Kovács and Ádány (2017), p. 193. Cf. Chap. 7: Annex, Table 7.1, Case No. 109.

[144] The New York Times (4 July 1990), Evolution in Europe; Albanians Take Refuge in Embassies; The Washington Post (4 July 1990), Albanians Seek Asylum in Embassies. Cf. Chap. 7: Annex, Table 7.1, Case No. 117.

[145] The New York Times (15 November 2018), Former Macedonian Leader Seeks Asylum in Hungary to Avoid Prison. Cf. Chap. 7: Annex, Table 7.1, Case No. 202.

[146] Yugoslavia ceased to be a state in the early 1990s. Its former territory is now composed of the following states: Serbia, Montenegro, Croatia, Slovenia, Bosnia and Herzegovina, Macedonia, Kosovo (though the statehood of the latter is still disputed).

[147] Cited by Moral Roncal (2013), p. 101. Cf. Chap. 7: Annex, Table 7.1, Case No. 11.

[148] Simándi (2015), p. 115; Kovács and Ádány (2017), p. 189. Cf. Chap. 7: Annex, Table 7.1, Case No. 53.

war in the years 1936 to 1939,[149] to a number of Cuban asylum seekers in Havana, Cuba in July 1990,[150] to its own citizens Max Goeldi and Rachid Hamdani in Tripoli, Libya for 17 months from summer 2008[151] and to Azerbaijani Emin Huseynov from August 2014 to June 2015.[152] It is likely that humanitarian considerations played a role in most, if not all, of these cases, rather than a sense of legal conviction.

5.3.3.6 Germany

Though Germany was separated into two states, the Federal Republic of Germany and the German Democratic Republic, from 1949 until 1990, for the purpose of this work the Federal Republic of Germany's historical practice will be considered as German practice owing to the German Democratic Republic being absorbed into the Federal Republic of Germany upon reunification.[153] The Federal Republic of Germany has therefore continually existed, with reunification denoting an expansion of its territory.

Table 7.1 provides for fifteen cases in which Germany has granted a right to diplomatic asylum, rendering it the European state with the most extensive modern state practice with regard to diplomatic asylum. Against the backdrop of the Spanish civil war, Germany granted diplomatic asylum to 80 (presumably all Spanish) asylees in the years 1936–1939.[154] In the context of the Second World War, Germany granted diplomatic asylum to Hungarians Ferenc Szálasi and some of his close collaborators in 1944.[155]

In 1984 the Federal Republic of Germany granted diplomatic asylum nine times, primarily to East German citizens. It granted diplomatic protection to 25 Czechs in its diplomatic mission in Prague in 1984.[156] In that very same year, it also granted

---

[149] Cited by Moral Roncal (2013), p. 101. Cf. Chap. 7: Annex, Table 7.1, Case No. 15.

[150] The New York Times (12 September 1990), Spanish-Cuban Asylum Battle Ends, Bitterly. Cf. Chap. 7: Annex, Table 7.1, Case No. 132.

[151] Denza (2016), Art. 22, p. 115.; N-tv (22 February 2010), Schweizer verlassen Botschaft. Cf. Chap. 7: Annex, Table 7.1, Case No. 173.

[152] Swiss Federal Department of Foreign Affairs, Media Release, 13th June 2015, Emin Huseynov arrives in Bern after 10 months at Swiss embassy in Baku. Cf. Chap. 7: Annex, Table 7.1, Case No. 193.

[153] Art. 1 Treaty of 31 August 1990 between the Federal Republic of Germany and the German Democratic Republic on the establishment of German unity (Unification Treaty), Adopted in Berlin on 31 August 1990, Entered into Force on 29 September 1990, BGBl. 1990 II, p. 889. This provision of Germany's reunification treaty provides that the territory of the German Democratic Republic will become part of the Federal Republic of Germany upon reunification. Cf. Craven (1998), p. 145.

[154] Cited by Moral Roncal (2013), p. 101. Cf. Chap. 7: Annex, Table 7.1, Case No. 13.

[155] Kovács and Ádány (2017), p. 186. Cf. Chap. 7: Annex, Table 7.1, Case No. 40.

[156] SBS News (3 September 2013), The bizzare history of embassy asylum. Cf. Chap. 7: Annex, Table 7.1, Case No. 92.

diplomatic asylum to: a group of twelve East Germans in Berlin in January;[157] to a prominent East German family (including the niece of Willi Stroph) in Prague for 4 weeks until 24 February;[158] to 48 East Germans in Berlin in February;[159] to over 50 East Germans in Prague in February;[160] to 161 East German refugees in Prague in October;[161] to seven East Germans and three Poles of German descent in Warsaw in November;[162] to fifteen East Germans in Budapest in November[163] and to a small number of East Germans in Bucharest in November.[164]

In July 1990, West Germany also granted diplomatic asylum to 162 Albanian asylum seekers in Tirana.[165]

Following reunification, Germany also granted diplomatic asylum to a North Korean man in Beijing in April 2002.[166] It also provided shelter to a further fifteen North Korean asylum seekers in September 2002.[167] Germany then granted diplomatic asylum to former Togolese Home Secretary Franois Boko in April 2005.[168]

Nine of the aforementioned cases involved West Germany granting protection to East Germans. West Germany did not recognise the division of Germany into two states on an international level and as such, East Germans generally also automatically received West German citizenship.[169] For this reason, the practice of Germany in this regard correlates to that of South Korea to a certain extent.[170] These cases are atypical and depict Germany extending diplomatic protection to individuals it regarded as its own citizens.

[157]The New York Times (1 February 1984), East Germany Tries Accommodation. Cf. Chap. 7: Annex, Table 7.1, Case No. 94.

[158]Roberts (1987), p. 234. Cf. Chap. 7: Annex, Table 7.1, Case No. 95.

[159]Roberts (1987), p. 234. Cf. Chap. 7: Annex, Table 7.1, Case No. 97.

[160]Riveles (1989), p. 157. Cf. Chap. 7: Annex, Table 7.1, Case No. 98.

[161]Roberts (1987), p. 234. Cf. Chap. 7: Annex, Table 7.1, Case No. 100.

[162]Roberts (1987), p. 234. Also see The New York Times (10 November 1984), West Germany is Demanding Rumania Recall 5 Diplomats. Cf. Chap. 7: Annex, Table 7.1, Case No. 101.

[163]Roberts (1987), p. 234. Also see The New York Times (10 November 1984), West Germany is Demanding Rumania Recall 5 Diplomats. Cf. Chap. 7: Annex, Table 7.1, Case No. 102.

[164]Roberts (1987), p. 234. Also see The New York Times (10 November 1984), West Germany is Demanding Rumania Recall 5 Diplomats. Cf. Chap. 7: Annex, Table 7.1, Case No. 103.

[165]The New York Times (4 July 1990), Evolution in Europe; Albanians Take Refuge in Embassies. Cf. Chap. 7: Annex, Table 7.1, Case No. 121.

[166]Chicago Tribune (27 April 2002), North Korean requests asylum at embassy. Cf. Chap. 7: Annex, Table 7.1, Case No. 149.

[167]In this case the asylum seekers sheltered in the German diplomatic compound rather than in the embassy itself: Chicago Tribune (4 September 2002), 15 seek refuge in German compound. Cf. Chap. 7: Annex, Table 7.1, Case No. 160.

[168]N-tv (24 April 2005), Unruhen in Togo, Zuflucht in deutscher Botschaft. Cf. Chap. 7: Annex, Table 7.1, Case No. 169.

[169]Cf. BVerfGE 77, 137, para. 31. Also see Fastenrath (1996), p. 28.

[170]See Chap. 5: Sect. 5.3.2.5.

5.3.3.7 Belgium

Belgium has granted diplomatic asylum on three separate occasions detailed by Table 7.1: to 287 (presumably all Spanish) asylees in the years 1936 to 1939 in the context of the Spanish civil war,[171] to Hungarians Ferenc B. Farkas and Judith Maléter from 4 to 8 November 1956[172] and to a number of Cuban asylum seekers in July 1990.[173] In the light of historical events, all of these cases are likely to have been motivated exclusively by human rights considerations, rather than a sense of legal conviction.

5.3.3.8 The Netherlands

Table 7.1 provides for two cases in which The Netherlands constitutes the state granting diplomatic asylum. It granted such asylum to 137 (presumably all Spanish) asylees in the context of the Spanish civil war in the years 1936 to 1939[174] and to Zimbabwean Morgan Tsvangira in June 2008.[175] Such cases, separated by nearly 70 years, in themselves lack commonality.

5.3.3.9 Romania

Table 7.1 provides for two distinct instances in which Romania has recognised and granted a right to diplomatic asylum: to 718 (presumably all Spanish) asylees in the context of the Spanish civil war in the years 1936 to 1939[176] and to its own citizens Adrian and Roman Mocanu from September 2008 to September 2009.[177] Such cases, separated by 70 years, lack commonality as the first denotes diplomatic asylum being granted based on humanitarian considerations and the second involves Romania granting diplomatic protection to its own citizens.

---

[171]Cited by Moral Roncal (2013), p. 101. Cf. Chap. 7: Annex, Table 7.1, Case No. 22.

[172]See Farkas (2016). Cf. Chap. 7: Annex, Table 7.1, Case No. 52.

[173]The New York Times (12 September 1990), Spanish-Cuban Asylum Battle Ends, Bitterly. Cf. Chap. 7: Annex, Table 7.1, Case No. 129.

[174]Cited by Moral Roncal (2013), p. 101. Cf. Chap. 7: Annex, Table 7.1, Case No. 18.

[175]The Telegraph (23 June 2008), Zimbabwe's Morgan Tsvangirai seeks refuge in Dutch embassy; The Telegraph (25 June 2008), Zimbabwe: Morgan Tsvangirai leaves embassy refuge to give ultimatum to Robert Mugabe. Cf. Chap. 7: Annex, Table 7.1, Case No. 174.

[176]Cited by Moral Roncal (2013), p. 101. Cf. Chap. 7: Annex, Table 7.1, Case No. 28.

[177]Moldova Azi (23 September 2009), Sons of Sergiu Mocanu quit Romanian Embassy. Cf. Chap. 7: Annex, Table 7.1, Case No. 176.

5.3.3.10 The Holy See

The Holy See, the central governing body of the Roman Catholic Church and a historic subject of international law, has granted diplomatic asylum on three occasions documented by Table 7.1: to the Hungarian Horthy Family in October 1944,[178] to Panamanian Manuel Noriega in December 1989[179] and to Venezuelan Nixon Moreno for 15 months until June 2008.[180] These three isolated incidents are separated by 55 years and 19 years respectively. Moreover, the cases are, particularly considering the nature of the Holy See, likely to have been motivated exclusively by human rights considerations rather than a sense of legal conviction.

5.3.3.11 Italy

Italy has granted diplomatic asylum on five occasions documented by Table 7.1, the first two in its diplomatic mission in Santiago in the context of the 1973 Chilean 1973 *coup d'état*: to Brazilian José Serra[181] and to 750 Chileans,[182] to twenty asylum seekers in Tirana, Albania in July 1990,[183] to a number of Cuban asylum seekers in Havana, Cuba in July 1990[184] and most recently to Américo de Grazia, Mariela Magallanes and five others in Caracas, Venezuela in May 2019.[185] These five cases all occurred in the midst of political upheaval in the receiving state.

[178] Kovács and Ádány (2017), p. 186. Cf. Chap. 7: Annex, Table 7.1, Case No. 41.

[179] BBC News (30 May 2017), Music torture: How heavy metal broke Manuel Noriega; The Telegraph (30 May 2017), How Panama's military dictator Manuel Noriega was defeated by rock'n'roll. Also see Chap. 3: Sect. 3.4.11. Cf. Chap. 7: Annex, Table 7.1, Case No. 113.

[180] Country Reports on Human Rights Practices for 2008, Vol. I, Report Submitted to the Committee on Foreign Relations US Senate and the Committee on Foreign Affairs US House of Representatives by the Department of State in Accordance with Sections 116(d) and 502B(b) of the Foreign Assistance Act of 1961, U.S. Government Printing Office, Washington 2010, p. 2781. Also see Chap. 3: Sect. 3.7.5.3. Cf. Chap. 7: Annex, Table 7.1, Case No. 171.

[181] China Daily (7 October 2002), Serra faces election struggle against workers' champion Lula. Also see Chap. 3: Sect. 3.4.4. Cf. Chap. 7: Annex, Table 7.1, Case No. 72.

[182] The Independent (3 March 2016), Chile honours Italian diplomats whose 'Schindler's List' saved 750 lives during Augusto Pinochet's brutal regime. Also see Chap. 3: 3.4.4. Cf. Chap. 7: Annex, Table 7.1, Case No. 73.

[183] The New York Times (4 July 1990), Evolution in Europe; Albanians Take Refuge in Embassies. Cf. Chap. 7: Annex, Table 7.1, Case No. 118.

[184] The New York Times (4 July 1990), Evolution in Europe; Albanians Take Refuge in Embassies. Cf. Chap. 7: Annex, Table 7.1, Case No. 131.

[185] El Pitazo (9 May 2019), Américo De Grazia se refugia en la embajada de Italia.

5.3.3.12 United Kingdom

Though the United Kingdom generally rejects the notion of diplomatic asylum,[186] it has been confronted with it in its own diplomatic missions on four occasions documented by Table 7.1: in the case of Romanian General Nicolae Rădescu in 1945,[187] in the case of South Africans Archie Gumede, Mewa Ramgobin, George Sawpershad, M. J. Naidoo, Billy Naier, Davades Paul Davids in September/October 1984,[188] in the case of dual South African and British citizen Olivia Forsyth for 6 months in 1988[189] and in the case of Afghan brothers Almadar and Muntazar on 18th July 2002, though this was very much shortlived.[190] These four cases are interesting, particularly as one atypical case involves the UK extending diplomatic protection to its own citizen and another involves a *de facto* case of diplomatic asylum very short in duration.

5.3.3.13 Sweden

Sweden has granted a right to diplomatic asylum on three occasions documented by Table 7.1: to 174 asylees (presumably all Spanish and including two priests, José Machiñena Austegui and Manuel Cavanillas Rodríguez) in the context of the Spanish civil war in the years 1936 to 1939,[191] to Chilean refugees after the 1973 *coup d'état*[192] and to two North Korean asylum seekers in December 2004.[193] It is likely that these three separate incidents were motivated by humanitarian considerations.

[186] Yearbook of the International Law Commission, 1949, 16th Meeting, 5 May 1949, p. 127, para. 85; William Hague, U.K. Foreign Secretary, Statement on Ecuadorian Government's Decision to Offer Political Asylum to Julian Assange (16th August 2012). Available at: https://www.gov.uk/government/news/foreign-secretary-statement-on-ecuadorian-government-s-decision-to-offer-political-asylum-to-julian-assange. Last Accessed 15 Dec 2020; Jeffery (1985), p. 15. Also see McNair (1956), p. 76 which holds that although the UK does not recognise the practice of diplomatic asylum, it has temporarily authorised it on occasion for humanitarian reasons.

[187] Dembinski (1988), p. 249. Cf. Chap. 7: Annex, Table 7.1, Case No. 43.

[188] See Riveles (1989). Cf. Chap. 7: Annex, Table 7.1, Case No. 99.

[189] AP (3 February 1989), Police Identify British Native As Spy. Cf. Chap. 7: Annex, Table 7.1, Case No. 108.

[190] R (B and Others) v Secretary of State for Foreign and Commonwealth Affairs (2004) EWCA 1344, paras. 4–17. Cf. Chap. 7: Annex, Table 7.1, Case No. 157.

[191] Cited by Moral Roncal (2013), p. 101. Cf. Chap. 7: Annex, Table 7.1, Case No. 19.

[192] Ensalaco (2000), p. 31; The Independent (3 March 2016), Chile honours Italian diplomats whose 'Schindler's List' saved 750 lives during Augusto Pinochet's brutal regime. Also see Chap. 3: Sect. 3.4.4. Cf. Chap. 7: Annex, Table 7.1, Case No. 71.

[193] Reuters (11 July 2007), Four North Koreans enter Danish embassy in Hanoi. Cf. Chap. 7: Annex, Table 7.1, Case No. 167.

5.3.3.14 Poland

Poland has granted diplomatic asylum on two occasions detailed by Table 7.1: to 350–400 (presumably all Spanish) asylees in the context of the Spanish civil war in the years 1936–1939[194] and to 25 Albanian asylum seekers in July 1990.[195] These two isolated incidents, which are separated by over 60 years, are likely to have been motivated exclusively by humanitarian considerations, rather than a sense of legal conviction.

5.3.3.15 Czechoslovakia[196]

Though Czechoslovakia has historically explicitly rejected recognising a right to diplomatic asylum,[197] it has granted such a right on three occasions documented by Table 7.1. In the context of the Spanish civil war in the years 1936–1939, Czechoslovakia granted diplomatic asylum to 204 (presumably all Spanish) asylees.[198] In July 1990, Czechoslovakia granted asylum to a number of asylum seekers in Tirana, Albania.[199] Furthermore, in July 1990 Czechoslovakia also granted a right to diplomatic asylum to a number of Cuban asylum seekers in Havana, Cuba.[200]

These three cases are all likely to have been motivated by humanitarian considerations, rather than a sense of legal conviction. Consequently and indeed considering Czechoslovakia has explicitly rejected the practice,[201] the *opinio juris* requirement would in any case not be fulfilled. Furthermore and importantly, since the dissolution of Czechoslovakia into Czech Republic and Slovakia in 1993, there is no evidence of either state having recognised a right to diplomatic asylum.

---

[194] Cited by Moral Roncal (2013), p. 101. Cf. Chap. 7: Annex, Table 7.1, Case No. 24.

[195] The New York Times (4 July 1990), Evolution in Europe; Albanians Take Refuge in Embassies. Cf. Chap. 7: Annex, Table 7.1, Case No. 119.

[196] Czechoslovakia ceased to be a state in 1992. Its successor states are Czech Republic and Slovakia.

[197] League of Nations Committee of Experts for the Progressive Codification of International Law, Report to the Council of the League of Nations on the Questions Which Appear Ripe for International Regulation, Questionnaires Nos 1 to 7, Adopted by the Committee at its Third Session, held in March–April 1927, Geneva, 20 April 1927, p. 254.

[198] Cited by Moral Roncal (2013), p. 101. Cf. Chap. 7: Annex, Table 7.1, Case No. 20.

[199] The New York Times (4 July 1990), Evolution in Europe; Albanians Take Refuge in Embassies. Cf. Chap. 7: Annex, Table 7.1, Case No. 125.

[200] The New York Times (12 September 1990), Spanish-Cuban Asylum Battle Ends, Bitterly. Cf. Chap. 7: Annex, Table 7.1, Case No. 130.

[201] League of Nations Committee of Experts for the Progressive Codification of International Law, Report to the Council of the League of Nations on the Questions Which Appear Ripe for International Regulation, Questionnaires Nos 1 to 7, Adopted by the Committee at its Third Session, held in March–April 1927, Geneva, 20 April 1927, p. 254.

5.3.3.16 Greece

Greece has granted diplomatic asylum on two separate occasions detailed by Table 7.1. In July 1990, Greece granted diplomatic asylum to a number of Albanian asylum seekers in Tirana, Albania.[202] Then in February 1999, Greece granted diplomatic asylum to Turkish Abdullah Öcalan.[203]

5.3.3.17 Denmark

Denmark has also granted diplomatic asylum on two occasions documented by Table 7.1, on both occasions to North Korean citizens in its diplomatic mission in Hanoi, Vietnam: in the first instance asylum was granted to four North Korean asylum seekers in July 2007,[204] on the second occasion, asylum was granted to nine North Korean asylum seekers in September/October 2009.[205] These two cases concern diplomatic asylum being granted to nationals of the same state. In the light of the political climate, it is also likely that the granting of asylum was in both cases motivated exclusively by human rights considerations rather than a sense of legal conviction.

5.3.3.18 Conclusion

There is extensive twentieth and twenty-first century state practice on the European continent to support a right to diplomatic asylum, encompassing twenty-one states[206] granting diplomatic asylum on 75 occasions. However, measured against the aforementioned high threshold of consistent practice required for regional custom,[207] this falls far short of the consistent practice required from European states in order to bind the entire continent. Indeed, European state practice in favour of the practice of diplomatic asylum encompasses only 42% of the European

---

[202]The New York Times (4 July 1990), Evolution in Europe; Albanians Take Refuge in Embassies. Cf. Chap. 7: Annex, Table 7.1, Case No. 128.

[203]CIA, Fiasco in Nairobi, Greek Intelligence and the Capture of PKK, Leader Abdullah Ocalan in 1999. Available at: https://www.cia.gov/library/center-for-the-study-of-intelligence/csi-publications/csi-studies/studies/vol53no1/fiasco-in-nairobi.html. Last Accessed 15 Dec 2020. Cf. Chap. 7: Annex, Table 7.1, Case No. 143.

[204]Reuters (11 July 2007), Four North Koreans enter Danish embassy in Hanoi. Cf. Chap. 7: Annex, Table 7.1, Case No. 171.

[205]Reuters (24 September 2009), North Koreans seek asylum at Danish embassy in Vietnam; Reuters (20 October 2009), North Koreans quit Danish embassy in Hanoi for South Korea. Cf. Chap. 7: Annex, Table 7.1, Case No. 181.

[206]Two of which have now ceased to exist in the cases of Yugoslavia and Czechoslovakia.

[207]Cf. Chap. 5: Sect. 5.2.

international community.[208] There is therefore insufficient regional state practice to give rise to regional custom in Europe.

Moreover, this practice in any case lacks a sufficiently general and consistent pattern. Though in most cases, diplomatic asylum was granted by European states in the midst of political unrest, some cases see humanitarian considerations playing a key role, while others do not. Furthermore, many European cases involve states exceptionally granting diplomatic asylum to one state, e.g. West Germany granting diplomatic asylum to East German citizens or even to their own citizens e.g. in the cases of Switzerland and the UK.

5.3.4 Latin America[209]

Though Latin American state practice with regard to the concept of diplomatic asylum has been described as erratic,[210] it is certainly extensive in terms of the number of state actors involved, particularly in relation to the size of the continent. Indeed, Table 7.1 provides for 74 cases in which Latin American states have granted a right to diplomatic asylum. It is also coherent, depicting a number of common features, for example that the individual in question is alleged to have committed a political offence, reservation for urgent cases, the granting of safe conduct etc.[211]

As much of the state practice of Table 7.1 with regard to Latin America has already been explored in the context of Chapter 3,[212] though here categorisation took place according to the receiving rather than the granting state,[213] the details of these cases will be spared repetition. Table 7.1 provides for: Argentina having granted such a right on two occasions,[214] Bolivia as having done so once,[215] Brazil as having

---

[208]There are 50 internationally recognised states with territory on the European continent.

[209]Latin America encompasses not only the South American continent, but also the Spanish, Portuguese or French-speaking Caribbean and Central American states, which belong to the continent of North America. For the purposes of this work, Latin America therefore consists of: Belize, Costa Rica, Cuba, Dominican Republic, El Salvador, Guatemala, Haiti, Honduras, Mexico, Nicaragua, Panama, Argentina, Bolivia, Brazil, Chile, Colombia, Ecuador, French Guiana, Guyana, Paraguay, Peru, Suriname, Uruguay and Venezuela.

[210]Rossitto (1987), p. 130. In this regard, it has been questioned whether the interruption of a set of concordant cases would prevent a rule of customary international law arising or simply constitute a violation of such a rule: Colombian-Peruvian Asylum Case (Colombia v Peru), Judgment of 20 November 1950, ICJ Reports 1950, No. 7, Dissenting Opinion by Judge Azevedo (translation), p. 336.

[211]Cf. Chap. 3: Sects. 3.4.2–3.4.14, 3.7 and 3.8.

[212]See Chap. 3: Sects. 3.1, 3.4 and 3.7.

[213]It is worth noting here that most Latin American state practice involves Latin American states granting a right to diplomatic asylum in other Latin American states. Cf. Chap. 7: Annex, Table 7.1.

[214]Cf. Chap. 7: Annex, Table 7.1, Case Nos 25 and 36.

[215]Cf. Chap. 7: Annex, Table 7.1, Case No. 16.

done so on fourteen occasions,[216] Chile as having done so on seven occasions,[217] Colombia as having done so on six occasions,[218] Costa Rica as having done so on one occasion,[219] Cuba as having done so on two occasions,[220] Dominican Republic as having done so on three occasions,[221] Ecuador as having done so on one occasion,[222] Haiti as having done so on one occasion,[223] Mexico as having done so on seventeen occasions,[224] Nicaragua as having done so on one occasion,[225] Panama as having done so on five occasions,[226] Paraguay as having done so on two occasions,[227] Peru as having done so on four occasions,[228] Venezuela as having done so on five occasions,[229] and Uruguay as having granted such a right on three occasions.[230]

This extensive state practice is also consistent insofar as Latin American states granted a right to diplomatic asylum in every decade from the 1930s, importantly this also coincides with the signing of the Montevideo Convention on Political Asylum 1933,[231] until the present day.

Indeed, state practice in Latin America entails the granting of a right to diplomatic asylum by seventeen of the twenty-three, as well as one overseas territory, Latin American states.[232] This is constitutive of over 70% of Latin American states with practice in favour of diplomatic asylum.

---

[216]Cf. Chap. 7: Annex, Table 7.1, Case Nos 3, 4, 12, 44, 58, 60, 65, 86, 89, 107, 168, 180,187 and 204.

[217]Cf. Chap. 7: Annex, Table 7.1, Case Nos 34, 38, 137, 198, 199, 201 and 205.

[218]Cf. Chap. 7: Annex, Table 7.1, Case Nos 6, 9, 47, 138, 141 and 152.

[219]Cf. Chap. 7: Annex, Table 7.1, Case No. 161.

[220]Cf. Chap. 7: Annex, Table 7.1, Case Nos 27 and 115. Though in Chap. 7: Annex, Table 7.1, Case No. 27, this was as Cuba-Haiti.

[221]Cf. Chapter 7: Annex, Table 7.1, Case Nos 14 and 110.

[222]Cf. Chap. 7: Annex, Table 7.1, Case No 188.

[223]In the aforementioned Chap. 7: Annex, Table 7.1, Case No. 27, together with Cuba.

[224]Cf. Chap. 7: Annex, Table 7.1, Case Nos 8, 29, 35, 42, 46, 48, 50, 70, 74–76, 80, 87, 105, 116 and 147.

[225]Cf. Chap. 7: Annex, Table 7.1, Case No. 178.

[226]Cf. Chap. 7: Annex, Table 7.1, Case Nos 30, 45, 69 and 200.

[227]Cf. Chap. 7: Annex, Table 7.1, Case Nos 23 and 51.

[228]Cf. Chap. 7: Annex, Table 7.1, Case Nos 26, 61, 83 and 114.

[229]Cf. Chapter 7: Annex, Table 7.1, Case Nos 49, 59, 68, 81 and 104.

[230]Cf. Chap. 7: Annex, Table 7.1, Case Nos 5, 21 and 203.

[231]See Chap. 4: Sect. 4.2.2.5 for further information.

[232]With state practice for El Salvador, Honduras, Guyana, French Guiana, Suriname, Guatemala and Belize being missing in this regard. However, in Chap. 7: Annex, Table 7.1, Case No. 34 a number of the asylees protected by Chile are noted as having previously been protected by Guatemala (200 refugees) and Honduras (36 refugees) respectively before both broke off diplomatic relations with Spain.

Such extensive and consistent state practice can be regarded as consistent in the context of Latin American states fulfilling the state practice element of customary international law for the participating states in the region of Latin America.[233] There is therefore sufficient state practice to fulfil the state practice requirement of regional custom for the participating states of Bolivia, Brazil, Chile, Colombia, Costa Rica, Cuba, Dominican Republic, Ecuador, Guatemala,[234] Haiti, Honduras,[235] Mexico, Nicargaua, Panama, Paraguay, Peru, Venezuela and Uruguay.[236] This state practice and its features correlate strongly to the established regional treaty law right in Latin America e.g. reservation for urgent cases, the practice being reserved for alleged political offences as opposed to common crimes. Whether or not this state practice is accompanied by *opinio juris* so as to constitute regional custom binding upon Latin America will be determined later in this chapter.[237]

5.3.5 Northern America[238]

Table 7.1 provides for 30 cases in which Northern American states granted a right to diplomatic asylum: with the U.S. having done so on 25 occasions documented by Table 7.1, whilst Canada has done so on five occasions. Due to to the multitude of cases, the state practice of these states will be examined in turn in the following sections.

[233]IACtHR, Advisory Opinion OC-25/18 of 30 May 2018 Requested by the Republic of Ecuador, The Institution of Asylum and its Recognition as a Human Right in the Inter-American System of Protection (Interpretation and Scope of Articles 5, 22.7 and 22.8 in Relation to Article 1(1) of the American Convention on Human Rights), p. 57, para. 162. It must be noted, however, that some authors see this differently: cf. Shah (2007), para. 7 providing that Latin American practice has been inconsistent.

[234]In Chap. 7: Annex, Table 7.1, Case No. 34 a number of the asylees protected by Chile are noted as having previously been protected by Guatemala (200 refugees).

[235]In Chap. 7: Annex, Table 7.1, Case No. 34 a number of the asylees protected by Chile are noted as having previously been protected by Honduras (36 refugees).

[236]Though importantly, Table 7.1 provides no evidence of state practice for El Salvador, Guyana, French Guiana, Suriname and Belize, which cannot therefore be held to be bound by any emerging regional custom.

[237]Cf. Chap. 5: Sects. 5.4.1.1, 5.4.2.4 and 5.4.3.

[238]In line with the aforementioned definition of Latin America as encompassing states in Central and North America, additional to the South American Continent, for the purposes of this work, the following geopolitical definition of Northern America will be adopted: Bermuda, Greenland, Saint-Pierre and Miquelon, the U.S. and Canada.

5.3.5.1 U.S.

Though the U.S. traditionally refutes the practice of diplomatic asylum,[239] a stance which may be viewed as a deterrent to would-be embassy asylum-seekers,[240] it has nevertheless granted such a right on various occasions detailed by Table 7.1: to Costa Rican Domingo González, his six sons and three daughters from 17th to 25th May 1917;[241] to Hungarian Cardinal József Mindszenty from 4th November 1956 to 28th September 1971;[242] to Soviet Reino Häyhänen from 4th to 10th May 1957;[243] to Chinese Tung Chi-Ping in the summer of 1964;[244] to Soviet Svetlana Alliluyeva (Stalin's daughter) from 9th March to April 1967;[245] to American Arthur from South Carolina for 6 weeks in the late 1970s;[246] to Soviet citizens Pyotr, Avgustina, Lydia, Lyubov and Liliya Vashchenko; Timofei and Maria Chmykhalov from 1978 to

[239] See U.S. Declaration made upon the approval of the Montevideo Convention on Political Asylum 1933; UN General Assembly, Question of Diplomatic Asylum, Report of the Secretary-General, 2 September 1975, A/10139 (Part I), Fn. 16 from 1975, which notes that no case of diplomatic asylum has been recorded on the North American continent; also see UN General Assembly, Question of Diplomatic Asylum, Report of the Secretary-General, 2 September 1975, A/10139 (Part I), para. 224; Esquirol (2012), p. 559; Jeffery (1985), p. 15; Leonhard (1968), pp. 679–680; Ronning (1965), p. 98 f.; Rossitto (1987), p. 115; IACtHR, Advisory Opinion OC-25/18 of 30 May 2018 Requested by the Republic of Ecuador, The Institution of Asylum and its Recognition as a Human Right in the Inter-American System of Protection (Interpretation and Scope of Articles 5, 22.7 and 22.8 in Relation to Article 1(1) of the American Convention on Human Rights), p. 57, para. 161.

[240] Cf. Rossitto (1987), p. 116, arguing that embassies would otherwise be overrun by such asylum-seekers. On this point, also see Kleiner (2010), p. 175.

[241] U.S. Department of State, Foreign Relations of the United States, Papers Relating to the Foreign Relations of the United States, With the Address of the President to Congress December 4, 1917, Doc. 399, 17 May 1917; U.S. Department of State, Foreign Relations of the United States, Papers Relating to the Foreign Relations of the United States, With the Address of the President to Congress December 4, 1917, Doc. 404, Chargé Johnson to the Secretary of State, Telegram, 25 May 1917. Cf. Chap. 7: Annex, Table 7.1, Case No. 2. Also see Chap. 3: Sect. 3.4.6.

[242] The New York Times (29 September 1971), Mindszenty Leaves Hungary, Goes to Rome. Also see Rossitto (1987), p. 118 f. Cf. Chap. 7: Annex, Table 7.1, Case No. 54. Kirchheimer holds that this case constitutes the U.S. having "a change of heart" regarding the institution of diplomatic asylum: Kirchheimer (1959), p. 1006.

[243] Following which he was granted safe passage to the United States: FBI, History, Famous Cases and Criminals, Hollow Nickel/Rudolph Abel. Available at: https://www.fbi.gov/history/famous-cases/hollow-nickel-rudolph-abel. Last Accessed 16 Dec 2020. Cf. Chap. 7: Annex, Table 7.1, Case No. 55.

[244] The New York Times (5 August 1964), Chinese Defector Says Peking Seeks to Take Over the Congo; Ex-Aide in Burundi Here, Asserts Regime's Goal is to Conquer Africa. For further reference thereto, also see Cohen and Chiu (1974), pp. 985–986; Evans (1965), p. 674. Cf. Chap. 7: Annex, Table 7.1, Case No. 63.

[245] The Independent (30 November 2011), Lana Peters: Stalin's daughter whose defection to the West did not bring peace of mind. Cf. Chap. 7: Annex, Table 7.1, Case No. 66.

[246] See Association for Diplomatic Studies and Training, A Thieving U.S. Citizen Wreaks Havoc at the U.S Embassy in Nicaragua. Available at: https://adst.org/2015/03/an-unwelcome-guest-at-embassy-managua/. Last Accessed 16 Dec 2020. Cf. Chap. 7: Annex, Table 7.1, Case No. 77.

1983;[247] to two Cuban soldiers from 23rd May 1980;[248] to East Germans Bernhard Marquardt and Angelika Machol for a week in April 1982;[249] to six East Germans from 20th to 22nd January 1984;[250] to four East Germans in February 1984;[251] to Soviet Private Aleksandr Vasilyevich Sukhanov from 31st October to 5th November 1985;[252] to Chinese citizens Fang Lizhi, Lu Shuxian, Fang Ke from early June 1989 until 25th June 1990;[253] to Cuban citizens Arturo Sandoval, his wife and son in July 1990;[254] to Cuban Alina Fernández Revuelta from 20th to 21st December 1993;[255] to 29 East Timorese Youths from 12th to 22nd December 1994;[256] to Burundian Sylvestre Ntibantunganya from 23rd July 1996 to 8th June 1997;[257] to Central African Republican Louis Pierre Gamba from May to August 2001;[258] to three North Korean asylum seekers in May 2002;[259] to a North Korean construction worker on 28th October 2004;[260] to American Sam Lahood from January to March 2012;[261] to Chinese Wang Lijun from 6th to 7th February 2012;[262] to

[247]Russia Beyond (15 August 2016), How did a group of Soviet Pentecostals end up living in the U.S. embassy? Also see Rossitto (1987), p. 120 f. Cf. Chap. 7: Annex, Table 7.1, Case No. 78.

[248]Sen (1988), p. 412. Cf. Chap. 7: Annex, Table 7.1, Case No. 85.

[249]The New York Times (1 February 1984), East Germany Tries Accommodation. Also see Roberts (1987), p. 233 f. Cf. Chap. 7: Annex, Table 7.1, Case No. 88.

[250]The New York Times (1 February 1984), East Germany Tries Accommodation. Cf. Chap. 7: Annex, Table 7.1, Case No. 93.

[251]Roberts (1987), p. 234. Cf. Chap. 7: Annex, Table 7.1, Case No. 96.

[252]Orlando Sentinel (5 November 1985), Soviet Soldier Goes Back to Army in Kabul. Rossitto (1987), p. 124 f. Cf. Chap. 7: Annex, Table 7.1, Case No. 106.

[253]Rubin (1990). Cf. Chap. 7: Annex, Table 7.1, Case No. 112.

[254]Los Angeles Times (23 April 1997), Trumpeter Arturo Sandoval Is Denied U.S. Citizenship. Cf. Chapter 7: Annex, Table 7.1, Case No. 133. Also see Chap. 3: Sect. 3.4.7.8.

[255]Los Angeles Times (23 December 1993), Fidel Castro's Daughter Gets U.S. Asylum: Defection: Longtime critic of the Cuban dictator flees island. She is now in Atlanta. Cf. Chap. 7: Annex, Table 7.1, Case No. 139. Also see Chap. 3: Sect. 3.4.7.9.

[256]Krieger (1997), p. 233. Cf. Chapter 7: Annex, Table 7.1, Case No. 140.

[257]The New York Times (25 July 1996), Burundi at the Edge; The Washington Post (8 June 1997), Former President of Burundi Leaves Shelter of Embassy. Cf. Chap. 7: Annex, Table 7.1, Case No. 142.

[258]Bradshaw and Fandos-Rius (2016), pp. 286–287. Cf. Chap. 7: Annex, Table 7.1, Case No. 145.

[259]BBC News (13 May 2002), Japan-China refugees row deepens. Cf. Chap. 7: Annex, Table 7.1, Case No. 150.

[260]Jeffries (2006), p. 100. Cf. Chap. 7: Annex, Table 7.1, Case No. 164.

[261]U.S. Department of State, Daily Press Briefing, 30 January 2012; The Washington Post (6 March 2012), Sam LaHood, NGO worker, hid in U.S. Embassy in Cairo for four weeks under 'real fear of arrest'. For further details on the case, also see Clooney (2017), p. 332. Cf. Chap. 7: Annex, Table 7.1, Case No. 183.

[262]The Telegraph (19 February 2013), Bo Xilai's police chief 'sought British protection'. Cf. Chap. 7: Annex, Table 7.1, Case No. 184.

Chinese Chen Guangcheng from late April to 2nd May 2012;[263] to Sudanese Meriam Ibrahim from 26th June to 1st August 2014[264] and to approximately 100 Burundian students on 25th June 2015.[265]

Interestingly two of the aforementioned cases involved the U.S. granting diplomatic protection to its own citizens, whilst three involved the U.S. extending diplomatic protection to citizens of its neighbour, Cuba, one to citizens of Costa Rica, one to a Hungarian, four to Soviet citizens, three to East German citizens, four to Chinese citizens, five to citizens of African states (East Timor, Burundi, Central African Republic and Sudan respectively) and two to citizens of North Korea. In this regard, U.S. practice is global and consistent, spanning every decade of the past 70 years.

Many U.S. cases were, however, motivated by human considerations rather than a sense of legal conviction and can thus be held to be consistent with the concept of humanitarian asylum.[266]

5.3.5.2 Canada

Canada has granted a right to diplomatic asylum on five occasions detailed by Table 7.1: to 50 Chileans after the 1973 *coup d'état*;[267] to six U.S. diplomats who escaped from the Tehran hostage crisis from November 1979 to January 1980;[268] to two North Korean asylum seekers on 11th May 2002;[269] to 44 North Korean asylum seekers from 29th September to December 2004[270] and to Ukrainian anti-government protesters for several days in February 2014.[271] Canada's practice is

---

[263]According to Foreign Ministry Spokesperson Liu Weimin's Remarks on Chen Guangcheng's Entering the US Embassy in China, 2nd May 2012; The Guardian (2 May 2012), Chen Guangcheng leaves US embassy in Beijing. Cf. Chap. 7: Annex, Table 7.1, Case No. 186.

[264]The Guardian (27 June 2014), Sudanese woman Meriam Ibrahim 'safe and well' in US embassy; The Telegraph (16 September 2014), Sudanese Christian Meriam Ibrahim tells for first time of her ordeal. Cf. Chap. 7: Annex, Table 7.1, Case No. 192.

[265]Fox News (26 June 2015), 100 students who sought refuge at US embassy in Burundi leave the premises. Cf. Chap. 7: Annex, Table 7.1, Case No. 194.

[266]Cf. Dahm et al. (1989), p. 291.

[267]Bassuener (2013), p. 429; Kovács and Ádány (2017), p. 182. Cf. Chap. 7: Annex, Table 7.1, Case No. 67. Also see Chap. 3: 3.4.4.

[268]Bassiouni (2014), p. 185. Cf. Chap. 7: Annex, Table 7.1, Case No. 82.

[269]BBC News (13 May 2002), Japan-China refugees row deepens; Chicago Tribune (13 May 2002), 2 North Koreans hole up in Canadian Embassy, Chicago Tribune (15 May 2002), China, Japan in feud over N. Koreans. Cf. Chap. 7: Annex, Table 7.1, Case No. 153.

[270]ABC News, The World Today (30 September 2004), North Korean asylum seekers break into Canadian Embassy in Beijing; Chicago Tribune (23 December 2004), N. Koreans leave Canadian Embassy; Jeffries (2006), p. 102. Cf. Chap. 7: Annex, Table 7.1, Case No. 163.

[271]CBC News (18 February 2014), Ukrainian protesters seek refuge in Canadian Embassy amid crackdown. Also see: National Post (13 July 2015), Investigation uncovers Canadian embassy in Ukraine used as a haven in 2014 by anti-government protesters. Cf. Chap. 7: Annex, Table 7.1, Case No. 191.

rather sporadic. It is also likely that human rights considerations played a role in Canada granting asylum in all five cases.

5.3.5.3 Conclusion

In conclusion, though the state practice of the U.S. is more extensive, that of Canada is less so and is limited to cases in which human rights considerations played a role.[272] There is also no evident state practice for the countries and territories of Greenland, Bermuda and St. Pierre and Miquelon. In sum, the state practice of Northern American states thus lacks the necessary extensiveness and consistency to fulfil the state practice requirement of customary international law for the region of Northern America. The state practice requirement of regional custom is therefore not fulfiled for Northern America.

5.3.6 *Oceania*

Table 7.1 contains only one case of a state from the continent of Oceania granting a right to diplomatic asylum: that of Australia granting asylum to Chinese (Taiwanese) citizen Hou Dejian from June to August 1989.[273] It is clear that this isolated case cannot be held to fulfil the requirement of state practice for Oceanic states. The state practice requirement of regional custom for the region of Oceania is therefore not fulfilled.

5.3.7 *Conclusion*

In conclusion, state practice with regard to diplomatic asylum from the Oceanic and African continents is near to non-existent, consisting of five states granting a right to diplomatic asylum on one single occasion. State practice with regard to Asian states is limited to 25 cases, encompassing twelve different states (including Taiwan, the status of which is internationally disputed and with one case depicting both Iran and Pakistan). State practice of European states is more extensive encompassing 75 cases and with twenty-one of the 50 European states having granted a right to diplomatic asylum in the twentieth and twenty-first Centuries. State practice in Northern America consists of 30 cases, encompassing two out of five states/territories. State practice in Latin America comprises 74 cases, with seventeen of the 23 Latin

[272]For further information on diplomatic asylum as a humanitarian obligation, see Chap. 6.

[273]Human Rights Watch, Repression in China since June 4, 1989, Cumulative Data, An Asia Watch Report, Embargoed for September 28, 1990, October 1990, United States, p. 7. Cf. Chap. 7: Annex, Table 7.1, Case No. 111.

American states having granted a right to diplomatic asylum in the twentieth and twenty-first Centuries.

In sum, state practice comprises of 209 twentieth and twenty-first century cases of diplomatic asylum, with 57 states having granted a *de facto* right to diplomatic asylum on at least one occasion. This falls far short of the aforementioned half of the international community benchmark required for the formation of universal customary international law.[274] State practice therefore lacks the extensiveness required for universal custom. Moreover, even upon alternatively applying the qualitative criterion of sufficiently widespread and representative practice,[275] with near to no state practice from two of the six major continents, the state practice element for universal custom can in any case not be held to be fulfilled.

Though a degree of uniformity in the aforementioned state practice—*de facto* asylum in the context of diplomatic premises being the key feature—is present, the vast variations in the duration of the asylum and the circumstances behind the asylum granted render the consistency of the practice in any case insufficient to fulfil the state practice requirement of customary international law,[276] for which general practice is constitutive.[277]

On a regional level, whilst the state practice of Asian, Northern American and European states is neither sufficiently consistent nor extensive to fulfil the state practice requirement of customary international law, the state practice of Latin America can be held to fulfil this requirement with regard to participating states.

5.4 *Opinio Juris* with Regard to the Practice of Diplomatic Asylum

Having established that the state practice requirement for the practice of diplomatic asylum is not fulfilled on a universal level, but on a regional level for Latin America's participating states, it is necessary to examine the *opinio juris* component of customary international law. In many of the aforementioned cases, a motivation behind the state granting the asylum, i.e whether or not the state feels legally compelled to do so, has proved hard to deduce as states granting asylum tend not to detail their reasons for doing so. This renders it more difficult for a state seeking to prove the positive existence of any such custom.

[274] Cf. Chap. 5: Sect. 5.1.1.

[275] ILC Draft conclusions on identification of customary international law, with commentaries, Adopted by the International Law Commission at its seventieth session, in 2018, and submitted to the General Assembly as a part of the Commission's report covering the work of that session (A/73/10), p. 136.

[276] See Chap. 5: Sects. 5.3.1–5.3.6. Also see UN General Assembly, Question of Diplomatic Asylum, Report of the Secretary-General, 2 September 1975, A/10139 (Part I), paras 24 and 282.

[277] Cf. Conclusion 8 ILC Draft conclusions on identification of customary international law, with commentaries, Adopted by the International Law Commission at its seventieth session, in 2018, and submitted to the General Assembly as a part of the Commission's report covering the work of that session (A/73/10), p. 135 f.

Opinio juris supporting the practice and evidence of states rebuking the practice will be detailed in turn in order to facilitate a conclusion. This *opinio juris* tends to be more general in nature, rather than relating to specific cases.

Though without the state practice requirement first being established, the presence of universal custom or regional custom for the remaining world regions, aside from Latin America's participating states, is precluded, in the interests of a comprehensive analysis *opinio juris* from around the world will be examined.

5.4.1 Opinio Juris *in Favour of the Practice*

5.4.1.1 Latin America

There is a variety of *opinio juris* from Latin America to support a legal right to diplomatic asylum. This includes *opinio juris* for the following states: Argentina,[278] Bolivia,[279] Brazil,[280] Chile,[281] Colombia,[282] Costa

[278] UN General Assembly, 14th Session, Sixth Committee, Summary Record of the 608th Meeting, Agenda Item 55, Report of the International Law Commission on the work of its eleventh session (A/4169, A/C.6/L.443) continued, A/C.6/SR.606, 5 October 1959, p. 28, para. 10.

[279] UN General Assembly, 14th Session, Sixth Committee, Summary Record of the 608th Meeting, Agenda Item 55, Report of the International Law Commission on the work of its eleventh session (A/4169, A/C.6/L.443) continued, A/C.6/SR.606, 5 October 1959, pp. 30–31, para. 35.

[280] The representative for Brazil described diplomatic asylum as "a corner-stone of Latin American international practice" and a "revered Latin American institution:" UN General Assembly, 28th Session, Sixth Committee, 1421st Meeting, Agenda Item 90, Draft convention on the prevention and punishment of crimes against diplomatic agents and other internationally protected persons, A/C.6/SR.1421, 23 October 1973, pp. 119–120, paras 11 and 14. See also UN General Assembly, 29th Session, Sixth Committee, Summary Record of the 1505th Meeting, Agenda Item 105, Diplomatic Asylum, A/C.6/SR.1505, 25 November 1974, p. 243, paras. 17–18.

[281] Cf. The League of Nations, Reports of the Representative of the Dominion of New Zealand on the 95th (Extraordinary), 96th and 97th Sessions of the Council of the League of Nations Held at Geneva in the Years 1936 to 1937, Appendix to the Journals of the House of Representatives, 1937 Session I, A-05b, p. 4. Also see UN General Assembly, 21st Session, Sixth Committee, Summary Record of the 920th Meeting, Agenda Item 85, Draft Declaration on the Right of Asylum, A/C.6/ SR.920, 27 October 1966, p. 115, para. 1; UN General Assembly, 29th Session, Sixth Committee, Summary Record of the 1505th Meeting, Agenda Item 105, Diplomatic Asylum, A/C.6/SR.1505, 25 November 1974, pp. 244–245, para. 26.

[282] Colombian-Peruvian Asylum Case (Colombia v Peru), Memorial Submitted by the Government of the Republic of Colombia, 10 January 1950, p. 13 f; UN General Assembly, 14th Session, Sixth Committee, Summary Record of the 608th Meeting, Agenda Item 55, Report of the International Law Commission on the work of its eleventh session (A/4169, A/C.6/L.443) continued, A/C.6/ SR.606, 5 October 1959, p. 31, paras 39 and 40; UN General Assembly, 28th Session, Sixth Committee, 1421st Meeting, Agenda Item 90, Draft convention on the prevention and punishment of crimes against diplomatic agents and other internationally protected persons, A/C.6/SR.1421, 23 October 1973, p. 118, para. 3; UN General Assembly, 29th Session, Sixth Committee, Summary Record of the 1505th Meeting, Agenda Item 105, Diplomatic Asylum, A/C.6/SR.1505, 25 November 1974, p. 243, para. 20.

Rica,[283] Cuba,[284] Ecuador,[285] El Salvador,[286] Mexico,[287] Paraguay,[288] Uruguay[289] and Venezuela.[290] There is also evidence of Caribbean state Grenada expressly aligning itself to Latin America and recognising the practice of diplomatic asylum.[291]

---

[283]UN General Assembly, 29th Session, Sixth Committee, Summary Record of the 1505th Meeting, Agenda Item 105, Diplomatic Asylum, A/C.6/SR.1505, 25 November 1974, p. 244, paras 24 and 25.

[284]Haya de la Torre Case (Colombia v Peru), Declaration of Intervention by the Government of Cuba, 13 March 1951, p. 118 f.

[285]In recognising a right to diplomatic asylum, Ecuador noted that it had granted such a right to 123 individuals over the course of the preceding year (please note that these cases could not be verified, hence they have been omitted from Table 7.1 of Chap. 7: Annex): UN General Assembly, 14th Session, Sixth Committee, Summary Record of the 604th Meeting, Agenda Item 55, Report of the International Law Commission on the work of its eleventh session continued, A/C.6/SR.604, 30 September 1959, p. 19, para. 24. See also UN General Assembly, 29th Session, Sixth Committee, Summary Record of the 1505th Meeting, Agenda Item 105, Diplomatic Asylum, A/C.6/SR.1505, 25 November 1974, p. 245, para. 27; Art. 41 Ecuadorian Constitution, Republic of Ecuador, Constitution of 2008, Last Updated 31 January 2011, Published in the Official Register, 20 October 2008, Political Database of the Americas; Statement of the Government of the Republic of Ecuador on the asylum request of Julian Assange, News Release, No. 1. https://web.archive.org/web/20130615201655/http://www.mmrree.gob.ec/eng/2012/com042.asp. Last Accessed 16 Dec 2020; IACtHR, Advisory Opinion OC-25/18 of 30 May 2018 Requested by the Republic of Ecuador, The Institution of Asylum and its Recognition as a Human Right in the Inter-American System of Protection (Interpretation and Scope of Articles 5, 22.7 and 22.8 in Relation to Article 1 (1) of the American Convention on Human Rights), p. 3 f.

[286]UN General Assembly, 14th Session, Sixth Committee, Summary Record of the 602nd Meeting, Agenda Item 55, Report of the International Law Commission on the work of its eleventh session (A/4169, A/C.6/L.443) continued, A/C.6/SR.602, 28 September 1959, p. 10, para. 9; General Assembly Resolution 1400 (XIV), Codification of the Principles and Rules of International Law Relating to the Right of Diplomatic Asylum, Note by the Secretariat, Document, A/CN.4/128, 4 March 1960, Yearbook of the International Law Commission 1960, Vol. II, p. 118.para. 2.

[287]UN General Assembly, 14th Session, Sixth Committee, Summary Record of the 608th Meeting, Agenda Item 55, Report of the International Law Commission on the work of its eleventh session, A/C.6/SR.608, 7 October 1959, p. 39, paras 18–20.

[288]UN General Assembly, 21st Session, Sixth Committee, Summary Record of the 923rd Meeting, Agenda Item 85, Draft Declaration on the Right of Asylum, A/C.6, SR.923, 31 October 1966, p. 140, para. 21.

[289]UN General Assembly, 14th Session, Sixth Committee, Summary Record of the 604th Meeting, Agenda Item 55, Report of the International Law Commission on the work of its eleventh session continued, A/C.6/SR.604, 30 September 1959, p. 18, paras 21 and 22.

[290]The principle of asylum, encompassing diplomatic asylum, is a constitutional principle of Venezuela: UN General Assembly, 28th Session, Sixth Committee, 1421st Meeting, Agenda Item 90, Draft convention on the prevention and punishment of crimes against diplomatic agents and other internationally protected persons, A/C.6/SR.1421, 23 October 1973, p. 119, para. 7.

[291]UN General Assembly, 29th Session, Sixth Committee, Summary Record of the 1505th Meeting, Agenda Item 105, Diplomatic Asylum, A/C.6/SR.1505, 25 November 1974, p. 242, paras 11–16.

5.4.1.2 Europe

There is also some, albeit limited, evidence of European states expressly recognising a right to diplomatic asylum. For example, in 1959 Spain stated that "diplomatic asylum had long been recognised and respected by Spain."[292] This, it may be argued, fulfils Spain's obligation to respect the Latin American custom due to its status as their mother-country.[293] Moreover, the UK, in the context of the draft for the codification of the law relating to diplomatic intercourse and immunities, held that mission premises should not be used for providing asylum except "to save life or prevent grave physical injury in the face of an immediate threat or emergency."[294]

5.4.1.3 Oceania

In 1974, Australia expressly declared itself amongst the states which believe "that the institution of diplomatic asylum was now recognized in international law for humanitarian reasons."[295] Nevertheless, Australia lacks the relevant state practice[296] for this to give rise to any customary rule binding upon Australia.

5.4.2 Evidence of States Rebuking the Practice

Despite the existence of *opinio juris* supporting a right to diplomatic asylum, there is also ample evidence of states rebuking the practice. Indeed, Section 9 (b) of the United Nations Headquarters Agreement between the UN and the United States 1947 expressly precludes the possibility of diplomatic asylum in the context of UN headquarters.[297]

---

[292] UN General Assembly, 14th Session, Sixth Committee, Summary Record of the 608th Meeting, Agenda Item 55, Report of the International Law Commission on the work of its eleventh session (A/4169, A/C.6/L.443) continued, A/C.6/SR.606, 5 October 1959, p. 31, para. 43.

[293] Colombian-Peruvian Asylum Case (Colombia v Peru), Judgment of 20 November 1950, ICJ Reports 1950, No. 7, Dissenting Opinion by Judge Azevedo (translation), p. 337.

[294] Yearbook of the International Law Commission, 1957, 394th Meeting, 3 May 1957, p. 54, para. 33. This is consistent with the idea of diplomatic asylum on the basis of humanitarian considerations. Cf. Chap. 6.

[295] UN General Assembly, 29th Session, Sixth Committee, Summary Record of the 1505th Meeting, Agenda Item 105, Diplomatic Asylum, A/C.6/SR.1505, 25 November 1974, p. 241, para. 1. On the Australian initiative to include an item on diplomatic asylum on the 1974 agenda of the GA, see Taylor (2019), pp. 376–396.

[296] See Chap. 5: Sect. 5.3.6.

[297] Agreement between the United Nations and the United States Regarding the Headquarters of the United Nations 1947, Adopted on 26 June 1947, Approved by the General Assembly on 31 October 1947, Entered into force on 21 November 1947, UNTS Vol. No. 147, p. 12.

5.4.2.1 Africa

Though African states have largely remained silent on the issue, there is evidence of at least one African state, Egypt, explicitly rejecting the notion of diplomatic asylum.[298]

5.4.2.2 Asia

Though Asian states have also largely remained silent on the issue, there is evidence of one Asian state expressly rejecting a right to diplomatic asylum—India.[299]

Rudolf holds that new rules of universal international law cannot emerge against the will of the so-called new states of Africa and Asia.[300] With regard to a rule providing for a right to diplomatic asylum, at least two African and Asian states have expressly rejected such a notion.

5.4.2.3 Europe

There is also evidence of several European states explicitly rejecting a right to diplomatic asylum. Austria rejected a legal basis for diplomatic asylum in general international law, though it upheld its regional legal basis in Latin America.[301] Poland has also held the right of diplomatic asylum to apply only to Latin America.[302] Switzerland has described diplomatic asylum as "an abuse of inviolability."[303] Czechoslovakia has furthermore held that the inviolability of the mission premises does not imply a right to asylum and that such asylees should be handed

---

[298] Cited by UN General Assembly, Question of Diplomatic Asylum, Report of the Secretary-General, 2 September 1975, A/10139 (Part I), para. 141.

[299] UN General Assembly, 29th Session, Sixth Committee, Summary Record of the 1505th Meeting, Agenda Item 105, Diplomatic Asylum, A/C.6/SR.1505, 25 November 1974, p. 244, para. 23.

[300] Rudolf (1976), p. 26.

[301] UN General Assembly, 28th Session, Sixth Committee, 1421st Meeting, Agenda Item 90, Draft convention on the prevention and punishment of crimes against diplomatic agents and other internationally protected persons, A/C.6/SR.1421, 23 October 1973, p. 119, para. 10.

[302] UN General Assembly, 21st Session, Sixth Committee, Summary Record of the 919th Meeting, Agenda Item 85, Draft Declaration on the Right of Asylum, A/C.6/SR.919, 26 October 1966, p. 112, para. 30.

[303] League of Nations Committee of Experts for the Progressive Codification of International Law, Report to the Council of the League of Nations on the Questions Which Appear Ripe for International Regulation, Questionnaires Nos 1 to 7, Adopted by the Committee at its Third Session, held in March–April 1927, Geneva, 20 April 1927, p. 243. Cf. Yearbook of the International Law Commission, 1957, 394th Meeting, 3 May 1957, p. 54, para. 38.

over to the local authorities.[304] The UK has also openly rejected diplomatic asylum on multiple occasions,[305] most recently with regard to the dispute which surrounded Julian Assange.[306] The Soviet Union[307] has stated that European countries have not accepted the view of Latin American states regarding diplomatic asylum.[308] Furthermore, the Soviet Union also categorised the issue of diplomatic asylum as being humanitarian in character.[309]

Moreover, there is also ample evidence of European scholars rejecting a right to diplomatic asylum.[310]

5.4.2.4 Latin America

Despite the wealth of *opinio juris* from Latin America with regard to diplomatic asylum,[311] there are still a number of scholars who deny that this is sufficient to give

---

[304]League of Nations Committee of Experts for the Progressive Codification of International Law, Report to the Council of the League of Nations on the Questions Which Appear Ripe for International Regulation, Questionnaires Nos 1 to 7, Adopted by the Committee at its Third Session, held in March–April 1927, Geneva, 20 April 1927, p. 254.

[305]Despite making an exception for diplomatic asylum granted for humanitarian reasons: cf. Yearbook of the International Law Commission, 1957, 394th Meeting, 3 May 1957, p. 54, para. 33.

[306]Yearbook of the International Law Commission, 1949, 16th Meeting, 5 May 1949, p. 127, para. 85; McNair (1956), p. 76; UN General Assembly, Question of Diplomatic Asylum, Report of the Secretary-General, 2 September 1975, A/10139 (Part I), paras 155, 191, 228; William Hague, U.K. Foreign Secretary, Statement on Ecuadorian Government's Decision to Offer Political Asylum to Julian Assange (16th August 2012). Available at: https://www.gov.uk/government/news/foreign-secretary-statement-on-ecuadorian-government-s-decision-to-offer-political-asylum-to-julian-assange. Last Accessed 16 Dec 2020.

[307]Though the majority of the Soviet Union's territory lay within the Asian continent, for the purposes of this book, it will be regarded as a European state due to its greater political affiliation thereto historically.

[308]96th Session of the Council of the League of Nations, First Meeting (Private), 21 January 1937, League of Nations Official Journal, February 1937, p. 67. On the Soviet Union rejecting a right to diplomatic asylum, also see: Yearbook of the International Law Commission, 1957, 394th Meeting, 3 May 1957, p. 54, para. 34; UN General Assembly, 3rd Session, Third Committee, 122nd Meeting, 4 November 1948, Draft International Declaration of Human Rights, p. 342; Jeffery (1985), p. 15. In this regard, it is important to note that there are no reports of any of the modern-day states, which used to form the Soviet Union (These being Russia, Georgia, Moldova, Belarus, Armenia, Azerbaijan, Kazakhstan, Uzbekistan, Turkmenistan, Kyrgyzstan and Tajikistan), ever recognising a right to diplomatic asylum.

[309]96th Session of the Council of the League of Nations, First Meeting (Private), 21 January 1937, League of Nations Official Journal, February 1937, p. 67. This issue will be discussed in greater depth in the context of Chap. 6.

[310]Boczek (2005), p. 51; Dupuy (1976), p. 747; Hobe (2020), p. 308; Schack (2014), p. 386; Värk (2012), pp. 256–257.

[311]Cf. Chap. 5: Sect. 5.4.1.1.

rise to regional custom in Latin America.[312] There is also evidence of Latin American scholars rejecting a right to diplomatic asylum.[313] The IACtHR has also recently held that *opinio juris* is lacking in Latin America.[314]

5.4.2.5 Northern America

The U.S. has also been vocal in its outright rejection of the principle of diplomatic asylum.[315] Equally, several U.S. authors have also expressly rejected a legal basis for such a right.[316] Canada has however not shared this vocalism, though it has also not expressly recognised such a right.

5.4.2.6 Oceania

Though there is evidence of Australia expressly recognising a right to diplomatic asylum on humanitarian grounds,[317] there is also evidence of Australian scholars rejecting a right to diplomatic asylum.[318]

[312] See for example Evans (1951), p. 761; Jeffery (1985), p. 14.

[313] See for example Corpeño (1963).

[314] IACtHR, Advisory Opinion OC-25/18 of 30 May 2018 Requested by the Republic of Ecuador, The Institution of Asylum and its Recognition as a Human Right in the Inter-American System of Protection (Interpretation and Scope of Articles 5, 22.7 and 22.8 in Relation to Article 1(1) of the American Convention on Human Rights), p. 57, para. 162.

[315] See Executive Order No. 5956, Unsanctioned Asylum, Herbert Hoover, White House, 1 December 1932, CDILR 2:104; U.S. Declaration made upon the approval of the Montevideo Convention on Political Asylum 1933; U.S. Department of State, Foreign Relations of the United States, 1949, The United Nations; The Western Hemisphere, Vol. II, Doc. 475, 20 December 1949 (though in relation to the Haya de la Torre case, the U.S. held that Peru had an international commitment to grant Haya de la Torre safe conduct); UN General Assembly, Question of Diplomatic Asylum, Report of the Secretary-General, 2 September 1975, A/10139 (Part I), Fn. 16 from 1975, which notes that no case of diplomatic asylum has been recorded on the North American continent; also see UN General Assembly, Question of Diplomatic Asylum, Report of the Secretary-General, 2 September 1975, A/10139 (Part I), para. 224; Dahm et al. (1989), p. 291; Jeffery (1985), p. 15; Cf. Kimminich (1961), pp. 237–238; Leonhard (1968), pp. 679–680; Ronning (1965), p. 98 f.; Rossitto (1987), p. 115.

[316] See for example Esquirol (2012), p. 559.

[317] See Chap. 5: Sect. 5.4.1.3.

[318] See e.g. Duxbury (2012), p. 1.

5.4.3 *Conclusion*

Though there is ample *opinio juris* with regard to diplomatic asylum for Latin America,[319] the same cannot be said for the other regions. Whilst there is evidence of Spain recognising a right to diplomatic asylum,[320] there is evidence of several European states, Poland, Austria, Switzerland, Czechoslovakia and the United Kingdom, rejecting such a right.[321] Though Australia has recognised the legality of diplomatic asylum in cases in which it is based upon humanitarian considerations,[322] its state practice is too insignificant to give rise to a rule of customary international law status. Though Asian states have largely remained silent on the issue, India has expressly rejected a right to diplomatic asylum.[323] The U.S. has also been vocal in its rejection of such a right, though Canada has remained silent.[324] So too has, for the most part, the African continent.[325] Despite the existence of minority views to the contrary,[326] it can be surmised that *opinio juris* and state practice is sufficient to give rise to a customary rule on diplomatic asylum for the participating states of Latin America.[327] In terms of general international law and the world regions outside of Latin America, *opinio juris* is insufficient to give rise to a rule of customary international law status.

5.5 Does Customary International Law Support a Right to Diplomatic asylum?

In summary, state practice and *opinio juris* are insufficient to support the practice of diplomatic asylum in customary international law on a universal level.

Owing to their extraordinary political, economic and geographical conditions facilitating the need for the practice, Latin American states may even be regarded as constituting specially affected states with regard to the formation of customary

---

[319]See Chap. 5: Sect. 5.4.1.1. Evidence of the practice being rebuked by Latin American states is in the minority.

[320]See Chap. 5: Sect. 5.4.1.2.

[321]See Chap. 5: Sect. 5.4.2.3.

[322]See Chap. 5: Sect. 5.4.1.3.

[323]See Chap. 5: Sect. 5.4.2.2.

[324]See Chap. 5: Sect. 5.4.2.5.

[325]Cf. Kimminich (1961), p. 237 holding that there is no evidence of a regional custom in Africa.

[326]See Chap. 5: Sect. 5.4.2.4.

[327]Colombian-Peruvian Asylum Case (Colombia v Peru), Judgment of 20 November 1950, ICJ Reports 1950, No. 7, Dissenting Opinion by Judge M. Caicedo Castilla (translation), p. 370; Yearbook of the International Law Commission, 1957, 394th Meeting, 3 May 1957, p. 56, para. 56; Barberis (1985), p. 41. Cf. Doehring (2004), p. 129, para. 293. On the participating states, see Chap. 5: Sect. 5.3.4.

international law on the right to diplomatic asylum. Nevertheless, there are still an insufficient number of states with both sufficiently general, consistent and uniform state practice alongside corresponding *opinio juris* for a customary international law rule with universal scope to be constituted. Moreover, a number of states have expressly rejected such a right. In summary, the right to diplomatic asylum fails to find a legal basis in customary international law on a universal level.

With regard to regional custom, such a right can be ascertained only with regard to the region of Latin America in respect of participating states. The scope of a right to diplomatic asylum under customary international law is therefore limited hereto.[328]

References

Akehurst M (1975) Custom as a source of international law. BYIL 47(1):1–53

Aust A (2010) Handbook of international law, 2nd edn. Cambridge University Press, Cambridge

Bailey N (1955) Asylum and Haya de la Torre. JIA 9(1):82–86

Balbastro AE (1959) Comments, the right of diplomatic Asylum. PJL 34(3):343–367

Barberis (1985) Asylum, Diplomatic. In: Biglieri E, Prati G (eds) Encyclopedia of public international law, Published under the Auspices of the Max Planck Institute for comparative public law and international law under the direction of Rudolf Bernhardt, 8: human rights and the individual in International Law, International Economic Relations, North Holland. Elsevier Science Publishers B.V., Amsterdam, pp 40–42

Bassiouni MC (2014) International extradition, United States law and practice, 6th edn. Oxford University Press, New York

Bassuener K (2013) The fall and rise of Chilean democracy: 1973–1989. In: Kinsman J, Bassuener K (eds) A diplomat's handbook for democracy development support, 3rd edn. Centre for International Governance Innovation, Waterloo, pp 417–431

Boczek BA (2005) International law, a dictionary, dictionaries of international law, No. 2. The Scarecrow Press Inc., Lanham

Bradley CA, Goldsmith JL (1997) Customary international law as Federal Common Law: a critique of the modern law position. HLR 110(4):815–876

Bradshaw R, Fandos-Rius J (2016) Historical dictionary of the Central African Republic. Rowman and Littlefield, Maryland

Cassese A (2005) International law, 2nd edn. Oxford University Press, Oxford

Cheng B (1997) Studies in international space law. Clarendon Press, Oxford

Choi G (2018) North Korean Refugees in South Korea: change and challenge in settlement support policy. KJIS 16(1):77–98

Clooney A (2017) Human rights. In: Roberts I (ed) Satow's diplomatic practice, 7th edn. Oxford University Press, Oxford, pp 305–334

Cohen JA, Chiu H (1974) People's China and international law, a documentary study, vol 2. Princeton University Press, Princeton

Corpeño VRS (1963) El asilo diplomático: su aspecto antijurídico e inhumano, Universidad de San Carlos de Guatemala USAC. Facultad de Ciencias Jurídicas y Sociales, Guatemala

[328] Case Concerning the Rights of Nationals of the United States of America in Morocco (France v United States of America), Judgment of 27 August 1952, ICJ Reports 1952, No. 11, p. 200.

Craven MCR (1998) The problem of state succession and the identity of states under International Law. EJIL 9:142–162
Crawford J (2019) Brownlie's principles of public international law, 9th edn. Oxford University Press, Oxford
Crawford J, Pellet A, Redgwell C (2013) Anglo-American and continental traditions in advocacy before international courts and tribunals. CJICL 2:1–23
D'Amato A (1969) The concept of special custom in international law. AJIL 63:211–223
Da Rocha FA, Carvalho C, Graeff Machry F, Barreto Vianna Rigon P (2013) Formation and evidence of customary international law. UFRGS Model United Nations J 1:182–201
Dahm G, Delbrück J, Wolfrum R (1989) Völkerrecht, vol I/1, 2nd edn. De Gruyter, Berlin
Danilenko GM (1993) Law-making in the international community. Martinus Nijhoff Publishers, Dordrecht
Dembinski L (1988) The modern law of diplomacy, external missions of States and International Organizations. Martinus Nijhoff Publishers, Dordrecht
Denza E (2016) Diplomatic law, Commentary on the Vienna Convention on Diplomatic Relations, 4th edn. Oxford University Press, Oxford
Doehring K (2004) Völkerrecht, 2nd edn. C. F. Müller, Heidelberg
Dumberry P (2016) The formation and identification of rules of customary international law in international investment law, Cambridge studies in international and comparative law. Cambridge University Press, Cambridge
Dupuy PM (1976) La position française en matière d'asile diplomatique. AFDI 22:743–755
Duxbury A (2012) Assange and the law of diplomatic relations. ASILI 16(32). https://www.asil.org/insights/volume/16/issue/32/assange-and-law-diplomatic-relations. Last Accessed 16 Dec 2020
East R, Thomas RJ (2003) Profiles of people in power: the World's Government leaders, 1st edn. Routledge, London
Elias O (1995) The nature of the subjective element in Customary International Law. ICLQ 44 (3):501–520
Ensalaco M (2000) Chile under Pinochet, recovering the truth. University of Pennsylvania Press, Philadelphia
Esquirol JL (2012) Latin America. In: Fassbender B, Peters A, Peter S, Högger D (eds) The Oxford handbook of the history of international law, 1st edn. Oxford University Press, Oxford, pp 553–577
Evans AE (1951) The Colombian-Peruvian Asylum case: termination of the judicial phase. AJIL 45 (4):755–762
Evans AE (1965) Reviewed Work(s): El Asilo Diplomatico: Su Aspecto Antijuridico e Inhumano. by Roberto S. Corpen. AJIL 59(3):674–675
Farhangi LS (1986) Insuring against abuse of diplomatic immunity. SLR 38(6):1517–1547
Farkas JA (2016) Sheltered by the Embassy of Belgium in Budapest, The Hungarian Review of 1956. Hungarian Rev VII(5). http://hungarianreview.com/article/20160924_sheltered_by_the_embassy_of_belgium_in_budapest. Last Accessed 16 Dec 2020
Fastenrath U (1996) Das Recht der Staatensukzession. In: Fastenrath U, Schweisfurth T, Ebonroth CT (eds) Das Recht der Staatensukzession (The Law of State Succession), BDGVR 35. C.F. Müller, Heidelberg, pp 9–48
Hobe S (2020) Einführung in das Völkerrecht, 11th edition, A. Francke Verlag, Tübingen
International Business Publications (2013) Haiti, Constitution and citizenship laws handbook. Strategic Information and Developments International Business Publications, Washington D.C
Jeffery AJ (1985) Diplomatic Asylum: its problems and potential as a means of protecting human rights. SAJHR 1:10–30
Jeffries I (2006) North Korea, a guide to economic and political developments. Routledge, Oxon
Kammerhofer J (2004) Uncertainty in the formal sources of international law: customary international law and some of its problems. EJIL 15(3):523–553
Kimminich O (1961) Asyl in Stützpunkten der UN Truppen. ZfP 8(3):235–240

Kirchheimer O (1959) Asylum. TAPSR 53(4):985–1016
Kleiner J (2010) Diplomatic practice, between tradition and innovation. World Scientific Publishing Company Limited, Hackensack
Kovács P, Ádány TV (2017) The non-customary practice of diplomatic Asylum. In: Behrens P (ed) Diplomatic law in a new millennium. Oxford University Press, Oxford, pp 179–203
Krieger H (ed) (1997) East Timor and the International Community, basic documents, Cambridge International Document Series, vol 10. Research Centre for International Law/University of Cambridge/Cambridge University Press, Cambridge/New York/Melbourne
Krüger H (1957) Souveränität und Staatengemeinschaft. In: Krüger H, Erler G (eds) Zum Problem der Souveränität, BDGVR 1. C.F.Müller, Karlsruhe, pp 1–28
Leonhard AT (1968) Regional particularism: the views of the Latin American Judges on the International Court of Justice. UMLR 2(3):674–685
Lepard BD (2010) Customary international law, a new theory with practical applications, ASIL studies in international legal theory. Cambridge University Press, New York
McNair A (1956) International law opinions, vol. II, Peace. Cambridge University Press, Cambridge
Moral Roncal AM (2013) An analysis of foreign diplomatic aid to the Catholic Clergy during the Spanish Civil War (1936–1939). Religions 4:96–115
Payendeh M, Saake C (2019) Diplomatisches Asyl als Einmischung? Venezuelas Oppositionsführer Leopoldo López in der spanischen Botschaft. In: Verfassungsblog. https://verfassungsblog.de/diplomatisches-asyl-als-einmischung-venezuelas-oppositionsfuehrer-leopoldo-lopez-in-der-spanischen-botschaft/. Last Accessed 16 Dec 2020
Peterson N (2008) Der Wandel des ungeschriebenen Völkerrechts im Zuge der Konstitutionalisierung. AdV 46(4):502–523
Riveles S (1989) Diplomatic Asylum as a Human Right: the Case of the Durban Six. HRQ 11:139–159
Roberts JB (1987) Notes and comments, diplomatic Asylum: an inappropriate solution for East Germans desiring to move to the West. TICLJ 1:231–261
Roberts A, Sivakumaran S (2018) The theory and reality of the sources of International Law. In: Evans MD (ed) International law, 5th edn. Oxford University Press, Oxford, pp 89–119
Romero Salvadó FJ (2013) Historical dictionary of the Spanish Civil War. The Scarecrow Press Inc., Lanham
Ronning CN (1965) Diplomatic Asylum: legal norms and political reality in Latin American relations. Martinus Nijhoff, The Hague
Rossitto AM (1987) Diplomatic Asylum in the United States and Latin America: a comparative analysis. BJIL 13:111–135
Rubin AP (1990) Diplomatic Asylum and Fang Lizhi. Diplomacy and Statescraft 1(1):84–89
Rudolf W (1976) Neue Staaten und das Völkerrecht. AdV 17(1):1–45
Ryu J (2016) A study on the current status of the support legislation for North Korean defectors and improvement proposals, Research Report. Korean Legislation Research Institute, Geumnam-myeon
Schack H (2014) Zugriff auf Potentatengelder – zwischen Vollstreckungsimmunität und Opferschutz. In: Paulus AL, Dethloff N, Giegerich T et al (eds) Internationales, nationales und privates Recht: Hybridisierung der Rechtsordnungen – Immunität, Issue 46, BDGIR. C.F. Müller, Heidelberg, pp 377–397
Scott JC (1989) Indochina's refugees, oral histories from Laos, Cambodia and Vietnam. McFarland & Company, Jefferson, North Carolina/London
Sen B (1988) A Diplomat's handbook of international law and practice, 3rd edn. Martinus Nijhoff, Dordrecht
Shah P (2007) Asylum, diplomatic. In: MPEPIL (Online). Oxford University Press, Oxford. https://opil.ouplaw.com/view/10.1093/law:epil/9780199231690/law-9780199231690-e756. Last Accessed 16 Dec 2020

Shahabuddeen M (1996) Precedent in the World Court, Hersch Lauterpacht Memorial Lectures. University of Cambridge Research Centre for International Law, Grotius Publications, Cambridge University Press, Cambridge/New York
Simándi I (2015) The tragedy of Prime Minister Imre Nagy and the Radio Free Europe – 1956–1958. WBHR 1:115–126. http://wbhr.cz/images/issues/WBHR_2015_1.pdf. Last Accessed 16 Dec 2020
Talmon S (2015) Determining customary international law: the ICJ's methodology between induction, deduction and assertion. EJIL 26(2):417–443
Taylor S (2019) Australia's diplomatic asylum initiative at the United Nations: comparing international law rhetoric with foreign policy practice. AJIA 73(4):376–396
Vági Z, Csösz L, Kádár G (2013) The Holocaust in Hungary, evolution of a Genocide. AltaMira Press, Plymouth
Värk R (2012) Diplomatic asylum: theory, practice and the case of Julian Assange. Sisekaitseakadeemia Toimetised 11:240–259
von Arnauld A (2019) Völkerrecht, 4th edn. C.F. Müller, Heidelberg
Voyiakis E (2011) Voting in the general assembly as evidence of customary international law. In: Allen S, Xanthaki A (eds) Reflections on the UN declaration on the rights of indigenous people. Hart Publishing, Oxford/Portland, pp 209–224
Weisburd AM (2009) The International Court of Justice and the concept of state practice. UPJIL 31 (2):295–372

Chapter 6
Diplomatic Asylum on the Basis of Humanitarian Considerations

Though a universal legal basis for the practice of diplomatic asylum could not be directly identified under either international treaty law or customary international law,[1] it is possible that such a practice could finds its legal basis on the grounds of human rights obligations. Indeed, many states have granted a right to diplomatic asylum motivated by the fundamental human rights of the individual concerned. Where a threat to life or limb is deemed to be immediate, this practice may be referred to as humanitarian asylum.[2] Hence, in the absence of *lex specialis,* relevant *lex generalis*, which may be applicable to the issue of diplomatic asylum, will be analysed. Owing to the modern-day trend of human rights obligations constituting the motivation for many states granting diplomatic asylum, the following chapter will explore whether or not human rights obligations suffice, in the absence of more specific *lex specialis*, to provide a legal basis for the practice of diplomatic asylum on a universal level.

6.1 Human Rights Considerations As a Source of Law

Against the backdrop of the post-war era and the birth of human rights denoted by the proclamation of the Universal Declaration on Human Rights,[3] even in the early days of the International Court of Justice, human rights considerations were already

[1]Cf. Chaps. 4 and 5.

[2]Marauhn and Simon (2012), p. 598. Cf. IACtHR, Advisory Opinion OC-25/18 of 30 May 2018 Requested by the Republic of Ecuador, The Institution of Asylum and its Recognition as a Human Right in the Inter-American System of Protection (Interpretation and Scope of Articles 5, 22.7 and 22.8 in Relation to Article 1(1) of the American Convention on Human Rights), p. 56, para. 155 describing diplomatic asylum as a "humanitarian practice."

[3]General Assembly Resolution 217 A (III), 183rd Plenary Meeting, 10 December 1948.

L. Hughes-Gerber, *Diplomatic Asylum*,
https://doi.org/10.1007/978-3-030-73046-8_6

recognised as a basis for legal obligations. For example, the Corfu Channel[4] judgment held:

> Such obligations are based…on certain general and well-recognized principles, namely: elementary considerations of humanity.[5]

Thus, humanitarian principles underpinned international obligations as early as 1949.

Similarly, in the context of the International Status of South-West Africa Advisory Opinion,[6] Judge Álvarez held:

> To achieve these purposes this law must lay stress on the notion of obligation of States, not only between themselves, but also toward the international community. It must limit absolute international sovereignty of States according to the new requirements of the life of peoples, and must yield to the changing necessities of that life.[7]

Therefore, the traditional notion of absolute state sovereignty has now become subject to the obligations a state owes to the entire international community, with human rights obligations constituting examples of such obligations. These human rights obligations have succeeded in securing increased institutional protection in the post-war period, particularly since the establishment of the United Nations.[8]

It is important to note the timing of both of these statements, in 1949 and 1950 respectively, long before the era of *erga omnes* obligations.[9] Nevertheless, this idea of general, well recognised principles owed to the entire international community paved the way for the later advent of *erga omnes* obligations. In this vein, the international legal order has continued to develop more and more of a human face.[10] Indeed, older more established principles of international law have to some degree been superseded by newly emerging principles of humanity. In this regard, former Secretary-General Kofi Annan held in 1999:

> State sovereignty, in its most basic sense, is being redefined by the forces of globalization and international cooperation. The State is now widely understood to be the servant of its people, and not vice versa.[11]

---

[4] See The Corfu Channel Case (United Kingdom of Great Britain and Northern Ireland v Albania), Merits, Judgment of 9 April 1949, ICJ Reports 1949, No. 1, p. 4 f.

[5] The Corfu Channel Case (United Kingdom of Great Britain and Northern Ireland v Albania), Merits, Judgment of 9 April 1949, ICJ Reports 1949, No. 1, p. 22.

[6] See International Status of South-West Africa, Advisory Opinion of 11 July 1950, ICJ Reports 1950, No. 10, p. 128 f.

[7] International Status of South-West Africa, Advisory Opinion of 11 July 1950, ICJ Reports 1950, No. 10, Dissenting Opinion by Judge Álvarez (translation), p. 176.

[8] Cf. Fremuth (2015), p. 16.

[9] First introduced by Case Concerning the Barcelona Traction, Light and Power Company, Limited (New Application: 1962) (Belgium v Spain), Second Phase, Judgment of 5 February 1970, ICJ Reports 1970, No. 50, p. 31, paras 33 and 34 in 1970.

[10] Cf. Hobe (1998), p. 219.

[11] United Nations, Secretary General Presents his Annual Report to General Assembly, Press Release, SG/SM/7136, GA/9596, 20 September 1999. https://www.un.org/press/en/1999/19990920.sgsm7136.html. Last Accessed 16 Dec 2020.

Indeed, state sovereignty is no longer understood as an absolute concept but as a relevant concept in the light of the international community's human rights obligations, particularly those with *jus cogens* status.[12] This coincides with the increasingly important role of the individual in international law.[13]

6.2 The Applicability of Human Rights Provisions and Principles to Diplomatic Asylum

The idea that diplomatic protection should extend to the protection of human rights is not universally accepted.[14] Nevertheless, Latin American states have long argued that their granting of a right to diplomatic asylum constitutes a humanitarian obligation.[15] As early as 1950, the Institute of International Law drafted a resolution protecting the right of diplomatic asylum on humanitarian grounds, safeguarding such a right where it was granted:

> to any person whose life, liberty or person is threatened by violence emanating from the local authorities or against which they are obviously powerless to protect him, or even which they tolerate or provoke.[16]

---

[12]See for example Peters (2009), pp. 514, 522; Simonovic (2002), pp. 371–381. Similarly, Tomuschat holds that the international legal order is no longer characterised solely by state sovereignty but that states are now required to protect human rights for the benefit of their citzens. Of these two fundamental concepts (state sovereignty and human rights), human rights have consistently increased in importance to render the current international legal system more individualistic compared to its state-centred origins: see Tomuschat (1999), pp. 161–162. Cf. Hobe (1998), p. 220 arguing that states are, by virtue of the institutionalisation of human rights, subject to increased international control.

[13]Orakhelashvli (2000), p. 241 f; Peters (2013), p. 1 f.

[14]Vermeer-Künzli (2007), p. 2.

[15]Cf. 96th Session of the Council of the League of Nations, First Meeting (Private), 21 January 1937, League of Nations Official Journal, February 1937, p. 65; Art. 2 Convention on Asylum; Art. 3 Montevideo Convention; UN General Assembly, 14th Session, Sixth Committee, Summary Record of the 608th Meeting, Agenda Item 55, Report of the International Law Commission on the work of its eleventh session, A/C.6/SR.608, 7 October 1959, p. 39, para. 24 with regard to Chile; UN General Assembly, 28th Session, Sixth Committee, 1421st Meeting, Agenda Item 90, Draft convention on the prevention and punishment of crimes against diplomatic agents and other internationally protected persons, A/C.6/SR.1421, 23 October 1973, pp. 119–120, paras 7 and 13 with regard to Venezuela and Brazil respectively; Accioly (1961), pp. 291, 293 from a Brazilian author. See also Colombian-Peruvian Asylum Case (Colombia v Peru), Counter-Memorial Submitted by the Government of the Republic of Peru, 21 March 1950, pp. 121–122. In this regard, states are regularly compelled by humanitarian considerations to admit refugees into their territories: cf. Kokott (1999), pp. 3–27; Martin and Schoenholtz (1999), p. 47.

[16]Art. 3 (2) Institute of International Law (5th Commission), Resolutions Adopted at its Bath Session, Asylum in Public International Law (Excluding Neutral Asylum), Sept 1950, AJIL: 45(2): Supplement: Official Documents (Apr.1951): 16.

Diplomatic asylum was therefore limited to situations in which a risk to the fundamental rights of the would-be asylee existed. This risk could emanate from the territorial authorities of the receiving state or even externally but which the receiving state is unable or unwilling to guard against. The right to territorial asylum was also linked to the "fulfilment of humanitarian duties.[17]"

Several authors have also argued for the recognition of a right to diplomatic asylum upon humanitarian grounds.[18] Furthermore, there is evidence of several states, aside from Latin American states, recognising a right to diplomatic asylum where it is granted for humanitarian reasons.[19] Moreover, this is also consistent with the idea of diplomatic protection as protecting individuals from the state in which they reside. In this regard, Borchard noted:

> Diplomatic protection, therefore, is a complementary or reserved right invoked only when the state of residence fails to conform with this international standard [*the performance of its international duties*].[20]

Thus, diplomatic protection only comes into play when an individual's state of residence is failing to comply with its international obligations, compelling the state granting diplomatic protection to act on that individual's behalf.

Traditionally, the ICJ has distinguished between reciprocal rights capable of diplomatic protection and *erga omnes* rights owed to the entire international community.[21] Rights with *erga omnes* status, such as fundamental human rights, were held to be incapable of being subject to diplomatic protection. However, this is changing. Indeed, Vermeer-Künzli holds in this respect that courts have displayed a

---

[17]Art. 2 (1) Institute of International Law (5th Commission), Resolutions Adopted at its Bath Session, Asylum in Public International Law (Excluding Neutral Asylum), Sept 1950, AJIL: 45(2): Supplement: Official Documents (Apr.1951): 16.

[18]Cf. Foakes and Denza (2017), p. 234; Jeffery (1985), p. 13; Porcino (1976), p. 448 f. Cf. McNair (1956), p. 76 stating that the UK has frequently authorised temporary asylum for humanitarian reasons. Also see Evans (1965), p. 674 stating that states granting diplomatic asylum may justify it as humanitarian so as not to acknowledge it as a lawful practice and von Arnauld (2019), p. 258, para. 586 providing that such a right is overwhelmingly accepted.

[19]For example, the UK and Australia respectively: Yearbook of the International Law Commission, 1957, 394th Meeting, 3 May 1957, p. 54, para. 33; UN General Assembly, 29th Session, Sixth Committee, Summary Record of the 1505th Meeting, Agenda Item 105, Diplomatic Asylum, A/C.6/SR.1505, 25 November 1974, p. 241, para. 1; McNair (1956), p. 76. Cf. The Soviet Union, though rejecting such a right, stated that such a right is humanitarian in nature: 96th Session of the Council of the League of Nations, First Meeting (Private), 21 January 1937, League of Nations Official Journal, February 1937, p. 67; cf. Chap. 7: Annex, Table 7.1, Case No. 179 with regard to the Republic of China. Cf. U.S. Department of State, United States: Policy Guidelines for Asylum Requests, General Policy for Dealing with Requests for Asylum by Foreign Nationals, 4 January 1972, ILM 11(1):228 and 231 with regard to the U.S. recognising the concept of temporary refuge. Also see Foakes and Denza (2017), p. 234 describing diplomatic asylum as a "humanitarian practice."

[20]Borchard (1915), p. 28.

[21]Case Concerning the Barcelona Traction, Light and Power Company, Limited (New Application: 1962) (Belgium v Spain), Second Phase, Judgment of 5 February 1970, ICJ Reports 1970, No. 50, p. 32, para. 33. Also see Gaja (2003), p. 375 f.

readiness to recognise the enforcement of human rights obligations by way of diplomatic protection.[22]

In the following section, various human rights obligations will be examined in order to determine whether their protection may justify states granting a right to diplomatic asylum, which would otherwise be illegitimate under general international law.

6.2.1 *Universal Declaration of Human Rights*

The Universal Declaration of Human Rights was proclaimed by the General Assembly in the context of Resolution 217 A. As it is contained within a General Assembly resolution, the declaration is not strictly legally binding,[23] nevertheless many of its provisions are now regarded as customary international law.[24]

The most important articles for the right to diplomatic asylum are Art. 3 UDHR, protecting the right to life, liberty and security of the person; Art. 5 UDHR, prohibiting torture or cruel, inhuman or degrading treatment or punishment; Art. 7 UDHR, protecting the right to equality before the law; Art. 9 UDHR, prohibiting arbitrary arrest, detention or exile; Art. 11 UDHR, concerning the right to a fair trial; Art. 12 UDHR, protecting against arbitrary interference; Art. 13 UDHR, protecting the right to freedom of movement; Art. 14 UDHR, protecting the right to asylum from persecution; Art. 18 UDHR, protecting the right to freedom of thought, conscience and religion; Art. 19 UDHR, protecting the right to freedom of expression; Art. 20 UDHR, protecting the right to freedom of assembly; Art. 21 UDHR, protecting the right to participate in government, the right of access to public service and democratic elections.

In declaring Julian Assange's enduring stay in the Ecuadorian embassy in London to constitute arbitrary detention, the UN Working Group on Arbitrary Detention relied on Assange's deprivation of liberty to result from his exercise of the rights guaranteed by the following UDHR provisions: Art. 7, 13, 14, 18, 19, 20, 21.[25] The UN Working Group on Arbitrary Detention also clarified that Assange was unable to rely on Art. 14 UDHR, protecting the right to asylum as he was being prosecuted for a non-political offence.[26]

---

[22]Vermeer-Künzli (2006), pp. 280–281.

[23]Cf. Art. 10 UN Charter.

[24]Glendon (2004), p. 5, Fn. 11; Goldsmith (1998), p. 366; Hannum (1996), p. 289; Alston and Goodman (2013), p. 532.

[25]Human Rights Council, Working Group on Arbitrary Detention, Opinions adopted by the Working Group on Arbitrary Detention at its seventy-fourth session, 30 November - 4 December 2015, Opinion No. 54/2015 concerning Julian Assange (Sweden and the United Kingdom of Great Britain and Northern Ireland). p. 1, para. 3.

[26]Art. 14 (2) UDHR; Human Rights Council, Working Group on Arbitrary Detention, Opinions adopted by the Working Group on Arbitrary Detention at its seventy-fourth session, 30 November–4 December 2015, Opinion No. 54/2015 concerning Julian Assange (Sweden and the United Kingdom of Great Britain and Northern Ireland).p. 6, para. 34.

Art. 14 UDHR, however, specifically excludes the possibility of diplomatic asylum in that it protects the right to asylum "in other countries".[27] Diplomatic asylum, of course, may and commonly does take place in an asylee's state of residence/nationality within the diplomatic premises of another state. The practice is thus inconsistent with this provision. In accordance with a systematic interpretation of the treaty-like instrument,[28] the Universal Declaration on Human Rights therefore cannot be held to constitute a legitimate legal basis for the right to diplomatic asylum.

6.2.2 European Convention on Human Rights[29]

The European Convention on Human Rights opened for signature in 1950 and entered into force in 1953. It is binding upon the 47 members of the Council of Europe. As it was based upon the UDHR,[30] the ECHR's provisions strongly correlate to those of the UDHR.

Relevant rights to the practice of diplomatic asylum include Art. 2 ECHR, protecting the right to life; Art. 3 ECHR, prohibiting torture and inhuman and degrading treatment; Art. 5 ECHR, protecting the right to liberty and security; Art. 6 ECHR, protecting the right to a fair trial; Art. 7 ECHR, guarding against arbitrary punishment; Art. 10 ECHR, protecting the right to freedom of expression and; Art. 13 ECHR, protecting the right to an effective remedy.

The scope of protection of the ECHR is of course limited to the Council of Europe member states. It could therefore, in any case, not provide a legal basis for a universal right to diplomatic asylum.

Though the ECtHR hasn't dealt with the issue of diplomatic asylum directly, it has already established that the Convention does not contain the right to political asylum, though it did hold that upon exercising the right to expel aliens, Art.

[27]Cf. IACtHR, Advisory Opinion OC-25/18 of 30 May 2018 Requested by the Republic of Ecuador, The Institution of Asylum and its Recognition as a Human Right in the Inter-American System of Protection (Interpretation and Scope of Articles 5, 22.7 and 22.8 in Relation to Article 1 (1) of the American Convention on Human Rights), p. 41, para. 115.

[28]On systematic interpretation of treaties see Art. 31 (1) VCLT. Also see Lo (2017), p. 196 f.

[29]Convention for the Protection of Human Rights and Fundamental Freedoms 1950, Opened for Signature on 04 November 1950, Entered into Force on 03 September 1953, UNTS Vol. No. 213, p. 221.

[30]Council of Europe, European Convention on Human Rights, Rights and Freedoms in Practice, Teaching Resources, p. 2. Available at: https://www.echr.coe.int/Documents/Pub_coe_Teaching_resources_ENG.pdf. Last accessed 16 Dec 2020; Council of Europe (1961), p. 676. Cf. Schabas (2015), pp. 5–8.

3 ECHR must be considered.[31] A state's jurisdiction within the context of Art. 1 ECHR ("The High Contracting Parties shall secure to everyone within their jurisdiction the rights and freedoms defined in Section I of this convention"), however, is—subject to very few limited exceptions[32]—to be understood as territorial jurisdiction.[33] The (largely military) context of the exceptions to the principle of territorial jurisdiction established to date can be vastly distinguished from the context in the case at hand i.e. a state's diplomatic mission. It would at least be fathomable to argue that a state exercises effective control over its embassy so as to constitute a jurisdictional link between an embassy and a receiving state. However, to permit diplomatic asylum in such a manner based upon the ECHR would be inconsistent with the use of the term effective control in ECtHR precedent to date,[34] the object and purpose of the ECHR[35] and the fundamental importance of the duty of non-interference in international law, particularly in the context of diplomatic relations.[36] Hence, a legal basis for the right to diplomatic asylum where motivated by human rights considerations cannot be found in the ECHR, even on a regional level.

[31]Salah Sheekh v The Netherlands, No. 1948/04, ECHR-2007-1, para. 135.

[32]Banković and Others v. Belgium and Others (dec.) [GC], No. 52207/99 ECHR-2001, para. 6 and M.N. and Others v Belgium (dec.) [GC], No. 3599/18, ECHR 2020, para. 102 holding that the court must assess whether exceptional circumstances exist so as to justify the exercise of a state's extraterritorial jurisdiction. Such an exception has, for example, been held to be constituted in an area in which the state exercises effective control so as to give rise to a jurisdictional link: cf. Loizidou v Turkey [GC], No. 15318/19, (Merits), Reports of Judgments and Decisions 1996-VI, No. 26, para. 56; Al-Skeini and Others v United Kingdom [GC], No. 55721/07, ECHR 2011, para. 149. Cf. IACtHR, Advisory Opinion OC-25/18 of 30 May 2018 Requested by the Republic of Ecuador, The Institution of Asylum and its Recognition as a Human Right in the Inter-American System of Protection (Interpretation and Scope of Articles 5, 22.7 and 22.8 in Relation to Article 1 (1) of the American Convention on Human Rights), p. 60, para. 175. In this vein, also see the argumentation of the Inter-American Commission of Human Rights on the extraterritorial application of the ACHR: Armando Alejandre Jr. et al. v. Cuba, Case 11.589, Inter-American Commission of Human Rights, Report No. 86/99, OAS/Ser.L/V/II.104 (1999), para. 23 f.

[33]Council of Europe/European Court of Human Rights, Guide on Article 1 of the European Convention on Human Rights, Obligations to Respect Human Rights—Concepts of "jurisdiction" and imputability, Updated on 31 August 2019, p. 7. Available at: https://www.echr.coe.int/Documents/Guide_Art_1_ENG.pdf. Last Accessed 16 Dec 2020.

[34]Cf. Loizidou v Turkey [GC], No. 15318/19, (Merits), Reports of Judgments and Decisions 1996-VI, No. 26, para. 56; Al-Skeini and Others v United Kingdom [GC], No. 55721/07, ECHR 2011, para. 149.

[35]The ECHR's preamble references "unity between its members", "justice and peace in the world" and "the rule of law" respectively. The nature of universal diplomatic asylum as creating bilateral discord between states and subverting the criminal jurisdiction of the receiving state is inconsistent with this object and purpose.

[36]Cf. Chap. 4: Sect. 4.1.3.

6.2.3 *International Covenant on Civil and Political Rights*[37]

The International Covenant on Civil and Political Rights was adopted by General Assembly Resolution 2200 (XXI) A on 16th December 1966 and opened for signature on 19th December 1966.[38] It entered into force on 23rd March 1976. It now has 173 state parties[39] and can thus be regarded as a universal treaty. For this reason, many of its provisions also have customary international law status.[40]

The provisions of the ICCPR relevant to the granting of a right to diplomatic asylum include: Art. 6 (1) ICCPR, protecting the right to life; Art. 7 ICCPR, prohibiting torture or cruel, inhuman or degrading treatment; Art. 9 ICCPR, protecting the right to liberty and security of the person and the right to a fair trial (components of which are also protected by Art. 14 ICCPR); Art. 12 ICCPR, protecting the right to liberty of movement; Art. 17 ICCPR, protecting against arbitrary or unlawful interference with privacy, family, home or correspondence; Art. 18 ICCPR, protecting the right to freedom of thought, conscience and religion; Art. 19 ICCPR, protecting the right to freedom of expression; Art. 21 ICCPR, protecting the right to peaceful assembly; Art. 22 ICCPR, protecting the right to freedom of association; Art. 25 ICCPR, protecting the right to take part in public affairs, the right to suffrage in fair elections and the right of equal access to the public service; Art. 26 ICCPR, protecting the right to equality before the law and; Art. 27 ICCPR, protecting minorities' rights to their own culture, religion and language.

In declaring Julian Assange's enduring stay in the Ecuadorian embassy in London to constitute arbitrary detention, the UN Working Group on Arbitrary Detention relied on Assange's deprivation of liberty to result from his exercise of the rights guaranteed by the following ICCPR provisions: Art. 12, 18, 19, 21, 22, 25, 26, 27.[41] Moreover the refusal of the Swedish authorities to consider Assange's time spent confined in the embassy in calculating his sentence, were he ever to be convicted of any crime in Sweden, was also held to violate Art. 14 (7) ICCPR.[42]

[37] International Covenant on Civil and Political Rights 1966, Adopted in New York on 16 December 1966, Opened for Signature on 19 December 1966, Entered into Force on 23 March 1976, UNTS Vol. No. 999, p. 171 and Vol. 1057, p. 407.

[38] General Assembly Resolution 2200 (XXI) A, International Covenant on Economic, Social and Cultural Rights, International Covenant on Civil and Political Rights and Optional Protocol to the International Covenant on Civil and Political Rights, 1496th Plenary Meeting, 16 December 1966.

[39] As of April 2021.

[40] See for example with regard to Art. 14 ICCPR: Hamdan v Rumsfeld, 548 U. S. 557 (2006), Opinion of Justice Stevens, pp. 70–71, Fn. 66; see also Filartiga v Pena-Irala, 630 F.2d 876, paras 83 - 85 with regard to the prohibition on torture; Lepard (2010), p. 330.

[41] Human Rights Council, Working Group on Arbitrary Detention, Opinions adopted by the Working Group on Arbitrary Detention at its seventy-fourth session, 30 November - 4 December 2015, Opinion No. 54/2015 concerning Julian Assange (Sweden and the United Kingdom of Great Britain and Northern Ireland), p. 1, para. 3.

[42] Human Rights Council, Working Group on Arbitrary Detention, Opinions adopted by the Working Group on Arbitrary Detention at its seventy-fourth session, 30 November–4 December 2015, Opinion No. 54/2015 concerning Julian Assange (Sweden and the United Kingdom of Great Britain and Northern Ireland), p. 4, para. 19.

Art. 2 (1) ICCPR stipulates that state parties to the ICCPR agree to guarantee the rights protected by the Convention within their own territory. This isn't, however, to say that states cannot be held to be bound by their obligations under the ICCPR outside of their own territory in areas in which they exercise jurisdiction.[43] This is, however, to be distinguished from states seeking to rely on such treaty provisions to give rise to a positive duty, which would otherwise be without a legal basis in general international law. A legal basis for the practice of diplomatic asylum, even where it is solely based on humanitarian considerations, can also not be found within the ICCPR.

6.2.4 EU Charter of Fundamental Rights[44]

The Charter of Fundamental Rights of the European Union became legally binding upon the entry into force of the Lisbon Treaty[45] on 1st December 2009. It applies in the first instance to EU institutions and, in the second, to member states in implementing EU law.[46]

Its provisions relevant to diplomatic asylum are as follows: Art. 1 EU Charter of Fundamental Rights, protecting human dignity; Art. 2 EU Charter of Human Rights, protecting the right to life; Art. 3 EU Charter of Human Rights, protecting the right to integrity of the person; Art. 4 EU Charter of Human Rights, prohibiting torture and degrading or inhuman treatment; Art. 6 EU Charter of Fundamental Rights, protecting the right to liberty and security; Art. 11 EU Charter of Fundamental Rights, protecting the right to freedom of expression; Art. 18 EU Charter of Fundamental Rights, protecting the right to asylum; Art. 19 (2) EU Charter of Fundamental Rights, protecting against extradition to a state in which there is a serious risk of the death penalty, torture or inhuman or degrading treatment or punishment; Art. 47 EU Charter of Fundamental Rights, protecting the right to an effective remedy and to a fair trial.

The scope of the EU Charter of Fundamental Rights is limited by Art. 51 thereof. This provision provides that the Charter is only applicable to member states when

[43]This was held by the ICJ in Legal Consequences of the Construction of a Wall in the Occupied Palestinian Territory, Advisory Opinion of 9 July 2004, ICJ Reports 2004, No. 131, p. 179 f, para. 109 f. On this point, also see Wilde (2013), p. 662, para. 48 f. It must also, however, be noted that the extraterritorial application of human rights treaties is not universally accepted by all states. See for example Hathaway et al. (2011), p. 1 f; Van Schaack (2014), p. 22 f.

[44]Charter of Fundamental Rights of the European Union 2000, Adopted on 7 December 2000, Entered into Force on 1 December 2009, 2012/C 326/02, Official Journal of the European Union, 26 October 2012, C 326/392.

[45]Treaty of Lisbon 2007, amending the Treaty on European Union and the Treaty establishing the European Community, Adopted in Lisbon on 13 December 2007, Entered into Force on 1 December 2009, 2007/C 306/01, Official Journal of the European Union, 17 December 2007, C 306/1.

[46]Cf. Art. 51 (1) EU Charter of Fundamental Rights.

they are implementing EU law. As granting diplomatic asylum can in any case not be considered an implementation of EU law, the EU Charter of Fundamental Rights also fails to provide a legal basis for the practice of diplomatic asylum when it is granted to protect human rights.

6.2.5 African (Banjul) Charter on Human and Peoples' Rights[47]

The African (Banjul) Charter on Human and Peoples' Rights was adopted on 27th June 1981 and entered into force on 21st October 1986. It currently has 54 state parties, encompassing nearly the entire African continent.[48]

Relevant provisions for the right to diplomatic asylum include: Art. 6 ACHPR, protecting the rights to security and liberty of the person and protecting against arbitrary detainment; Art. 7 ACHPR, protecting the right of an individual to have his cause heard; Art. 9 (2) ACHPR, protecting an individual's right to express an opinion, though importantly this must be within the law; Art. 10 ACHPR, protecting the right to free association; Art. 11 ACHPR, protecting the right to free assembly; Art. 12 ACHPR, protecting the rights to free movement, residence and asylum and; Art. 19 ACHPR, protecting the right to equality.

The scope of the African Charter of Human and Peoples' Rights is of course limited to the African continent. It could therefore, in any case, not provide a legal basis for a universal right to diplomatic asylum.

Art. 12 (3) ACHPR provides that individuals have the right to asylum "in other countries in accordance with the laws of those countries and international conventions." Diplomatic asylum, which involves subverting the local laws of the receiving state, is therefore inconsistent with this provision. In accordance with a systematic interpretation of the Charter,[49] the ACHPR therefore cannot be held to constitute a legitimate legal basis for the right to diplomatic asylum.

6.2.6 American Convention on Human Rights

The American Convention on Human Rights was adopted at the Inter-American Specialized Conference on Human Rights on 22 November 1969 in San José, Costa

---

[47] African (Banjul) Charter on Human and Peoples' Rights 1981, Adopted in Nairobi on 27 June 1981, Entered into Force on 21 October 1986, UNTS Vol. No. 1520, p. 217.

[48] As of April 2021. The only state on the African continent which is not party to the Banjul Charter is Morocco.

[49] On systematic interpretation see Art. 31 (1) VCLT. Also see Lo (2017), p. 196 f.

Rica. It entered into force on 18 July 1978. The convention currently has 24 state parties.[50]

The right to asylum is included in Art. 22 ACHR. Other relevant rights include the right to life under Art. 4 ACHR, the right to humane treatment under Art. 5 ACHR, the right to personal liberty under Art. 7 ACHR, the right to a fair trial under Art. 8 ACHR, freedom of thought and expression under Art. 13 ACHR, freedom of association under Art. 16 ACHR, freedom of movement under Art. 22 ACHR and the right to equal protected under Art. 24 ACHR.

The scope of the American Convention on Human Rights is of course geographically limited. It could therefore, in any case, not provide a legal basis for a universal right to diplomatic asylum.

In its 2018 Advisory Opinion, the IACtHR was tasked with answering various asylum-related questions submitted by the Republic of Ecuador, *inter alia* regarding the status of diplomatic asylum as an individual right.[51] The Court, in its Advisory Opinion, affirmed that diplomatic asylum does not fall within the mearning of asylum under Art. 22 (7) ACHR, primarily due to the provision's use of the term "in foreign territory" and both in line with a systematic interpretation of the provision[52] and despite the ACHR's *pro homine* approach.[53] The Court, furthermore, noted that the exclusion of the right to diplomatic asylum can be ascribed to the desire to maintain the right as a state right subject to discretion rather than a right owed to an individual.[54] In line with this rationale, in particular a systematic interpretation of the ACHR, a legal basis for the right of a state to grant diplomatic asylum cannot be identified in the ACHR. The issue, however, remains treaty governed on a regional level by the treaty law framework explored in Chap. 4: Sect. 4.2.[55]

---

[50] As of April 2021.

[51] IACtHR, Advisory Opinion OC-25/18 of 30 May 2018 Requested by the Republic of Ecuador, The Institution of Asylum and its Recognition as a Human Right in the Inter American System of Protection (Interpretation and Scope of Articles 5, 22.7 and 22.8 in Relation to Article 1(1) of the American Convention on Human Rights), p. 3 f.

[52] IACtHR, Advisory Opinion OC-25/18 of 30 May 2018 Requested by the Republic of Ecuador, The Institution of Asylum and its Recognition as a Human Right in the Inter-American System of Protection (Interpretation and Scope of Articles 5, 22.7 and 22.8 in Relation to Article 1(1) of the American Convention on Human Rights), p. 53, para. 147 f.

[53] IACtHR, Advisory Opinion OC-25/18 of 30 May 2018 Requested by the Republic of Ecuador, The Institution of Asylum and its Recognition as a Human Right in the Inter-American System of Protection (Interpretation and Scope of Articles 5, 22.7 and 22.8 in Relation to Article 1(1) of the American Convention on Human Rights), p. 54, para. 149 f.

[54] IACtHR, Advisory Opinion OC-25/18 of 30 May 2018 Requested by the Republic of Ecuador, The Institution of Asylum and its Recognition as a Human Right in the Inter-American System of Protection (Interpretation and Scope of Articles 5, 22.7 and 22.8 in Relation to Article 1(1) of the American Convention on Human Rights), p. 55, para. 154 f.

[55] IACtHR, Advisory Opinion OC-25/18 of 30 May 2018 Requested by the Republic of Ecuador, The Institution of Asylum and its Recognition as a Human Right in the Inter-American System of Protection (Interpretation and Scope of Articles 5, 22.7 and 22.8 in Relation to Article 1(1) of the American Convention on Human Rights), p. 57, para. 163.

6.2.7 Temporary Shelter

Diplomatic asylum may, based *inter alia* upon the aforementioned human rights provisions,[56] correlate with the concept of temporary shelter or refuge in which a state grants temporary refuge in its diplomatic premises to a person facing grave danger to life or limb for humanitarian reasons.[57] Such shelter tends to occur only in the midst of extraordinary circumstances.[58]

Temporary shelter may be distinguished from diplomatic asylum in that safe-conduct is not strived towards.[59] States may be permitted or indeed compelled to grant such a right on the basis of general international law.[60] Indeed, Peru has described the concept of temporary shelter as preferential to states wishing to balance the protection of human rights with the desire not to breach another state's sovereignty and the functioning of its justice system.[61]

One example which has been categorised as a case of such temporary shelter being granted is the case of Cardinal Mindszenty—despite the long duration of his residence in the diplomatic premises.[62] Other examples include refuge granted to GDR refugees in 1989 and to Albanians in 1990.[63] Arguably, all of the cases in which shelter was granted in the context of the U.S. diplomatic mission constitute cases of temporary shelter rather than diplomatic asylum being granted.[64] Indeed, states have certainly in modern times displayed a greater willingness to grant an individual such refuge, where their fundamental human rights have been at stake. An analysis of many of the cases from Table 7.1[65] depicts the frequent use of the practice of temporary shelter as many of the diplomatic asylum cased listed are equally indicative of the practice of temporary shelter.[66]

In this regard, the right to such shelter/asylum stems from the responsibility of states for protecting basic human rights such as those detailed above.[67] In particular,

---

[56]In this regard, states may also rely on human rights obligations under customary international law.

[57]Cf. U.S. Department of State, United States: Policy Guidelines for Asylum Requests, General Policy for Dealing with Requests for Asylum by Foreign Nationals, 4 January 1972, ILM 11 (1):231; Colombian-Peruvian Asylum Case (Colombia v Peru), Counter-Memorial Submitted by the Government of the Republic of Peru, 21 March 1950, p. 121..Also see Dahm et al. (1989), p. 291; Hobe (2020), p. 308; Jully (1951), p. 25; Kimminich (1961), p. 238; Ronning (1965), p. 8; Shah (2007), paras 1, 8.

[58]Oelfke et al. (2018), Art. 22, p. 144. Cf. Hackworth (1941), p. 622.

[59]Oelfke et al. (2018), Art. 22, p. 144.

[60]Kimminich (1961), p. 238; von Arnauld (2019), p. 258, para. 586.

[61]Colombian-Peruvian Asylum Case (Colombia v Peru), Counter-Memorial Submitted by the Government of the Republic of Peru, 21 March 1950, p. 121.

[62]Kimminich (1961), p. 238.

[63]For further information on this concept, see Richtsteig (2010), Art. 22, p. 47.

[64]Kimminich (1961), p. 238.

[65]See Chap. 7: Annex.

[66]Cf. Chap. 3: Sects. 3.1–3.4 and 3.7; Chap. 5: Sect. 5.3.1–5.3.6.

[67]Cf. Art. 56 UN Charter; Dahm et al. (1989), p. 291.

an asylee will be facing persecution due to race, religion, nationality or their political opinions.[68] It is important to note that this practice does not violate the rights of the host state but instead prevents harm from occurring.[69]

This idea of temporary shelter may be regarded as a form of limited recognition of the practice of diplomatic asylum.[70] An important distinction between diplomatic asylum and temporary shelter has, however, been made by Kimminich, holding that temporary shelter, unlike diplomatic asylum, does not compel the receiving state to grant safe conduct to the sheltered individual(s).[71] However, both diplomatic asylum and temporary shelter may give rise to a later claim for territorial asylum if the individual concerned is able to leave the country.[72]

There is, however, no evidence of states granting such temporary shelter based upon the conviction that they have a legal obligation to do so i.e. fulfilling the *opinio juris* element of customary international law.[73] Hence the concept of temporary shelter, whilst indicative of state practice relating to diplomatic asylum, cannot in any case be held to constitute a rule of customary international law status.

6.2.8 *Deriving from the Principle of Humanitarian Intervention*

A legal basis for diplomatic asylum granted due to humanitarian considerations has also been held to emerge from the principle of humanitarian intervention.[74]

Humanitarian intervention, of course, in the classical sense denotes the use of military force by a state as a response to grave human rights breaches by another state.[75] Whilst traditionally humanitarian intervention developed as an exception to the general principle of non-intervention, it now constitutes an exception to the prohibition on the use of force.[76] The principle of humanitarian intervention is

[68] Riveles (1989), p. 158.

[69] Dahm et al. (1989), p. 291.

[70] Riveles (1989), p. 158. Cf. U.S. Department of State, United States: Policy Guidelines for Asylum Requests, General Policy for Dealing with Requests for Asylum by Foreign Nationals, 4 January 1972, ILM 11(1):231-232; Cf. Kau (2019), pp. 197–198, para. 74. See also Dahm et al. (1989), p. 291 referring to diplomatic asylum as a special form of such humanitarian asylum.

[71] Kimminich (1961), p. 238.

[72] Cf. Kimminich (1961), p. 239.

[73] Cf. Shah (2007), para. 10. Also see von Arnauld (2019), p. 258, para. 586 providing that state practice is lacking in this regard.

[74] See for example von Pollern (1980), p. 95.

[75] Cf. Lowe and Tzanakopoulos (2011), para. 3.

[76] Wolf (1988), p. 338.

regarded by some scholars as constituting a rule of customary international law status.[77]

As with temporary shelter, such asylum is granted on the basis of a threat to life, limb or liberty stemming from the territorial authorities of the host state.

The practice of granting diplomatic asylum as a form of humanitarian intervention cannot, however, be held to constitute a rule with customary international law status.[78] This owes to a distinct lack of state practice and *opinio juris* in this regard.

6.2.9 Non-refoulement

The principle of non-refoulement in international law provides that no individual should be returned to a country in which they may force torture, cruel, inhuman or degrading treatment or punishment or any other irreparable harm,[79] including detention, arrest or any other deprivation of liberty.[80] The right is protected by a wide range of international treaties, with both regional and universal scope.[81]

The principle of non-refoulement is not, however, directly relevant to the issue of diplomatic asylum as the sending state (and the state granting asylum), being outside of its own jurisdiction, does not have the authority to extradite an individual.[82] Therefore, a state granting diplomatic asylum cannot be subject to a legal obligation

[77]See for example Adjei (2005), p. 21; Merriam (2001), p. 119; Modibo Ocran (2002), p. 44. Rejecting a customary international law status for the principle, see: Deutscher Bundestag, Wissenschaftliche Dienste, Völkerrechtliche Grundlagen der humanitären Hilfe unter besonderer Berücksichtigung Syriens, WD 2—3000—043/13, 2016 p. 12; Heintze (1998), p. 186; Henke (2002), p. 96; Oeter (2009), p. 45.

[78]Von Pollern (1980), p. 95.

[79]Cf. Art. 22 (8) American Convention on Human Rights; Art. 3 (1) Convention against Torture (Convention against Torture and Other Cruel, Inhuman, Degrading Treatment or Punishment 1984, Adopted in New York on 10 December 1984, Entered into Force on 26 June 1987, UNTS Vol. No. 1465, p. 85); Art. 3 Inter-American Convention to Prevent and Punish Torture (Inter-American Convention to Prevent and Punish Torture 1985, Adopted at the 15th Regular Session of the General Assembly of the Organisation of American States in Cartagena de Indias, Colombia on 12 September 1985, Entered into Force on 28 February 2007, OAS Treaty Series No. 67); Art. 19 (2) EU Charter of Fundamental Rights.

[80]Art. 2 and 16 International Convention for the Protection of all Persons Against Enforced Disappearance (International Convention for the Protection of all Persons Against Enforced Disappearance 2006, Adopted in New York on 20 December 2006, Entered into Force on 23 December 2010, UNTS Vol. No. 2176, p. 3).

[81]Cf. Art. 31 Convention relating to the Status of Refugees 1951 (which has 146 state parties as of April 2021); Art. 22 (8) ACHR (which has twenty-four state parties as of April 2021); Art. 3 Convention against Torture (which has 171 parties as of April 2021); Art. 3 Inter-American Convention to Prevent and Punish Torture (which has eighteen state parties as of April 2021); Art. 19 (2) EU Charter of Fundamental Rights; Art. 16 International Convention for the Protection of all Persons Against Enforced Disappearance (which has 63 parties as of April 2021).

[82]Cf. Kau (2019), p. 197, para. 74.

not to extradite an individual based upon protection of their human rights. However, the non-refoulement principle has been held to be applicable to persons in an embassy being removed and handed over to the territorial authorities.[83] Nevertheless, whilst this may oblige a state to provide an individual with protection, it does not oblige such a state to provide an individual with diplomatic asylum.[84] In any case, the principle of non-refoulement is not absolute and is subject to exceptions.[85]

The principle of non-refoulement cannot be held to constitute a legal basis for the principle of diplomatic asylum even where it is motivated by human rights considerations.

6.2.10 Conclusion

In conclusion, neither treaty (or in the case of the UDHR treaty-like) provisions, nor customary international law provide a legal basis for a right to diplomatic asylum based on humanitarian considerations.[86] Furthermore, and importantly, diplomatic protection is certainly not the only means available to a state wishing to respond to human rights violations.[87] It is arguably also not even an appropriate vehicle for invoking responsibility. Art. 48 ILC Draft Articles on the Responsibility of States for Internationally Wrongful Acts endows states with legal standing with regard to breaches of *erga omnes* norms[88]—many human rights boast *erga omnes* status.[89]

---

[83] European Commission on Human Rights, W.M. v. Denmark, No. 17392/90. Decision on Admissibility of 14 October 1992, para. 1, and Human Rights Committee, Case of Mohammad Munaf v. Romania (Communication No.1539/2006), UN Doc. CCPR/C/96/D/1539/2006, Views adopted on 21 August 2009, paras. 14.2 and 14.5; IACtHR, Advisory Opinion OC-25/18 of 30 May 2018 Requested by the Republic of Ecuador, The Institution of Asylum and its Recognition as a Human Right in the Inter-American System of Protection (Interpretation and Scope of Articles 5, 22.7 and 22.8 in Relation to Article 1(1) of the American Convention on Human Rights), p. 65; para. 189.

[84] IACtHR, Advisory Opinion OC-25/18 of 30 May 2018 Requested by the Republic of Ecuador, The Institution of Asylum and its Recognition as a Human Right in the Inter-American System of Protection (Interpretation and Scope of Articles 5, 22.7 and 22.8 in Relation to Article 1(1) of the American Convention on Human Rights), p. 67, para. 198.

[85] Hailbronner (2002), p. 53.

[86] Cf. Stein et al. (2017), p. 278 arguing that neither of the requirements for customary international law are fulfilled.

[87] Cf. Vermeer-Künzli (2013), p. 499.

[88] Armed Activities on the Territory of the Congo (Democratic Republic of the Congo v Uganda), Judgment of 19 December 2005, ICJ Reports 2005, No. 116, Separate Opinion by Judge Simma, pp. 347-348, para. 35.

[89] Cf. Case Concerning the Barcelona Traction, Light and Power Company, Limited (New Application: 1962) (Belgium v Spain), Second Phase, Judgment of 5 February 1970, ICJ Reports 1970, No. 50, p. 31, para. 34; Armed Activities on the Territory of the Congo (Democratic Republic of the Congo v Uganda), Judgment of 19 December 2005, ICJ Reports 2005, No. 116, Separate Opinion by Judge Simma, p. 348, para. 35.

Thus, invoking state responsibility would be the more appropriate vehicle for a state wishing to respond to grave human rights violations. Admittedly, however, this would require a state to wait for a human rights violation to occur instead of extending diplomatic protection to an individual in order to prevent such human rights violations from occurring.

6.3 Diplomatic Asylum As a Human Rights Conundrum

States not only regularly rely on their human rights obligations to justify granting diplomatic asylum, at the same time fundamental human rights obligations may be breached by a granting state *vis-à-vis* the diplomatic asylee by virtue of their residence in the diplomatic premises. Such a human rights violation may be posed, for example, by the duration of a case of diplomatic asylum in cases such as Cardinal Mindszenty, resident in the U.S embassy in Budapest for 15 years,[90] or that of Julian Assange, resident in Ecuador's embassy in London for nearly 7 years.[91]

In such cases, an asylee's fundamental rights, such as the right to liberty,[92] the prohibition on inhuman or degrading treatment,[93] freedom of movement,[94] freedom of thought, conscience and religion,[95] freedom of expression,[96] freedom of assembly,[97] freedom of association,[98] the right to asylum from persecution,[99] the right to participate in government and the right of access to the public service and democratic elections,[100] the right to equality before the law[101] or the prohibition on arbitrary detention[102] may be put at risk of breach or actually breached by virtue of the diplomatic asylum granted.

Moreover, in such lengthy diplomatic asylum cases, access to medical facilities may be limited. In particular, in the case of Julian Assange it was noted that Assange had suffered health defects, e.g. vitamin deficiency and vision problems, as a direct result of his time in the embassy, due to limited exposure to sunlight. Assange was

[90] Cf. Chap. 7: Annex, Table 7.1, Case No. 54.

[91] Cf. Chap. 7: Annex, Table 7.1, Case No. 188.

[92] Protected by Art. 3 UDHR; Art. 5 ECHR and Art. 9 ICCPR.

[93] Protected by Art. 5 UDHR; Art. 3 ECHR and Art. 7 ICCPR.

[94] Protected by Art. 13 UDHR and Art. 12 ICCPR.

[95] Protected by Art. 18 UDHR and Art. 18 ICCPR.

[96] Protected by Art. 19 UDHR; Art. 10 ECHR and Art. 19 ICCPR.

[97] Protected by Art. 20 UDHR and Art. 21 ICCPR.

[98] Protected by Art. 22 ICCPR.

[99] Protected by Art. 14 UDHR.

[100] Protected by Art. 21 UDHR and Art. 25 ICCPR.

[101] Protected by Art. 26 ICCPR.

[102] Protected by Art. 9 UDHR.

also noted as living in a very small confined space, designed for office use.[103] This is thought to also have taken its toll on Assange's psychological well-being.[104]

In holding that Assange was being arbitrarily detained in 2015, the UN Working Group on Arbitrary Detention relied on human rights treaty obligations emerging from the UDHR and the ICCPR in alleging that Assange's rights to equality before the law; culture, language and religion; asylum from persecution; freedom of movement; thought, conscience and religion; expression; assembly; association; participation in government and access to public service and democratic elections had been breached by his so-called detention.[105]

This is interesting as states rely on rights contained in these very same human rights treaties/treaty-like instruments in order to justify granting diplomatic asylum, for example the right to life or the security of the person. Indeed, states are often motivated by the protection of such fundamental human rights in granting an individual diplomatic asylum. The mechanism of diplomatic asylum may consequently prevent an individual's human rights from being breached by the receiving state. In such cases, were diplomatic asylum not to be granted, the asylee's fundamental human rights e.g. to life and security of the person would be at risk of being breached by the receiving state.

Thus, human rights treaties and treaty-like instruments can simultaneously provide an albeit not universally accepted basis for granting diplomatic asylum in that the protection of rights contained within can motivate states to grant diplomatic asylum, as well as a basis to argue that such asylum facilitates a violation of the diplomatic asylee's fundamental human rights, for example an asylee's freedom of movement. For this reason, it is this author's view that diplomatic asylum constitutes a human rights conundrum as both the failure to grant diplomatic asylum and the decision to grant diplomatic asylum may result in the breach of the fundamental human rights of the asylee.

References

Accioly H (1961) Das Asylrecht. AdV 9(3):289–293

Adjei E (2005) The legality of humanitarian intervention, Dissertation. University of Georgia, Athens

Alston P, Goodman R (2013) International human rights, the successor to International Human Rights in context, text and materials. Oxford University Press, Oxford

[103]Cf. CNET (11 April 2019), Julian Assange finally leaves his tiny room, but what was it like in there?; The New York Times (11 April 2019), Julian Assange's Seven Strange Years in Self-Imposed Isolation.

[104]Cf. CNET (11 April 2019), Julian Assange finally leaves his tiny room, but what was it like in there?; El País (14 April 2019), The life of Julian Assange, according to the Spaniards who watched over him.

[105]Cf. Chap. 6: Sects. 6.2.1 and 6.2.3.

Borchard EM (1915) The diplomatic protection of citizens abroad or the law of International Claims. The Banks Law Publishing Co., New York

Council of Europe (1961) Yearbook of the European Convention on Human Rights, the European Commission and European Court of Human Rights, 1960. Martinus Nijhoff Publishers, The Hague

Dahm G, Delbrück J, Wolfrum R (1989) Völkerrecht, vol I/1, 2nd edn. De Gruyter, Berlin

Evans AE (1965) Reviewed Work(s): El Asilo Diplomatico: Su Aspecto Antijuridico e Inhumano. by Roberto S. Corpen. AJIL 59(3):674–675

Foakes J, Denza E (2017) Privileges and immunities of diplomatic missions. In: Roberts I (ed) Satow's diplomatic practice, 7th edn. Oxford University Press, Oxford, pp 222–245

Fremuth M (2015) Menschenrechte, Grundlagen und Dokumente, Schriftenreihe, vol 1650. Bundeszentrale für politische Bildung, Bonn

Gaja G (2003) Is a state specially affected when its Nationals Human Rights are infringed? In: Vohrah LC, Pocar F, Featherstone Y, Fourmy O, Graham C, Hocking J, Robson N (eds) Man's inhumanity to man, essays in International Law in Honour of Antonio Cassese. Kluwer Law International, The Hague, pp 373–382

Glendon MA (2004) The rule of law in the universal declaration of Human Rights. NJIHR 2 (1):2–19

Goldsmith J (1998) International Human Rights law and the United States double standard. The Green Bag 1(4):365–373

Hackworth GH (1941) Digest of International Law, Vol. II, Chapters VI – VIII, Department of State Publication 1521. United States Government Printing Office, Washington

Hailbronner K (2002) Kommentar: Die Genfer Flüchtlingskonvention vor den Herausforderungen des 21. Jahrhunderts. In: Hailbronner K, Klein E (eds) Flüchtlinge – Menschenrechte – Staatsangehörigkeit, Menschenrechte und Migration. C. F. Müller, Heidelberg

Hannum H (1996) The status of the Universal Declaration of Human Rights in National and International Law. GJICL 25:287–397

Hathaway O, Levitz P, Nielsen E, Nowlan A, Perdue W, Purvis C, Solow S, Spiegel J (2011) Human Rights abroad: when do Human Rights Treaty obligations apply extraterritorially? ASLJ 43:1–38

Heintze H (1998) Interventionsverbot, Interventionsrecht und Interventionspflicht im Völkerrecht. In: Reiter E (ed) Maßnahmen zur internationalen Friedenssicherung, Schriftenreihe: Forschungen zur Sicherheitspolitik, vol 3. Büro für Sicherheitspolitik, Vienna, pp 163–194

Henke C (2002) Die humanitäre Intervention: Völker- und verfassungsrechtliche Probleme unter besonderer Berücksichtigung des Kosovo-Konflikts, Dissertation. Westfälische Wilhelms-Universität Münster, Münster

Hobe S (1998) Der offene Verfassungsstaat zwischen Souveränität und Interdependenz. Duncker & Humboldt, Berlin

Hobe S (2020) Einführung in das Völkerrecht, 11th edition, A. Francke Verlag, Tübingen

Jeffery AJ (1985) Diplomatic Asylum: its problems and potential as a means of protecting Human Rights. SAJHR 1:10–30

Jully L (1951) L'asile diplomatique devant la Cour internationale de Justice. Die Friedens-Warte 51:20–58

Kau M (2019) Der Staat und der Einzelne als Völkerrechtssubjekte. In: Vitzthum W, Proelß A (eds) Völkerrecht, 7th edn. DeGruyter, Berlin, pp 159–318

Kimminich O (1961) Asyl in Stützpunkten der UN Truppen. ZfP 8(3):235–240

Kokott J (1999) Die Aufnahme "humanitärer Flüchtlinge" Temporary Protection: U.S. and European responses to mass migration, referat. In: Hailbronner K, Klein E (eds) Einwanderungskontrolle und Menschenrechte – Immigration Control and Human Rights, Beiträge anläßlich des Symposiums am 29./30. Juni 1998 in Potsdam. C. F. Müller, Heidelberg, pp 3–27

Lepard BD (2010) Customary international law, a new theory with practical applications, ASIL studies in international legal theory. Cambridge University Press, New York

Lo C (2017) Treaty interpretation under the Vienna Convention on the Law of Treaties, a new round of codification. Springer, Singapore

Lowe V, Tzanakopoulos A (2011) Humanitarian intervention. In: MPEPIL online. Oxford University Press, Oxford. https://opil.ouplaw.com/view/10.1093/law:epil/9780199231690/law-9780199231690-e306?prd=EPIL. Last Accessed 29 Apr 2021

Marauhn T, Simon S (2012) Diplomatisches Asyl für Julian Assange. ZJS 5:593–601

Martin SF, Schoenholtz A (1999) Die Aufnahme "humanitärer Flüchtlinge" temporary protection: U.S. and European responses to mass migration, Referat. In: Hailbronner K, Klein E (eds) Einwanderungskontrolle und Menschenrechte – Immigration Control and Human Rights, Beiträge anläßlich des Symposiums am 29./30. Juni 1998 in Potsdam. C. F. Müller, Heidelberg, pp 29–50

McNair A (1956) International law opinions, vol. II, Peace. Cambridge University Press, Cambridge

Merriam J (2001) Kosovo and the law of Humanitarian intervention. CWRJIL 33(1):111–154

Modibo Ocran T (2002) The Doctrine of humanitarian intervention in light of robust peacekeeping. BCICLR 25(1):1–58

Oelfke C, Pröpstl T, Raasch H, Wagner N (2018) Wiener Übereinkommen über diplomatische Beziehungen vom 18. April 1961, Kommentar für die Praxis. Berliner Wissenschaftsverlag, Berlin

Oeter S (2009) Humanitäre Intervention und die Grenzen des völkerrechtlichen Gewaltverbots — Wen oder was schützt das Völkerrecht: Staatliche Souveränität, kollektive Selbstbestimmung oder individuelle Autonomie? In: Münkler H, Malowitz K (eds) Humanitäre Intervention, Ein Instrument außenpolitischer Konfliktbearbeitung, Grundlagen und Diskussion. Verlag für Sozialwissenschaften, Wiesbaden, pp 29–64

Orakhelashvli A (2000) The position of the individual in International Law. CWILJ 31(2):241–276

Peters A (2009) Humanity as the A and Ω of sovereignty. EJIL 20(3):513–544

Peters A (2013) Der Mensch im Mittelpunkt des Völkerrechts. MPICPLIL 27:1–9

Porcino P (1976) Toward codification of diplomatic Asylum. NYUJILP 8:435–456

Richtsteig M (2010) Wiener Übereinkommen über diplomatische und konsularische Beziehungen, Entstehungsgeschichte, Kommentierung, Praxis, 2nd edn. Nomos, Baden-Baden

Riveles S (1989) Diplomatic Asylum as a Human Right: the case of the Durban six. HRQ 11:139–159

Ronning CN (1965) Diplomatic Asylum: legal norms and political reality in Latin American relations. Martinus Nijhoff, The Hague

Schabas WA (2015) The European Convention on Human Rights: a commentary. Oxford University Press, Oxford

Shah P (2007) Asylum, Diplomatic. In: MPEPIL (Online). Oxford University Press, Oxford. https://opil.ouplaw.com/view/10.1093/law:epil/9780199231690/law-9780199231690-e756. Last Accessed 16 Dec 2020

Simonovic I (2002) Relative sovereignty of the twenty first century. HICLR 25(3):371–381

Stein T, Von Buttlar C, Kotzur M (2017) Völkerrecht, 14th edn. Verlag Franz Vahlen, Munich

Tomuschat C (1999) 'International law: ensuring the survival of mankind on the eve of a new century: general course on public international law', Collected Courses of the Hague Academy of International Law, vol 281. Brill, Nijhoff, Leiden/Boston, pp 9–438

Van Schaack B (2014) The United States' position on the extraterritorial application of Human Rights Obligations: now is the time for change. ILS 90:20–65

Vermeer-Künzli A (2006) Restricting discretion: judicial review of diplomatic protection. NJIL 75:279–307

Vermeer-Künzli AMH (2007) The protection of individuals by means of diplomatic protection: diplomatic protection as a Human Rights Instrument, Dissertation. Leiden University, Leiden

Vermeer-Künzli A (2013) Diallo: between diplomatic protection and Human Rights. JIDS 4 (3):487–500

von Arnauld A (2019) Völkerrecht, 4th edn. C.F. Müller, Heidelberg
von Pollern H (1980) Das moderne Asylrecht, Völkerrecht und Verfassungsrecht der Bundesrepublik Deutschland, Schriften zum Völkerrecht, Band 67. Duncker & Humblot, Berlin
Wilde R (2013) Human Rights beyond borders at the World Court: the significance of the International Court of Justice's jurisprudence on the extraterritorial application of International Human Rights Law Treaties. CJIL 12(4):639–677
Wolf D (1988) Humanitarian intervention. MJIL 9(1):333–366

Chapter 7
Conclusion

Having defined the concept of diplomatic asylum as the practice of states granting asylum in the context of their diplomatic premises,[1] and having established that the practice has a long-standing history,[2] it is necessary to tackle the question at hand i.e. whether or not general international law supports a right to diplomatic asylum.

7.1 Does International Law Support the Granting of a Right to Diplomatic Asylum?

7.1.1 Treaty Law[3]

Treaty law does not provide a universal legal basis for the practice of diplomatic asylum.[4] Firstly, treaty law with a universal scope does not provide a legal basis for diplomatic asylum as such a legal basis can neither be found in international legal provisions codifying a general right to territorial asylum, nor can it be found in the VCDR. Though the absolute nature of the inviolability of the mission premises under Art. 22 VCDR facilitates the practice, a sending state nevertheless has the legal obligation both to respect the laws of the host state and not to interfere in its domestic affairs.[5] Moreover, a sending state also has the obligation not to use the mission premises for any purpose incompatible with the functions of the mission.[6]

[1]See Chap. 2.
[2]See Chap. 3.
[3]See Chap. 4.
[4]Cf. Chap. 4.
[5]Art. 41 (1) VCDR.
[6]Art. 41 (3) in combination with Art. 3 VCDR.

L. Hughes-Gerber, *Diplomatic Asylum*,
https://doi.org/10.1007/978-3-030-73046-8_7

In the context of the regional treaty law of Latin America, there is a wealth of treaty law relevant to the issue of diplomatic asylum.[7] This includes the Treaty on International Penal Law 1889, the Treaty of Peace and Friendship 1907, the Bolivarian Agreement on Extradition 1911, the Convention on Asylum 1928, the Montevideo Convention on Political Asylum 1933, the Treaty on Political Asylum and Refuge 1939 and the Convention on Diplomatic Asylum of Caracas from 1954. The most important of these treaties in terms of participation are the Convention on Asylum 1928, the Montevideo Convention on Political Asylum 1933 and the Convention on Diplomatic Asylum of Caracas from 1954. From these treaties, the following common themes have emerged: diplomatic asylum is reserved for political offenders and for cases of urgency. The applicability of such treaties is, however, limited to state parties thereto. Therefore, the relevance of such treaties is limited to Latin America.

7.1.2 Customary International Law[8]

A universal legal basis for the practice of diplomatic asylum also cannot be found in customary international law.[9]

With regard to the African, Oceanic, Northern American and Asian regions, state practice is sparse and sporadic. With regard to the European continent, state practice is much more extensive though it is ultimately not extensive enough to fulfil the state practice requirement of customary international law for regional custom, with state practice also lacking in uniformity in this respect. State practice in Latin America is also extensive, even more so in relation to the size of the continent. Moreover, in Latin America state practice is sufficiently consistent to satisfy the state practice requirement of customary international law in relation to participating states.

Opinio juris in favour of the practice of diplomatic asylum can be identified for Latin America, Europe (only in the form of Spain) and Oceania (in the form of Australia). Evidence of states rebuking the practice is, however, much more widespread and can be identified for Asia, Europe, Northern America, Oceania and even Latin America, albeit to a limited extent.

Only in the context of Latin America is state practice and *opinio juris* sufficient for the practice to give rise to a rule of customary international law status and thus become legally binding as a regional custom.[10] This regional custom can only be held to be binding upon those states which participate in it and recognise it.[11]

---

[7]See Chap. 4: Sect. 4.2.2.

[8]See Chap. 5.

[9]Cf. Chap. 5.

[10]Crawford even holds diplomatic asylum to be "the best known example of a regional custom": Crawford (2019), p. 28. Cf. Doehring (2004), p. 129, para. 293; Kimminich (1961), p. 236; Roberts and Sivakumaran (2018), p. 97.

[11]Cf. Kimminich (1961), p. 236 holding that diplomatic asylum is without legal foundation in general international law.

7.1.3 *Diplomatic Asylum on the Basis of Humanitarian Considerations*[12]

A right to diplomatic asylum could also not be ascertained in the context of humanitarian considerations.

In the absence of a universal treaty provision or customary rule providing directly for a right to diplomatic asylum, relevant *lex generalis* in the form of fundamental human rights provisions and principles were examined in order to determine the extent to which a right to diplomatic asylum could find its basis therein. Having established that humanitarian considerations can constitute a source of law, various relevant human rights provisions were examined in order to determine their applicability to the practice of diplomatic asylum.

The UDHR, the ECHR, the ICCPR, the EU Charter of Fundamental Rights and the ACHPR all contain provisions protecting fundamental human rights. Common provisions relevant to the question of diplomatic asylum include, *inter alia,* the right to life, the right to liberty and security of the person, the right to asylum, the right not to be subjected to cruel, inhuman or degrading treatment or punishment and the right to freedom of expression. These provisions cannot, however, be held to give rise to a right to diplomatic asylum on human rights grounds owing to a systematic and/or teleological interpretation of the treaties/treaty-like instruments in question preventing their extraterritorial application.

The concept of temporary shelter, which denotes a state granting temporary refuge to an individual in order to protect their fundamental rights, is not a rule of customary international law status. Furthermore, deriving the practice of diplomatic asylum from the principle of humanitarian intervention also falls short of achieving customary international law status. The principle of non-refoulement is also of little assistance as it requires a state to have the jurisdiction to extradite an individual, which a sending state granting diplomatic asylum lacks.

Consequently, neither international treaty law nor customary international law provides a legal basis for a right to diplomatic asylum even where this is granted to protect the fundamental human rights of the diplomatic asylee.

7.2 The Problem of Diplomatic Asylum

It has been established that no legal basis for the practice of diplomatic asylum exists under general international law,[13] save for the existence of the practice under both the treaty and customary law of Latin America.[14] The conundrum therefore remains

[12]See Chap. 6.

[13]See Chaps. 4, 5 and 6.

[14]See Chap. 4: Sect. 4.2 and Chap. 5: Sects. 5.3.4, 5.3.7, 5.4.1.1, 5.4.2.4 and 5.4.3.

as to the inviolability of the mission premises, protected by Art. 22 VCDR, facilitating the *de facto* universal practice of diplomatic asylum[15] albeit without any form of legitimate legal basis. This is highly undesirable as it constitutes a legal loophole in which states, which are not permitted by the VCDR or other international treaty/ customary international law to use the diplomatic premises to house diplomatic asylees nevertheless continue to do so as there is no effective remedy preventing them from granting such a *de facto* right and no effective sanction to deter such conduct.

This legal loophole has resulted in the over 200 twentieth and twenty-first Century diplomatic asylum cases detailed by Table 7.1, the majority of which did not take place on the Latin American continent i.e. on the territory of a state recognising the right to diplomatic asylum by way of customary international law and/or treaty law mechanisms. Where diplomatic asylum takes place in such an unsanctioned manner, it constitutes both an abuse of the diplomatic premises contrary to Art. 41 (3) VCDR and an interference into the domestic affairs of the receiving state contrary to Art. 41 (1) VCDR.

Such abuse of the diplomatic premises ultimately runs contrary to the efficient functioning of the mission, with longstanding cases of diplomatic asylum such as that of Julian Assange notably impeding the work of the diplomatic mission.[16] It is therefore crucial to find a solution to curtail such abuses of the diplomatic premises from continuing to occur. Interference in the domestic affairs of another state equally undermines the efficient functioning of the mission.

Furthermore, states continue to grant diplomatic asylum motivated by fundamental human rights considerations. Currently, there is no codified right permitting states to do so, rendering legal certainty lacking in this regard. It is therefore also imperative to bolstering human rights protection that this situation is addressed in order to ensure that an individual's fundamental rights are protected by states when neccessary.

7.3 Potential Solutions to Address the Problem

The following section will moot potential solutions in order to bridge the legal lacuna and prevent the continuation of the practice and thus the abuse of the inviolability of the diplomatic mission. Additionally, some of the solutions mentioned will tackle the problem of a lack of legal certainty, particularly in cases of diplomatic asylum motivated by human rights considerations.

---

[15]This statement is supported by the wealth of state practice evidenced in Table 7.1, This Chap: Annex.

[16]Cf. El País (14 April 2019), The life of Julian Assange, according to the Spaniards who watched over him.

7.3.1 *Declaring* Persona Non Grata *and the Severance of Diplomatic Relations*

The most obvious solution to the problem of an abuse of diplomatic immunity, by way of an abuse of the premises of the diplomatic mission, would be to utilise the sanctions foreseen by the Vienna Convention on Diplomatic Relations. These are declaring the agents of the mission involved to be *persona non grata*[17] and the severance of diplomatic relations by the host state.[18] Indeed, this option was utilised by the UK following the killing of PC Yvonne Fletcher by a bullet emanating from the Libyan embassy in London in 1984—depicting another example of an abuse of the diplomatic premises.

However, this option would be unlikely to be effective in the case of diplomatic asylum as Art. 45 (a) VCDR provides that a host state must protect and respect the premises of the mission even after a severance of diplomatic relations between the host state and the receiving state. Thus, even after a unilateral severance of diplomatic relations between the host state and the sending state, the duty to respect the inviolability of the mission premises would remain and a case of diplomatic asylum could therefore perpetuate unhindered. This option also has the disadvantage of a necessary deterioration in relations between the sending state and the receiving state.

7.3.2 *Depriving Mission Premises of Diplomatic Status*

One option to prevent the problem of *de facto* diplomatic asylum from continuing to reoccur and thus to prevent the premises of the mission from being used contrary to Art. 3 VCDR is for states to deprive such mission premises of their diplomatic status.[19] Section 1 (3) (b) of the UK Diplomatic and Consular Premises Act 1987[20] would seem to provide for this opportunity in that it allows for the Secretary of State to withdraw his/her acceptance or consent to the land in question being used for the purposes of the mission.[21] Moreover, in this regard ICJ Judge Giorgio Gaja has held:

> The relevant provisions of the Vienna Convention do not imply that, once a building has been used for a diplomatic mission, the sending State is entitled to continue to use it indefinitely for that purpose... Except for what may be provided for in a treaty, there is no

[17]Art. 9 VCDR.

[18]Art. 45 VCDR.

[19]In this regard, Herdegen speaks of "forfeiture of the mission status:" Herdegen (1986), p. 756.

[20]Diplomatic and Consular Premises Act 1987, C. 46.

[21]On this point, see Akande (2012) with regard to the case of Julian Assange.

> obligation for the receiving State to let the sending State continue to use a specific building for its mission.[22]

Therefore, a building could be deprived of diplomatic status forcing the diplomatic mission to vacate the premises, along with the diplomatic asylee.

This option would certainly put political pressure on the sending state, and the state granting diplomatic asylum, to surrender the diplomatic asylee. However, this option would also leave open the possibility of the sending state transporting the diplomatic asylee via diplomatic vehicle.[23] Such transport could involve complete removal of the diplomatic asylee from the territory of the host state or transport to alternative diplomatic premises of the sending state. This option may also endanger the fundamental human rights of the diplomatic asylee and has the disadvantage of a necessary deterioration in relations between the sending and receiving states.

7.3.3 Codification of the Question of Diplomatic Asylum

Another option to prevent further disputes surrounding the issue of diplomatic asylum would be codification of the issue. This option would boost legal certainty and as such, is advocated by scholars.[24] Such codification could, for example, provide that save for in the context of Latin America, states are not permitted to grant asylum within the premises of their diplomatic missions. Equally, at some point in the future when a universal consensus on granting a right to diplomatic asylum may emerge, such codification could also take the form of cementing the universal rules applicable to the right to diplomatic asylum. Nevertheless, such codification has, despite copious attempts and discussions surrounding the issue, so far eluded international law. Furthermore, considering the increasing difficulty in achieving international consensus in international law more generally,[25] this could prove difficult to achieve.

Codification could take the form of a new treaty or an amendment to the pre-existing VCDR.[26] Alternatively, codification could be undertaken by the ILC,

---

[22]Immunities and Criminal Proceedings (Equatorial Guinea v France), Judgment of 6 June 2018, No. 163, Declaration by Judge Gaja. In the context of the same case, France argued that the term "premises of the mission" in Art. 1 (i) VCDR is descriptive and does not provide for any criteria or stipulations to be met by such premises. Accordingly, the characterisation of diplomatic premises must occur in accordance with customary international law: Immunities and Criminal Proceedings (Equatorial Guinea v France), Preliminary Objections, Judgment of 6 June 2018, No. 163, p. 37, para. 126.

[23]The diplomatic vehicle also enjoys immunity as property of the diplomatic agent: Art. 30 (2) VCDR.

[24]Cf. Porcino (1976), p. 451; Riveles (1989), p. 159.

[25]Characterised for example by an increase in the role of soft law.

[26]Cf. Evans (1951), p. 761; Farhangi (1986), p. 1536.

though its numerous unsuccessful codification attempts to date[27] would indicate that this may prove difficult.

Codification could also, at least initially, be prohibitory in order to increase the likelihood of achieving a universal consensus. For example, those accused of common crimes or deserters of the armed forces could be held to be exempt from the practice of diplomatic asylum. This would be consistent with existing regional Latin American treaty law.[28] Importantly, several historical documents establishing such basic legal rules applicable to the issue of diplomatic asylum were also adopted by states outside of Latin America,[29] indicating that a very basic consensus on the issue could be possible to achieve even if it was prohibitory in nature. Going forward, states could proceed to continually exclude further constellations from the practice of diplomatic asylum by way of codification instruments, hereby gradually providing improved legal certainty.

This codification option would boost legal certainty and in doing so decrease the risk of conflict occurring between the receiving and sending states in a diplomatic asylum case as both states would be informed as to their rights and obligations. This would ultimately promote friendly relations between states and the maintenance of international peace and security.[30]

In light of the general difficulty in achieving international consensus sufficient to generate an international treaty/ customary rule, a soft law instrument could provide another option for codification, which may prove more favourable to states. Soft law instruments typically take the form of guidelines or codes of conduct and have already been influential in the field of International Environmental Law.[31] The difficulty, of course, with such soft law instruments is in ensuring implementation and in the inability to invoke state responsibility for violations.[32]

7.3.4 Interpreting the Vienna Convention on Diplomatic Relations to Provide for a More Restrictive Diplomatic Immunity

Moreover, another option, which would circumvent the need to obtain express international consensus on the issue, would be to interpret the VCDR to provide for a more restrictive form of diplomatic immunity.[33] This option has the advantage of preserving the existing international legal framework.[34]

[27] See Chap. 3: Sect. 3.5.
[28] Cf. Chap. 4: Sect. 4.2.
[29] Cf. Chap. 4: Sect. 4.2.1.
[30] Cf. Art. 1 (1) and (2) UN Charter; Preamble to the VCDR.
[31] Cf. Dupuy (1991), p. 422.
[32] Klabbers (1998), p. 381 f.
[33] Farhangi (1986), p. 1533 f.
[34] Farhangi (1986), p. 1533.

This option would rely on a relevant case being brought before the ICJ in order to enable an authoritative interpretation to be made in this regard.

However, as the provisions of the VCDR relevant to the issue of diplomatic asylum[35] are clear and unambiguous,[36] such an interpretation would arguably breach the VCDR, particularly as any waiver of the immunity of diplomatic agents is required to be express.[37] Furthermore, such an interpretation may additionally undermine the purpose of privileges and immunities i.e. ensuring the efficient performance of the functions of the diplomatic mission.[38] Such an interpretation may also undermine legal certainty and lead to conflict between the sending and receiving states as to the nature of their rights and obligations under the convention. It is also highly unlikely that the ICJ would interpret the VCDR in this manner, considering its existing jurisprudence relating to diplomatic asylum[39] and its affinity with the fundamental nature of diplomatic immunity.[40]

7.3.5 Isolating States Which Breach the Vienna Convention on Diplomatic Relations

Another option to prevent states from granting a right to diplomatic asylum is the isolation of states which breach the VCDR in order to exert political pressure upon them. This was also an option, at least unilaterally, utilised by the United Kingdom following the killing of PC Yvonne Fletcher in 1984.[41] However, this option has the disadvantage that it would provide no clarity on the legal situation and is reliant upon a sending state reacting to political pressure. It is also likely to lead to a deterioration in multilateral diplomatic relations as the granting state would face international alienation.

---

[35]Art. 22, 41 (1), in combination with Art. 3 and 41 (3) VCDR. See Chap. 4: Sects. 4.1.2–4.1.4.

[36]Particularly Art. 22 VCDR in providing for the absolute inviolability of the mission premises. Granting diplomatic asylum also cannot be held to be consistent with the functions of the diplomatic mission: cf. Chap. 4: Sect. 4.1.4.

[37]Art. 32 (2) VCDR. According to a systematic interpretation of the VCDR (cf. Art. 21 (1) VCLT), any waiver of the inviolability of the diplomatic premises would require an express waiver by the sending state.

[38]Provided for in the Preamble to the VCDR.

[39]Cf. Chap. 3: Sect. 3.4.13.1.

[40]Cf. Case Concerning United States Diplomatic and Consular Staff in Tehran (United States of America v Iran), Request for the Indication of Provisional Measures, Order of 15 December 1979, No. 64, p. 19, para. 38.

[41]The UK is described as "freezing out" Libya: Cameron (1985), p. 611. Cf. Farhangi (1986), pp. 1528–1529.

7.3.6 *Respecting the Principle of Non-interference*[42] *Whilst Protecting the Asylee*

Another option, put forward by Switzerland in the context of the League of Nations, is for a sending state to respect the principle of non-interference,[43] whilst simultaneously protecting the asylee.[44] Quite how this option would work in practice is unclear. Moreover, in cases of diplomatic asylum, it is exactly the protection of the asylee, that from the point of view of the host state blocks the ordinary process of its justice system, which constitutes interference in the host state's domestic affairs. Hence, this option is not viable to solve the dispute. Moreover, even if it was somehow viable, it would be unlikely to boost legal certainty and would create the potential for dispute.

7.3.7 *Countermeasures*

Furthermore, if the granting of diplomatic asylum by states other than those in Latin America can be held to constitute an internationally wrongful act,[45] a host state may be able to respond by way of the use of countermeasures.[46]

However, as diplomatic law is held to constitute a self-contained regime,[47] states may only respond to breaches of diplomatic law by way of mechanisms provided for by diplomatic law.[48] Moreover, Art. 50 (2) lit. b ILC Draft Articles on the Responsibility

[42] Cf. Art. 41 (1) VCDR.

[43] Cf. Art. 41(1) VCDR.

[44] Cf. League of Nations Committee of Experts for the Progressive Codification of International Law, Report to the Council of the League of Nations on the Questions Which Appear Ripe for International Regulation, Questionnaires Nos 1 to 7, Adopted by the Committee at its Third Session, held in March - April 1927, Geneva, 20 April 1927, p. 243.

[45] Cf. Art. 2 Draft Articles on Responsibility of States for Internationally Wrongful Acts, Text adopted by the International Law Commission at its fifty-third session, in 2001, and submitted to the General Assembly as a part of the Commission's report covering the work of that session, Annex to General Assembly resolution 56/83 of 12 December 2001, and corrected by document A/56/49 (Vol. I)/Corr.4.

[46] Cf. Art. 22 ILC Draft Articles on Responsibility of States for Internationally Wrongful Acts 2001. On the use of countermeasures, see Fiedler (1998), pp. 9–38; Klein (1998), pp. 39–71.

[47] Case Concerning United States Diplomatic and Consular Staff in Tehran (United States of America v Iran), Judgment of 24 May 1980, ICJ Reports 1980, No. 64, p. 40, para. 86. For critique on the status of diplomatic law as a self-contained regime and an alternative interpretation of the judgment see Marschik (1997), p. 107.

[48] In this regard, the ICJ held: "This is because diplomatic law itself provides the necessary means of defence against, and sanction for, illicit activities by members of diplomatic or consular missions:" Case Concerning United States Diplomatic and Consular Staff in Tehran (United States of America v Iran), Judgment of 24 May 1980, ICJ Reports 1980, No. 64, p. 38, para. 83.

of States for Internationally Wrongful Acts 2001 explicitly prohibits states from infringing the inviolability of diplomatic premises in their exercise of countermeasures.

In any case, the use of countermeasures would lead to a deterioration in diplomatic relations between the sending and receiving states.

This would leave a host state wishing to respond to diplomatic asylum being granted on its territory with the following mechanisms foreseen by the VCDR: declaring members of the mission *persona non grata*[49] and/or the severance of diplomatic relations.[50]

7.3.8 Conclusion

In summary, potential solutions to address the problem of *de facto* diplomatic asylum persisting without a legal basis include: a host state declaring the diplomatic agents involved *persona non grata* under Art. 9 VCDR, and severing diplomatic relations with the sending state; depriving mission premises of their diplomatic status; codification of the issue; interpreting the VCDR to provide for a more restrictive form of diplomatic immunity; isolating states which breach the VCDR; respecting the principle of non-interference whilst protecting the asylee and countermeasures.

Whilst the latter is prohibited given the status of diplomatic law as a self-contained regime, respecting the principle of non-interference whilst protecting the asylee is contradictory in nature. Furthermore, isolating such states is a purely political option with no prospect of widespread success. Interpreting the VCDR to provide for a more restrictive form of diplomatic immunity would arguably breach the VCDR itself and would certainly risk undermining the purpose of diplomatic privileges and immunities i.e. to ensure the efficient functioning of the mission. Moreover, many of these options are not viable solution options as they create the potential for further dispute between the receiving and sending states and would thus conflict with several of the fundamental principles of the UN Charter, reflected also in the VCDR.[51]

It is this author's view that codification of the issue would be the best option in terms of achieving legal certainty and preventing further disputes around the issue of diplomatic asylum. This is because it is the only solution capable of providing both legal certainty and transparency. Both are vital to preventing further disputes and indeed to boosting human rights protection by way of the mechanism of diplomatic asylum where (and when) permissible.

---

[49]Cf. Art. 9 VCDR, this Chapter: Sect. 7.3.1.

[50]This Chapter: Sect. 7.3.1.

[51]These being the promotion of friendly relations between states and the maintenance of international peace of security: Art. 1 (1) and (2) UN Charter and Preamble to the VCDR.

Nevertheless, such codification has so far eluded the international community and given the increasing difficulty in achieving consensus in general in international law, coupled with the long-standing nature and inconsistent usage of the practice, it is likely to continue to do so. Negative codification, i.e. codification of the constellations in which diplomatic asylum is not permitted, may provide an easier avenue to achieving consensus. However, it is likely to prove a slow process until adequate legal certainity can be won.

For this reason, codification by way of a soft law instrument may provide a more favourable means of achieving codification. The difficulty in the implementation of soft law obligations is, however, well-known. Despite this, the drafting of guidelines governing the issue of diplomatic asylum under general international law would provide states with a specific point of reference containing applicable principles. Whilst acknowledging the lack of an enforcement mechanism, not all states would adhere to the guidelines, their general use would streamline the practice and provide it with a greater degree of uniformity than ever before. This form of codification would also be much easier to achieve, not requiring the explicit consent of a large number of states as a traditional universal treaty law instrument would.

Soft law codification of the right to diplomatic asylum under general international law could be undertaken by way of a resolution from a non-profit organisation, for example the Institute of International Law or the International Law Association, in which principles of international law are purported to be established.[52] The influence of such a resolution would of course be greatly limited without state endorsement, rendering the problem of obtaining widespread consent again the key issue.

Soft law codification could also take the form of a non-binding agreement between states.[53] However, again considering the difficulty in achieving a universal state consensus on the issue of diplomatic asylum, even in the form of a non-binding agreement, this is likely to still prove difficult to achieve.

Soft law codification could alternatively take the form of a General Assembly resolution. General Assembly resolutions do not generally require a vote to have taken place before they are adopted, this is only the case for very important questions primarily regarding peace and security, and thus the issue of obtaining universal consent would be circumvented.[54] General Assembly resolutions have also, in the past, proved highly influential in the development of customary international law, with notable examples including the UDHR,[55] the Declaration on the Elimination of

[52]Cf. Chinkin (1989), p. 851.

[53]Thürer (2009), para. 15 f.

[54]Cf. Art. 18 (2) UN Charter; Rule 83, Rules of Procedure of the General Assembly, embodying amendments and additions adopted by the General Assembly up to September 2016, A/520/Rev.1, Reissued for technical reasons on 21 February 2017, United Nations, New York, 2016.

[55]General Assembly Resolution 217 A (III), 183rd Plenary Meeting, 10 December 1948.

Discrimination against Women[56] or the Declaration on the Granting of Independence to Colonial Countries and People.[57]

For the aforementioned reasons, it is this author's view that soft law codification of the legal principles applicable to the issue of diplomatic asylum would be most effective through the UN General Assembly.

Failing this, and acknowledging that they lack guarantee of success, the mechanisms envisaged by the VCDR, i.e. declaring diplomatic agents *persona non grata* in line with Art. 9 VCDR and the severance of diplomatic relations by the host state, constitute the best alternative options for a host state to respond to the illegitimate granting of *de facto* diplomatic asylum upon its territory.

7.4 A Developmental Perspective of the Concept of Diplomatic Asylum

Although a right to diplomatic asylum has yet to crystallise in general international law, the regionally established right to diplomatic asylum has been utilised in a similar form globally—though notably in most cases without the guarantee of safe-conduct from the host state. The frequency of the practice provokes the question as to whether the development of the practice is such so as to permit a regional custom being applied universally, for example under customary international law. Indeed, the recent case of Assange denotes Ecuador evoking a rule of regional custom, and also regional treaty law, status in a jurisdiction outside of the rule's territorial scope.[58]

The notion of applying regional custom universally would of course be consistent with the extraterritoriality theory, allowing states to exercise territorial jurisdiction, and therefore also implement rules with only territorial scope, in the premises of their diplomatic missions.

It would, however, be inconsistent with the principle of state consent, emanating from the fundamental notion of state sovereignty,[59] providing that states should explicitly consent before being bound by a rule.[60]

[56] General Assembly Resolution 2263 (XXII), Declaration on the Elimination of Discrimination against Women, 1597th Plenary Meeting, 7 November 1967.

[57] General Assembly Resolution 1514 (XV), Declaration on the granting of independence to colonial countries and peoples, 947th Plenary Meeting, 14 December 1960.

[58] Cf. Chap. 1: Sect. 1.2.

[59] Cf. Art. 2 (1) UN Charter. For further information on state consent in customary international law, see Lobo de Souza (1995), p. 521 f.

[60] Cf. Art. 34 VCLT with regard to treaty law.

There is a distinct lack of international judicial precedent relating to the application of regional custom elsewhere, which could assist in providing an answer to this question. That is not to say that the idea of regional rules being influential upon the universal legal framework or vice versa is a novel one, particularly in the field of human rights.[61] Moreover, regional human rights frameworks have also been influential upon other regions' development, for example the European Court of Human Rights has acted as a model for the later established Inter-American Court of Human Rights and African Court on Human and People's Rights.[62] However, in such cases regional rules inspired the establishment or development of a similar normative legal basis in other regions, rather than being applied directly extraterritorially.

The development of international law does not yet support the universal application of rules with purely regional scope. Nevertheless, with regard to diplomatic asylum, the development of human rights law and the rigidity of the VCDR facilitate the *de facto* application of this regional rule universally. Going forward, this could serve as a dangerous precedent for other areas of international law. It is therefore of crucial importance to the preservation of legal certainty to solve the problem of diplomatic asylum.[63]

Balancing fundamental traditional principles of international law such as state sovereignty and non-intervention with newer human rights obligations has proved increasingly difficult for states to achieve.[64] Though this general tension between conflicting norms of international law shows no sign of subsiding, equally the classic fundaments of the international legal system coming to be entirely replaced by notions of humanity seems a remote prospect.

The problem of diplomatic asylum provides a classic example of this friction, with conventional principles of international law—specifically the principle of territorial jurisdiction and the duty of non-interference—prohibiting the practice on a universal level whilst human rights obligations motivate states to continue to facilitate it regardless. Recent cases, such as those of Assange and Guangcheng, show that with regard to diplomatic asylum, human rights considerations are superseding traditional principles of international law. The status of diplomatic law as a self-contained regime also leaves receiving states with few methods of redress in this regard.

---

[61]See Ronning (1965), p. 24 ascribing the development of diplomatic asylum in Latin America to "the result of a conscious application of European patterns." In the field of human rights, the ECtHR has inspired universal and regional human rights institutions alike: cf. Amos (2017), p. 770; von Arnauld (2006), p. 258. Furthermore, the UDHR had a significant influence on the development of the African (Banjul) Charter of Human and Peoples' Rights: cf. International Commission of Jurists, African Conference on the Rule of Law, Lagos, Nigeria, 3 -7 January 1961, Report on the Proceedings of the Conference, Geneva, 1961, p. 11. Available at: https://www.icj.org/wp-content/uploads/1961/06/Africa-African-Conference-Rule-of-Law-conference-report-1961-eng.pdf. Last Accessed 16 Dec 2020.

[62]Cf. Amos (2017), p. 770; Hamm (2003), p. 101; von Arnauld (2006), p. 258.

[63]Cf. This Chapter: Sects. 7.2 and 7.3.

[64]Cf. Wagner (2017), p. 44.

With the volume of diplomatic asylum cases ever increasing,[65] the cases of Assange and Guangcheng are indicative of the transformative period in which the practice finds itself, with cases no longer being reserved for political unrest or disturbance but instead for the immediate protection of an individual's fundamental human rights in cases in which a threat thereto emanates from the host state. Whether or not this will eventually result in a right to diplomatic asylum being recognised on a universal level under customary international law in cases in which fundamental human rights are threatened remains to be seen.

Nevertheless, the concept of diplomatic asylum has evolved and developed based upon centuries of practice and discussion. Regardless as to whether codification of the topic takes place, the practice will likely continue to develop and evolve in the future, shaping and evolving customary international law on both a universal and a regional level. In doing so, increased clarity and transparency may be won with regard to the practice's legal parameters under general international law. Perhaps then, diplomatic premises could legitimately serve not only as places of representation of sending states, but also as guarantors of fundamental human rights.[66]

Currently the issue of diplomatic asylum under international law is shrouded in decades—if not centuries—of uncertainty and inconsistency. Whilst it would certainly be desirable to quell the dispute once and for all by comprehensively codifying its legal parameters, consensus is not yet sufficient to facilitate this. Perhaps in time, consensus may emerge but until then a soft law instrument may serve as an interim means of codification to at least establish a limited right to diplomatic asylum where fundamental human rights are at stake.

Annex

[65]Table 7.1 records 63 cases as having occurred in the twenty years since the millennium: cf. This Chapter: Annex, Table 7.1, Case No. 145 onwards. As a point of comparison, the previous 144 cases occurred in the twentieth century.

[66]Cf. IACtHR, Advisory Opinion OC-25/18 of 30 May 2018 Requested by the Republic of Ecuador, The Institution of Asylum and its Recognition as a Human Right in the Inter-American System of Protection (Interpretation and Scope of Articles 5, 22.7 and 22.8 in Relation to Article 1 (1) of the American Convention on Human Rights), p. 56, para. 155 providing that diplomatic asylum may provide an effective mechanism in cases in which fundamental human rights considerations are at stake.

Table 7.1 Twentieth/Twenty-first century examples of individuals being granted asylum in the context of diplomatic[a] premises[b]

No.	Name	Nationality	Location of diplomatic premises (Host state)	Granting state	Time span
1	Jean Vilbrun Guillaume Sam	Haitian	Port-au-Prince, Haiti	France	Ca. 27 July 1915[c]
2	Domingo González, his six sons and three daughters	Costa Rican	San José, Costa Rica	U.S.	17[d]–25 May 1917[e]
3	Mario G. Menocal and his nephew, Martín Menocal	Cuban	Havana, Cuba	Brazil	24 May–2 July 1932[f]
4	(Pedro) Martínez Fraga	Cuban	Havana, Cuba	Brazil	24 May–ca. 9 July 1932[g]
5	Carlos Manuel de la Cruz and Pedro Cué y Abreu	Cuban	Havana, Cuba	Uruguay	October 1932 onwards[h]
6	Eliseo Arguelles, Jr., and Julio Rabell	Cuban	Havana, Cuba	Colombia	October 1932 onwards[i]
7	Gabriel and Marío Menocal y Moreno	Cuban	Havana, Cuba	Spain	October 1932 onwards[j]
8	Ricardo Dolz and Eliceo Arguelles, Sr.	Cuban	Havana, Cuba	Mexico	October 1932 onwards[k]
9	Eight asylees	Presumed to all be Spanish	Madrid, Spain	Colombia	In the years 1936–1939 (exact length of stay unknown)[l]
10	Eighteen asylees	Presumed to all be Spanish	Madrid, Spain	Hungary	In the years 1936–1939 (exact length of stay unknown)[m]
11	Twenty-one asylees (including four members of the clergy)	Presumed to all be Spanish	Madrid, Spain	Yugoslavia	In the years 1936–1939 (exact length of stay unknown)[n]
12	71 asylees (including three members of the clergy)	Presumed to all be Spanish	Madrid, Spain	Brazil	In the years 1936–1939 (exact length of stay unknown)[o]
13	80 asylees (among them three members of the clergy)	Presumed to all be Spanish	Madrid, Spain	Germany	From the outbreak of the Spanish civil war until November 1936[p]
14	82 asylees (including four members of the clergy)	Presumed to all be Spanish	Madrid, Spain	Dominican Republic	In the years 1936–1939 (exact length of stay unknown)[q]
15	85 asylees	Presumed to all be Spanish	Madrid, Spain	Switzerland	In the years 1936–1939 (exact length of stay unknown)[r]
16	124 asylees	Presumed to all be Spanish	Madrid, Spain	Bolivia	In the years 1936–1939 (exact length of stay unknown)[s]
17	137 asylees	Presumed to all be Spanish	Madrid, Spain	Austria	In the years 1936–1939 (exact length of stay unknown)[t]

(continued)

Table 7.1 (continued)

No.	Name	Nationality	Location of diplomatic premises (Host state)	Granting state	Time span
18	137 asylees	Presumed to all be Spanish	Madrid, Spain	The Netherlands	In the years 1936–1939 (exact length of stay unknown)[u]
19	174 asylees (including two priests, José Machiñena Austegui and Manuel Cavanillas Rodríguez)	Presumed to all be Spanish	Madrid, Spain	Sweden	In the years 1936–1939 (exact length of stay unknown)[v]
20	204 asylees	Presumed to all be Spanish	Madrid, Spain	Czechoslovakia	In the years 1936–1939 (exact length of stay unknown)[w]
21	257 asylees (including six members of the clergy)	Presumed to all be Spanish	Madrid, Spain	Uruguay	In the years 1936–1939 (exact length of stay unknown)[x]
22	287 asylees (among them five members of the clergy)	Presumed to all be Spanish	Madrid, Spain	Belgium	In the years 1936–1939 (exact length of stay unknown)[y]
23	322 asylees (including six members of the clergy)	Presumed to all be Spanish	Madrid, Spain	Paraguay	In the years 1936–1939 (exact length of stay unknown)[z]
24	350–400 asylees (including one member of the clergy)	Presumed to all be Spanish	Madrid, Spain	Poland	In the years 1936–1939 (exact length of stay unknown)[aa]
25	428 asylees	Presumed to all be Spanish	Madrid, Spain	Argentina	In the years 1936–1939 (exact length of stay unknown)[ab]
26	600 asylees (including three members of the clergy)	Presumed to all be Spanish	Madrid, Spain	Peru	In the years 1936–1939 (exact length of stay unknown)[ac]
27	600 asylees (including twelve members of the clergy)	Presumed to all be Spanish	Madrid, Spain	Cuba-Haiti	In the years 1936–1939 (exact length of stay unknown)[ad]
28	718 asylees (including five members of the clergy)	Presumed to all be Spanish	Madrid, Spain	Romania	In the years 1936–1939 (exact length of stay unknown)[ae]
29	807 asylees (including seven members of the clergy)	Presumed to all be Spanish	Madrid, Spain	Mexico	In the years 1936–1939 (exact length of stay unknown)[af]
30	847 asylees (including four members of the clergy)	Presumed to all be Spanish	Madrid, Spain	Panama	In the years 1936[ag]–4 April 1939[ah]
31	900 asylees (including sixty-five members of the clergy)	Presumed to all be Spanish	Madrid, Spain	Norway	In the years 1936–1939 (exact length of stay unknown)[ai]

32	900 asylees (including 213 members of the clergy)	Presumed to all be Spanish	Madrid, Spain	France	In the years 1936–1939 (exact length of stay unknown)[aj]
33	923 asylees (including 25 members of the clergy)	Presumed to all be Spanish	Madrid, Spain	Turkey	In the years 1936–1939 (exact length of stay unknown)[ak]
34	2000 asylees (including 26 members of the clergy)	Presumed to all be Spanish	Madrid, Spain	Chile	In the years 1936–1939 (exact length of stay unknown)[al]
35	Many Spanish Republicans	Spanish	Spain/France	Mexico	For indeterminate periods of time between 1936 and 1942[am]
36	Pilar Primo de Rivera Y Sáenz de Heredia	Spanish	Madrid, Spain	Argentina	From the outbreak of the Spanish civil war in 1936 (length of stay unknown)[an]
37	José Ungría Jiménez	Spanish	Spain (presumably Madrid)	France	From sometime after the outbreak of the Spanish civil war until April 1937[ao]
38	Seventeen Spanish Republicans	Spanish	Madrid, Spain	Chile	Sometime between 27 and 31 March 1939[ap] until 12 October 1940 when the remaining Republicans left[aq]
39	Miklós Kállay	Hungarian	Hungary	Turkey	March[ar]–19 November 1944as
40	Ferenc Szálasi and some of his close collaborators	Hungarian	Hungary	Germany	27 September–15 October 1944[at]
41	The Horthy Family	Hungarian	Budapest, Hungary	The Holy See	16 October 1944[au]
42	Juan José Arévalo Bermejo	Guatemalan	Guatemala City, Guatemala	Mexico	18 October 1944 onwards[av]
43	General Nicolae Rădescu	Romanian	Bucharest, Romania	United Kingdom	1945[aw]
44	Augusto Roa Bastos	Paraguayan	Asunción, Paraguay	Brazil	40 days in 1947[ax]
45	Captain Francisco (Panchito) Aguirre Baca and his brother Horacio	Nicaraguan	Managua, Nicaragua	Panama	May 1947[ay]
46	Leonardo Argüello Barreto	Nicaraguan	Managua, Nicaragua	Mexico	From May 1947 (length of stay unknown)[az]
47	Víctor Raúl Haya de la Torre	Peruvian	Lima, Peru	Colombia	3 January 1949–6 April 1954[ba]
48	Carlos Prío Socarrás	Cuban	Havana, Cuba	Mexico	10–13 March 1952[bb]
49	Alfonso López Pumarejo and Dr. Carlos Lleras Restrepo	Colombian	Bogota, Colombia	Venezuela	Ca. 12 September 1952 (length of stay unknown)[bc]
50	Jacobo Árbenz Guzmán and family	Guatemalan		Mexico	27 June–8 September 1954[bd]

(continued)

Table 7.1 (continued)

No.	Name	Nationality	Location of diplomatic premises (Host state)	Granting state	Time span
			Guatemala City, Guatemala		
51	Juan Domingo Perón	Argentinian	Buenos Aires, Argentina	Paraguay	September 1955[be]
52	Ferenc B. Farkas and Judith Maléter	Hungarian	Budapest, Hungary	Belgium[bf]	Ca. 4–8 November 1956[bg]
53	Imre Nagy	Hungarian	Budapest, Hungary	Yugoslavia	4–21 November 1956[bh]
54	József Mindszenty	Hungarian	Budapest, Hungary	U.S.	4 November 1956–28 September 1971[bi]
55	Reino Häyhänen	Soviet	Paris, France	U.S.	4–10 May 1957[bj]
56	Sharif Ali bin al-Hussein and family	Iraqi	Baghdad, Iraq	Saudi Arabia	1958[bk]
57	Alfredo B. Saulo	Filipino	Manila, Phillippines	Indonesia	12 November–18 November 1958[bl]
58	Humberto Delgado	Portuguese	Lisbon, Portugal	Brazil	12 January–20 April 1959[bm]
59	Manuel Urrutia	Cuban	Havana, Cuba	Venezuela	July 1959 onwards[bn]
60	Olga Morgan (also known as Olga María Rodríguez Farinas and later known as Olga Goodwin)	Cuban	Havana, Cuba	Brazil	4 January–March 1961[bo]
61	Five Military Prisoners including two army officers	Assumed to be Venezuelan	Caracas, Venezuela	Peru	1 October 1961–ca. 17–23 March 1962[bp]
62	Twenty-two opponents of the governing regime	Haitian	Port-au-Prince, Haiti	Dominican Republic	May 1963[bq]
63	Tung Chi-Ping	Chinese	Bujumbura, Burundi	U.S.	26 May–ca. August 1964[br]
64	Kong Le	Laotian	Vientiane, Laos	Indonesia	1966[bs]
65	Leon Veillard	Haitian	Port au Prince, Haiti	Brazil	For eight months ca. 1967[bt]
66	Svetlana Alliluyeva (Stalin's daughter)	Soviet	New Delhi, India	U.S.	9 March–April 1967[bu]
67	About 50 persons	Chilean	Santiago, Chile	Canada	For 2 months after the 1973 *coup d'état*[bv]
68	100 persons with links to the overthrown Allende government	Chilean	Santiago, Chile	Venezuela	After the 1973 *coup d'état* for the following months[bw]

69	250 persons with links to the overthrown Allende government	Chilean	Santiago, Chile	Panama	After the 1973 *coup d'état* for the following months[bx]
70	300[by]–500 +[bz] (reports differ) persons with links to the overthrown Allende government	Chilean	Santiago, Chile	Mexico	After the 1973 *coup d'état* for the following months
71	A number of refugees	Chilean	Santiago, Chile	Sweden	After the 1973 *coup d'état*[ca]
72	José Serra	Brazilian	Santiago, Chile	Italy	For 6 months after the 1973 *coup d'état*[cb]
73	Up to 750 persons	Chilean	Santiago, Chile	Italy	After the 1973 *coup d'état*[cc]
74	Rodolfo Puiggrós and his wife	Argentinian	Buenos Aires, Argentina	Mexico	23 September 1974[cd]
75	Héctor Cámpora	Argentinian	Buenos Aires, Argentina	Mexico	1976[ce] until late 1979[cf]
76	Juan Abal Medina	Argentinian	Buenos Aires, Argentina	Mexico	29 April 1976[cg]–late May 1982[ch]
77	Arthur (from South Carolina)	American	Managua, Nicaragua	U.S.	Six weeks in the late 1970s[ci]
78	Pyotr, Avgustina, Lydia, Lyubov and Liliya Vashchenko; Timofei and Maria Chmykhalov	Soviet	Moscow, Soviet Union	U.S.	1978–1983 (when the last of them left)[cj]
79	A Soviet Citizen of Armenian origin	Soviet	Moscow, Soviet Union	France	July–October 1978[ck]
80	Sergio Ramírez Mercado	Nicaraguan	Managua, Nicaragua	Mexico	Ca. September–December 1978[cl]
81	Cuban refugees	Cuban	Havana, Cuba	Venezuela	On three separate occasions on 25 May, 9 June and 14 December 1979[cm]
82	Six U.S. diplomats who escaped from the Tehran hostage crisis	American	Tehran, Iran	Canada	November 1979–January 1980[cn]
83	The "Mariel Cuban" Exodus (over 10,000 Cubans)	Cuban	Havana, Cuba	Peru	March–June 1980[co]
84	Adolphus Tolbert	Liberian	Monrovia, Liberia	France	15 April–14 June 1980[cp]
85	Two Cuban Soldiers	Cuban	Addis Ababa, Ethiopia	U.S.	23 May 1980 (length of stay unknown)[cq]
86	Hugo Céspedes	Bolivian	La Paz, Bolivia	Brazil	March 1981[cr]
87	Gabriel García Márquez	Colombian	Bogota, Colombia	Mexico	26 March 1981[cs]
88	Bernhard Marquardt and Angelika Machol	East German (GDR)	Berlin, East Germany	U.S.	A week in April 1982[ct]

(continued)

Table 7.1 (continued)

No.	Name	Nationality	Location of diplomatic premises (Host state)	Granting state	Time span
89	Francisco Bobadilla Palomo	Guatemalan	Guatemala City, Guatemala	Brazil	April 1982–29 August 1983[cu]
90	Ange-Félix Patassé	Central African Republic	Bangui, Central African Republic	France	April 1982[cv]
91	O Nam Chol	North Korean	New York City, U. S.	North Korea	10 months[cw] until 26 July 1983[cx]
92	25 Czechs	Czechoslovakian	Prague, Czechoslovakia	West Germany (FRG)	1984[cy]
93	Six East Germans	East German (GDR)	Berlin, East Germany	U.S.	20–22 January 1984[cz]
94	Twelve East Germans	East German (GDR)	Berlin, East Germany	West Germany (FRG)	24 January 1984 (exact length of stay unknown)[da]
95	A prominent East German family (including the niece of Willi Stroph)	East German (GDR)	Prague, Czechoslovakia	West Germany (FRG)	Four weeks until 24 February 1984[db]
96	Four East Germans	East German (GDR)	Berlin, East Germany	U.S.	Ca. February 1984 (exact length of stay unknown)[dc]
97	48 East Germans	East German (GDR)	Berlin, East Germany	West Germany	Ca. February 1984 (exact length of stay unknown)[dd]
98	Over 50 East Germans	East German (GDR)	Prague, Czechoslovakia	West Germany (FRG)	February 1984[de]
99	Archie Gumede, Mewa Ramgobin, George Sawpershad, M. J. Naidoo, Billy Naier, Davades Paul Davids (who joined later)	South African	Durban, South Africa	United Kingdom	13 September–October 1984[df]
100	161 refugees	East German (GDR)	Prague, Czechoslovakia	West Germany (FRG)	Ca. October–mid November 1984[dg]
101	Seven East Germans and Three Poles of German descent	East German (GDR)/ Polish	Warsaw, Poland	West Germany (FRG)	November 1984 (length of stay unknown)[dh]
102	Fifteen East Germans	East German (GDR)	Budapest, Hungary		November 1984 (length of stay unknown)[di]

				West Germany (FRG)	
103	A small number of East Germans	East German (GDR)	Bucharest, Romania	West Germany (FRG)	November 1984 (length of stay unknown)[dj]
104	Lt. Roberto Granera	Nicaraguan	Managua, Nicaragua	Venezuela	1985[dk]
105	José Efrén Martínez Mondragón (and nine other persons)	Nicaraguan	Tegucigalpa, Honduras	Mexico	ca. March–May 1985[dl]
106	Private Aleksandr Vasilyevich Sukhanov	Soviet	Kabul, Afghanistan	U.S.	31 October–5 November 1985[dm]
107	Albert Pierre, Gener Crotin, Edner Pageotte et al	Haitian	Port au Prince, Haiti	Brazil	Ca. 11 February–ca. 23 February 1986[dn]
108	Olivia Forsyth	South African/British	Luanda, Angola	United Kingdom	Six months in 1988[do]
109	12 people of the Hungarian minority from Romania	Assumed to be Romanian	Sofia, Bulgaria	Hungary	14 September 1988–17 February 1989[dp]
110	Franck Romain	Haitian	Port au Prince, Haiti	Dominican Republic	17 September 1988[dq]–January 1989[dr]
111	Hou Dejian	Chinese (Taiwanese)	Beijing, China	Australia	June–August 1989[ds]
112	Fang Lizhi, Lu Shuxian, Fang Ke	Chinese	Beijing, China	U.S.	Early June 1989–25 June 1990[dt]
113	Manuel Noriega	Panamanian	Panama City, Panama	The Holy See	December 1989–3 January 1990[du]
114	Heraclides Sucre and Gonzalo González	Panamanian	Panama City, Panama	Peru	December 1989–11 May 1990[dv]
115	Luis Gomez	Panamanian	Panama City, Panama	Cuba	December 1989–11 May 1990[dw]
116	Rafael Arosemena	Panamanian	Panama City, Panama	Mexico	December 1989–11 May 1990[dx]
117	Four Albanian asylum seekers	Albanian	Tirana, Albania	Hungary	July 1990 (length of stay unknown)[dy]
118	Twenty Albanian asylum seekers	Albanian	Tirana, Albania	Italy	July 1990 (length of stay unknown)[dz]
119	25 Albanian asylum seekers	Albanian	Tirana, Albania	Poland	July 1990 (length of stay unknown)[ea]
120	32 Albanian asylum seekers	Albanian	Tirana, Albania	Turkey	July 1990 (length of stay unknown)[eb]
121	162 Albanian asylum seekers	Albanian	Tirana, Albania	West Germany (FRG)	July 1990 (length of stay unknown)[ec]

(continued)

Table 7.1 (continued)

No.	Name	Nationality	Location of diplomatic premises (Host state)	Granting state	Time span
122	A number of Albanian asylum seekers	Albanian	Tirana, Albania	Algeria	July 1990 (length of stay unknown)[ed]
123	A number of Albanian asylum seekers	Albanian	Tirana, Albania	Bulgaria	July 1990 (length of stay unknown)[ee]
124	A number of Albanian asylum seekers	Albanian	Tirana, Albania	China	July 1990 (length of stay unknown)[ef]
125	A number of Albanian asylum seekers	Albanian	Tirana, Albania	Czechoslovakia	July 1990 (length of stay unknown)[eg]
126	A number of Albanian asylum seekers	Albanian	Tirana, Albania	Egypt	July 1990 (length of stay unknown)[eh]
127	A number of Albanian asylum seekers	Albanian	Tirana, Albania	France	July 1990 (length of stay unknown)[ei]
128	A number of Albanian asylum seekers	Albanian	Tirana, Albania	Greece	July 1990 (length of stay unknown)[ej]
129	A number of Cuban asylum seekers	Cuban	Havana, Cuba	Belgium	Ca. July 1990[ek]
130	A number of Cuban asylum seekers	Cuban	Havana, Cuba	Czechoslovakia	Ca. July 1990[el]
131	A number of Cuban asylum seekers	Cuban	Havana, Cuba	Italy	Ca. July 1990[em]
132	A number of Cuban asylum seekers	Cuban	Havana, Cuba	Switzerland	Ca. July 1990[en]
133	Arturo Sandoval, his wife and son	Cuban	Rome, Italy	U.S.	July 1990[eo]
134	At least 18 Cuban asylum seekers	Cuban	Havana, Cuba	Spain	Ca. 9 July–4 September 1990[ep]
135	Ca. 1800 people	Presumed to be Liberian	Monrovia, Liberia	Nigeria	Ca. August 1990[eq]
136	Michel Aoun	Lebanese	Beirut, Lebanon	France	October 1990–30 August 1991er
137	Erich Honecker (former GDR politician)	German	Moscow, Soviet Union/Russia	Chile	December 1991–29 July 1992[es]
138	Alan García Pérez	Peruvian	Lima, Peru	Colombia	31 May–2 June 1992[et]
139	Alina Fernández Revuelta	Cuban	Madrid, Spain	U.S.	20–21 December 1993[eu]
140	29 East Timorese Youths	East Timorese	Jakarta, Indonesia	U.S.	12–22 November 1994[ev]
141	Prosper Avril	Haitian	Port-au-Prince, Haiti	Colombia	From 7 November 1995[ew] (length of stay unknown)[ex]
142	Sylvestre Ntibantunganya	Burundian	Bujumbura, Burundi	U.S.	23 July 1996[ey]–8 June 1997[ez]
143	Abdullah Öcalan	Turkish (Kurdish)	Nairobi, Kenya	Greece	2–15 February 1999[fa]
144	João Bernardo Vieira	Bissau-Guinean	Bissau, Guinea Bissau	Portugal	May[fb]–June 1999[fc]

145	Louis Pierre Gamba	Central African Republic	Bangui, Central African Republic	U.S.	May–August 2001[fd]
146	Alassane Ouattara	Ivorian	Abidjan, Ivory Coast	France	2002[fe]
147	Ca. Twenty-one Cuban Asylum Seekers	Cuban	Havana, Cuba	Mexico	From 27 February 2002 (length of stay unknown)[ff]
148	25 North Korean Asylum Seekers	North Korean	Beijing, China	Spain	March 2002[fg]
149	A North Korean Man	North Korean	Beijing, China	Germany	26 April 2002 onwards (length of stay unknown)[fh]
150	Three North Korean Asylum Seekers	North Korean	Shenyang, China	U.S.	May 2002[fi]
151	Five North Korean Asylum Seekers[fj]	North Korean	Shenyang, China	Japan	May 2002[fk]
152	Pedro Carmona	Venezuelan	Caracas, Venezuela	Colombia	May 2002[fl]
153	Two North Korean Asylum Seekers (a married couple)	North Korean	Beijing, China	Canada	Saturday 11 May 2002 onwards (length of stay unknown)[fm]
154	A Single Man and A Couple Seeking Asylum	North Korean	Beijing, China	South Korea	23/24 May 2002 (length of stay unknown)[fn]
155	A Male North Korean Asylum Seeker	North Korean	Beijing, China	South Korea	27 May 2002 (length of stay unknown)[fo]
156	Twenty-one North Korean Asylum Seekers	North Korean	Beijing, China	South Korea[fp]	June–September 2002[fq]
157	Brothers Almadar and Muntazar	Afghan	Melbourne, Australia	United Kingdom	Ca. 10.00–16.00 on 18 July 2002[fr]
158	Twenty North Korean Asylum Seekers	North Korean	Beijing, China	South Korea	September–11 October 2002[fs]
159	29 North Korean Asylum Seekers	North Korean	Beijing, China	Japan	1 September 2004 onwards (length of stay unknown–in December nine still remained in the embassy)[ft]
160	Fifteen North Korean Asylum Seekers	North Korean	Beijing, China	Germany	3 September 2002 (length of stay unknown)[fu]
161	Carlos Ortega	Venezuelan	Caracas, Venezuela	Costa Rica	14 March 2003 (length of stay unknown)[fv]
162	130 North Korean Asylum Seekers	North Korean	Beijing, China	South Korea	October 2003[fw]
163	44 North Korean Asylum Seekers	North Korean	Beijing, China	Canada	29 September[fx]–December 2004[fy]
164	A North Korean Construction Company Worker	North Korean	Vladivostock, Russia	U.S.	From 28 October 2004[fz]
165	A North Korean Translator	North Korean	Vladivostock, Russia	South Korea	From 15 November 2004[ga]
166	Four North Korean Asylum Seekers	North Korean	Hanoi, Vietnam	France	December 2004[gb]

(continued)

Table 7.1 (continued)

No.	Name	Nationality	Location of diplomatic premises (Host state)	Granting state	Time span
167	Two North Korean Asylum Seekers	North Korean	Hanoi, Vietnam	Sweden	December 2004[gc]
168	Lucio Gutiérrez Borbúa	Ecuadorian	Quito, Ecuador	Brazil	20–24 April 2005[gd]
169	Franois Boko	Togolese	Lomé, Togo	Germany	From 22 April 2005 (length of stay unknown)[ge]
170	Seven North Korean Asylum Seekers	North Korean	Hanoi, Vietnam	Thailand	June 2005[gf]
171	Nixon Moreno	Venezuelan	Caracas, Venezuela	The Holy See	Fifteen months up to June 2008 when he was granted political asylum[gg]
172	Four North Korean Asylum Seekers	North Korean	Hanoi, Vietnam	Denmark	11 July 2007[gh]
173	Max Goeldi and Rachid Hamdani	Swiss	Tripoli, Libya	Switzerland	For seventeen months from summer 2008[gi]
174	Morgan Tsvangirai	Zimbabwean	Harare, Zimbabwe	The Netherlands	22 June[gj]–25 June 2008[gk]
175	Anwar Ibrahim	Malaysian	Kuala Lumpur, Malaysia	Turkey	29–30 June 2008[gl]
176	Adrian and Roman Mocanu	Romanian (presumed to also hold Moldovan citizenship)	Chişinău, Moldova	Romania	25 September 2008–23 September 2009[gm]
177	Andry Rajoelina	Madagascan	Antananarivo, Madagascar	France	3–9 March 2009[gn]
178	Alberto Pizango	Peruvian	Lima, Peru	Nicaragua	Ca. 6[go]–17[gp] June 2009
179	Xiomara Hortensia Zelaya (José Manuel Zelaya Rosales' daughter) and her 5-year-old child	Honduran	Tegucigalpa, Honduras	Republic of China (Taiwan)	28 June–10 July 2009[gq]
180	José Manuel Zelaya Rosales (and an indeterminate number of Honduran citizens)[gr]	Honduran	Tegucigalpa, Honduras	Brazil	21 September 2009[gs]–27 January 2010[gt]
181	Nine North Korean Asylum Seekers	North Korean	Hanoi, Vietnam	Denmark	24 September[gu]–20 October 2009[gv]
182	Shahram Amiri	Iranian	Washington D.C., U.S.	Pakistan (Iranian Interest Section)	12–14 July 2010[gw]
183	Sam Lahood	American	Cairo, Egypt	U.S.	January[gx]–March 2012[gy]

184	Wang Lijun	Chinese	Chengdu, China	U.S.	6–7 February 2012[gz]
185	Amadou Toumani Toure	Malian	Bamako, Mali	Senegal	18[ha]–20 April 2012[hb]
186	Chen Guangcheng	Chinese	Beijing, China	U.S.	Late April[hc]–2 May 2012[hd]
187	Roger Pinto	Bolivian	La Paz, Bolivia	Brazil	452 days from 2012 until August 2013[he]
188	Julian Assange	Australian[hf]	London, United Kingdom	Ecuador	19 June 2012[hg]–11 April 2019[hh]
189	Mohamed Nasheed	Maldivian	Male, Maldives	India	13–23 February 2013[hi]
190	An aide to Jang Song Thaek	North Korean	China	South Korea[hj]	December 2013 (length of stay unknown)
191	Several Anti-Government Protesters	Ukrainian	Kiev, Ukraine	Canada	Several days in February 2014[hk]
192	Meriam Ibrahim	Sudanese	Khartoum, Sudan	U.S.	26 June[hl]–1 August 2014[hm]
193	Emin Huseynov	Azerbaijani	Baku, Azerbaijan	Switzerland	18 August 2014–ca. 13 June 2015[hn]
194	Approximately 100 Burundian students	Burundi	Bujumbura, Burundi	U.S.	25 June 2015[ho]
195	Kim Ryen-hi	North Korean	Seoul, South Korea	Vietnam	Two hours on 7 March 2016[hp]
196	An eighteen year old North Korean	North Korean	Hong Kong, China	South Korea	July 2016[hq]
197	Hyon Kwang Song, Kim Uk Il, Ri Ji U	North Korean	Kuala Lumpur, Malaysia	North Korea	Ca. February[hr]–30 March 2017[hs]
198	Roberto Enríquez and Eduardo Vetancourt	Venezuelan	Caracas, Venezuela	Chile	From 5 April 2017[ht] (length of stay unknown)
199	Judges Beatriz Ruiz Marín, Zuleima Del Valle González, Elenis Rodríguez Martínez, José Fernando Núñez Sifontes and Luis Manuel Marcano Salazar	Venezuelan	Caracas, Venezuela	Chile	August–19 October 2017[hu]
200	Judges Gustavo Sosa Izaguirre and Manuel Antonio Espinoza Melet	Venezuelan	Caracas, Venezuela	Panama	From ca. 4 August 2017[hv] (length of stay unknown)
201	Freddy Guevara	Venezuelan	Caracas, Venezuela	Chile	4 November 2017[hw]–9 September 2020[hx]
202	Nikola Gruevski	Macedonian	Tirana, Albania	Hungary	Ca. November 2018[hy]
203	Alan García	Peruvian	Lima, Peru	Uruguay	17 November–ca. 3 December 2018[hz]
204	25 armed Guaido supporters	Presumed to all be Venezuelan	Caracas, Venezuela	Brazil	Ca. April 2019 (exact length of stay unknown)[ia]
205	Leopoldo López, his wife Lilian Tintori and their daughter	Venezuelan	Caracas, Venezuela	Chile	Several hours on 30 April 2019[ib]
206	Leopoldo López and his wife Lilian Tintori	Venezuelan	Caracas, Venezuela	Spain	30 April 2019[ic]–ca. 25 October 2020[id]

(continued)

Table 7.1 (continued)

No.	Name	Nationality	Location of diplomatic premises (Host state)	Granting state	Time span
207	Eighteen national guardsmen	Presumed to all be Venezuelan	Venezuela	Panama	May 2019 (length of stay unknown)[ie]
208	Américo de Grazia, Mariela Magallanes and five others	Presumed to all be Venezuelan	Caracas, Venezuela	Italy	May 2019 (length of stay unknown)[if]
209	Franco Manuel Casella	Venezuelan	Caracas, Venezuela	Mexico	14 May[ig]–20 September 2019[ih]

[a]Whilst the vast majority of the cases listed here depict examples of individuals being granted asylum in the context of diplomatic premises, several involve individuals being granted asylum in the context of consulates. As such asylum is consistent with a broader definition of the term diplomatic asylum, such cases were not omitted here. Moreover, several cases detailed here also involve an individual being sheltered in the context of an ambassador's residence, consistent with the historical origins of the practice

[b]Please note that this list is by no means intended to be exhaustive but merely indicative of the scale of the practice. Further examples are, for example, cited by Klepper (2009), pp. 130–201; Ronning (1965), p. 225 f. Those cases, which could not be verified by way of e.g. news reports, have been omitted here. The existence of further undiscovered and unreported cases is also very much assumed. Furthermore, Table 7.1 additionally encompasses several attempts to obtain diplomatic asylum in cases in which the purported asylee was not immediately expelled from the mission premises and thus a short-term *de facto* case of diplomatic asylum ensued. This list accounts for cases up to December 2020

[c]The American Conservative (1 April 2010), Haitian-Building

[d]U.S. Department of State, Foreign Relations of the United States, Papers Relating to the Foreign Relations of the United States, With the Address of the President to Congress December 4, 1917, Doc. 399, 17 May 1917

[e]U.S. Department of State, Foreign Relations of the United States, Papers Relating to the Foreign Relations of the United States, With the Address of the President to Congress December 4, 1917, Doc. 404, Chargé Johnson to the Secretary of State, Telegram, 25 May 1917. Also see Chap. 3: Sect. 3.4.6

[f]U.S. Department of State, Foreign Relations of the United States Diplomatic Papers, 1932, The American Republics, Vol. V, Cuba, Political Unrest in Cuba, Doc. 602. Also see Chap. 3: Sect. 3.4.7.1

[g]U.S. Department of State, Foreign Relations of the United States Diplomatic Papers, 1932, The American Republics, Vol. V, Cuba, Political Unrest in Cuba, Doc. 602. Also see Chap. 3: Sect. 3.4.7.1

[h]U.S. Department of State, Foreign Relations of the United States Diplomatic Papers, 1932, The American Republics, Vol. V, Cuba, Political Unrest in Cuba, Doc. 608. Also see Chap. 3: Sect. 3.4.7.2

[i]U.S. Department of State, Foreign Relations of the United States Diplomatic Papers, 1932, The American Republics, Vol. V, Cuba, Political Unrest in Cuba, Doc. 608. Also see Chap. 3: Sect. 3.4.7.2

[j]U.S. Department of State, Foreign Relations of the United States Diplomatic Papers, 1932, The American Republics, Vol. V, Cuba, Political Unrest in Cuba, Doc. 608. Also see Chap. 3: Sect. 3.4.7.2

[k]U.S. Department of State, Foreign Relations of the United States Diplomatic Papers, 1932, The American Republics, Vol. V, Cuba, Political Unrest in Cuba, Doc. 608. Also see Chap. 3: Sect. 3.4.7.2

[l]Cited by Moral Roncal (2013), p. 101. Cf. Chap. 3: Sect. 3.4.1
[m]Cited by Moral Roncal (2013), p. 101. Cf. Chap. 3: Sect. 3.4.1
[n]Cited by Moral Roncal (2013), p. 101. Cf. Chap. 3: Sect. 3.4.1
[o]Cited by Moral Roncal (2013), p. 101. Cf. Chap. 3: Sect. 3.4.1
[p]Cited by Moral Roncal (2013), p. 101. Cf. Chap. 3: Sect. 3.4.1
[q]Cited by Moral Roncal (2013), p. 101. Cf. Chap. 3: Sect. 3.4.1
[r]Cited by Moral Roncal (2013), p. 101. Cf. Chap. 3: Sect. 3.4.1
[s]Cited by Moral Roncal (2013), p. 101. Cf. Chap. 3: Sect. 3.4.1
[t]Cited by Moral Roncal (2013), p. 101. Cf. Chap. 3: Sect. 3.4.1
[u]Cited by Moral Roncal (2013), p. 101. Cf. Chap. 3: Sect. 3.4.1
[v]Cited by Moral Roncal (2013), pp. 101, 103. Cf. Chap. 3: Sect. 3.4.1
[w]Cited by Moral Roncal (2013), p. 101. Cf. Chap. 3: Sect. 3.4.1
[x]Cited by Moral Roncal (2013), p. 101. Cf. Chap. 3: Sect. 3.4.1
[y]Cited by Moral Roncal (2013), p. 101. Cf. Chap. 3: Sect. 3.4.1
[z]Cited by Moral Roncal (2013), p. 101. Cf. Chap. 3: Sect. 3.4.1
[aa]Cited by Moral Roncal (2013), p. 101. Cf. Chap. 3: Sect. 3.4.1
[ab]Cited by Moral Roncal (2013), p. 101. Cf. Chap. 3: Sect. 3.4.1
[ac]Cited by Moral Roncal (2013), p. 101. Cf. Chap. 3: Sect. 3.4.1
[ad]It is not clear why Cuba and Haiti are grouped together though it seems likely that the two shared diplomatic premises: Cited by Moral Roncal (2013), p. 101. Cf. Chap. 3: Sect. 3.4.1
[ae]Cited by Moral Roncal (2013), p. 101. Cf. Chap. 3: Sect. 3.4.1
[af]Cited by Moral Roncal (2013), p. 101. Cf. Chap. 3: Sect. 3.4.1
[ag]Cited by Moral Roncal (2013), p. 101. Cf. Chap. 3: Sect. 3.4.1
[ah]This case of diplomatic asylum ended rather abruptly with troops of General Franco storming the embassy and arresting the asylees present: Sinha (1971), p. 34
[ai]Cited by Moral Roncal (2013), p. 101. Cf. Chap. 3: Sect. 3.4.1
[aj]France also assisted in the evacuation of hundreds of other refugees: Cited by Moral Roncal (2013), p. 101. Cf. Chap. 3: Sect. 3.4.1
[ak]Cited by Moral Roncal (2013), p. 101. Cf. Chap. 3: Sect. 3.4.1
[al]This included the asylees of the following legations, which sheltered their asylees under the Chilean flag after breaking off diplomatic relations with Spain: Guatemala (200 persons), Honduras (36 people) and El Salvador: Cited by Moral Roncal (2013), p. 101. Cf. Chap. 3: Sect. 3.4.1
[am]Lajous (2001), p. 9. This may also be classified as a case of collective shelter: Denza (2016), Art. 22, pp. 116–117. Cf. Chap. 3: Sect. 3.4.1
[an]Romero Salvadó (2013), p. 266. Cf. Chap. 3: Sect. 3.4.1
[ao]Romero Salvadó (2013), p. 332. Cf. Chap. 3: Sect. 3.4.1
[ap]Grugel and Quijada (1990), p. 359. Cf. Chap. 3: Sect. 3.4.1
[aq]Grugel and Quijada (1990), p. 371
[ar]Vági et al. (2013), p. 149
[as]Kovács and Ádány (2017), p. 185

(continued)

Table 7.1 (continued)

[at]Kovács and Ádány (2017), p. 186
[au]Kovács and Ádány (2017), p. 186
[av]Fry (2018), p. 50. Also see Chap. 3: Sect. 3.4.8.1
[aw]Dembinski (1988), p. 249
[ax]Prior to obtaining political asylum in Argentina: Augusto Roa Bastos, Instituto Cervantes https://cvc.cervantes.es/actcult/roa/cronologia/cronologia01.htm. Last Accessed 16 Dec 2020. For further information on the case also see: Chap. 3: Sect. 3.4.12
[ay]U.S. Department of State, Foreign Relations of the United States Diplomatic Papers, 1947, The American Republics, Vol. VIII, Nicaragua, Political Upheaval in Nicaragua: United States policies of nonintervention and nonrecognition, Doc. 731. Also see Chap. 3: Sect. 3.4.10.1
[az]U.S. Department of State, Foreign Relations of the United States Diplomatic Papers, 1947, The American Republics, Vol. VIII, Nicaragua, Political Upheaval in Nicaragua: United States policies of nonintervention and nonrecognition, Doc. 731. Also see Chap. 3: Sect. 3.4.10.1
[ba]U.S. Department of State, Foreign Relations of the United States, 1949, The United Nations; The Western Hemisphere, Vol. II, Doc. 475, 20 December 1949. For further information on this case and the legal dispute surrounding it see: Chap. 3: Sect. 3.4.13.1; Colombian-Peruvian Asylum Case (Colombia v Peru), Judgment of 20 November 1950, ICJ Reports 1950, No. 7, p. 266 f.; Request for Interpretation of the Judgment of November 20th 1950 in the Asylum Case (Colombia v Peru), Judgment of 27 November 1950, ICJ Reports 1950, No. 13, p. 395 f.; Haya de la Torre Case (Colombia v Peru), Judgment of 13 June 1951, ICJ Reports 1951, No. 14, p. 71 f
[bb]Leonard (2004), p. 16
[bc]The New York Times (13 September 1952), 2 Colombian Liberal Chiefs Get Asylum in Venezuelan Embassy; Take Refuge in Venezuelan Embassy EMBASSY ASYLUM FOR 2 COLOMBIANS
[bd]It was also noted that the time Árbenz Guzmán spent at the Mexican embassy was uncomfortable due to the 300 people seeking refugee there at the time: Garcia Ferreira (2008), p. 62; Lajous (2001), p. 10. Also see Chap. 3: Sect. 3.4.8.2
[be]MercoPress (12 September 2013), Argentina thanks Paraguay for granting General Peron asylum in 1955. Also see Chap. 3: Sect. 3.4.2.1
[bf]In the case of Farkas, having unsuccessfully attempted to obtain asylum at both the Swiss and Austrian embassies. For further information, see: Farkas (2016)
[bg]In the light of the Hungarian revolution, it was noted that a total of nineteen people seeking refuge arrived at the Belgian embassy on 4th November 1956: Farkas (2016), p. 1
[bh]Simándi (2015), p. 115. Nagy is said to have fled with several members of his government and their relatives: Kovács and Ádány (2017), p. 189. Though he was promised safe passage from the embassy, Nagy was apprehended by Soviet authorities upon exiting the embassy and was subsequently executed
[bi]The New York Times (29 September 1971), Mindszenty Leaves Hungary, Goes to Rome. Also see Rossitto (1987), p. 118 f
[bj]Following which he was granted safe passage to the United States: FBI, History, Famous Cases and Criminals, Hollow Nickel/Rudolph Abel. Available at: https://www.fbi.gov/history/famous-cases/hollow-nickel-rudolph-abel. Last accessed 16 Dec 2020
[bk]See The New York Times (2 April 2001), London Journal; If Iraq Ever Needs a King, Here's a Dapper Hopeful; The New York Times (28 January 2005), The King Is Dead (Has Been for 46 Years) but Two Iraqis Hope: Long Live the King!
[bl]This case caused widespread protests and unrest in the Philippines: Balbastro (1959), p. 350 f. Also see: Official Gazette (14 November 1958), Statement: President Garcia at his regular weekly press conference; The Official Gazette (17 November 1958), Official Week in Review: November 9–November 15, 1958
[bm]For more information on this case, see Ribeiro de Meneses (2009), p. 440
[bn]See Cuzán (1999), p. 185. Also see Chap. 3: Sect. 3.4.7.4

[bo]Toledo Blade (5 March 2002), An escape from Cuba: Olga comes home to Toledo. Also see Chap. 3: Sect. 3.4.7.5
[bp]Whiteman (1968), pp. 494–495. Also see Rossitto (1987), pp. 130–131
[bq]Die Zeit (24 May 1963), Tyrann mit sanften Augen; Kitschenberg (1965), Einleitung. Cf. Chap. 3: Sect. 3.4.9.1
[br]The New York Times (5 August 1964), Chinese Defector Says Peking Seeks to Take Over the Congo; Ex-Aide in Burundi Here, Asserts Regime's Goal is to Conquer Africa. For further reference thereto, also see Cohen and Chiu (1974), pp. 985–986; Evans (1965), p. 674
[bs]Scott (1989), p. 162
[bt]Orlando Sentinel (28 December 1991), He Raises His Voice for Haiti; Gainesville Sun (27 July 1987), Ex-militiaman, clergyman vie to lead Haitian exiles. Also see Chap. 3: Sect. 3.4.9.2
[bu]The Independent (30 November 2011), Lana Peters: Stalin's daughter whose defection to the West did not bring peace of mind
[bv]Bassuener (2013), p. 429; Kovács and Ádány (2017), p. 182. Also see Chap. 3: Sect. 3.4.4
[bw]Dembinski (1988), p. 249. Also see Chap. 3: Sect 3.4.4
[bx]Dembinski (1988), p. 249. Also see Chap. 3: Sect. 3.4.4
[by]Dembinski (1988), p. 249. Also see Chap. 3: Sect. 3.4.4.for further information on this case
[bz]Bassuener (2013), p. 429; Kovács and Ádány (2017), p. 182
[ca]Ensalaco (2000), p. 31; The Independent (3 March 2016), Chile honours Italian diplomats whose 'Schindler's List' saved 750 lives during Augusto Pinochet's brutal regime. Also see Chap. 3: Sect. 3.4.4
[cb]China Daily (7 October 2002), Serra faces election struggle against workers' champion Lula. Also see Chap. 3: Sect. 3.4.4
[cc]The Independent (3 March 2016), Chile honours Italian diplomats whose 'Schindler's List' saved 750 lives during Augusto Pinochet's brutal regime. Also see Chap. 3: Sect. 3.4.4
[cd]The New York Times (25 September 1974), Argentines Given Embassy Refuge. Also see Behrens (2014), p. 330. Also see Chap. 3: Sect. 3.4.2.2
[ce]Sen (1988), p. 410.
[cf]UPI (19 December 1980), Former Argentine President Hector Campora, who paved the way... Also see Chap. 3: Sect. 3.4.2.3
[cg]UPI (3 September 1981), Peronist holds Latin American record for asylum. Also see Chap. 3: Sect. 3.4.2.4 for further information on this case
[ch]UPI (25 May 1982), Argentina increases pressure on U.S. over Falklands
[ci]See Association for Diplomatic Studies and Training, A Thieving U.S. Citizen Wreaks Havoc at the U.S Embassy in Nicaragua. Available at: https://adst.org/2015/03/an-unwelcome-guest-at-embassy-managua/. Last Accessed 16 Dec 2020
[cj]Russia Beyond (15 August 2016), How did a group of Soviet Pentecostals end up living in the U.S. embassy? Also see Rossitto (1987), p. 120 f
[ck]Dembinski (1988), p. 249
[cl]The New York Times (16 July 1979) Sergio Ramirez Mercado
[cm]Dupes Hawk et al. (2014), p. 29. Also see Chap. 3: Sect. 3.4.7.6
[cn]Bassiouni (2014), p. 185
[co]Costa Rica and the U.S. also offered to grant political asylum to some of the group. See von Glahn and Taulbee (2017), p. 366 and Global Security, Mariel Boatlift. https://www.globalsecurity.org/military/ops/mariel-boatlift.htm. Last Accessed 16 Dec 2020. Also see Chap. 3: Sect. 3.4.7.6
[cp]Dembinski (1988), p. 249
[cq]The U.S. refused to surrender the soldiers without assurance of safe-conduct: Sen (1988), p. 412
[cr]UPI (21 March 1981), CBS' 60 Minutes influences coup attempt. Also see Chap. 3: Sect. 3.4.3
[cs]UPI (26 March 1981), Gabriel Garcia Marquez, Colombia's best-known novelist, sought political asylum... Also see Chap. 3: Sect. 3.4.5.2

(continued)

Table 7.1 (continued)

[ct]The New York Times (1 February 1984), East Germany Tries Accommodation. Also see Roberts (1987), p. 233 f
[cu]UPI (31 August 1983), Five members of council quit in protest. Also see Chap. 3: Sect. 3.4.8.3
[cv]East and Thomas (2003), p. 97
[cw]Farhangi (1986), p. 1525. For further information on Chol's stay, also see The New York Times (9 December 1982), U.S. Stand on Envoy Backed by U.N. Aide; The New York Times (22 July 1983), U.S. Threatens to Expel Envoy in Assault Case
[cx]The New York Times (29 July 1983), The Region; Korean Diplomat Heads for Home. In this case, the asylee was both a national of the protecting state and also a member of its diplomatic mission, sought by the territorial authorities due to allegations of sexual assault
[cy]SBS News (3 September 2013), The bizzare history of embassy asylum
[cz]The New York Times (1 February 1984), East Germany Tries Accommodation
[da]The New York Times (1 February 1984), East Germany Tries Accommodation
[db]Roberts (1987), p. 234
[dc]The group's request for political asylum was rejected: Roberts (1987), p. 234
[dd]The group was eventually granted political asylum and thus permitted to travel to West Germany: Roberts (1987), p. 234
[de]Riveles (1989), p. 157
[df]For further information see Riveles (1989), p. 139 f
[dg]Roberts (1987), p. 234
[dh]Roberts (1987), p. 234. Also see The New York Times (10 November 1984), West Germany is Demanding Rumania Recall 5 Diplomats
[di]Roberts (1987), p. 234. Also see The New York Times (10 November 1984), West Germany is Demanding Rumania Recall 5 Diplomats
[dj]Roberts (1987), p. 234. Also see The New York Times (10 November 1984), West Germany is Demanding Rumania Recall 5 Diplomats
[dk]Behrens (2014), p. 331, Fn. 70. Also see Chap. 3: Sect. 3.4.10.3
[dl]The Washington Post (8 May 1985), A Defecting Nicaraguan Contra's Tale. Also see Chap. 3: Sect. 3.4.10.4
[dm]Orlando Sentinel (5 November 1985), Soviet Soldier Goes Back to Army in Kabul; Rossitto (1987), p. 124 f
[dn]UPI (24 February 1986), Former Duvalier Supporters said to flee Haiti. Also see Chap. 3: Sect. 3.4.9.3
[do]AP (3 February 1989), Police Identify British Native As Spy
[dp]Kovács and Ádány (2017), p. 193
[dq]AP (21 January 1989), Former Mayor Franck Romain Indicted for Massacre
[dr]OAS, Inter-American Commission on Human Rights, Annual Report of the Inter-American Commission on Human Rights 1988–1989, 18 September 1989; Haiti, Doc. 10, OEA/Ser.L/V/II.76. Available at: http://www.cidh.org/annualrep/88.89eng/chap.4c.htm. Last Accessed 16 Dec 2020
[ds]Human Rights Watch, Repression in China since June 4, 1989, Cumulative Data, An Asia Watch Report, Embargoed for September 28, 1990, October 1990, United States, p. 7
[dt]See Rubin (1990), pp. 84–89
[du]For further information on the unusual methods employed to extract Noriega from the Apostolic Nunciature of the Holy See (the diplomatic mission of the Holy See and equivalent to an embassy), see for example: BBC News (30 May 2017), Music torture: How heavy metal broke Manuel Noriega; The Telegraph (30 May 2017), How Panama's military dictator Manuel Noriega was defeated by rock'n'roll. Also see Chap. 3: Sect. 3.4.11

[dv]UPI (11 May 1991), Former Noriega associates allowed to leave country. Also see Chap. 3: Sect. 3.4.11
[dw]UPI (11 May 1991), Former Noriega associates allowed to leave country. Also see Chap. 3: Sect. 3.4.11
[dx]UPI (11 May 1991), Former Noriega associates allowed to leave country. Also see Chap. 3: Sect. 3.4.11
[dy]The New York Times (4 July 1990), Evolution in Europe; Albanians Take Refuge in Embassies; The Washington Post (4 July 1990), Albanians Seek Asylum in Embassies
[dz]The New York Times (4 July 1990), Evolution in Europe; Albanians Take Refuge in Embassies
[ea]The New York Times (4 July 1990), Evolution in Europe; Albanians Take Refuge in Embassies
[eb]The New York Times (4 July 1990), Evolution in Europe; Albanians Take Refuge in Embassies; The Washington Post (4 July 1990), Albanians Seek Asylum in Embassies: at least 26 of the 32 were granted safe-conduct
[ec]The New York Times (4 July 1990), Evolution in Europe; Albanians Take Refuge in Embassies
[ed]The New York Times (4 July 1990), Evolution in Europe; Albanians Take Refuge in Embassies; The Washington Post (4 July 1990), Albanians Seek Asylum in Embassies
[ee]The New York Times (4 July 1990), Evolution in Europe; Albanians Take Refuge in Embassies; The Washington Post (4 July 1990), Albanians Seek Asylum in Embassies
[ef]The New York Times (4 July 1990), Evolution in Europe; Albanians Take Refuge in Embassies; The Washington Post (4 July 1990), Albanians Seek Asylum in Embassies
[eg]The New York Times (4 July 1990), Evolution in Europe; Albanians Take Refuge in Embassies
[eh]The New York Times (4 July 1990), Evolution in Europe; Albanians Take Refuge in Embassies; The Washington Post (4 July 1990), Albanians Seek Asylum in Embassies
[ei]The New York Times (4 July 1990), Evolution in Europe; Albanians Take Refuge in Embassies; The Washington Post (4 July 1990), Albanians Seek Asylum in Embassies
[ej]The New York Times (4 July 1990), Evolution in Europe; Albanians Take Refuge in Embassies
[ek]The New York Times (12 September 1990), Spanish-Cuban Asylum Battle Ends, Bitterly
[el]The New York Times (12 September 1990), Spanish-Cuban Asylum Battle Ends, Bitterly
[em]The New York Times (12 September 1990), Spanish-Cuban Asylum Battle Ends, Bitterly
[en]The New York Times (12 September 1990), Spanish-Cuban Asylum Battle Ends, Bitterly
[eo]Los Angeles Times (23 April 1997), Trumpeter Arturo Sandoval Is Denied U.S. Citizenship. Also see Chap. 3: Sect. 3.4.7.8
[ep]The New York Times (12 September 1990), Spanish-Cuban Asylum Battle Ends, Bitterly
[eq]The New York Times (11 August 1990), 5 Nations Moving Troops to Liberia
[er]The New York Times (30 August 1991), Lebanese General Is Spirited to France
[es]This diplomatic crisis only came to an end after Chile refused Honecker a visa and threatened to relocate its mission's premises to force his exit: The New York Times (2 August 1992), JULY 26 - AUG. 1: Nowhere Else to Turn; Rebuffed by Chile, Honecker Returns to Germany for Trial
[et]Los Angeles Times (3 June 1992), Ex-Peruvian President Garcia Arrives in Colombia for Asylum. For further information on the case also see: Chap. 3: 4.13.2. For further information as to the reasoning behind García's asylum, also see: OAS, Inter-American Commission on Human Rights, Report Number 1/95, Case 11.006, Peru, 7 February 1995. Available at: https://www.cidh.oas.org/annualrep/94eng/Peru11006.htm. Last Accessed 16 Dec 2020
[eu]Los Angeles Times (23 December 1993), Fidel Castro's Daughter Gets U.S. Asylum: Defection: Longtime critic of the Cuban dictator flees island. She is now in Atlanta. Also see Chap. 3: Sect. 3.4.7.9
[ev]Krieger (1997), p. 233
[ew]Stotzky (1997), p. 162. Also see U.S. Department of State, Country Reports on Human Rights Practices for 1995, Vols 8 to 15, 1 March 1996, p. 445

(continued)

Table 7.1 (continued)

[ex]Though Avril is noted as still being in the embassy at the end of the year: U.S. Department of State, Country Reports on Human Rights Practices for 1995, Vols. 8 to 15, Report Submitted to the Committee on International Relations, U.S. House of Representatives and the Committee on Foreign Relations, U.S. Senate, U.S. Government Printing Office, 1 March 1996, p. 370

[ey]The New York Times (25 July 1996), Burundi at the Edge

[ez]The Washington Post (8 June 1997), Former President of Burundi Leaves Shelter of Embassy

[fa]For further information on this case see for example: CIA, Fiasco in Nairobi, Greek Intelligence and the Capture of PKK, Leader Abdullah Ocalan in 1999. Available at: https://www.cia.gov/library/center-for-the-study-of-intelligence/csi-publications/csi-studies/studies/vol53no1/fiasco-in-nairobi.html. Last Accessed 16 Dec 2020

[fb]BBC News (13 May 1999), Portugal says ex-president safe

[fc]BBC News (6 June 1999), Ousted Bissau president leaves country

[fd]Bradshaw and Fandos-Rius (2016), pp. 286–287

[fe]BBC News (22 September 2002), France sends troops to Ivory Coast

[ff]The New York Times (1 March 2002), Cubans Set on Asylum Crash a Bus into Embassy

[fg]BBC News (13 May 2002), Japan-China refugees row deepens; Chicago Tribune (15 March 2002), North Korean defectors leave Beijing. See also: Human Rights Watch, The Invisible Exodus: North Koreans in the People's Republic of China, A Human Rights Watch Report, November 2002, Vol. 14, No. 8 (C)., p. 3, Fn. 3

[fh]Chicago Tribune (27 April 2002), North Korean requests asylum at embassy

[fi]BBC News (13 May 2002), Japan-China refugees row deepens

[fj]Two family members were inside the embassy and three further asylum seekers were outside when they were detained by Chinese police: Chicago Tribune (10 May 2002), Beijing defends raid to seize N. Koreans

[fk]Chicago Tribune (10 May 2002), Beijing defends raid to seize N. Koreans; The New York Times (10 May 2002), Japan Protests China's Arrest of Koreans at Consulate

[fl]Carmona fled to the ambassador's actual residence in Caracas: BBC News (27 May 2002), Venezuelan Coup Leader Given Asylum. Also see Chap. 3: Sect. 3.7.5.1

[fm]BBC News (13 May 2002), Japan-China refugees row deepens; Chicago Tribune (13 May 2002), 2 North Koreans hole up in Canadian Embassy, Chicago Tribune (15 May 2002), China, Japan in feud over N. Koreans

[fn]Chicago Tribune (29 May 2002), China tells S. Korea to give up migrants

[fo]Chicago Tribune (29 May 2002), China tells S. Korea to give up migrants

[fp]Upon the group departing, South Korea conceded that at least another twenty-four North Korean asylum seekers were still present in its Beijing embassy pending permission to leave China: Chicago Tribune (12 September 2002), 36 defectors arrive near Seoul

[fq]Human Rights Watch, The Invisible Exodus: North Koreans in the People's Republic of China, A Human Rights Watch Report, November 2002, Vol. 14, No. 8 (C), p. 3, Fn. 3

[fr]R (B and Others) v Secretary of State for Foreign and Commonwealth Affairs (2004) EWCA 1344, paras 4–17. In the context of this case and in the light of a number of provisions under the Human Rights Act (1998, C.42), transposing the ECHR into UK law, the brothers asked the court to declare the unlawfulness of the consulate's decision to ask the brothers to leave and to facilitate their journey to UK consular premises (paras 22 and 23)

[fs]Chicago Tribune (13 October 2002), Koreans reach Seoul from China via Philippines

[ft]Jeffries (2006), pp. 101–102

[fu]In this case the asylum seekers sheltered in the German diplomatic compound rather than in the embassy itself: Chicago Tribune (4 September 2002), 15 seek refuge in German compound
[fv]Deseret News (15 March 2003), Venezuelan strike leader given asylum. Also see Chap. 3: Sect. 3.7.5.2
[fw]It is unclear how long the asylum seekers had been in the embassy's consular section before it closed in October 2003 in order to organise their removal: Chicago Tribune (7 October 2003), S. Korea Embassy shuts to clear out defectors
[fx]ABC News, The World Today (30 September 2004), North Korean asylum seekers break into Canadian Embassy in Beijing
[fy]Chicago Tribune (23 December 2004), N. Koreans leave Canadian Embassy; Jeffries (2006), p. 102
[fz]Jeffries (2006), p. 100
[ga]Jeffries (2006), p. 100
[gb]Reuters (11 July 2007), Four North Koreans enter Danish embassy in Hanoi
[gc]Reuters (11 July 2007), Four North Koreans enter Danish embassy in Hanoi
[gd]ABC News (24 April 2005), Ecuador's former president leaves country for Brazil: report. Also see Chap. 3: Sect. 3.7.2
[ge]N-tv (24 April 2005), Unruhen in Togo, Zuflucht in deutscher Botschaft
[gf]Reuters (11 July 2007), Four North Koreans enter Danish embassy in Hanoi
[gg]Country Reports on Human Rights Practices for 2008, Vol. I. Report Submitted to the Committee on Foreign Relations US Senate and the Committee on Foreign Affairs US House of Representatives by the Department of State in Accordance with Sections 116(d) and 502B(b) of the Foreign Assistance Act of 1961, U.S. Government Printing Office, Washington 2010, p. 2781. Also see Chap. 3: Sect. 3.7.5.3
[gh]Reuters (11 July 2007), Four North Koreans enter Danish embassy in Hanoi
[gi]Denza (2016), Art. 22, p. 115.; N-tv (22 February 2010), Schweizer verlassen Botschaft
[gj]The Telegraph (23 June 2008), Zimbabwe's Morgan Tsvangirai seeks refuge in Dutch embassy
[gk]The Telegraph (25 June 2008), Zimbabwe: Morgan Tsvangirai leaves embassy refuge to give ultimatum to Robert Mugabe
[gl]Reuters (30 June 2008), Malaysia's Anwar leaves Turkish embassy
[gm]Moldova Azi (23 September 2009), Sons of Sergiu Mocanu quit Romanian Embassy
[gn]He was held to have been under UN protection here: France24 (9 March 2009), Opposition leader leaves French embassy
[go]The Guardian (9 June 2009), Peruvian indigenous leader seeks asylum in Nicaragua's embassy
[gp]The San Diego Union-Tribune (17 June 2009), Peru Indian protest leader arrives in Nicaragua. For further information on the case see Chap. 3: Sect. 3.7.4.1
[gq]Taiwan Today (30 September 2009), Deposed Honduran leader's daughter granted asylum. Cf. Chap. 3: Sect. 3.7.3
[gr]See Certain Questions concerning Diplomatic Relations (Honduras v Brazil) Application Instituting Proceedings by the Republic of Honduras against the Federative Republic of Brazil, 28 October 2009; Certain Questions concerning Diplomatic Relations (Honduras v Brazil), Order of 12 May 2010, No. 147, ICJ Reports 2010, pp. 303–305. Cf. Chap. 3: Sect. 3.7.3
[gs]The Guardian (25 October 2009), Manuel Zelaya undergoes strange siege inside Brazilian embassy
[gt]Reuters (27 January 2010), Honduras' Zelaya leaves Brazilian embassy
[gu]Reuters (24 September 2009), North Koreans seek asylum at Danish embassy in Vietnam
[gv]Reuters (20 October 2009), North Koreans quit Danish embassy in Hanoi for South Korea
[gw]Interestingly this case involved the opposite practice to usual diplomatic asylum cases as Amiri was seeking to flee the U.S. by way of repatriation to his home country of Iran: The Guardian (14 July 2010), Iranian nuclear scientist Shahram Amiri heads home

(continued)

Table 7.1 (continued)

[gx]U.S. Department of State, Daily Press Briefing, 30 January 2012
[gy]The Washington Post (6 March 2012), Sam LaHood, NGO worker, hid in U.S. Embassy in Cairo for 4 weeks under 'real fear of arrest'. For further details on the case, also see Clooney (2017), p. 332
[gz]The Telegraph (19 February 2013), Bo Xilai's police chief 'sought British protection'
[ha]BBC News (18 April 2012), Mali's Amadou Toumani Toure in Senegal's embassy
[hb]BBC News (20 April 2012), Mali's ex-leader Amadou Toumani Toure flees to Senegal
[hc]According to Foreign Ministry Spokesperson Liu Weimin's Remarks on Chen Guangcheng's Entering the US Embassy in China, 2nd May 2012
[hd]The Guardian (2 May 2012), Chen Guangcheng leaves US embassy in Beijing
[he]The Guardian (27 August 2013), Brazil foreign minister loses job in diplomatic fiasco over Bolivian senator. Also see Chap. 3: Sect. 3.7.1
[hf]Assange was also granted Ecuadorian nationality in January 2018: The Guardian (10 January 2018), Julian Assange's bid for diplomatic status rejected by Britain. This citizenship was revoked before Ecuador invited British police into the embassy in order to arrest Assange: Yahoo News (11 April 2019), Quito withdraws Assange's Ecuador citizenship
[hg]The New York Times (15 August 2012), Ecuador to Let Assange Stay in Its Embassy
[hh]The Guardian (11 April 2019), Julian Assange arrested at Ecuadorian embassy in London
[hi]The Hindu (23 February 2013), Nasheed leaves Indian embassy after 'deal'
[hj]Though it is unconfirmed whether South Korea actually sheltered the aide in its Chinese embassy, he was reported as being under the (diplomatic) protection of South Korean officials in a secret location in China: Reuters (6 December 2013), Aide to North Korean leader's ousted uncle seeks asylum in South: media
[hk]CBC News (18 February 2014), Ukrainian protesters seek refuge in Canadian Embassy amid crackdown. Also see: National Post (13 July 2015), Investigation uncovers Canadian embassy in Ukraine used as a haven in 2014 by anti-government protesters
[hl]The Guardian (27 June 2014), Sudanese woman Meriam Ibrahim 'safe and well' in US embassy
[hm]The Telegraph (16 September 2014), Sudanese Christian Meriam Ibrahim tells for first time of her ordeal
[hn]Swiss Federal Department of Foreign Affairs, Media Release, 13th June 2015, Emin Huseynov arrives in Bern after 10 months at Swiss embassy in Baku
[ho]Fox News (26 June 2015), 100 students who sought refuge at US embassy in Burundi leave the premises
[hp]Ms Ryen-hi entered the embassy to request political asylum in an attempt to ultimately be repatriated to her home country, North Korea, contrary to the domestic law provisions of her resident country, South Korea. This is, however, to be seen as an attempt by Ms Ryen-hi to gain diplomatic asylum as Vietnam requested South Korean officials enter the embassy in order to escort Ms Ryen-hi out, hence her stay was limited to a number of hours: The New York Times (7 March 2016), North Korean Defector in South Seeks Vietnam's Help to Return Home
[hq]BBC News (28 July 2016), North Korean 'seeks asylum at S Korean consulate in Hong Kong'; The Telegraph (28 July 2016), North Korean defector seeks asylum at South Korean consulate in Hong Kong
[hr]The Telegraph (22 February 2017), Exclusive: North Korean suspects in Kim Jong-nam murder 'hiding' in Pyongyang's embassy in Kuala Lumpur
[hs]The Seattle Times (31 March 2017), Malaysia interviewed, cleared 3 N. Koreans before they left
[ht]Reuters (6 April 2017), Chile says will give Venezuelan politician asylum if requested. Also see Chap. 3: Sect. 3.7.5.4 for further information on this case
[hu]EFE (19 October 2017), Venezuelan judges granted asylum by Chile arrive in Santiago. Also see Chap. 3: Sect. 3.7.5.5 for further information on this case
[hv]Panama Today (4 August 2017), Panama grants asylum to two Venezuelans magistrates seeking protection. Also see Chap. 3: Sect. 3.7.5.5 for further information on this case

[hw]In this case Guevara was granted refuge in the ambassador's home: Reuters (5 November 2017), Venezuela opposition leader Guevara seeks refuge in Chile ambassador's home. Also see Chap. 3: Sect. 3.7.5.6 for further information on this case
[hx]RTL Today (10 September 2020), Maduro opponent exits Chilean embassy in Caracas
[hy]From here, Gruevski was transported via diplomatic vehicle to Montenegro before travelling on to Hungary: The New York Times (15 November 2018), Former Macedonian Leader Seeks Asylum in Hungary to Avoid Prison
[hz]BBC News (3 December 2018), Peru corruption: Ex-President Alan García denied asylum
[ia]RT (30 April 2019), Coup fizzles? Guaido's mentor takes refuge in Chilean embassy as 25 military seek asylum in Brazil's. Cf. Chap. 3: Sect. 3.7.5.7
[ib]RT (30 April 2019), Coup fizzles? Guaido's mentor takes refuge in Chilean embassy as 25 military seek asylum in Brazil's. Cf. Chap. 3: Sect. 3.7.5.8
[ic]RT (30 April 2019), Coup fizzles? Guaido's mentor takes refuge in Chilean embassy as 25 military seek asylum in Brazil's. Also see Payendeh and Saake (2019). Cf. Chap. 3: Sect. 3.7.5.8
[id]The Guardian (25 October 2020), Leopoldo López flees Venezuela vowing to continue fighting Maduro regime
[ie]The Japan Times (13 May 2019), Maduro's foes fill foreign embassies in Caracas as Venezuela crisis deepens. Cf. Chap. 3: Sect. 3.7.5.6
[if]El Pitazo (9 May 2019), Américo De Grazia se refugia en la embajada de Italia. Cf. Chap. 2, VII, 5, 7
[ig]Rappler (15 May 2019), Mexico gives 'protection' to Venezuelan opposition lawmaker. Cf. Chap. 3: Sect. 3.7.5.7
[ih]Effecto Cocuyo (20 September 2019), Diputado Casella abandona residencia diplomática de México en Caracas

References

Akande D (2012) The Julian Assange affair: may the UK terminate the diplomatic status of Ecuador's Embassy? UPDATED. In: EJIL Blog https://www.ejiltalk.org/may-the-uk-terminate-the-diplomatic-status-of-ecuadors-embassy/. Last Accessed 16 Dec 2020

Amos M (2017) The value of the European Court of Human Rights to the United Kingdom. EJIL 28 (3):763–785

Balbastro AE (1959) Comments, the right of diplomatic Asylum. PJL 34(3):343–367

Bassiouni MC (2014) International extradition, United States law and practice, 6th edn. Oxford University Press, New York

Bassuener K (2013) The fall and rise of Chilean Democracy: 1973–1989. In: Kinsman J, Bassuener K (eds) A Diplomat's handbook for democracy development support, 3rd edn. Centre for International Governance Innovation, Waterloo, pp 417–431

Behrens P (2014) The law of diplomatic Asylum – a contextual approach. MJIL 35:319–367

Bradshaw R, Fandos-Rius J (2016) Historical dictionary of the Central African Republic. Rowman and Littlefield, Maryland

Cameron I (1985) First report of the Foreign Affairs Committee of the House of Commons. ICLQ 34(3):610–620

Chinkin CM (1989) The challenge of soft law: development and change in International Law. ICLQ 38(4):850–866

Clooney A (2017) Human Rights. In: Roberts I (ed) Satow's diplomatic practice, 7th edn. Oxford University Press, Oxford, pp 305–334

Cohen JA, Chiu H (1974) People's China and International Law, a documentary study, vol 2. Princeton University Press, Princeton

Crawford J (2019) Brownlie's principles of Public International Law, 9th edn. Oxford University Press, Oxford

Cuzán AG (1999) Fidel Castro: a Machiavellian Prince? Proc ASCE 9:178–191

Dembinski L (1988) The modern law of diplomacy, external missions of states and International Organizations. Martinus Nijhoff Publishers, Dordrecht

Denza E (2016) Diplomatic law, Commentary on the Vienna Convention on Diplomatic Relations, 4th edn. Oxford University Press, Oxford

Doehring K (2004) Völkerrecht, 2nd edn. C. F. Müller, Heidelberg

Dupes Hawk K, Villella R, Leyva de Varona A, Cifers K (2014) Florida and the Mariel Boatlift of 1980, the first twenty days. The University of Alabama Press, Tuscaloosa

Dupuy P (1991) Soft law and the international law of the environment. MJIL 12(1):420–435

East R, Thomas RJ (2003) Profiles of people in power: the World's Government Leaders, 1st edn. Routledge, London

Ensalaco M (2000) Chile under Pinochet, recovering the truth. University of Pennsylvania Press, Philadelphia

Evans AE (1951) The Colombian-Peruvian Asylum case: termination of the judicial phase. AJIL 45 (4):755–762

Evans AE (1965) Reviewed Work(s): El Asilo Diplomatico: Su Aspecto Antijuridico e Inhumano. by Roberto S. Corpen. AJIL 59(3):674–675

Farhangi LS (1986) Insuring against abuse of diplomatic immunity. SLR 38(6):1517–1547

Farkas JA (2016) Sheltered by the Embassy of Belgium in Budapest, The Hungarian Review of 1956. Hungarian Rev VII(5). http://hungarianreview.com/article/20160924_sheltered_by_the_embassy_of_belgium_in_budapest. Last Accessed 16 Dec 2020

Fiedler W (1998) Gegenmaßnahmen. In: Fiedler W, Klein E, Schnyder AK (eds) Gegenmaßnahmen (Counter Measures), BDGVR 37. C.F. Müller, Heidelberg, pp 9–38

Fry MF (2018) Historical dictionary of Guatemala. Rowman and Littlefield, Lanham

Garcia Ferreira R (2008) The CIA and Jacobo Arbenz: history of a disinformation Campaign. J Third World Stud XXV(2):59–81

Grugel J, Quijada M (1990) Chile, Spain and Latin America: the right of Asylum at the onset of the Second World War. JLAS 22(2):353–374

Hamm B (2003) Menschenrechte, Ein Grundlagenbuch. Leske + Budrich, Opladen

Herdegen M (1986) The abuse of diplomatic privileges and countermeasures not covered by the Vienna Convention on Diplomatic relations, some observations in the light of recent British experience. ZaöRV 46:734–757

Jeffries I (2006) North Korea, a guide to economic and political developments. Routledge, Oxon

Kimminich O (1961) Asyl in Stützpunkten der UN Truppen. ZfP 8(3):235–240

Kitschenberg H (1965) Das diplomatische Asyl unter besonderer Berücksichtigung des Asylstreits zwischen Kolumbien und Peru, Dissertation. Universität zu Köln

Klabbers J (1998) The undesirability of soft law. NJIL 67(4):381–391

Klein E (1998) Gegenmaßnahmen. In: Fiedler W, Klein E, Schnyder AK (eds) Gegenmaßnahmen (Counter Measures), BDGVR 37. C.F. Müller, Heidelberg, pp 39–71

Klepper I (2009) Diplomatisches Asyl, Zulässigkeit und Grenzen, Dissertation, Universität zu Köln, vol 4814. Peter Lang Verlag, Frankfurt am Main

Kovács P, Ádány TV (2017) The non-customary practice of diplomatic Asylum. In: Behrens P (ed) Diplomatic law in a new millennium. Oxford University Press, Oxford, pp 179–203

Krieger H (ed) (1997) East Timor and the International Community, basic documents, Cambridge International Document Series, vol 10. Research Centre for International Law/University of Cambridge/Cambridge University Press, Cambridge/New York/Melbourne

Lajous R (2001) Mexico's diplomatic Asylum policy. Voices Mexico 54:7–11. http://www.revistascisan.unam.mx/Voices/pdfs/5402.pdf. Last Accessed 16 Dec 2020

Leonard TM (2004) Fidel Castro: a biography. Greenwood Press, Westport

Lobo de Souza IM (1995) The role of state consent in the customary process. ICLQ 44(3):521–539

Marschik A (1997) Subsysteme im Völkerrecht: ist die europäische Union ein "self-contained regime"?, Schriften zum europäischen Recht, Band 44. Ducker & Humboldt, Berlin

Moral Roncal AM (2013) An analysis of foreign diplomatic aid to the catholic clergy during the Spanish Civil War (1936–1939). Religions 4:96–115

Payendeh M, Saake C (2019) Diplomatisches Asyl als Einmischung? Venezuelas Oppositionsführer Leopoldo López in der spanischen Botschaft. In: Verfassungsblog. https://verfassungsblog.de/diplomatisches-asyl-als-einmischung-venezuelas-oppositionsfuehrer-leopoldo-lopez-in-der-spanischen-botschaft/. Last Accessed 16 Dec 2020

Porcino P (1976) Toward codification of diplomatic Asylum. NYUJILP 8:435–456

Ribeiro de Meneses F (2009) Salazar: a political biography, 1st edn. Enigma Books, New York

Riveles S (1989) Diplomatic Asylum as a Human Right: the case of the Durban Six. HRQ 11:139–159

Roberts JB (1987) Notes and comments, diplomatic Asylum: an inappropriate solution for East Germans desiring to move to the West. TICLJ 1:231–261

Roberts A, Sivakumaran S (2018) The theory and reality of the sources of International Law. In: Evans MD (ed) International law, 5th edn. Oxford University Press, Oxford, pp 89–119

Romero Salvadó FJ (2013) Historical dictionary of the Spanish civil war. The Scarecrow Press Inc., Lanham

Ronning CN (1965) Diplomatic Asylum: legal norms and political reality in Latin American relations. Martinus Nijhoff, The Hague

Rossitto AM (1987) Diplomatic Asylum in the United States and Latin America: a comparative analysis. BJIL 13:111–135

Rubin AP (1990) Diplomatic Asylum and Fang Lizhi. Diplomacy Statescraft 1(1):84–89

Scott JC (1989) Indochina's refugees, oral histories from Laos, Cambodia and Vietnam. McFarland & Company, Jefferson

Sen B (1988) A diplomat's handbook of international law and practice, 3rd revised edition. Martinus Nijhoff, Dordrecht

Simándi I (2015) The tragedy of Prime Minister Imre Nagy and the Radio Free Europe – 1956–1958. WBHR 1:115–126. http://wbhr.cz/images/issues/WBHR_2015_1.pdf. Last Accessed 16 Dec 2020

Sinha SP (1971) Asylum and International Law. Martinus Nijhoff, The Hague

Stotzky IP (1997) Silencing the Guns in Haiti: the promise of deliberative democracy. The University of Chicago Press, Chicago

Thürer D (2009) Soft law. MPEPIL Online. Oxford University Press, Oxford. https://opil.ouplaw.com/view/10.1093/law:epil/9780199231690/law-9780199231690-e1469. Last Accessed 29 Apr 2021

Vági Z, Csösz L, Kádár G (2013) The Holocaust in Hungary, evolution of a genocide. AltaMira Press, Plymouth

von Arnauld A (2006) Rechtsangleichung durch allgemeine Rechtsgrundsätze? Europäisches Gemeinschaftsrecht und Völkerrecht im Vergleich. In: Riesenhuber K, Takayama K (eds) Rechtsangleichung: Grundlagen, Methoden und Inhalte, Deutsch-Japanische Perspektiven, Schriften zum Europäischen und Internationalen Privat-, Bank- und Wirtschaftsrecht, vol 10. De Gruyter Recht, Berlin, pp 247–278

von Glahn G, Taulbee JL (2017) Law Among Nations: an introduction to Public International Law, 11th edn. Routledge, Taylor and Francis Group, Abingdon/New York

Wagner L (2017) Menschenrechte in der Entwicklungspolitik, Extraterritoriale Pflichten, der Menschenrechtsansatz und seine Umsetzung. Springer VS, Wiesbaden

Whiteman MM (1968) Digest of international law, vol 6. Department of State Publication 8350, U.S. Government Printing Office, Washington D.C